The Religions of Man

The Religions of Man

HUSTON SMITH

PERENNIAL LIBRARY

Harper & Row, Publishers
New York, Cambridge, Philadelphia, San Francisco
London, Mexico City, São Paulo, Singapore, Sydney

Contents

Preface

In the spring of 1955 I gave a course on *The Religions of Man* over KETC, the St. Louis educational television station. The response revealed a real hunger on the part of Americans to know the great faiths that have motivated and continue to motivate the peoples of the world. Over 1200 men and women in this one community enrolled as tuition-paying students while the viewing audience rose to the neighborhood of 100,000.

The second thing the response revealed was the need for a different kind of book on world religions, a book which without sacrificing depth would move more rapidly than the usual survey into the *meaning* these religions carry for the lives of their adherents. Letters from all parts of the country which came to me as the series was subsequently shown by kinescopes in approximately twenty other cities almost invariably asked either for transcripts of the lectures themselves or for a book along the same lines. Transcripts were not available for the lectures had not been delivered from script. Nor was there a single book I felt would directly meet the needs of these inquirers. For, despite innumerable masterful books in the field, I knew of none which took this as its single object; against the backdrop of critical scholarship to carry the intelligent layman into the heart of the world's great living faiths to the point where he might see and even feel why and how they guide and motivate the lives of those who live by them.

This is the book I have tried to write. I have, in the process, received inestimable help from a number of directions. Swami Satprakashananda, Leader of the Vedanta Society of St. Louis, has not only taught me almost everything I know about Hinduism, but has also labored painstakingly over the chapter by that title. Arthur Waley's writings have helped structure the feel for China built up during my seventeen years in that land of my birth, while Dr. Henry Platov has corrected a number of inaccuracies in the first drafts of my chapters on Buddhism and Taoism. Special debts relating to my discussion of Zen Buddhism will be acknowledged in that section. Professor Joseph Kitagawa of the University of Chicago has improved the chapters on Confucianism and Islam; in the latter chapter his suggestions have been supplemented by those of Professor Fouad El Ehwany of Cairo University. Rabbis Robert Jacobs and Bernard Lipnick and the Rev. Dr. Allen Miller of St. Louis have been most helpful critics of the chapters on Judaism and Christianity respectively. Lewis Hahn, Chairman of the Department of Philosophy at Washington University, has improved the manuscript as a whole by his careful reading, while Mrs. Lorna Garmany as secretary and typist has been a cheerful and unflagging pace-setter. On reading the completed manuscript I am struck by how many of its ideas first came to me in lectures which for two semesters Gerald Heard gave in my course on comparative religions. To each of these my sincerest thanks and a waiver of responsibility for what has actually carried through into print.

In addition to the above, all but one of whom has contributed directly to the manuscript itself, I wish to thank the following for providing contexts of stimulus, encouragement, and provocation which urged this book forward: Professor Lewis Hahn, Dean Thomas Hall, and my students in Philosophy 221-222 over the past decade at Washington University; President Thomas Spragens, Dean James Rice, and Professor Ralph Leyden at Stephens College where the material was presented over closed-circuit television during the spring of 1956; the Danforth Fellows before whom portions were delivered in The Danforth Fellow Lectures of September 1956 at Camp Miniwanca, and the Danforth Foundation for providing a seven month trip around the world to corroborate and revise the manuscript's original contents.

I reserve two names for mention in special categories. The first is that of Mayo Simon who was producer and director of the television series from which this book has grown most directly. Mayo and I were at ease together; we respected each other; we got fresh ideas from each other.

As we struggled with the enormous problems involved in trying to convey over a mass communication medium some of the profoundest insights that have occurred to man, the material came to new life for us. In view of the quickening effect this had on the lectures, it was our original hope to write this book together as well. Mayo's subsequent involvement as a playwright made this impossible, but if here and there the book speaks directly to the mind of the reader it will be in large part due to his ideas as they have continued to bubble up in every chapter and nearly every page.

When authors acknowledge a wife's help the picture usually conjured up is that of a patient spouse respectfully tiptoeing through the household tasks, exuding, perhaps, an ineffable aura of admiration and support. While these virtues are not absent from my wife, something must be added to the image; a partner happily involved in every sentence, pruning with zeal, revising with skill and imagination. It is because of this that "her husband is known in the gates, when he sitteth among the elders of the land."

HUSTON SMITH

St. Louis, Mo.
October 1957

The Religions of Man

1

Point of Departure

I WRITE these opening lines on a day widely celebrated throughout Christendom as World-Wide Communion Sunday. The sermon in the service I attended this morning dwelt on Christianity as a world phenomenon. From mud huts in Africa to igloos in Labrador Christians are kneeling today to receive the elements of the Holy Eucharist. It was an impressive picture.

Still, as I listened with half my mind the other half wandered to the wider company of God-seekers. I thought of the Yemenite Jews as I watched them six months ago in their Synagogue in Jerusalem: dark-skinned men sitting shoeless and cross-legged on the floor, wrapped in the prayer-shawls their ancestors wore in the desert. They are there today, at least a quorum of ten, morning and evening, swaying backwards and forwards like camel-riders as they recite their Torah, following a form they inherit unconsciously from the centuries when their fathers were forbidden to ride the desert-horse and developed this pretense in compensation. Yalcin, the Muslim architect who guided me through the Blue Mosque in Istanbul, has completed his month's Ramadan fast that was beginning while we were together, but he too is praying today, five times as he prostrates himself toward Mecca. Swami Ramakrishna in his tiny house by the Ganges at the foot of the Himalayas will not speak today. He will continue the devotional silence which, with the exception of three days each year, he has kept for five years. By this hour U Nu is probably facing the delegations, crises,

1

and cabinet meetings that are the lot of a Prime Minister, but from four to six this morning, before the world broke upon him, he too was alone with the eternal in the privacy of the Buddhist shrine that adjoins his home in Rangoon. At that, Dai Jo and Lai San, Zen monks in Kyoto, were ahead of him an hour. They have been up since three this morning, and until eleven tonight will spend most of the day sitting cross-legged and immovable as they seek with intense absorption to plumb the Buddha-nature that lies at the center of their being.

What a strange fellowship this is: the God-seekers of every clime, lifting their voices in the most diverse ways imaginable to the God of all men. How does it all sound to Him? Like bedlam? Or, in some mysterious way, does it blend into harmony? Does one faith carry the melody, the lead, or do the parts share in counterpoint and antiphony when not in solid chorus?

We cannot know. All we can do is try to listen, carefully and with full attention, to each voice in turn as it is raised to the divine.

This defines the purpose of this book. It may be wondered if it is not too broad. The religions we propose to consider belt the world. Their histories stretch back thousands of years, in addition to which they are motivating more men today than ever before. Is it possible to listen seriously to them within the compass of a single book?

The answer is that it is, because we shall be approaching them with special and limited intents. These must be seen and kept in mind or the picture that emerges from the pages that follow will mislead and distort.

Before saying what this book is, or at least tries to be, let us make as clear as possible what it is not.

1. It is not a textbook in the history of religions. This will explain the scarcity of names, dates, movements, and social crosscurrents in what follows. There are excellent books that focus on precisely this material.[1] They are invaluable. This book, too, could have been swollen prodigiously with the facts they present. But it is not its intent to do their job in addition to its own. Historical facts, as a consequence, have been held to the minimum needed to give the ideas discussed some grounding in space and time. Beyond this, every fact to escape deletion has had to be one that made an appreciable difference to the outlook in question. The book is written against the background of what scholars have uncovered about the history of religions, but their material has been built upon without allowing it to clutter or eclipse the meaning the religions held and hold for human life. Every attempt has been made to keep

scholarship in the foundations, essential to the strength of the structure but out of sight, instead of letting it rise in scaffolding which would obstruct the view of the mansions themselves.

2. Even in the realm of meaning, the book does not attempt to give a rounded view of the religions discussed. To do so would have required writing either a huge book or a choppy one. For people differ even when nurtured by the same culture, and as religion must try to speak to the needs of them all it has no choice but to spread out in almost endless diversity even within the same tradition. One need think only of Christianity. Eastern Orthodox Christians worship in ornate cathedrals while Quakers regard even a steeple as a desecration. St. Thomas finds no theological doctrine acceptable if it goes against reason while Tertullian cries "I believe because it is absurd." There are Christian mystics and Christians who denounce mysticism as beginning in 'mist,' centering in 'I,' and ending in 'scism.' Albertus Magnus finds religious meaning in cracking the hard nut of a theological argument, St. Francis in preaching to birds and flowers. There are Christian Holy Rollers and Christian Unitarians. How is it possible to say in a single chapter what Christianity means to all Christians?

The answer, of course, is that it is not possible. Selection is unavoidable. The question facing an author is not whether to select among points of view within a given religion; the questions are *how many* to present and *which ones*. In this book the first question has been answered by the principle of economy. Forced to choose, the attempt has been to do reasonable justice to a modest array of perspectives instead of crowding in, catalogue fashion, a more complete spectrum. In some cases (for example Islam) this has meant confining myself to a single statement, ignoring differences between Sunnis and Shiites or between traditionalists and modernists. In other cases (the Big and Little Rafts of Buddhism, for instance) two or three of the most important differences within a religion have been set forth. The number never goes above three lest the trees obscure the wood. Put the matter this way: if you were trying to describe Christianity to an intelligent and interested but busy Thailander, how many versions would you include? You could hardly pass over the differences between Roman Catholic, Greek Orthodox, and Protestant. But you would probably not try to bring in at one sitting what divides Presbyterians, Baptists, Methodists, and Episcopalians.

When we turn to the second question—which views are to be presented—the guiding principle has been relevance to the interests of the intended readers. Such relevance has been determined by weighing three considerations. The first is sheer numbers. There are some faiths with which every alert world citizen should be acquainted, simply because of the hundreds of millions of persons who live by them. Second, there is the question of relevance to the modern mind. Because the ultimate good that might come from a book like this, even beyond that of world understanding, is help to the reader in ordering and quickening his own life, priority has been given to what, with caution yet a certain confidence, we may regard as these religions' contemporary expressions. The third consideration is universality. Every religion is a blend of universal principles and local setting. The former, when lifted out and made clear, speak to man as man, whatever his time or place. The latter, a rich compound of myth and rite, can never make its way into the emotional life of an outsider and can reach his understanding only with the help of a poet or skilled anthropologist. It is one of the illusions of rationalism that the universal principles of religion are more important than the rites and rituals from which they grow. To say this is like saying that a tree is more important than the sun and soil from which it draws its life. But for this book principles are more important than contexts if for no other reason than that they are what the author has been trained to work with.

I have read books that have transplanted contexts themselves, an entire ecological environment of the spirit, and made them live: *Nectar in a Sieve* for India, *My Country and My People* for China, *The Old Country* for Eastern European Jews. Someday I hope someone will write a book on the religions of man which conveys these intimate living contexts out of which they have grown. But this is a book I shall read not write. I know my limitations and stick to those perspectives where ideological elements either predominate or can be readily extracted.

3. This book is not a balanced view of its subject. The warning is important. I wince to think of the shock if the reader were to close the chapter on Hinduism and step directly into the Hinduism described by Nehru as "a religion that enslaves you": her Kali Temple in Calcutta, the curse of her caste system, her two million cows revered to the point of nuisance, her fakirs deliberately offering their bodies as living sacrifice to bedbugs. Or what if he were to find himself in the streets of the leading city of Bali with one of its two movie houses named the Vishnu-Hollywood after the second god in the Hindu trinity and bookstores doing brisk business in *KLASIK COMIKS* in which Hindu gods and goddesses mow down hosts of unsightly demons with cosmic ray guns?

I know the contrast. I feel it vividly between what I have written of Taoism and the Taoism that surrounded me during the years of my youth in China: its almost complete submergence in augury, necromancy, and superstition. It is like the contrast between the Silent Christ and the Grand Inquisitor, between the Sermon on the Mount and the wars of Christendom, between the stillness of Bethlehem and department stores blaring "Silent Night" in the rush of Christmas shopping. The full story of religion is not rose-colored. It is not all insight and inspiration. It is often crude; charity and wisdom are often rare, and the net expressions bizarre when not revolting. A balanced view of man's religions would record its perversions as well as its glories. It would include human sacrifice and scapegoating, fanaticism and persecution, the Christian Crusades and the holy wars of Islam. It would include witch hunts in Massachusetts, monkey trials in Tennessee, and snake worship in the Ozarks—the list would have no end.

Why then are these things not included in the pages that follow? My answer is so simple that it may sound ingenuous. This is a book about values. Probably as much bad music as good has been written in the course of human history, but we do not ask that a course in music appreciation give it equal space. Time being limited, we expect no apology for spending it with the best. I have taken a similar position with regard to religion. A recent book on legal science carries the author's confession that he has written lovingly of the law. If something as impersonal as the law has captured one author's love, it should be no surprise that religion has captured another's. Others will be interested in trying to balance the record to determine if religion in its entirety has been more of a blessing than a curse. This has not been my concern.

4. This is not a book on comparative religions in the sense of speaking of their comparative worth. Comparisons among things men hold dear always tend to be odious, those among religions most odious of all. Hence there is no assumption in this book either that one religion is or is not superior to others. Comparative religion which takes such questions for its concern usually degenerates into competitive religion. What is more, the growth in knowledge of all religions together with the appearance of new sects in many make the standard contrasts which have been built up thus far daily more insecure. "There is no one alive today," observes Arnold Toynbee, "who knows enough to say with confidence whether one religion has been greater than all others." Coming from the man who should be able to pronounce on this point if anyone could,

the statement carries weight. For my part I have approached all the religious history treated in these pages as sacred history: questions of
degree I have, with Toynbee, felt I had not the God's eye-view to speak
to. I have tried to let the best in each religion come through; the reader
may draw his own comparisons from there.

Thus far we have been saying what this book is not. Now we must
say what it is.

1. It is a book that seeks to embrace the world. In one sense, of course,
such a wish must remain frustrated. Being finite, man's arms even when
spread to the maximum reach only a certain distance and his feet
must be planted somewhere; there must always be some base on which
he stands and from which his vision proceeds. To begin with the obvious, this book is written in English which from the start anchors it
to some extent. Next come cross-references introduced to facilitate entry
into the reader's understanding. There are proverbs from China, myths
from India, paradoxes from Japan, but most of the illustrations come
from the West. A line from Shakespeare, a verse from the Bible, a suggestion from psychoanalysis, the idiom is Western throughout. Beyond
idiom, however, the book is inescapably Western in being directed to
the mind-set of the contemporary Western reader. This has been due
to necessity; this being the writer's own mind-set, it was the only book he
could write. But one must recognize it as a limitation and understand
that the book would have been different if written by a Zen Buddhist,
a Muslim Sufi, or a Polish Jew.

This book, then, has a home—a home whose door swings freely both
in and out, a base from which to journey forth and return only to hit
the road again in study and imaginings when not in actual fact. If it is
possible to be homesick for the world, even places one has never been
and suspects one will never see, this book is the child of such home-
sickness.

We live in a fantastic century. I leave aside the incredible discoveries
of science, the narrow ridge between doom and fulfillment onto which
they have pushed us, and speak only of the new situation among peoples.
Lands across the planet have become our neighbors, China across the
street, Egypt at our doorstep. Radio and air traffic have shriveled space
until the only barrier is cost. Even where plane fare is lacking there is a
never-ending stream of books, documentaries, and visitors from abroad.
A random issue of a metropolitan daily carries word of yesterday's doings
in seventeen countries. We hear on all sides that East and West are
meeting but it is an understatement. They are being flung at one an-

other, hurled with the force of atoms, the speed of jets, the restlessness of minds impatient to learn of ways that differ from their own. From the perspective of history this may prove to be the most important fact about the twentieth century. When historians look back upon our years they may remember them not for the release of nuclear power nor the spread of Communism but as the time in which all the peoples of the world first had to take one another seriously.

The change in role this new situation requires of us all—we who have been suddenly catapulted from town and country onto a world stage—is enormous. Twenty-five hundred years ago it took an exceptional man like Socrates to say on his deathbed, "I am not an Athenian or a Greek but a citizen of the world." Today we must all be struggling toward these words. We have come to the point in history when anyone who is only a Japanese or only an American, only an Oriental or only a Westerner, is but half human; the other half of his being which beats with the pulse of all mankind has yet to be born.

To borrow Nietzsche's image, we have all been summoned to become Cosmic Dancers who do not rest heavily in a single spot but lightly turn and leap from one position to another. We shall all have our own perspectives, but they can no longer be cast in the hard molds of oblivion to the rest. The Cosmic Dancer, the World Citizen, will be an authentic child of his parent culture but related closely to all. He will not identify his whole being with any one land however dear. Where he prides himself on his culture or nationality, as he well may, his will be an affirming pride born of gratitude for the values he has gained, not a defensive pride whose only device for achieving the sense of superiority it pathetically needs is by grinding down others through invidious comparison. His roots in his family, his community, his civilization will be deep, but in that very depth he will strike the water table of man's common humanity and thus nourished will reach out in more active curiosity, more open vision, to discover and understand what others have seen. For is he not also man? If only he might see what has interested others, might it not interest him as well? It is an exciting prospect. The classic ruts between native and foreign, barbarian and Greek, East and West, will be softened if not effaced. Instead of crude and boastful contrasts there will be borrowings and exchange, mutual help, cross-fertilization that leads sometimes to good strong hybrids but for the most part simply enriches the species in question and continues its vigor.

The motives that impel us toward world understanding may be

several. Recently I was taxied by bomber to the Air Command and Staff College at the Maxwell Air Force Base outside Montgomery, Alabama, to lecture to a thousand selected officers on the religions of other peoples. I have never had students more eager to learn. What was their motivation? Individually I am sure it went beyond this in many cases, but as a unit they were concerned because someday they were likely to be dealing with the peoples they were studying as allies, antagonists, or subjects of military occupation. Under such circumstances it would be crucial for them to predict their behavior, conquer them if worse came to worst, and control them during the aftermath of reconstruction. This is one reason for coming to know people. It may be a necessary reason; certainly we have no right to disdain it as long as we ask the military to do the job we set before it.

Nevertheless one would hope that there are motives for understanding more elevated than that of national security. President Eisenhower moved into these when he remarked, "With everyone a loser in any new war, a better understanding than ever before is essential among people and among nations." These simple words give expression to world impulses, world dangers, world destinies. Here the motive for understanding is not military success; it is to make military action unnecessary. In a word, the motive is peace. The word rings so sweet that our first impulse is to clasp it as the final goal of all our seekings. But this would be wrong. Peace as we usually use the word is the absence of war and as such, however indispensable, is essentially negative. The final argument for understanding another cannot be to keep out of trouble with him; it is to enjoy the wider angle of vision such understanding affords. The vision can carry a thousand derivative benefits, silent harvests of the yield of wisdom, but the basic reward is the view itself.

We are, of course, speaking of vision and view in the mental sense but an analogy from physical sight is applicable. Experiments in the psychology of sense perception have shown that without the use of both eyes, without binocular vision, there can be no awareness of space's third dimension. Step up the power of a single eye as much as you please, without convergence from more than one angle the world would look as flat as a postcard. There would be above and below, right and left, but no near and far, no thickness, no substance, no body; the roundness of an orange would be a circle not a sphere. The rewards of having two eyes are intensely practical. They keep us from bumping into things and enable us to judge the speed of approaching cars. But the final reward is the deepened view of the world they make possible, the panoramas they unroll before us, the vistas they spread at our feet. It is the same with mental vision. "What do they know of England who only England know?"

The practical gains that come from being able to look at the world through the eyes of another people are enormous. They can enable industry to do business with Iran; they can keep a nation from tripping so often in a crowded and busy world. But the greatest gains need no tally. To glimpse what belonging means to a Chinese; to sense with a Burmese grandmother what passes in life and what endures; to understand how a Hindu can regard his personality as only a mask overlaying and obscuring the Infinite beneath and see how he can accept personal and impersonal views of God as equally true; to crack the paradox of a Zen monk in Kyoto who will assure you there is no difference between thieving and charity but who would never dream of thieving himself— to swing such things into view is to introduce a whole new dimension into the glance of spirit. It is to have another world to live in. The only thing good without qualification is not as Kant argued the good will— a will can mean well within terribly narrow confines. The only thing good without qualification is extended vision, the enlargement of one's understanding and awareness of what reality is ultimately like.

These thoughts about world understanding, its necessity, its incentives, and its rewards, lead directly to the religions of man. The surest way to the heart of a people is through their religion, assuming it is still alive and has not fossilized. Which distinction, between religion dead and religion alive, brings us to the second affirmative characteristic of this book.

2. It is a book that takes religion seriously. To begin with, it will be no tourist guide. There will be no hustling through men's faiths to light on what has shock value for the curiosity seeker; no dwelling on the strange, the bizarre, and the fantastic; no ascetics on beds of nails, no crucifixions among Indians in New Mexico, no Parsi Towers of Silence where the dead are dumped to be eaten by vultures, no absorption with cults like Indic tantra which uses sex as a means to salvation. Such material is a part of the religions of man. But to focus on it, lifting it out of context and waving it before the public drool, is, where not straight sacrilege, the crudest kind of vulgarization.

There are more refined ways not to take religion seriously. One way is to stress its importance, but for other people—people of the past, people of other cultures, people whose ego strength needs bolstering. This, too, will not be our approach. The parts of speech we use will be those of the third person. We shall be talking about Hindus, Buddhists, Confucianists, Muslims—it will be "they," and "them" most of the way. But behind these the tacit concern will be for "we" and "us." The chief reason I find myself returning to the religions of man is for help on questions I have not been able to get away from even when I have tried to ignore and forget. Given the essential similarity of human nature, it is safe to assume that they are questions that will not have escaped the reader either.

Nor will we fall into the other indirect way of belittling religion which also affirms its importance but this time as an instrument for achieving ends other than those of religion itself: artistic inspiration, for example, or health, success, personal adjustment, group loyalty. This is a book about religion that exists, in William James' contrast, not as a dull habit but as an acute fever. It is about religion alive. And wherever religion comes to life it displays a startling quality; it takes over. All else, while not silenced, becomes subdued and thrown without contest into a supporting role.

Religion alive confronts the individual with the most momentous option this world can present. It calls the soul to the highest adventure it can undertake, a proposed journey across the jungles, peaks, and deserts of the human spirit. The call is to confront reality, to master the self. Those who dare to hear and follow this secret call soon learn the dangers and difficulties of its lonely journey.

> A sharpened edge of a razor, hard to traverse,
> A difficult path is this—the poet's declare![2]

Science, as Justice Holmes was fond of saying, makes major contributions to minor needs. Religion, whether or not it comes up with anything, is at least at work on the things that matter most. When, then, a lone spirit succeeds in breaking through to major conquests here, he becomes more than a king—he becomes a world redeemer. His impact stretches for milennia blessing the tangled course of human history. "Who are. . . . the greatest benefactors of the living generation of mankind?" asks Toynbee. "I should say: 'Confucius and Laotze, the Buddha, the Prophets of Israel and Judah, Zoroaster, Jesus, Mohammed and Socrates.' "[3]

The answer should not surprise. Authentic religion is the clearest opening through which the inexhaustible energies of the cosmos can pour into human existence. What then can rival its power to touch and inspire the deepest creative centers of man's being? Moving outward from there into myth and rite it provides the symbols that carry history forward, until at length its power too is spent against the world's backwash and life awaits a new redemption. This recurrent pattern leads even the unpious like George Bernard Shaw to conclude that religion is the only real motive force in the world. It is religion in this sense that will be our object in the chapters ahead.

3. Finally, this book makes a real effort to communicate. I think of it as a work of translation, a work that has been concerned not only to penetrate the worlds of Hindu, Buddhist, and Muslim, but also to throw a bridge from these to the reader's world. The study of religion can be as technical and academic as any, but I have tried not to lose sight of the relevance this material has for the problems that men face today. "If you cannot—in the long run—tell everyone what you have been doing," writes a great contemporary scientist who is also a superb translator, "your doing has been worthless."[4]

This concern for translation accounts for the book's stance with respect to historical scholarship.

As far as I am aware, there is nothing in these pages contrary to the facts historians have discovered. But beyond this avoidance of straight inaccuracy, the relation of my presentation to historical evidence is less simple. I have deleted enormously, simplifying matters where historical details seemed to clog the meaning I was trying to get at. I have occasionally supplied corollaries where these seemed clearly implied but were not stated, and have occasionally introduced examples which seemed in keeping with the spirit of the material but were not actually found in the traditions in question.

These liberties may lead some historians to feel that the book "sits loose on the facts." But the problem has been more complicated than one of straight history. Religion is not primarily a matter of facts in the historical sense; it is a matter of meanings. An account may speak endlessly of gods and rites and beliefs, but unless it leads us to see how these things help men to meet such problems as isolation, tragedy, and death it may be impeccably accurate, but religion has not been touched at all. I have tried to keep this account of man's religions religiously translucent.

In sum, I have tried to let the book make religious sense without violating any other sense it might be happy enough to make in addition. Religion is not precisely history, but, as it is not fiction either, a book on the religions of man is no more at liberty to violate fact than to violate the human spirit by burying it under dead fact. What it takes fact and spirit to be are, of course, its ultimate gamble.

We are about to begin a voyage in space and time and eternity. The places will often be distant, the times remote, the themes beyond space and time altogether. We shall have to use words that are foreign— Sanskrit, Chinese, and Arabic. We shall describe conditions of the soul that words can only hint at. We shall have to use logic to try to corner perspectives that laugh at our attempt. And ultimately we shall fail; being ourselves of a different cast of mind, we shall never quite understand those of these religions that are not our own. But if we take those religions seriously we need not fail badly. And to take them seriously we need do only two things. One, we need to see their adherents as men and women confronted with problems like ourselves. Second, we must rid our minds of all preconceptions that will dull their sensitivity or alertness to fresh insights. If we lay aside our preformed ideas about these religions, see each as the work of men who were struggling to see something that would give help and meaning to their lives, and then try ourselves, without prejudice, to see what they saw—if we do these things the veil that separates us from them, while not removed, can be reduced to gauze.

A great anatomist used to close his first lecture to beginning medical students with some words whose tenor applies equally well to our own undertaking. "In this course," he would say, "we shall be dealing with flesh and bones and cells and sinews, and there are going to be times when it's all going to seem terribly cold blooded. But never forget—it's alive!"

2

Hinduism

If I were asked under what sky the human mind . . . has most deeply
pondered over the greatest problems of life, and has found solutions of some
of them which well deserve the attention even of those who have studied
Plato and Kant—I should point to India. And if I were to ask myself from
what literature we . . . who have been nurtured almost exclusively on the
thoughts of Greeks and Romans, and of one Semitic race, the Jewish, may
draw the corrective which is most wanted in order to make our inner life
more perfect, more comprehensive, more universal, in fact more truly human
a life, not for this life only, but a transfigured and eternal life—again I
should point to India.

Max Muller

On July 16, 1945, in the deep privacy of a New Mexico desert an event
occurred which may prove to be the most important single happening of
the twentieth century. A chain reaction of scientific discoveries that
began at the University of Chicago and centered at 'Site Y' at Los
Alamos was culminated. The first atomic bomb was, as we say, a success.

No one had been more instrumental in this achievement than Robert
Oppenheimer, director of the Los Alamos project. An observer who was
watching him closely that morning has given us the following account:
"He grew tenser as the last seconds ticked off. He scarcely breathed.
He held on to a post to steady himself. . . . When the announcer shouted
'Now!' and there came this tremendous burst of light, followed . . . by
the deep-growling roar of the explosion, his face relaxed in an expression
of tremendous relief." This much from the outside. But what flashed

through his mind during those moments, Mr. Oppenheimer recalled later, were two lines from the *Bhagavad-Gita* in which God is the spokesman:

> I am become death, the shatterer of worlds;
> Waiting that hour that ripens to their doom.

This incident is a profound symbol of our times. Like its predecessors, our generation was brought up on the first half of Kipling's quatrain only:

> Oh, East is East and West is West,
> And never the twain shall meet . . .

Today we are discovering its sequel:

> Till earth and sky stand presently
> At God's great Judgment Seat.

Kipling's "presently" has arrived. Certainly nuclear weapons have brought all earth if not sky to some sort of Judgment. It is a remarkable vindication of the poet's prophecy that at precisely the fateful moment which announced this Judgment there flashed through the mind of a man who stands as a symbol of the scientific West lines drawn not from his own tradition but from the scriptures of the East, the Hindu *Bhagavad-Gita*, or *Song of God*.

Not that East and West or (to speak explicitly of that part of the East with which we are concerned in this chapter) India and the West have not met at all in the past. A century ago, Thoreau could testify that his mind had been made by two books, Emerson's *Essay on Nature* and the *Bhagavad-Gita*. At almost the same time, Arthur Schopenhauer could write of the basic Hindu scriptures, "In the whole world there is no study so beautiful and so elevating as that of the *Upanishads*. It has been the solace of my life, it will be the solace of my death." But men like these were exceptional. Only in our generation has there developed in the West a widespread presentiment of a spiritual greatness in India which we have yet to comprehend and from which we might indeed draw profit.

Most responsible for awakening the West to this recognition was a little man who weighed not much more than a hundred pounds and whose worldly possessions when he died totaled under two dollars. If his picture were to appear on this page it would be recognized immediately. How many other portraits would be recognized so universally? Someone ventured a few years ago that there were only three: those of Charlie Chaplin, Mickey Mouse, and Mahatma Gandhi, Gandhi "whose essence of being is great" as the title Mahatma would be literally translated. In an age in which violence and peace faced each other more fatefully than ever before, his name became the counterpoise to Stalin and Hitler. The achievement for which the world credited him was the British withdrawal from India in peace. What is not as well known is that among his own people he lowered a barrier much more formidable than that of race in the United States, renaming the "untouchables" *harijan*, God's People, and raising them to human status. As General Marshall said on learning of his assassination: "Mahatma Gandhi was the spokesman for the conscience of mankind." Christians instinctively spoke of him as the most Christ-like man alive, and it is true that he was profoundly influenced by the Sermon on the Mount. But his basic inspiration came from his native India. Early in his *Autobiography* Gandhi wrote, "such power as I possess for working in the political field (has) derived (from) my experiments in the spiritual field," adding that in the latter "truth is the sovereign principle," and that the *Bhagavad-Gita* is "the book *par excellence* for the knowledge of Truth."

Precisely to what extent contemporary Western interest in India's spiritual heritage is due to Mahatma Gandhi cannot, of course, be measured. But the interest itself is unmistakable. That one of the most acclaimed poems of our generation, T. S. Eliot's *The Waste Land*, should end with the classic Hindu benediction, "*Shantih, shantih, shantih*," meaning "Peace, peace, peace," may be no more than a scrap of bilingualism, but there are other notable authors who make no secret of the fact that they have drawn as much personal inspiration and meaning from India as from their native heritage: Aldous Huxley, Christopher Isherwood, Vincent Sheean, Louis Fischer, Gerald Heard, and John Van Druten. Scholars, too, could be added to the list: René Guenon of France, Joseph Campbell of Sarah Lawrence College, and Heinrich Zimmer of Columbia University whose *Philosophies of India*, a book concerned with "the world-reverberating jungle roar of India's wisdom," opens with the striking conviction that "We of the Occident are about to arrive at a crossroads that was reached by the thinkers of India some seven hundred years before Christ." In an address delivered at Edinburgh University in 1952, Arnold Toynbee predicted that in fifty years the world would be under the hegemony of the United States but that in the twenty-first century, as religion captures the place of technology, it is possible that "India the conquered will conquer its conquerors."

Our task in this chapter is to discover what Hinduism says that can interest the mind of a Huxley, inspire a life like Gandhi's, and lead Toynbee to believe that even in a Westernizing world it has a future to be watched.

THE WANTS OF MAN

If we were to take Hinduism as a whole—its vast literature, its opulent art, its elaborate rituals, its sprawling folkways—if we were to take this enormous outlook in its entirety and epitomize it in a single, central affirmation we would find it saying to man: You can have what you want.

This sounds good but it throws the problem back in our laps. For what *do* we want? It is easy to give a simple answer but hard to give a good one. India has been with this question a long time, and has her answer waiting. The wants of man, she says, are four.

He begins by wanting pleasure. This is natural. We are all born with built-in pleasure-pain reactors. If we ignored these completely, leaving our hands on hot stoves or stepping out of second-story windows, we would read ourselves out of existence. What could be more obvious, then, than to follow these friendly leads of pleasure and make them our guiding principle and ultimate goal?

Having heard—for this is a common Western view—that India is ascetic, other-worldly, and life-denying, we might expect her attitude toward hedonists who set pleasure as their goal to be sharply scolding, but it is not. True, India has not taken pleasure as life's highest value, but this is different from condemning enjoyment as itself evil. To the person who wants pleasure, India says in effect: Go after it—there is nothing wrong with it. It is one of the four legitimate ends of life. The world holds immense possibilities for enjoyment. It is awash with beauty and heavy with delights for all our senses. Moreover, there are other worlds above this where pleasures mount by a factor of a million at each successive round; we shall experience these worlds too at later stages in our becoming. Of course, hedonism like everything else calls for good sense. Not every impulse can be followed with impunity; small immediate goals must be sacrificed for the sake of greater future ones, and impulses that would injure others must be checked if for no other reason than to avoid antagonisms without and a troubled conscience within. Only the ignorant will lie, steal, or cheat for the sake of seeming advantage or fall into gross addictions. But as long as the basic rules of morality are observed you are free to seek all the pleasure you wish. Far from condemning pleasure, Hindu texts abound in pointers on how to increase it to the full. For the simple peasant whose aspirations are still in this direction, virtually all religion, from its rites and rituals to its ethical dictates, is presented as something that can protect his prosperity and good fortune, bring rain, heal the sick, and in general insure good fortune. Even for the sophisticate there is in accepted Hindu philosophy a hedonism which, in its combined subtlety and frankness, often shocks the West. If pleasure is what you want, says India, don't suppress this desire. See instead that it is fulfilled as richly and esthetically as possible.

She says this—and waits. She waits for the time (it will come to everyone, though not to everyone in his present life) when one realizes that pleasure *isn't* all one wants. The reason everyone eventually comes to this discovery is not because pleasure is wicked—we have seen that it is not—but because it is enervating and too narrow and trivial to satisfy man's total nature. Pleasure is essentially private, and the self is too small an object for perpetual enthusiasm. Kierkegaard tried for a while what he called the esthetic life which made enjoyment its principle, only to experience its radical failure which he so lucidly described in *Sickness Unto Death*. "In the bottomless ocean of pleasure, I have sounded in vain for a spot to cast anchor," he wrote in his *Journal*. "I have felt the almost irresistible power with which one pleasure drags another after it, the kind of adulterated enthusiasm which it is capable of producing, the boredom, the torment which follow." Even New York city's colorful playboy, Jimmy Walker, accused of many things but never of profundity, is said to have remarked in his later years, "The glamour of yesterday I have come to see as tinsel." Such discoveries, India would say, are typical. Sooner or later, everyone wants to be more than a kaleidoscope of private, momentary pleasures however exquisite and subtle.

When this time comes the individual's interests usually shift to the second great goal of life which is worldly success,[1] with its three aspects of wealth, fame, and power. This too is a worthy goal, to be neither scorned nor condemned. Moreover its satisfactions last longer, for, unlike pleasure, success is a social achievement substantially meshed with the lives of others. In this respect it commands a scope and importance that the playboy's pleasure cannot pretend.

This point does not have to be argued for an American audience. The Anglo-American world is not voluptuous; visitors from other cultures are almost unanimous in their impression that, despite superficial appearances to the contrary, English-speaking peoples do not enjoy life a great deal and are not really intent upon doing so—they are in too much of a hurry. The impress of Calvinism and Puritanism is still deep. What has conquered the West is the gospel not of sensualism but of success. What takes arguing for the West is not that achievement carries rewards beyond sensualism but rather that success too has its limitations, that man has never been able to live by bread alone and that the question "What is he worth?" can have a deeper reference than "How much has he got?"

India acknowledges that drives for possessions, status, and power run deep. Nor should they be disparaged per se. A modicum of worldly success is indispensable for the upkeep of a household, raising a family, and discharge of civic duties. Beyond this minimum, worldly achievements bring to many a sense of dignity and self-respect. In the end, however, these too are found wanting. For beneath the surface of each lurk the following limitations:

1. Wealth, fame, and power are exclusive, hence competitive, hence precarious. Unlike values associated more directly with man's mind and spirit, these do not multiply when shared; they cannot be distributed without one's own portion being diminished. If I own a dollar, that dollar cannot be yours. As long as I am sitting on a chair, you cannot sit on it too. Fame and power are similarly exclusive. The idea of a nation in which everyone is famous is a contradiction in terms; if power were distributed equally no one would be powerful in the sense in which we customarily use the word. Fame consists in standing out from one's fellows and power is control over them. From the competitiveness of these values to their precariousness is a short step. As other people of ability want them too, who knows when success will change hands? One can never be certain that one's competitors will not gain the advantage; hence a position of unassailable security is never reached.

2. The second contradiction within worldly success when this is taken as life's objective is the sense in which it can never be satisfied. While it is not true to say that men can never get enough money, fame, and power, it is true to say that men can never get enough of these things when they want them greedily, when they make them the supreme forces of their lives. These are not the things men really want, and man can never get enough of what he does not really want. As the Hindus say, "to try to extinguish the drive for riches with money is like trying to quench a fire by pouring butterfat over it."

The West, too, has of course known this point well. "Poverty consists, not in the decrease of one's possessions, but in the increase of one's greed," writes Plato for the philosophers. "Could you from all the world all wealth procure, more would remain, whose lack would leave you poor," adds St. Gregory Nazianzen for the theologians. Abram Kardiner speaks for the psychologists, "Success is a goal without a satiation point," while the Lynds in their first sociological study of Middletown note that "both business men and working men seem to be running for dear life in this business of making the money they earn keep pace with the even more rapid growth of their subjective wants." Each of these men is testifying from his own professional perspective to the point India, characteristically, puts in a parable, the parable of the donkey before which the driver dangled a luscious carrot hanging from a stick fastened to its own harness. The more the animal ran to get at the carrot, the further the carrot receded.

3. The third weakness of worldly success is identical with that of hedonism. Though less obviously trivial than pleasure, it too centers value and meaning in the self which must eventually be sensed in the silences of subjectivity to be too small for the heart's eternal trust. Neither fortune nor position can shut out the awareness that the possessor lacks so much else. In the end everyone asks more from life than a ranch home in the suburbs, two cars in the garage, and a plush annuity.

4. The final reason worldly success cannot satisfy man completely is because its achievements are ephemeral. Man knows well that wealth, fame, and power do not survive bodily death. "You can't take it with you," has become the familiar way of putting this point in the West. And since he cannot, this fact must keep these things from satisfying man wholly, for he is a creature who can envision eternity and must instinctively rue by contrast the brief purchase on time his worldly successes command.

Before proceeding to the other two things Hinduism sees men wanting it will be well to summarize the ones considered thus far. Pleasure and success are described by the Hindus as the twin goals of the Path of Desire. They use this phrase because the personal desires of the individual have thus far been uppermost in charting life's course. Other goals lie ahead but this does not mean that our attitude toward the ones already recounted should be negative. Nothing can possibly be gained by repressing desires wholesale or pretending we do not have them. As long as pleasure and success are what we think we want we should go after them, remembering only the instrumentalities of prudence and fair play already noted.

In short, Hinduism regards the objects of the Path of Desire as if they were toys. If we ask ourselves whether there is anything wrong with toys our answer must be: on the contrary, there is something tragic in the picture of children deprived of them. Even sadder, however, is that of adults who fail to move on to interests more significant than dolls and electric trains. A mature adult takes interest in such things not from his own need but for the sake of children who prize them and move through their enjoyment of them to a point beyond. By the same token, in the perspective of man's total career the individual whose development is not arrested will work his way through full delight in success and the senses to the point where these pulls have been largely outgrown. Unless he does, his energies must remain locked forever in life's banal, outmoded nursery.

But what more significant concerns does life afford? Two, answers Hinduism. In contrast with the Path of Desire, they make up the Path of Renunciation.

The word renunciation has a negative ring, and India's frequent use of it has undoubtedly been one of the factors in earning for her the reputation of being life-denying and pessimistic. Renunciation, however, can be prompted by disillusionment and despair, in which case it represents life's foreclosing, the liquidation proceedings of the human spirit in withdrawal and decline. But renunciation can also be a clearer sign of exhilaration and confidence in life's high calling than any amount of momentary indulgence. In this category falls discipline of every form, the sacrifice of a trivial now for a momentous then, the turning away from an easy this toward a beckoning yet-to-be. When not perverted, religious renunciation is on a continuum with that of the athlete in training who turns his back upon every indulgence that would deflect from his prize. Precisely the opposite of disillusionment, it is the only evidence that can be given of life's confidence in the existence of values beyond those it is experiencing at the moment.

We must never forget that in Hinduism the Path of Renunciation comes *after* the Path of Desire. If men could be satisfied by following their initial wants the idea of renunciation would never have arisen. Nor does it occur only to those who have failed on the former path—the young man who enters a monastery because he has been jilted, for example. We can agree with the disparagers of renunciation that such persons may resort to it only to rationalize or to compensate for personal inadequacies. What forces us to listen attentively to Hinduism's hypothesis of other goals is the testimony of those who have followed the Path of Desire with brilliant success only to find themselves wishing desperately that life could give them something more. These people —not the ones who renounce but the ones who see nothing to renounce for—are the world's real pessimists. For to live a man must believe in that for the sake of which he lives. If he sees no futility in pleasure and success he can believe in these as worth living for. But if, as Tolstoy points out in his *Confession,* he can no longer have faith in the value of the finite, he will believe in the infinite or die.

Let us be clear. Hinduism does not say that everyone in his present life will find the Path of Desire inadequate. For against a vaster time scale Hinduism draws a distinction with which we have all become familiar between chronological and psychological age. Two men both forty-six are the same age chronologically but psychologically one may be still a child whereas the other is a mature adult. The Hindus accept this distinction but extend it to cover multiple life spans, a point we shall take up explicitly when we come to the idea of reincarnation. We will, consequently, find men and women who play the game of desire with all the zest of nine-year-olds at cops and robbers; though they know nothing else they will die with the sense of having lived to the full and will leave as their verdict that life is good. But equally there will be others who play this game just as ably yet find the laurels inadequate. Why the difference? The difference, say the Hindus, lies in the fact that the enthusiasts are caught in the flush of novelty whereas the others, having played and won the game more often, are instinctively feeling out for other worlds to conquer.

We can describe the typical experience of this second type. The world's visible rewards still attract him strongly. He throws himself into enjoyment, building up his holdings and advancing his status. But neither the pursuit nor the attainment of these things brings him true happiness. Some of the things he wants he fails to get and this makes him miserable. Some he gets and holds for a while only to have them suddenly snatched from him—and again he is miserable. Some he both gets and keeps only to find, like the experience of so many Christmases in adolescence, that they do not bring the joy he expected. Many experiences that thrilled on first encounter pall on the hundredth. Throughout, each attainment seems only to fan the fire of new desire; none satisfies fully and all, he perceives, perish with time. Eventually there comes over him a suspicion that he is caught on a nonstop treadmill, having to race faster and faster for rewards that mean less and less.

When this condition is reached and he finds himself crying, "Vanity,

vanity, all is vanity!" it may occur to him that his trouble lies in the fact that his satisfactions are limited by the smallness of the self he has been scrambling to serve. What if the focus of his concern were shifted? Might not becoming a part of a larger, more significant whole relieve his life of its oppressive triviality?

This question, once it arises, brings the beginning of religion. For though in some watered down sense there may be a religion which makes of the self its own god, true religion begins with the quest for meaning and value beyond privacy—with renunciation of the ego's claims to finality.

But for what is this renunciation to be made? The question brings us to the two specific ingredients in the Path of Renunciation. The human community suggests itself as the first candidate. In supporting at once our own life and the lives of myriads of others, the community has an importance no single life can command. Let us, then, transfer our allegiance to it, giving its claims priority over our own.

This is the first great step in religion. It produces the religion of duty, the third great aim of life in the Hindu outlook. Its power over those who have matured enough to feel its pull is tremendous. Countless persons have passed beyond the wish to win into the wish to be of service, beyond the wish to gain to the wish to give. Not to triumph but to do their best, to acquit themselves as men in whatever task life puts before them, has become their deepest objective.

Hinduism abounds in directives to the man or woman who would put his shoulder to the human enterprise. It sets forth in elaborate detail the duties which go with age, disposition, and social status. We shall be looking into these in subsequent sections. Here we need only repeat for this third life-objective what was said in connection with the previous two: it, too, yields notable rewards, but in the end fails to satisfy the human heart completely. Its rewards require maturity to be appreciated, but given this they are substantial. Faithful performance of duty brings the praise of peers. More gratifying than this, however, is the self-respect that comes from having done one's part, of having contributed. But in the end even this realization cannot provide joy adequate to man's desiring. For even when elongated through history, the human community, as long as it stands alone, remains both finite and tragic; tragic not only in the sense that it must eventually come to an end, but also in its implacable resistance to perfection. The final want of man must still lie elsewhere.

What Men Really Want

"There comes a time," writes Aldous Huxley, "when one asks even of Shakespeare, even of Beethoven, is this all?"

It is difficult to think of a sentence that puts its finger more precisely on Hinduism's attitude toward the world. The things of this world are not bad. By and large they are good. Some of them are so wonderful that they can command man's admiration and enthusiasm for many lifetimes. Eventually, however, every human being comes to realize with Simone Weil "that there is no true good here below, that everything that appears to be good in this world is finite, limited, wears out, and once worn out, leaves necessity exposed in all its nakedness."[2] When this point is reached, he will find himself asking even of the finest this world can offer—not only the peaks of esthetic experience but the highest reaches of love and knowledge and duty as well, "Is this all?"

This is the moment Hinduism has been waiting for. As long as a person is content with the prospects of pleasure, success, or dutiful living, the Hindu sage will not be likely to disturb him beyond offering some suggestions as to how to proceed toward these goals more effectively. The critical point in life comes when these things lose their original charm and one finds oneself wishing that life had something more to offer. Whether life does or does not hold more is probably the question which divides men more sharply than any other.

The Indic answer to this question is unequivocal. Life definitely holds other possibilities. To see what these are we must return to the question of what men want. Thus far, Hinduism would say, we have been answering this question too superficially. Pleasure, success, and duty are never man's ultimate goals; at best they are means which we assume will take us in the direction of what we really want. What we really want are things which lie on a deeper level.

First, we want being. Everyone wants to be rather than not be. Normally nobody wants to die. Toward the close of his own life, Ernie Pyle, the great correspondent of World War II, described the atmosphere of a room in which were gathered thirty-five men who had been assigned to a bombing mission the following day. On an average only one-fourth of those who went out on this particular run returned. What he felt in those men, Ernie Pyle wrote, was not really fear. Rather, it was "a profound reluctance to give up the future." This is true of us all, the Hindus would say; none of us take happily to the thought of the future proceeding without us. Occasionally an individual may find himself driven by desperation to suicide but no one really feels happy about dying.

Second, we want to know, to be aware. People are endlessly curious. Whether it be a scientist probing the mysteries of nature, a businessman scanning the morning paper, a teen-ager glued to television to find out who won the ball game, or neighbors catching up on the local news over a cup of coffee, we are all insatiably curious. Experiments have shown that monkeys will work longer and harder to find out what is on the other side of a trap door than they will for rewards of either food or sex. If curiosity is this strong in monkeys, how much stronger in human beings!

The third thing men seek is joy, a resolution of feelings in which the basic motifs are the opposite of frustration, futility, and boredom.

These are the real desires of men. To which if we are to complete the picture, says Hinduism, we must add one further point. Not only are these the things man wants; he wants each of them in infinite degree. One of the most distinctive and significant features of man is the fact that he can conceive the idea of infinity. This capacity colors his entire life, as Chirico's painting "Nostalgia of the Infinite" poignantly suggests. Mention any good and man can always imagine a bit more of it and in doing so wish for that more. Medical science has doubled man's life expectancy, but is man today more ready to die once that expectancy is reached? To state the full truth, then, we must say that what man would really like is infinite being, infinite knowledge, and infinite joy. Disregarding for the moment what he might have to settle for, these are what he would really like. To gather them together in a single word, what man really wants is liberation (*mukti*)—complete release from the countless limitations that press so closely upon his present existence.

Pleasure, success, responsible discharge of duty, and liberation—we have completed the circuit of what man thinks he wants and what he really wants. And now we come back to India's staggering conclusion with which we began; what man most wants, that he can have. Infinite being, infinite awareness, and infinite joy are within his reach. The most startling statement, however, comes next. Not only are these within his reach, Hinduism argues; they are already his.

For what is man? A body? Certainly, but anything else? A personality that includes his mind, memories, and the propensities that have accumulated from his own unique pattern of life experiences? This, too, but anything more? Some would say no, but Hinduism disagrees. Underlying man's personality and animating it is a reservoir of being that never dies, is never exhausted, and is without limit in awareness and bliss. This infinite center of every life, this hidden self or *Atman*, is no less than *Brahman*, the Godhead. Body, personality, and *Atman-Brahman*—man is not completely accounted for until all three have been named.

But if this is true, if we really are infinite in our being, why is this not apparent? Why do we not act accordingly? "I don't happen to feel particularly unlimited today," one may be prompted to observe. "And my neighbor—I haven't noticed his behavior as exactly Godlike." How can the Hindu thesis possibly withstand the evidence of the morning paper?

The answer, say the Hindus, lies in the extent to which the Eternal is buried under the almost impenetrable mass of distractions, false ideas, and self-regarding impulses that comprise our surface being. A lamp may be so covered with dust and dirt that its light will be invisible. The problem life puts to man is to cleanse the dross of his being to the point where its infinite center will be fully manifest.

This, clearly, is a thesis that must be explored further.

The Beyond that is Within

"The aim of life," Justice Holmes used to say, "is to get as far as possible from imperfection." Hinduism says its purpose is to pass beyond imperfection altogether.

If we were to set out to compile a catalogue of the specific imperfections that hedge our lives, it would have no end. We lack strength and imagination to effect our dreams; we fall ill; we grow tired; we make mistakes; we are ignorant; we fall and become discouraged; we grow old and die. Lists of this sort could be extended indefinitely but there is no need, for all specific limitations reduce to three basic variants. We are limited in being, knowledge, and joy, the three things men really want.

Is it possible to pass beyond the strictures that separate us from these things? Is it feasible to seek to rise to a quality of life which, because less circumscribed, would be life indeed?

The strictures on our joy fall into three groups: physical pain, the frustration from the thwarting of desire, and boredom with life as a whole. The first is the least troublesome. As its intensity is due in large part to the fear which accompanies it, the conquest of fear can reduce pain appreciably. When seen to have a purpose, pain can be accepted, as one welcomes the return of life and feeling to a frozen arm even though painful. Again, pain can be forgotten in the urgency of purpose. In extreme cases of useless pain it may be possible simply to turn it off through anesthesia induced either externally through drugs or internally through mastery of the senses. Ramakrishna, the greatest Hindu saint of the nineteenth century, died of cancer of the throat. A doctor who was examining him in the last stages of this dreadful disease probed the degenerating tissue and Ramakrishna started in pain. "Wait a minute," he said, then, "Go ahead." After which the doctor could probe without resistance. He had placed himself in a state of mind in which the nerve sensations did not break through on his awareness at all or barely did so. One way or another it seems possible to rise to a point where physical pain ceases to be a serious limitation.

Far more serious is the psychological pain which arises from the thwarting of specific desires. We want to win a golf tournament but don't; we want to make money on a deal but lose; we want to be promoted but are not; we want to be invited but are snubbed. Life is so filled with disappointments that we are likely to assume that they are embedded in the condition of being human. As we look, however, we discover something all disappointments share in common. Each lets down some personal expectation of the individual ego. If the ego were to have no expectations, there would then be nothing to disappoint.

Or, if this sounds like ending an ailment by killing the patient, put the same point in positive terms. What if the interests of the self were expanded to the point of approximating a God's-eye view of the human scene. Seeing, thus, all things "under the aspect of eternity," would not one become completely objective toward oneself, accepting failure as being as natural an occurrence as success in the stupendous human drama of yes and no, positive and negative, push and pull—as little cause for worry and concern as having to play the role of a loser in a summer theater performance? How can defeat disappoint if one feels the joy of the victor as if it were one's own? How can failure to be promoted touch one if the rival's success can be enjoyed vicariously with equal force? Instead of crying "Impossible" we ought perhaps to content ourselves with observing how different this would be from life as it is usually lived, for the lives of the greatest spiritual geniuses suggest that they rose to precisely this condition. "Inasmuch as ye have done it unto the least of these, ye have done it unto me." Are we to suppose that Jesus was posturing when he uttered these words? We are told that Ramakrishna once

howled with pain when he saw two boatmen quarrelling angrily. He came to identify himself with the sorrows of the whole world, however impure and murderous they might be, until his heart was scored with scars. But he knew that even the differences leading to strife among men are the daughters of the same Mother; that the 'Omnipotent Differentiation' is the face of God Himself; that he must love God in all sorts and conditions of men, however antagonistic and hostile, and in all forms of thought controlling their existence and often setting them at variance to one with the other.[3]

Detachment from the finite self or attachment to reality as a whole—we can state the phenomenon in either positive or negative terms. When it occurs life is lifted above the possibility of frustration. Above ennui as well, for the cosmic drama is too spectacular to permit boredom in the face of such intensive identification.

The second great limitation of human life is ignorance. The Hindus claim this, too, is removable. The *Upanishads* speak of "knowing That the knowledge of which brings knowledge of everything." It is difficult to know whether this means that there is a discovery which, if made, would bring literally a detailed simultaneous awareness of everything that has ever happened or ever will. More likely it refers to some blinding insight which so illumines the cosmic scene that its stupendous point is laid bare. In the presence of this shattering vision of wholeness, to ask of details would be as irrelevant as asking the number of atoms in a particular patch of blue in a Picasso painting, or the number of vibrations per second in the lowest note of a chord climaxing a Bach chorale. When the point is grasped, who cares about details?

But is transcendent knowledge even in this second sense open to man? Certainly the mystics are unanimous in their reports that it is. Academic psychology has not followed their claims all the way and often seems to look in a different direction, but it too has become convinced that there is far more to our minds than we see on the surface. Our minds are like icebergs, most of which lie below the waterline of visibility. What lies in this vast, submerged continent we call the subconscious? Some think it harbors every memory and experience that has come to us, absolutely nothing being lost to this deep mind that never sleeps. Others like Carl Jung think it includes racial memories, a collective unconscious that summarizes the wisdom of the human race. The purpose of psychoanalysis is to throw a few pinpoints of light onto those vast, opaque regions of our minds that are invisible until specially approached. But suppose this submerged continent could be fully conquered. Who can predict how far the horizons of our awareness would be pushed back?

As for life's third limitation, its finitude, to profitably consider this we have first to ask how the boundary of the self is to be defined. Not, certainly, by the amount of physical space our bodies occupy, the amount of water we displace when we submerge in the bathtub. It would make more sense if we were to gauge a man's being by the size of his spirit, that is, the range of reality with which he identifies himself. A man who identifies himself with his family, finding his joys in theirs, would have that much reality; one who could really identify himself with mankind as a whole would be proportionately greater. By this criterion, if a man could identify himself with being in general, being as a whole, his own being would be unlimited. Still this seems hardly right, for no extent of such identification could keep him from dying at which time his being would be cut off abruptly. The object of his concern would continue, but he would be gone.

We need, therefore, to approach this question of being not only spatially, so to speak, but also in terms of time. Our everyday experience provides a wedge for doing so. Strictly speaking every moment in our lives is a dying. The I of that moment dies, never to live again. Yet despite the fact that in this sense my experience consists of nothing but funerals, I do not think that I am dying in these, for I do not equate myself with any one of my experiences. I think of myself enduring through these, witnessing them, but not in my entirety identical with any. Hinduism pushes this concept back to another level. It posits a self that underlies my entire present life as that endures through my individual experiences.

A child's heart is broken by misfortunes we consider trivial. He *is* each incident, being unable to see it against the backdrop of a whole, variable lifetime. A great deal of experience is required before the child shifts his self-identification away from the individual moment and becomes an adult. Compared with children we are mature, but compared with saints we are children. No more capable of seeing our total selves in perspective than a three-year-old who has broken her doll, our attention is fixated on our present lifespan. If only we could grow up completely we would discover that our total being is more vast than we suppose. We would find that it is infinite.

This is the basic point in the Hindu estimate of man. Contemporary

psychology, as we have seen, has accustomed us to
is more to ourselves than we suspect. Like the earth
ago, our minds have their own darkest Africas, their
and Amazonian basins. Indeed, their bulk still w
According to Hinduism, mind's hidden continen
touch infinity. Infinite in being, infinite in awareness, there
outside them waiting to be known. Infinite in joy, too, for again there
is nothing external or contradictory which could intrude to interrupt
their eternal self-content.

Hindu literature is full of parables and metaphors designed to open
our imaginations to this infinite which lies concealed in the depths of
every life. We are like a king who, falling victim to amnesia, wanders
his kingdom in tatters not knowing who he really is. We are like a lion
cub who, having become lost from his mother at birth, grows up by
accident among sheep and takes to grazing and bleating like them,
assuming that he too is a sheep. We are like a lover who, dreaming,
searches the world in despair for his beloved, oblivious to the fact that
she is lying at his side.

What the realization of our total being is like can be known only by
actual experience; it can no more be described than a sunset to one born
blind. The biographies of those who have made this supreme discovery
provide us, however, with important clues. These men are wiser; they
have more personal strength and joy. They seem free, not in the sense
that they go around breaking the laws of nature (though the power to
do exceptional things which could only seem like miracles to us is
usually ascribed to them) but in the sense that they never find the
natural order frustrating. This being so, nothing binds them nor shakes
them. Nothing disrupts their peace of mind. They feel no lack, no
misery, no fear, and find no cause for strife or grief. They seem always
to be in good spirits, agreeable, even gay. As their egos need no bolstering, their love can flow outward, alike to all. Contact with them imparts
strength, purity, and encouragement.

Four Paths to the Goal

All of us dwell on the brink of the infinite ocean of life's creative
power. We all carry it within us; supreme strength, the fullness of wisdom, unquenchable joy. It is never thwarted and cannot be destroyed.
But it is hidden deep, which is what makes life a problem. The infinite
is down in the darkest, profoundest vault of our being, in the forgotten

e, the deep cistern. What if we could discover it again and
rom it unceasingly?

is question became India's obsession. Her people sought religious
uth not simply to increase their store of general information; they
sought it as a chart to guide them to a higher state of being. The religious person was one who was seeking to transform his nature, remake
it into a superhuman pattern through which the infinite could shine with
fewer obstructions. One feels the urgency of the quest in a metaphor
encountered in Hindu texts under many variations: Just as a man
carrying on his head a load of wood that has caught fire would go rushing to a pond to quench the flames, even so will the seeker of truth,
scorched with the mad pains of the fire of life in the world, its birth,
its death, its self-deluding futility, go rushing to a teacher learned in the
things that matter most.

Hinduism's specific directions for actualizing man's fullest nature
come under the heading of *yoga*. The word is not unknown to the West.
Apart from its fortuitous association with the name of a big league ball
player, Yogi Berra, it is not at all unusual to pick up the morning paper
and find that another Hollywood actress has taken it up, that Yehudi
Menuhin is standing on his head in moving railway compartments, or
that Marlon Brando has studied it enough to make his belly muscles
flow rhythmically around his navel. What connection can capers and
contortions like these have to do with the life of the spirit—to say
nothing of the usual pictures the word *yoga* brings to mind, pictures of
shaggy men in loin cloths turning themselves into human pretzels and
brandishing strange psychic powers?

There is a connection, though sometimes it is no more than etymo-
logical. The word *yoga* comes from the same root as the English word
yoke. Yoke carries a double connotation: to unite (yoke together) and
to place under discipline or training (to bring under the yoke, take my
yoke upon you). Both connotations are present in the Sanskrit word.
Defined generally, then, *yoga* is a method of training designed to lead to
integration or union. But integration of what?

Some persons are chiefly interested in coordinating their bodies.
Needless to say, they have their Indian counterparts—men who take
mastery of the body as their basic interest. Out of centuries of experiment and practice, India has built up the most fantastic school of
physical culture the world has ever seen.[4] Not that she has been more
interested in the body than the West, but her interest has taken a different turn. Whereas the West has sought strength and beauty, India

has been interested in precision and control, ideally complete control over the body's every function. How many of her incredible claims in this area can be scientifically corroborated remains to be seen; suffice it to note here that even such a hard-headed empiricist as Julian Huxley has ventured cautiously that India appears to have discovered some things about what the body can be brought to do of which the West has no inkling.[5] This extensive body of instruction comprises an authentic *yoga, hatha yoga.* Originally it was practiced as preliminary to spiritual Yoga, but as it has largely lost this connection it need not concern us here. The judgment of the Hindu sages on this matter can be ours as well; incredible things can be done with the body if this is what interests you and you are willing to give your life to it. But these things have little to do with enlightenment. In fact, if they grow out of a desire to show off, their mastery makes for pride and so is inimical to spiritual progress.

The *yogas* that do concern us are those designed to unite man's spirit with God who lies concealed in its deepest recesses. "Since all the Indian spiritual [as distinct from bodily] exercises are devoted seriously to this practical aim—not to a merely fanciful contemplation or discussion of lofty and profound ideas—they may well be regarded as representing one of the most realistic, matter-of-fact, practical-minded systems of thought and training ever set up by the human mind. How to come to Brahman and remain in touch with it; how to become identified with Brahman, living out of it; how to become divine while still on earth—transformed, reborn adamantine while on the earthly plane; that is the quest that has inspired and deified the spirit of man in India through the ages."[6]

The spiritual trails that Hindus have blazed toward this goal are four. At first this may seem surprising. If there is one goal, should there not be one path to it? This might be true if we were all starting from the same point, though even then different modes of transport—walking, driving, flying—might dictate alternate routes. As it is, men approach the goal from different directions. Their different starting points require, therefore, that they follow different paths if they are to reach the same summit.

One's starting point is determined by the kind of person one is, the specific complex of aptitudes, interests, and temperament that constitutes one's personality or nature. Actually this idea of there being different paths to God for different kinds of people is well known among spiritual directors of the West. "There are directors," writes Father Surin in his Spiritual Catechism, "who get an idea and a plan into their heads, which they think much of, and apply to all the souls who come to them, thinking that they will accomplish something great if they bring them into line with it. So they have no other object than of carrying out what they have imagined like one who should wish all to wear the same clothes." St. John of the Cross makes the same point in *The Living Flame*. The aim of spiritual directors should be "not to guide souls by a way suitable to themselves, but to ascertain, if they can, the way by which God Himself is guiding them." The unique thing about Hinduism is the amount of attention her seers have given to identifying and marking the major alternative paths. Almost every spiritual director has been concerned with the problem. The result is a general understanding shared by even the average, non-professional Hindu, not only that there are multiple paths to God but also what these paths are. It is as if Hinduism prescribes Quaker worship for one person and the rich imagery of the Mass for another.

There are, according to the Hindu analysis, four general kinds of persons. Some are basically reflective. Others are primarily emotional. Still others are essentially active. Finally some are most accurately characterized as empirical or experimental. For each of these personality types a distinct *yoga* is recommended and designed to capitalize on the endowments at the individual's disposal.

All four paths begin with certain moral preliminaries. The aim in each case being to render the surface self transparent to the divinity beneath, it is obvious that this self must first be cleansed of its gross moral impurities. Religion is always more than morality, but if its structure is to stand it has to be built on a strong moral base. Selfish acts coagulate the finite self instead of allaying it; bad habits keep mind and body roiled like a torrent. As the first step to any *yoga*, then, the aspirant must seek to cultivate habits and practices such as non-injury, truthfulness, non-stealing, self-control, cleanliness, contentment, self-discipline, and a compelling desire to reach the goal.

Keeping in mind this common preliminary step we are now ready for the distinctive features of the four *yogas*.

THE WAY TO GOD THROUGH KNOWLEDGE

Jnana yoga, intended for spiritual aspirants who have a strong intellectual bent, is the path to oneness with the Godhead through knowledge. There are persons who are by nature philosophical. Ideas to them are of first importance. When such persons become convinced of something it makes a real difference in their living, for their lives follow where their minds lead. Socrates and Buddha are classic examples of men of this type. For persons of their disposition and aptitude, Hinduism proposes a series of meditations and logical demonstrations designed to convince the thinker that there is more to him than his finite self; once this kind of person sees this he will shift his central concern to the deeper reaches of his being.

The aim of this *yoga* is "to cleave the domain of ignorance with the sword of discrimination." What is needed is the power to distinguish between the surface self that crowds the foreground of our being and the larger self that lies behind it. The path that leads to this power consists of three steps. The first is hearing. Here, through listening to sages and scripture and philosophic treatises comparable to St. Thomas Aquinas' *Summa Theologica*, the aspirant becomes acquainted with the basic hypothesis that, unbeknownst, there lies at the center of his being the infinite unthwartable fount of being itself.

The second step is thinking. By prolonged, intensive reflection, that which in the first step was raised as an abstract possibility must take on life; the *Atman* must be transformed in our outlook from an empty concept to a momentous reality. A number of lines of reflection are suggested. For example, the disciple is advised to examine the language he uses every day and ponder its implications. The word "my" always implies a distinction between the possessor and what is possessed. When I speak of my book or my coat, there is no thought that I am these things. But I also speak of my body, my mind, or my personality, giving evidence thereby that in some sense I think of myself as standing apart from these also. What is this I that is the possessor of my body and mind but cannot be equated with them?

Again, science tells me there is nothing in my body that was with me seven years ago. In the course of my lifetime my mind and personality have undergone changes that are in their own way equally radical. Yet through all these revisions I have remained on some level the same person, the person who had this body at one time, that at another, who once was fair but now is faded, who once was young and now is old. What is this something in our make-up deeper than either body or personality that provides this continuity in the midst of incessant change?

Our word "personality" comes from the Latin *persona* which originally meant the mask an actor donned as he stepped onto the stage to play his role, the mask through (*per*) which he sounded (*sonat*) his part. The mask carried the make-up of the role, while the actor behind it remained hidden and anonymous, aloof from the emotions enacted. This, say the Hindus, is perfect. This is precisely what our personalities are—the roles into which we have been cast for the moment in this greatest drama of all, the comic-tragedy of life itself in which we are simultaneously both co-authors and actors. As a good actor gives his best to his part, we too should play ours as close to perfection as possible. The disturbing fact, however, is that we have lost sight of the distinction between our true self and the veil of personality that is its present costume, its current shroud, but which will be laid aside when the play is over. We have come completely under the fascination of our present lines, unable to remember previous roles we have played or to anticipate future ones. The task of the *yogi* is to correct this false identification. Turning his awareness inward he must pierce and dissolve the innumerable layers of the manifest personality until, all strata of the mask at length cut through, he arrives finally at the anonymous and strangely unconcerned actor who stands beneath.

The distinction between self and Self can come through another image. Imagine someone playing chess. The board represents his world. There are pieces to be moved, men to be won and lost, an objective to be gained. The game can be won or lost but not the player himself. His pieces may be captured one by one, but if he has played the game to the best of his ability he has developed his faculties; in fact, he is somewhat more likely to profit by defeat than by victory. As the contestant is related to the total person, so is the finite self of any particular lifetime related to the *Atman*.

Sometimes the *yogi* is counseled to drop argument entirely and turn his mind over to metaphor. One of the most beautiful is found in the Upanishads, as also, by interesting coincidence, in Plato. There is a rider who sits serene and motionless in his chariot. Having delegated responsibility for the journey to his charioteer, he is free to sit back and give full attention to the passing landscape. In this image lies a metaphor of life. The body is the chariot. The road over which the chariot is drawn represents sense objects. The horses that pull the chariot over the road are the senses themselves. The mind that controls the senses when they are disciplined is the reins. The decisional faculty of the mind is the driver, and the master of the chariot who is in full authority but need never lift a finger is the Omniscient Self.

If the *yogi* is able and diligent, such reflections will in due time build up a lively sense of the abiding Self that underlies his phenomenal personality. The two will be distinct in his mind, related as oil and water, not milk and water as formerly. He is then ready for the third step which consists in shifting his self-identification from the passing to the eternal part of his being. The most direct way of doing this, of course, is simply to meditate as profoundly as possible on one's identity with the Eternal Spirit, trying to think of oneself as such even while going about the tasks of the day. This, however, is not easy; it is a high, exacting art. The aspirant first needs a wedge to be driven between his self-identification and the body and personality with which it has become so thoroughly involved. An effective way to do this is to think of one's finite self in the third person. Walking down the street, the *yogi*, instead of thinking "I am doing this" should say to himself, "There goes Jones down Fifth Avenue." He should even try to visualize himself as seen from a distance. Neither agent nor patient, his unwavering approach to all experience should be "I am the Witness." He observes his unsubstantial history with calm detachment, as one might let one's hair blow in the wind. Just as a lamp that lights a room is unconcerned with what goes on within it, so the witness watching what goes on in this house of protoplasm, this person, this on-stage mask. Its processes are simply permitted to proceed. Even inertia is to be felt as something separate, not part of one's real self which is infinite. Pain likewise. Seated in the dentist's chair, the *yogi* should be no more than an onlooker: "Poor Jones. Too bad. He'll feel better tomorrow." Practice can bring surprising detachment even here. One still feels the pain but in a different way; it does not touch one's will, and as pain is three-fourths fear, it becomes less acute. A serious *yogi*, however, must practice his discipline equally when fortune smiles and he would normally love to identify himself with the individual self upon which the honor is being bestowed.

Thinking of oneself in the third person does two things simultaneously. It drives a wedge between one's self-identification and one's surface self and at the same time forces this self-identification to a deeper level until at last, through a knowledge identical with being, one becomes in full what one always was at heart. "That thou art, other than Whom there is no other seer, hearer, thinker, or agent."[7]

The Way to God Through Love

The *yoga* of knowledge is said to be the shortest path to divine realization. It is also the steepest, however. Requiring as it does a rare combination of rationality and spirituality, it is for the select few. In most persons the rational component is too weak to carry them to God by its exercise alone.

On the whole, life is motored not so much by reason as by emotion, and of the many emotions that crowd man's life, the most powerful and pervasive is love. Even hate can be interpreted as a rebound from the thwarting of this impulse. Moreover, men tend to become like that which they love, with the name thereof progressively written on their brows. The aim of *bhakti yoga* is to direct toward God the geyser of love that lies at the base of every heart. "As the waters of the Ganges flow incessantly toward the ocean," says God in the *Bhagavata Purana*, "so do the minds of [the *bhaktas*] move constantly toward Me, the Supreme Person residing in every heart, immediately they hear about My qualities."

Unlike *jnana yoga*, *bhakti yoga* has countless followers, being, indeed, the most popular of the four. Though it originated in antiquity, one of its best known proponents was a sixteenth century mystical poet named Tulsidas. During his early married life he was inordinately fond of his wife to the point that he could not abide her absence even for a day. One day she went to visit her parents. Before the day was half over Tulsidas turned up at her side, whereupon his wife exclaimed, "How passionately attached to me you are! If only you could shift your attachment to God, you would reach him in no time." "So I would," thought Tulsidas. He tried it, and it worked.

All the basic principles of *bhakti yoga* are richly exemplified in Christianity. Indeed from the Hindu point of view Christianity is one great brilliantly lit *bhakti* highway toward God, other paths being not neglected but not as clearly marked. Along this path God must be conceived in a way different from the way he was conceived by the *jnana yogi*. In *jnana yoga* the guiding image was an infinite sea of being underlying the tiny waves of our finite selves. God was thought of as the all-pervading Self, as fully present within us as without. The task was to recognize our identity with him. Moreover, God was conceived primarily in impersonal terms, for the characteristic of ultimate reality that most impresses the philosopher is his infinity in comparison with which personality, embodying as it must certain properties to the exclusion of others, must always seem in some respects a limitation. For one to whom love means more than mind God must appear different on each of these counts. First, as love when healthy is an out-turning emotion the *bhakti* will reject all suggestion that the God he loves is himself, even his deepest Self, and insist instead on his otherness. As a Hindu devotional classic puts the point, "I want to taste sugar; I don't want to be sugar."

> Can water quaff itself?
> Can trees taste of the fruit they bear?
> He who worships God must stand distinct from Him,

So only shall he know the joyful love of God;
For if he say that God and he are one,
That joy, that love, shall vanish instantly away.

Pray no more for utter oneness with God:
Where were the beauty if jewel and setting were one?
The heat and the shade are two,
If not, where were the comfort of shade?
Mother and child are two,
If not, where were love?
When after long being sundered, they meet,
What joy do they feel, the mother and child!
Where were joy, if the two were one?
Pray, then, no more for utter oneness with God.[8]

Second, because of this sense of God's otherness the *bhakta's* goal, too, will differ from the *jnani's*; his aim will not be to perceive his identity with God but to adore him with every element of his being. The words of Bede Frost, though written in another tradition, are directly applicable to this side of Hinduism: "The union . . . is no Pantheistic absorption of the man in the one . . . but is essentially personal in character. . . . More, since it is preeminently a union of love, the kind of knowledge which is required is that of friendship in the very highest sense of the word."[9] Finally, in such a context God's personality, far from being a limitation, is indispensable. Philosophers may be able to love pure being, infinite beyond all attributes, but they are exceptions. The normal object of human love is personality, however exalted its attributes of wisdom, compassion, and grace may be.

All we have to do in this *yoga* is to love God dearly—not just say we love him but love him in fact; love him only (loving other things because of him), and love him for no ulterior reason (not even from the desire for liberation) but for love's sake alone. Insofar as we succeed we will know joy, for no experience can compare with that of being authentically and fully in love. Moreover, every strengthening of our affections toward God will weaken the world's grip. The saint may, indeed will, love the world far more than the addict, but he will love it in a very different way, seeing in it the reflected glory of the God he adores.

How is this love of God to be developed? Obviously the task will not be easy. The things of this world clamor for our affection so incessantly that it may be marveled that a Being who can neither be seen nor heard can ever become their competitor.

Enter Hinduism's myths, her magnificent symbols, her several hundred images of God, her rituals that keep turning night and day like a never-ending prayer wheel. Valued as ends in themselves these could, of course, usurp God's place, but this is not their intent. They are matchmakers, responsible for introducing man's heart to what they represent but themselves are not. It is clumsy to confuse Hinduism's images with idolatry and her many images with polytheism. They are but runways from which man's heavily sense-embodied spirit can take off for its "flight of the alone to the Alone." Even village priests will frequently open their temple worship with the following beloved invocation:

O Lord, forgive three sins that are due to my human limitations:
Thou are everywhere, but I worship you here;
Thou are without form, but I worship you in these forms;
Thou needest no praise, yet I offer you these prayers and salutations.
Lord, forgive three sins that are due to my human limitations.

A symbol such as a multiarmed image graphically portraying God's astounding versatility and superhuman might, can epitomize an entire philosophy through condensation and concentration. Myths plumb depths which the intellect can see only obliquely. Parables and legends present ideals in such a way as to make the hearer long to embody them in his own life, vivid support for Irwin Edman's contention that "it is a myth, not a mandate, a fable, not a logic . . . by which men are moved." The value of these things lies in their power to recall our minds from the world's distractions to the thought of God and thereby progressively to his love. In singing God's praises, in praying to him with wholehearted devotion, in meditating on his majesty and glory, in reading about him in the scriptures, in regarding the entire universe as his handiwork, we move our affections steadily in his direction. "Those who . . . meditate on Me and worship Me without any attachment to anything else," says the *Bhagavad-Gita*, "those I soon lift from the ocean of death."

Three features of the *bhakta's* approach deserve mention: *japam*, ringing the changes on love, and the worship of one's chosen ideal.

Japam is the practice of repeating the name of God. It finds a close Christian parallel in one of the classics of Russian Orthodoxy, *The Way of a Pilgrim*.[10] This book is the story of an unnamed peasant whose first concern is to fulfill the Biblical injunction to "Pray without ceasing." He wanders through Russia and Siberia with a knapsack of dried bread for food and the charity of men for shelter, consulting many authorities only to come away empty-hearted until at last he meets a holy man who teaches him "a constant, uninterrupted calling upon the divine Name of Jesus with the lips, in the spirit, in the heart . . . during every occupation, at all times, in all places, even during sleep." The peasant's teacher trains him until he can repeat the name of Jesus more than 12,000 times a day without strain. "This frequent service of the lips imperceptibly becomes a genuine appeal of the heart." The prayer becomes a constant, warming presence within him that brings a "bubbling joy." "Keep the name of the Lord spinning in the midst of all your activities" is the Hindu statement of the same point. Washing or weaving, shopping or planting, imperceptibly but indelibly these verbal droplets of aspiration will soak down into the subconscious, turning the total self toward the divine.

Ringing the changes on love puts to religious use the fact that love has different shades and nuances depending on the relationship in which it is involved. The love of the parent for child carries overtones of protectiveness in contrast to the love of a child for its parent which is blended with dependence. The love of friends is different from the conjugal love of man and wife. Differing from each of these, again, is the love of a devoted servant for his benevolent master. According to Hinduism, man's full capacities for love require that each of these modes be tapped. It encourages *bhaktas*, therefore, to adopt each of these attitudes of love toward God.

Hindu psychology classifies the stages of devotion in a hierarchy of increasing intimacy and reciprocity of love. First comes the attitude of the protected toward the protector, the receiver toward the giver, the servant toward his master. At this stage we should think of God as mother, father, lord or master. Next comes the stage of friendship. Here God is approached more intimately, in the role of companion and even playmate. Third comes the attitude of the parent in which the devotee looks on God as if He were his child. Finally, there is the attitude of the lover in which God is the beloved. Of these roles the ones in which God has most often been depicted by the Western religious consciousness are Father and Lord, but the others are not lacking. "What a Friend we have in Jesus" is a familiar Christian hymn; another draws upon two responses simultaneously as one of its stanzas closes with the line "My Master and my Friend." God figures in the guise of the spouse in the Song of Songs as well as in the writings of the mystics where the marriage of the soul to Christ is a standing image. The attitude of regarding God as one's child is the one likely to sound the most foreign to the West, yet much of the magic of Christmas stems precisely from the fact that this is the one time in the year when God enters the heart as a child, eliciting thereby the special tenderness that flows from the parental impulse.

We come finally to the worship of God in the form of one's chosen ideal. The Hindus have represented God in innumerable forms. This, they say, is appropriate. Each is but a symbol that points to something beyond, and as none exhausts the fullness of God's actual nature the entire array can be regarded as depicting God in his innumerable aspects and manifestations. But though a number of representations can point to God equally, it is advisable for each devotee to attach himself on a lifelong basis to some particular aspect or manifestation. Only so can its meaning deepen and its full power become accessible. This manifestation will be one's chosen ideal. The *bhakta* need not shun all others, but this one will never be forsaken and will always have a special place in his heart. The best ideal for most persons will be one of God's human incarnations. God can be loved most readily when he manifests himself in human form, for our hearts are already tuned to love people. Many Hindus acknowledge Christ as such a God-man while believing that there have been others as well, Rama, Krishna, Buddha. The list varies in length according to different schools. Whenever the world falls into decay and the ascent of man towards divinity is seriously endangered, God descends to earth to release the jammed wheels of history.

> When goodness grows weak,
> When evil increases,
> I make myself a body.
>
> In every age I come back
> To deliver the holy,
> To destroy the sin of the sinner,
> To establish the righteous.[11]

THE WAY TO GOD THROUGH WORK

The third path toward God, intended for persons of active bent, is *karma yoga*, the path toward God through work.

An examination of the anatomy and physiology of the human organism discloses an interesting fact. All organs of digestion and respiration serve to feed the blood with nutritive materials. The circulatory apparatus delivers this nourishing blood throughout the body maintaining bones, joints, and muscles. Bones provide a framework without which the muscles could not operate while joints supply the flexibility needed for movement. The brain envisions the movements that are to be made and the spinal nervous system executes them. The vegetative nervous system helped by the endocrine system maintains the harmony of the viscera on which the motor muscles depend. In short, the entire body except for its reproductive apparatus converges toward muscles and their movements. All human life when looked at from the angle of the body converges on action. "The human machine," writes a contemporary physician, "seems indeed to be made *for action*."[12]

Work is the staple of human life. The point is not simply that all but the few who are born into the truly leisure class have to work. Ultimately the impulse to work is psychologically, not economically, motivated. Forced to be idle most persons become irritable; forced to retire they decline. Included are the Marthas trotting from chore to chore, as well as captains of industry. To such persons Hinduism says, You don't have to retire to a cloister to realize God. You can find him in the world of everyday affairs as readily as anywhere.[13] Throw yourself into your work with everything you have, only do so wisely, in a way that will bring the highest rewards, not just trivia. Learn the secret of work by which every movement can carry you Godward even while other things are being accomplished, like a wristwatch that winds itself as other duties are being attended to.

How this is to be done depends on other components in the worker's nature. By assuming this path he has already indicated his predominantly active disposition, but there remains the question of whether in other respects he is inclined more in a reflective or affective direction. The path of work has alternate routes depending on whether it is approached philosophically or in the attitude of love. In the language of the four *yogas, karma yoga* can be practiced under the mode either of *jnana* (knowledge) or *bhakti* (devotion).

As we have seen, the point of life is to transcend the smallness of the finite self. This can be done either by shifting the center of interest and affection to a personal God experienced as distinct from oneself or by identifying oneself with the impersonal Absolute that resides at the core of one's being. The first is the way of the *bhakta*, the second the *jnani*. Work can be a vehicle for self-transcendence by either approach. For according to Hindu doctrine every action performed upon the external world has its correlative internal reaction upon the doer. If I chop down a tree that blocks my view, each stroke of the ax unsettles the tree but leaves its mark on me as well, driving deeper into my being my determination to have my way in the world. Every deed I do for the sake of my own private welfare adds another coating to the ego and in thus thickening it insulates it further from God within or without. Correlatively, every act done without thought of self diminishes self-centeredness until finally no barrier remains to cloud one from the divine.

The best way for the emotionally inclined to render his work selfless is to bring his ardent and affectionate nature into play and work for God's sake instead of his own. "He who performs actions without attachment, resigning them to God, is untainted by their effects as the lotus leaf by water."[14] Such a one is just as active as before, but he works for a completely different reason. His whole orientation toward the tasks of his daily life has become one of devotion. Every act of his diurnal routine is performed without concern for its effect upon himself. Not only is it performed as a service to God; it is regarded as prompted by God's will, executed for God's sake, and transacted by God's own energy which is being channeled through the devotee. "Thou art the Doer, I the instrument." Performed in this spirit actions lighten the ego instead of encumbering it. Each task becomes a sacred ritual, lovingly fulfilled as a living sacrifice to God and his glory without thought of profit that might redound to the individual. "Whatever you do, whatever you eat, whatever you offer in sacrifice, whatever you give away, whatever austerity you practice, O Son of Kunti, do this as an offering to Me. Thus shall you be free from the bondages of actions that bear good and evil results."[15] "They have no desire for the fruits of their actions," echoes the *Bhagavata Purana*: "These persons would not accept even . . . the state of union with Me; they would always prefer My service."

A young man, newly married and in love, works not for himself alone. As he works the thought of his beloved is in the back of his mind giving meaning and purpose to all his labors. So too with a devoted servant. He claims nothing for himself. Regardless of personal cost he does his duty for his master's satisfaction. Just so is God's will the sole joy and satisfaction of the devotee. Surrendering himself to the Lord of all, he remains untouched by the uncertainties of life over which he has no control. Such persons' backs never break. They never grow discouraged for they do not ask to win; they ask only to be on the side where they belong. They know that if history ever changes it will not be men who will change it but its Author—when men come to the point that they want it changed. Men in history lose their centering in eternity when they grow anxious for the outcome of their deeds. As long as they rest them on the knees of the Living God they are released by them from the bondages of the sea of death. "Do without attachment the work you have to do. . . . Surrendering all action to Me . . . freeing yourself from longing and selfishness, fight—unperturbed by grief."[16]

Once he has forsaken every claim on his acts including all claims for success, the *karma yogi's* deeds no longer boomerang to litter and increase his ego. They leave no mark on his mind to produce future effects, good or evil. In this way he works out the accumulated impressions of previous deeds without acquiring new ones. Whatever one's reaction to this imagery, it is not difficult to see the psychological truth of such a description. A man who is completely at the disposal of others does not exist. When Negro slaves accidentally hurt their feet or their hands, they used to say wryly, "It does not matter, it is the master's foot, the master's hand." He who has no sense of possessiveness around which selfhood can crystallize does not exist. The Spanish put the point nicely: "Would you like to become invisible? Have no thought of yourself for two years and no one will notice you."

Work as a path toward God takes a different turn for persons whose dispositions are more reflective than emotional. For these too the key is work done unselfishly, but the psychological framework is different. Philosophers tend to find the idea of Infinite Being at the center of one's self more meaningful than the thought of a personal Heavenly Father who stands over and above men and the world ruling them with a love that is eternal. It is only intelligent, therefore, that their approach to work should be adapted to this perspective.

The secret of this *jnana* approach to work consists in discrimination. Specifically it consists in drawing a sharp line between the empirical self immersed in action and the eternal self which stands aloof from it. Man's usual interest in work relates to the consequences it will have for his empirical self, the pay or acclaim it will bring. Such interests obviously inflate the ego and thicken the insulation between our conscious selves and the Infinite that is beneath them.

The way that leads to enlightenment is work performed in the spirit of complete detachment, almost dissociation, from the empirical self. Identifying himself securely with the Eternal, the worker goes about his duties, but as these are being effected by his empirical self, his True Self is in no way involved with them. "The knower of Truth, [being] centered [in the Self] should think, 'I do nothing at all'—though seeing, hearing, touching, smelling, eating, going, sleeping, breathing, speaking, letting go, holding, opening and closing the eyes—convinced that it is the senses that move among sense objects."[17]

As the *yogi's* identification shifts from his finite to his infinite self, he will become increasingly indifferent to the consequences that flow from his work for the former. More and more he will recognize the truth of the *Gita's* dictum: "To work you have the right, but not to the fruits thereof." Duty for duty's sake becomes his sole concern in action.

> He who does the task
> Dictated by duty,
> Caring nothing
> For the fruit of the action,
> He is a yogi.[18]

Hence the story of the *yogi* who as he sat meditating on the banks of the Ganges saw a scorpion fall into the water before him. He scooped it out, only to have it bite him. Presently the scorpion fell into the river again. Once more the *yogi* rescued him, only to be bitten a second time. The sequence was repeated twice more, whereupon a bystander asked the *yogi*, "Why do you keep rescuing that scorpion when the only gratitude it shows is to bite you?" "It is the nature of scorpions to bite," was the reply, "It is the nature of *yogis* to help others when they can."

The *karma yogi* will try to do each thing as it comes as if it were the only thing he has to do, and having done it or being forced to leave it to go on to another duty, to do so in the same spirit. He will seek to concentrate fully and calmly on each duty as it presents itself, resisting all impatience, excitement, and the vain attempt to do or think of half a dozen things at once.[19] Into the various tasks that fall his lot he will put all the strokes he can, for to do otherwise would be to yield to laziness which is simply a variety of selfishness; but once he has done this he will dissociate himself from the act and let the chips fall where they may.

> One to me is loss or gain,
> One to me is fame or shame,
> One to me is pleasure, pain.[20]

A mature individual does not resent correction, for he identifies himself more with the long-range self that grows through correction than with the momentary self that is being indicted. Similarly the *yogi* accepts pain, loss, and shame with equanimity because such things touch only the surface self whereas his identification is being transferred to the underlying immutable self whose limitless joy and serenity cannot possibly be ruffled by momentary turns of fortune. Once his self-identification becomes thus permanently poised in the Eternal, he experiences calm even in the midst of intense activity. Like the center of a rapidly spinning wheel, he has the appearance of rest even in the most concentrated endeavors. It is like the stillness of absolute motion.

Though the conceptual frameworks in terms of which philosophic and affectionate natures approach the practice of *karma yoga* differ sharply, it is not difficult to see that they aim at the same result. Both are engaged in a radical reducing diet that is designed to starve the finite personality to death by deflecting it from the consequences of the actions on which it feeds. Neither gives the slightest purchase to that native egoism which the world considers healthy selfishness, indispensable if any living creature is to compete successfully in the struggle for existence. Both *yogis* aim at a prize that transcends creaturely existence altogether. The *bhakta* seeks his "self-naughting" by giving his heart and will to the Eternal Companion and finding them again therein a thousandfold enriched. The *jnani* is equally concerned to wither the self because of his conviction that in proportion to its recession there will come into view a nucleus of our being that is radically unaffected by anything we connect with our individual personalities: "a sublime inhabitant and onlooker, transcending the spheres of the former conscious-unconscious system, aloofly unconcerned with the tendencies that formerly supported the individual biography. This anonymous 'diamond being' is not at all what we were cherishing as our character and cultivating as our faculties, inclinations, virtues, and ideals; for it transcends every horizon of unclarified and partly clarified consciousness. It was enwrapped within the sheaths of the body and personality; yet the dark, turbid, thick [layers of the surface self] could not disclose its image. Only the translucent essence of [a self in which all private wants have been dispersed] permits it to become visible—as through a glass, or in a quiet pond. And then, the moment it is recognized, its manifestation bestows an immediate knowledge that this is our true identity. The life-monad is remembered and greeted, even though it is distinct from everything in this phenomenal composite of a body and psyche, which, under the delusion caused by our usual ignorance and undiscriminating consciousness we had crudely mistaken for the real and lasting essence of our being."[21]

The Way to God Through Psychological Exercises

Because of the dazzling heights to which it leads, *raja yoga* has been known in India as "the royal road to re-integration." Designed for persons who are basically scientific in bent, it is the way to God through psychological experiment.

The West has honored the empiricist in the laboratory but often distrusted his approach in things of the spirit,[22] accusing him of prideful deification of personal experience as the final test of truth. India has had no such fear. Affairs of the spirit, she holds, can be approached just as empirically as outer nature. Consequently persons who have the inclination and self-discipline needed to approach God in this way are given full encouragement. Theirs is the fourth path to the goal, the royal way of *raja yoga*. All that is required is a strong suspicion that our true selves are vastly more wonderful than we now realize and a passion for direct experience of their full reach. Without these dispositions the empiricist will either lack the patience to carry through or turn his experiments toward the outer world and become a research student in the conventional sense. Given a basically spiritual orientation and outreach, however, all that is proposed is that the *yogi* undertake a series of experiments with all the patience and rigor of a frontier experiment in physics and carefully observe the outcome. If it is nil, and the experiments have been performed ably and with diligence, the hypothesis has been disproved, at least as far as this experimenter is concerned. The expectation, however, is that they will lead to experiences which will progressively confirm the hypothesis as the experiment proceeds.

Unlike the bulk of experiments in Western science, the experiments called for by *raja yoga* are on one's self rather than on the world of external nature. Even where Western science does turn to self-experiment—as, for example, in medicine, where ethics prescribes that dangerous experiments may be performed only on oneself—the Indic emphasis is different; in *raja yoga* one experiments not on one's body (though as we shall see the body is definitely involved in the act) but on one's spirit. The experiments take the form of practicing certain prescribed mental exercises and observing the effects of these on one's spiritual condition.

The *raja yogi* is not required to swallow any dogmas. Nevertheless, experiment cannot proceed except on the basis of some hypothesis which the results either support or negate. The hypothesis underlying *raja yoga* is the Hindu doctrine of man and, though it has been recurrently referred to already, it needs to be restated here as the conceptual background in terms of which the *raja* experiments have been drawn up.

The Hindu concept of man rests on the basic thesis that he is a layered being. We need not here go into the detailed Hindu analyses of these layers; the accounts are extremely technical and involved and may (in the light of growing scientific knowledge) turn out to be more meta-phorically than literally accurate. It will suffice for our purposes to sum-marize the hypothesis by reducing the principal layers to four. First and most obviously, man has a body. Next comes that portion of his mind and experience that he is aware of, his conscious personality. Underlying these two is a third region, the realm of his individual subconscious. This has been built up out of his private past experiences down through the years. Though it is hidden to his normal awareness, it shapes his life in profound ways that contemporary psychoanalysis is beginning to detail. These three parts of man are paralleled in the contemporary Western view. The distinctive point in the Hindu hypothesis is its postulation of a fourth part. Underlying the other three, more unperceived by the con-scious mind than even its private subconscious though as vitally related to it, stands Being Itself, infinite, unthwarted, eternal. "I am smaller than the minutest atom, likewise greater than the greatest. I am the whole, the diversified-multicolored-lovely-strange universe. I am the An-cient One. I am Man, the Lord. I am the Being-of-Gold. I am the very state of divine beatitude."[23]

Hinduism agrees with psychoanalysis that if only we could dredge up a portion of our lost individual totality—the third part of our being—we would experience a remarkable expansion of our powers, a vivid re-freshening of life. But this is only the beginning of its hypothesis. If only we could resurrect something forgotten not only by ourselves but also by mankind as a whole, something which provides the clue not simply to our private compulsions and idiosyncracies but to all life and all existence, what then? Would we not have discovered something of historical moment? Would we not become true boon-bringers to hu-manity?

The call, clearly, is to retreat from the world's inconsequential pan-orama to the deep-lying causal zones of the psyche where the real prob-lems and answers lie. Beyond this, however, *raja yoga's* response cannot be described, quite, as an answer to any articulated call. Rather, it is a determined refusal to allow the pitter-patter of daily existence to dis-tract from the unknown demands of some waiting void within: a kind of total strike against the terms of routine, prosaic existence. The suc-cessful *yogi* succeeds in carrying life's problem to this plane of new magnitude and there resolving it. The insights of such a one will be eloquent not so much to passing personal and social predicaments as to the unquenchable source by which all men and societies are renewed, for his inspiration will be drawn from direct contact with this primary spring. In body he will remain an individual; in spirit he will have become eternal man, unspecific, universal, perfected.

The purpose of *raja yoga* is to demonstrate the validity of this four-fold estimate of man by leading the inquirer to direct personal experience of "the beyond that is within." Its method is willed introversion, one of the classic implements of creative genius in any line of endeavor but here carried to logical completion. Its intent is no less than to drive man's psychic energy into the deepest part of his being and activate the lost continent of his true self. Risks are, of course, involved; if the venture is bungled, at best considerable time will have been lost, at worst consciousness can disintegrate into neurosis or psychosis. Rightly done, however, under a director who knows what he is about, the personality will be able to absorb and integrate the new forces that are being tapped and will experience an almost superhuman degree of self-awareness and masterful control.

With the hypothesis *raja yoga* proposes to test before us we are now prepared to indicate the eight steps of the experiment itself.

1 and 2. The first two are concerned with moral preliminaries. Anyone who sits down to this task of trying to discover his true and total self through introspection will soon discover that he is beset by a host of distractions which seem bent on crashing his attention to prevent it from making headway. The most obvious two are bodily addictions and social inquietude. Just as the conference is about to get underway in earnest, the *yogi* may find his attention summoned abruptly from the room in answer to the annoyingly trivial urge for a cigarette or a drink. Or, he may find the atmosphere of the conference jammed by the inter-personal static of resentments, envies, and conscience. The first two steps of *raja yoga* seek to clear this atmosphere and lock the door against outside intrusions to the point where serious introspection can begin. The first step involves the practice of five abstentions: from injury, lying, stealing, sensuality, and greed. The second involves the practice of five observances: of cleanliness, contentment, self-control, studiousness, and contemplation of the divine. Together they constitute the five finger exercises of the spirit in anticipation of more intricate renditions that are to follow. Chinese and Japanese officers, who used to practice variations of *raja yoga* in Buddhist monasteries with no religious interest at all but simply to increase their mental clarity and vitality, discovered that even in their case a certain amount of moral discipline was a necessary condition of success.

3. *Raja yoga* works with the body even though its ultimate concern is with the mind. More precisely, it works through the body to the mind. Its chief concern with the body, beyond general health, is to keep it from intruding to distract the mind from its concentrations. This, however, is no small assignment, for an untrained body cannot go for long without itching or fidgeting in some way. Each sensation it interposes is a demand for attention and hence a distraction from our central concern. The object of this third step is to shut out this third kind of distraction—to get Brother Ass, as St. Francis affectionately called his body, properly tethered and out of the way, or, in the words of a lesser saint, to see that the body does in fact respond to Harry Lauder's adjuration to "Stop your ticklin', Jock!" Obviously what is needed is a bodily state midway between the stimulations of discomfort and the adjournments of drowsiness and sleep. The Hindu discoveries for achieving this mid-point balance are called *asanas*, a word usually translated "postures" but carrying connotations of ease and comfort. The physical and psychological benefits of at least some of these postures are now universally recognized. That the Hindu texts describe eighty-four indicates extensive experimentation in the area; but only about five are considered conducive to meditation.

Of these, the one that has proved most popular is the world-famous lotus position in which the *yogi* sits, ideally on a doeskin as symbol of calm, with his legs crossed in such a way that each foot rests sole up on its opposing thigh. The spinal column, right up to the base of the brain, is completely erect. Hands are placed with palms up in the lap, one on top of the other, thumbs touching. In contrast to Christianity, which advocates closing the eyes completely during prayer so all external distractions may be shut out, the East, fearing internal distractions of imaginings as much as external ones of sense, recommends that the eyes be left half open and focused on a point between the eyes, at the base of the nose, or at the pit of the stomach.[24] Persons who undertake the lotus position after their bodies have reached maturity find it painful, for it imposes at the start a terrific strain on the tendons which requires months of conditioning to be overcome. When the body has become accustomed to it, however, it is astonishingly comfortable, the reason being that the nerve centers of the lower limbs are partially numbed causing a restful relaxation which in turn settles the mind for concentration. Considering the fact that reclining tends toward sleep, there may be no other position in which the body can be kept both quiescent and alert for so long.

4. The postures of *yoga* are intended to guard the contemplative's awareness against intrusions from his muscular system in its static aspect. There remain its actions, such as breathing. A *yogi* cannot stop breathing and live; at the same time uncontrolled breathing can shatter his mind's repose. Those who have not ventured into meditation cannot imagine the extent to which unbridled respiration can intrude upon this work. Bronchial irritations and congestions trigger coughs and clearings of the throat. Each time the breath sinks too low a deep sigh breaks in to shatter the spell. Nor are such obvious irregularities the sole offenders; through the concentrated silence of a *yogi's* interior a "normal" breath can rip like a crosscut, sending the hush shivering, flying. The purpose of *raja yoga's* fourth step is to prevent such intrusions by developing complete mastery of the breathing mechanism. The exercises prescribed toward this end are numerous and varied. Some, like learning to breathe in one nostril and out the other, seem extremely bizarre until we remember that complete control is the overall aim. On the whole, however, the exercises work toward protracted breath suspension, regularity of inhalation and exhalation, and reduction in air supply needed. A typical exercise, for example, calls for breathing so gently and evenly across goose down touching the nostrils that an observer cannot tell if the air is moving in or out. Breath suspension is particularly important, for only when the breath is held can the body be brought to the maximum stillness of which it is capable. When, for example, the *yogi* is doing a cycle of sixteen counts in, sixty-four holding, and thirty-two out, there is a considerable period during which animation is virtually suspended and the mind is startlingly disembodied. These are moments of true opportunity for the task at hand. "The light of a lamp," says the *Bhagavad-Gita*, "does not flicker in a windless place."

5. Composed, his body at ease, his breathing regular, the *yogi* sits wrapped in contemplation. Suddenly a door creaks, a sliver of moonlight shimmers on the ground before him, a mosquito settles on his neck—and he is back again in the world.

> Restless man's mind is,
> So strongly shaken
> In the grip of the senses. . . .
> Truly I think
> The wind is no wilder.[25]

Man's senses turn outward. As bridges to the physical world they are invaluable. The *yogi*, however, is concerned with something else. On the track of a more interesting world, the interior universe of man himself within which (so he has heard) is to be found the final secret to life's mystery, he is at the moment impatient with the incessant reports of his senses. The outer world has, to be sure, its own fascination, but on the problem with which he is absorbed it has nothing to contribute but gibberish. For what the *yogi* is bent on discovering is what lies behind life's facade. Behind its material front where we experience the play of life and death, is there a deeper life which knows no death? Beneath our surface accounting of objects and things, is there a dimension of awareness different not just in degree but in kind? The *yogi* is testing an hypothesis: that the deepest truth is opened only to those who turn their attention inward; and in this experiment the physical senses, so useful elsewhere, can be nothing but busybodies. "The senses turn outward," observe the *Upanishads*. "Man, therefore, looks toward what is outside, and sees not the inward being. Rare is the wise man who . . . shuts his eyes to outward things and so beholds the glory of the Atman within." Five hundred years later the *Bhagavad-Gita* takes up the theme like an echo:

> Only that yogi
> Whose joy is inward,
> Inward his peace,
> And his vision inward
> Shall come to Brahman
> And know Nirvana.[26]

It is against the background of three millenia of this hypothesis that Mahatma Gandhi made his proposal to our own time. "Turn the spotlight," he said simply, "inward."

The final, transitional step in the process of effecting this radical transfer from the external to the internal world is to close the windows of the senses; only so can the clatter of the world's boiler factory be effectively shut out. That this can be done and without bodily mutilation is a common experience of everyone. A wife calls her husband to dinner. Five minutes later he insists, despite the fact that he was in the adjoining room, that he did not hear her; she, that her call was so clear that he must have. Neither lies; it is a matter of definition. If hearing means that sound waves of considerable volume beat upon healthy eardrums, he heard; if it means that they were admitted to awareness, he did not. There is nothing in the least esoteric about such a phenomenon: the explanation is simply concentration; the husband was preoccupied with what he was reading. Similarly this fifth step in *raja yoga* has no catch. It seeks to carry the *yogi* beyond the point the husband had reached, first, by turning his absorption from a chance phenomenon into a power he can turn on and off at will; second, by raising his talent to a point where, if he wishes, he can be oblivious to drums beating in the same room. But the technique is identical; if sufficiently intense, concentration on one thing will eclipse all others.

6. At last the *yogi* is alone with his thoughts. The five steps enumerated thus far have all aimed at this eventuality; one by one the intrusions of addiction, the troubled conscience, body, breath, and sense have been retired. But the battle is not yet won; indeed, in its direct intent it is just beginning. For the mind's fiercest antagonist is itself. Alone with itself it still shows not the slightest inclination to settle down. Memories, anticipations, daydreams, streams of consciousness, chains of revery held together by the flimsiest, most fortuitous links imaginable close in from a thousand sides, placing the mind in continuous ripple, like the face of a lake beneath a breeze, shimmering with broken, ever-changing, self-shattering reflections. Left to itself the mind would never stand unruffled, smooth as a mirror, crystal clear, reflecting the Sun of all life in perfect replica. For such a condition to be realized it is not enough that the entering rivulets be dammed; this the five preceding steps have effectively accomplished. There remain lake bottom springs to be stopped, the bubblings of memories, emotional pressures, and imaginings, not to mention breezes of sheer irrelevancy that must be stilled. Obviously much remains to be done.

Or change the metaphor to one less serene. The motions of the average mind, say the Hindus, are about as purposeful and orderly as those of a crazed monkey cavorting about its cage. Nay, more; like the prancings of a drunk, crazed monkey. Even so we have not conveyed its full restlessness; the mind is like a drunk, crazed monkey that has St. Vitus' dance. If we are to be truly accurate to its frenzy we must go a final step; it is like a drunk, crazed monkey with St. Vitus' dance who has just been stung by a wasp.

Few who have seriously tried to meditate will think this analogy extreme. The trouble with the advice to "leave your mind alone" is the unimpressive spectacle that remains. I tell my hand to rise and it obeys; I tell my mind to be still and it taunts me with impertinence. How long can the average mind think about one thing—purely one thing, without slipping first into thinking about *thinking about* that thing and taking off from there on an absolutely inconsequential and humiliating chain of irrelevancies? About three and a half seconds, the psychologists tell us. Like a ping pong ball, a mind will light where its owner directs it, but only to take off immediately on a jittery flight of staccato bounces which are out of hand completely.

What, though, if it could be turned from a ping pong ball into a lump of dough which, thrown, sticks to its object until deliberately removed? Would not its power over any problem it tackled increase enormously if it could be thus stayed and focused? Would not its intensity be compounded, even as a lamp's when surrounded by reflectors? A normal mind can be held to a reasonable extent by the world's objects. A psychotic mind cannot; it slips at once into uncontrollable fantasy. What if a third condition of mind could be developed as much above the normal as the psychotic's is below it, a condition in which the individual could hold his mind to objects to penetrate them more deeply? This is the aim of concentration, the sixth step of *raja yoga*. An elephant's trunk, which sways to and fro as the elephant walks and reaches out for objects to either side will become steady if given an iron ball to hold. The purpose of concentration is to teach the restless mind to hold unwaveringly to the objects it is presented. "When all the senses are stilled, when the mind is at rest, when the intellect wavers not—that, say the wise, is the highest state."[27]

The method proposed for reaching this state is not exotic, only arduous. One begins by relaxing the mind completely to let thoughts that need out bubble up from the subconscious and thus exorcise themselves. Then one selects something to concentrate on—the glowing point of a stick of incense, the tip of one's nose, an imagined sea of infinite light, the object does not much matter—and practices keeping the mind on it until success gradually increases.

7. The last two steps are stages in which this process of concentration progressively deepens. In the preceding step the mind was brought to the point where it would flow steadily toward its object, but it did not lose consciousness of itself as distinct from the objects it knew. In this seventh step in which concentration deepens into meditation the union between the two is tightened to the point where separateness vanishes: "The subject and the object are completely merged so that the self-consciousness of the individual subject has disappeared altogether."[28] In this moment, the duality of knower and known is resolved into a perfect unity. In the words of Schelling, "the perceiving self merges in the self-perceived. At that moment we annihilate time and the duration of time; we are no longer in time, but time, or rather eternity itself, is in us."

8. There remains the final, climactic state for which the Sanskrit word *samadhi* should be retained. Etymologically *sam* parallels the Greek prefix *syn* as in synthesis, synopsis, syndrome. It means "together with." *Adhi* in Sanskrit is usually translated Lord, paralleling the Hebrew word for Lord in the Old Testament, *Adon* or *Adonai*. *Samadhi*, then, names the state in which man's mind is completely absorbed in God. In the seventh step, that of meditation, concentration was intensified to the point where the self dropped out of sight entirely, all attention having been riveted on the object being known. The distinctive feature of *samadhi* is that all forms fall away from this object. For forms limit; to be one, others must be excluded, whereas the object of our knowledge now is precisely Being unlimited. The mind is thinking of no thing, but this does not mean that it is thinking of nothing—it has perfected the paradox of seeing the invisible. It is filled with that which is "separated from all qualities, neither this nor that, without form, without a name."[29]

We have come a long way from Lord Kelvin's statement that he could not imagine anything of which he could not construct a mechanical model. By that mode in which the knower is united with what is known, the individual has been brought to the knowledge of total being and dissolved into it. He has plunged at last into the one reality, the brimming ocean of utter being, boundless as the sky, indivisible, absolute.[30] He has attained what he started out to seek—personal proof of the existence of *Brahman* and his identity with it. By strict experiment he too has reached the final insight: "That, verily, That are thou."

We have presented these four *yogas* as four alternative pathways to God. This does not, however, mean that they are exclusive. No man is solely reflective, emotional, active, or experimental, and different occasions call for different responses. While most persons will, on the whole, find travel on one road more satisfactory than on others and will consequently tend to keep closest to it, Hinduism encourages men to test all four and combine them as best suits their needs. The major division is between *jnana* and *bhakti*, the reflective and the emotional types in men. Work, as we have seen, can be adapted to either mode, and some meditation is valuable in any case. The normal pattern, therefore, will be for the individual to cast his religion in either a philosophical or a devotional mold, adapt his work to the mold he chooses, and meditate to the extent that he can make time for it.

We read in the *Bhagavad-Gita* that some "realize the Atman through contemplation. Some realize the Atman philosophically. Others realize it by following the *yoga* of right action. Others worship God as their teachers have taught them. If these faithfully practice what they have learned, they will pass beyond death's power."

THE FOUR STAGES

People are different. Few observations could be more banal, yet serious attention to it is one of Hinduism's distinctive features. The preceding sections traced its insistence that differences in human nature call for a variety of paths toward life's fulfillment. We have now to note the same insistence pressed in a different direction. Not only does each life taken as a whole differ from others, but also each life taken in itself moves through several distinct stages each of which calls for its own unique response. As each day passes from morning through noon and afternoon into evening, so every life, too, passes through four phases with different aptitudes each calling for its own appropriate mode of behavior. If we ask, therefore, how should we live? Hinduism would answer, that depends not only on what kind of person you are but also in which stage of life you are.

The first stage India marked off as that of the student. Traditionally this stage began after the rite of initiation between the ages of eight and twelve and lasted for twelve years during which the student usually lived in the home of his teacher, serving him in return for the instruction he received. Life's prime responsibility at this stage was to learn, to open the pores of one's being to all that one's teacher, standing as it were on the pinnacle of the past, could transmit to him. There would be time later to contribute to society; for the present, this one gloriously suspended moment in which his only obligation was to learn, the greatest service he could render was to receive, to store up against the years when much would be expected of him. What was to be learned included factual information, but more; for India, dreamy, unpractical India, has never been much interested in knowledge for its own sake. The successful student was not to emerge an encyclopedia on two legs, a reference library wired for sound. Habits were to be cultivated, character acquired. Indeed the entire training was more like an apprenticeship in which information became incarnated in skill. The liberally educated student was to emerge as equipped to turn out a good and effective life as the potter's apprentice to turn out a well-wrought urn.

The second stage, beginning with marriage, was that of the householder. Here during life's noonday, with physical powers poised at their zenith, man's interests and energies turn naturally outward. There are three fronts on which they can play with satisfaction: his family, his

vocation, and the community to which he belongs. Normally his attention will include all three. This is the time for satisfying the first three
wants of man: pleasure through the family primarily, success through
his vocation, and duty through his responsibilities as a citizen.

Hinduism smiles on the happy fulfillment of these wants but does not
try to prime them when they begin to ebb. That they should in due
course dwindle is altogether appropriate; what a shock it would be if
life had to come to a stop while work and desire were in full swing. It is
not so ordained. If we follow the seasons as they come, we shall notice
a time when sex and the delights of the senses (pleasure) as well as
achievement in the game of life (success) no longer yield any novel and
surprising turns; when, further, the responsible discharge of the tasks
of a respectable human career (duty) begins to pall, having become
repetitious and stale. When this season arrives, it is time for the individual to move on to a third stage in life's passage.

Some never do. Their spectacle is not a pretty one, for pursuits appropriate in their day become grotesque when prolonged beyond. A playboy of twenty-five may have considerable appeal, but preserve us from
the playboys of fifty. How hard they work at their pose, how little they
receive in return. Similarly with men who cannot bring themselves to
relinquish key positions when younger men with more energy and new
ideas should be stepping into them.

Still such persons cannot be censured, for seeing no other frontier
to life they have no option but to hang on to what they know. The
question they pose is simply, "Is old age worthwhile?" With medical
science stepping up the average life expectancy annually, more and more
persons are having to ask that question. Poets have always given a bow in
the direction of "the evening of our lives," "the sunset years," "the
crimson hues of autumn," but their phrases sound suspect. Simply as
poetry, "Grow old along with me, the best is yet to be" carries not half
the conviction of "While we are but decaying, Come my Corinna,
come, let's go a Maying."

Whether life has a future beyond middle age depends in the end not
on poetry but on fact, on what the values of life really are. If they are
supremely those of body and sense, we may as well resign ourselves to
the fact that all experience after youth must be downhill. If gross motor
activity in the affairs of man is preeminent, middle age, the stage of the
householder, will be life's peak. But if vision and self-understanding
carry rewards equal to or surpassing these others, old age has its own

opportunities and we can come to happiness at the time when the rivers of our lives run gently.

Whether or not they do hold such rewards depends on the scene to be disclosed when the curtain of ignorance lifts. If reality is a monotonous and depressing wasteland and self no more than subtle cybernetics, the rewards of vision and self-knowledge cannot possibly rival the ecstasies of sense or the satisfactions of social achievement. We have seen, however, that in Hinduism they are held to be more. "Leave all and follow Him! Enjoy his inexpressible riches," say the *Upanishads*. No joy can approximate the beatific vision, and the Self to be discovered is great beyond all report. It follows that succeeding the stages of student and householder Hinduism will mark with confidence a third stage into which life should move.

This is the stage of retirement. Anytime after the arrival of his first grandchild, the individual may avail himself of the license of age and withdraw from the social obligations he has thus far shouldered with a will. For twenty to thirty years he has enacted his due role in the world; now replacements are in order lest life be over before it is grasped. Thus far society has required the individual to specialize; there has been little time to read, to think, to ponder life's meaning without interruption. This is not resented; the game has carried its own satisfactions. But must man's spirit be indentured to society forever? The time has come for the individual to begin his true adult education, to discover who he is and what life is about. What is the secret of the "I" with which he has been on such intimate terms all these years yet which remains a stranger, full of inexplicable quirks, baffling surds, irrational impulses? What lurks behind the world's facade, animating it, ordering it—to what end? Beyond the plains of life's routine that has become familiar and boring these ultimate mysteries rise and tower, the final challenge, intrigue, and fascination of the human mind.

Traditionally those who responded fully to this lure of spiritual adventure were known as forest dwellers, for, man and wife together if she wished to go, man alone after providing for her if she did not, they would pull up stakes and plunge into the forest solitudes to launch their program of self-discovery. At last their responsibilities were to themselves alone. "Business, family, secular life, like the beauties and hopes of youth and the successes of maturity, have now been left behind; eternity alone remains. And so it is to that—not to the tasks and worries of this life, already gone, which came and passed like a dream—that the mind is turned."[31] Retirement looks beyond the stars, not to the village streets. It is the time for working out a philosophy and then working that philosophy into oneself, the time for transcending the senses to find and dwell at one with the timeless reality that underlies the dream of life in this natural world.

Beyond retirement the final stage in which the goal is actually reached is the state of the *sannyasin*, defined by the *Bhagavad-Gita* as "one who neither hates nor loves anything."

The pilgrim is now free to return to the world for, the intent of his forest discipline achieved, time and place have lost all hold upon him. Where in all the world can one be totally free if not everywhere? The Hindus likened the *sannyasin* to a wild goose or swan "which has no fixed home but wanders, migrating with the rain-clouds north to the Himalayas and back south again, at home on every lake or sheet of water, as also in the infinite, unbounded reaches of the sky." The market place has now become as hospitable as the forests. But though the *sannyasin* is back, he is back a different person. Having discovered that complete release from every limitation is synonymous with absolute anonymity, he has learned the art of keeping the finite self dispersed lest it eclipse the infinite.

Far from wanting to "be somebody," the *sannyasin's* wish is the exact reverse: to remain a complete nonentity on the surface that he may be joined to all in his depths. How could he possibly wish to make himself up again as an individual, restore the superimpositions, colorings, besmearings of the actor's mask that conceals the purity and radiance of his intrinsic self? The outward life that fits this total freedom best is that of a homeless mendicant. Others might seek to be economically independent in their old age; the *sannyasin* proposed to become independent of economics. With no fixed place on earth, no obligations, no goal, no belongings, the expectations of body are nothing. Social pretensions likewise have no soil from which to sprout and interfere. No pride remains in the man who, begging bowl in hand, finds himself at the back door of one over whom he was once master; and would not have it otherwise.

The *sannyasin* saints of Jainism, an offshoot of Hinduism, went about "clothed in space," stark naked. Buddhism, another offshoot, dressed its counterparts in ochre, the color worn by the criminal ejected from society and condemned to death. Good that all status be whisked away at a stroke, for all determinations are negations by specialization, preventing total identification with the ubiquitous and imperishable ground of all existence. "Taking no thought of the future and looking with indifference upon the present," read the Hindu texts, the *sannyasin* "lives identified with the eternal Self and beholds nothing else." "He no more cares whether his body falls or remains, than does a cow what becomes of the garland that someone has hung around her neck; for the faculties of his mind are now at rest in the Holy Power, the essence of bliss."[32]

The unwise life is one long struggle with death the intruder—an uneven battle in which life is beaten back at every stage. When youth slips away, the ignorant would hold it back by force. When the fervor of desire slackens, they would revive it with fresh fuel of their own devising. Even when their grip relaxes of necessity, they are reluctant to let go. Unable to recognize the inevitable as not only natural but also good, they cannot give up gracefully what must go and should go to make room for what is better; they wait, therefore, in fear until it is snatched away. But as Tagore remarked, truth comes as conqueror only to those who have lost the art of receiving it as friend.

THE STATIONS OF LIFE

People are different—we are back a third time to this cardinal Hindu contention. We have traced its import for the different paths men should follow toward God and the different patterns of life appropriate at various stages in the arc of the human career. We come now to its implications for the station the individual should occupy in the social order.

This brings us to the Hindu concept of caste. On no other score is Hinduism better known or more roundly condemned by the outside world. Caste contains both point and perversion. Everything in the discussion of this subject depends on being able to distinguish between them.

How caste came into being is one of the most complicated and confused topics in history. Central, certainly, was the fact that during the second millenium B.C., a host of Aryans possessing a different language, culture, and physiognomy (tall, fair-skinned, blue-eyed, straight-haired) migrated into India. The clash of differences that followed burgeoned the caste system if it did not actually create it. The extent to which ethnic differences, color, trade guilds with professional secrets, sanitation restrictions between groups with greater and less immunity to disease, and magico-religious taboos concerning pollution and purification contributed to the pattern that emerged may never be confidently unraveled. In any event the outcome was a society clearly divided into four groups: seers, administrators, producers, and followers.

Let us record at once the perversions that entered in time however they may have originated. To begin with, a fifth group—of outcastes or untouchables—appeared. Even in speaking of this institution there are mitigating points to be remembered: in dealing with her lowest social group India never sank to slavery as have most civilizations; outcastes who, having pressed through to the fourth stage of life, renounced the world for God, were regarded as super-social and to be revered and learned from even by Brahmins;[33] from Buddha through Dayananda to Gandhi, many religious reformers have sought to remove untouchability and heredity from the caste system; and contemporary India's constitution has outlawed untouchability. However, the outcaste's lot through the bulk of India's history cannot be defended and must be regarded as the basic perversion that entered the caste system. A second deteriorating development lay in the proliferation of castes into subcastes of which there are today over three thousand. Third, proscriptions against intermarriage and interdining came to complicate social intercourse enormously, a fact responsible for much of Prime Minister Nehru's feeling against caste. Fourth, privileges entered the scale with top castes profiting at the expense of the low. Finally, caste became hereditary; one remained in the caste into which one was born.

With these sharp counts against it, it may come as a surprise to find contemporary Indians thoroughly familiar with Western alternatives who defend caste in any sense.[34] What lasting values could such a system possibly contain?

What is needed here is recognition that with respect to the ways they can best contribute to society and develop their own potentialities people fall into four groups. (1.) The first group India called Brahmins or seers. Reflective, with a passion to understand and a keen intuitive grasp of the values that matter most in human life, these are civilization's intellectual and spiritual leaders. Into their province fall the functions which in our specialized society have been distributed among philosophers, artists, religious leaders, and teachers. (2.) Others are born administrators[35] with a genius for organizing and promoting the affairs of men in such a way as to bring the best results out of the human materials involved. (3.) Others find their vocation as producers; they are craftsmen, artisans, farmers, skillful at creating the material things on which life depends. (4.) Finally there are some who are best described as followers. Unskilled laborers would be another name for them. These are persons who, if they had to carve out a career, submit to a long period of training, or go into business for themselves, would flounder. Their time sense is short, which makes them unwilling to sacrifice much in the present for the sake of the future. Under supervision, however, they are capable of hard work and devoted labor. Such persons are better off and actually happier working for others than being on their own. We with our democratic sentiments do not like to admit that there are such people by nature. The orthodox Hindu replies, What you would *like* people to be is not the point. The question is what they *are*.

Few contemporary Hindus defend the lengths to which India eventually went to keep the castes distinct. Her proscriptions regulating intermarriage, eating, and many other forms of social contact have made her, in Nehru's wry comment, "the least tolerant nation in social forms while the most tolerant in the realm of ideas." Yet even here a certain point lies behind the accursed proliferations. That proscriptions against different castes drinking from the same source were especially firm suggests that differences in immunity levels may have been part of the reason. But the reason as a whole is broader than this. Unless unequals are kept differentiated by some device, the weak will be matched with the strong all the way down the line and can stand no chance of winning anywhere. Between castes there was no equality, but within each caste the individual's rights were safer than if he had been forced to fend for them alone in the world at large. Each caste was self-governing, and in trouble a man could be sure of being tried by his peers. Within each caste was equality, opportunity, and social insurance.

Inequality between the castes themselves aimed for due compensation for services rendered. The well-being of society requires that some persons assume, at the cost of considerable self-sacrifice, responsibilities far beyond average. While most young persons will plunge early into marriage and earning, some must postpone these joys for as much as a decade longer that they may give themselves to their specialized studies. When the wage earner checks out at five o'clock he is through. His employer meanwhile must take home the ever-present insecurities of management and probably a briefcase of homework as well. The question is not so much whether they would be willing to continue their services without tangible returns as whether it is right for society to ask them to. India never confused democracy with egalitarianism. Justice was defined as a state in which privileges were proportionate to responsibilities. In salary and social power, therefore, the second caste, the administrators, rightly stood supreme; in honor and psychological power, the Brahmins. But only, according to the ideal, because their responsibilities were proportionately greater. In precise reverse of the European doctrine that the king could do no wrong, the orthodox Hindu view came very near holding that the Sudras or lowest caste could do no wrong, for they were as children from whom more could not justly be expected. Caught in the same offense, the punishment of a producer was twice as heavy as that of a follower, that of an administrator twice as heavy again, and that of a Brahmin twice or even four times heavier still. In India the lowest caste was free of many of the forms of probity and self-denial to which the upper castes were expected to conform. Its widows, for example, might remarry, and proscription against the eating of meat were less strict.

Stated in modern idiom the ideal of caste emerges something like this: At the bottom of the social scale is a class of routineers—factory workers and hired hands—who can put up with an unvaried round of duties but whose self-discipline is so small that they must punch time clocks if they are to get in a day's work, and whose time sense is so short that they cannot be counted on to forego many present pleasures for future rewards. Above them is a class of technicians. Craftsmen in pre-industrial societies, in an industrial age they are the men who understand the machines, repair them, and keep them running. Next comes Burnham's managerial class. In its political wing it includes state officials, chief executives, and civil servants; in its military branch, generals and chiefs-of-staff; in its industrial arm, supply and distribution experts, managing directors, and corporation executives who allot products, foresee consumption, and plan expansion.

If, however, society is to be complicated and good, efficient, wise, and inspired, there must be above the administrators in esteem (though not in pay, for one of the defining marks of this class must lie precisely in its orientation to values beyond the material) a fourth class which in our specialized society would include teachers, religious leaders, writers, and other artists. Such persons are rightly called seers in the literal sense of this word, for they are the eyes of the community. As the head (administrators) rests on the body (laborers and technicians) so the eyes are placed at the top of the head.[36] The members of this class must be equipped with will power sufficient to restrain the egotism and impulse that inhibit insight and vision. They command respect because others recognize both their own incapacity for such restraint and the validity of what the seers report back to them. The seer "sees what lower types can only smell." But such vision is a tender plant, capable of flowering only when carefully protected. Needing leisure for unhurried reflection, the seer must be protected from over-involvement in the day to day exigencies that clutter and cloud the distant scene, as starwatching lookout men are kept on the bridge, free of hold and galley, while others who entrust the steersmanship to them serve tables. Above all, this final caste must be protected from temporal power. Its members must never be executives. The Brahmin was supposed to renounce all pretentions to secular authority; when this vow was forgotten his caste became corrupt. For temporal power always subjects its wielder to pressures and temptations which to some extent refract judgment and distort it. The role of the seer is not to crack down but to counsel, not to drive but to show; his power is persuasion not force. Like a compass needle, guarded that it may point, his function is to indicate the true north of life's meaning and purpose; he becomes thereby the poet of history, inspiring and luring as he points the direction of civilization's advance.

When it has died, caste is as offensive as any other decaying body. Whatever its character at the start, it came in time to neglect Plato's crucial insight that "a golden parent may have a silver son, or a silver parent a golden son, and then there must be a change of rank; the son of the rich must descend, and the child of the artisan rise, in the social scale; for an oracle says 'that the State will come to an end if governed by a man of brass or iron.' " As one of the most thoughtful contemporary advocates of the basic idea of caste has written, "we may expect that the coming development . . . will differ chiefly . . . in permitting intermarriage and choice or change of occupation under certain conditions, though still recognizing the general desirability of marriage within the group and of following one's parent's calling."[37] Insofar as caste has come to mean rigidity, exclusiveness, and undeserved privilege, Hindus today are working to clear this corruption from their polity. But there remain many who are convinced that to the problem no country has yet solved, the problem of how society ought to be ordered so as to insure to a maximum the virtues of both fair play and creativity, the basic theses of caste still have something to contribute to modern thought.

Up to this point we have approached Hinduism in terms of its practical import for man. Beginning with its analysis of what man wants, we have traced its suggestions concerning the ways these wants might be met and the responses appropriate to various stages and stations of human life. The remaining sections of this chapter shift the focus from

practice to theory, indicating the principal philosophical concepts that
rib the Hindu religion.

"He Before Whom All Words Recoil"

Arnold Toynbee tells of criticizing his mother for omitting a foreground detail in the landscape she was drawing. She replied that in
sketching the first principle to learn is what to leave out.

This is also the first principle to be learned in speaking of God, the
Hindus would insist. Man is forever trying to lay hold of Reality with
words, only in the end to find mystery rebuking his speech and his
syllables swallowed by silence. The problem is not that our minds are
not bright enough. The problem lies deeper. Our minds, taken in their
conscious, surface sense, are the wrong kind of instrument for the undertaking. The effect, as a result, is like trying to ladle the ocean with a net
or lasso the wind with rope. The awe inspiring prayer of Shankara, the
St. Thomas Aquinas of Hinduism, begins with the invocation, "Oh
Thou, before whom all words recoil."

Man's mind has been evolved to facilitate his survival in this natural
world. It is adapted to deal with finite objects. God, on the contrary,
is infinite and of a completely different order of being from what our
minds can grasp. To expect man to corner the infinite with his finite
mind is like asking a dog to understand Einstein's equation with his
nose. This analogy becomes misleading if, pressed in a different direction,
it suggests that man can never know the Abysmal God. The *yogas*, as
we saw, are roads to precisely such knowledge. But the knowledge to
which they lead transcends the knowledge of the rational mind, rising
to the deep yet dazzling darkness of the mystical consciousness.[38] The
only literally accurate description of the Unsearchable of which man's
surface mind is capable is *neti . . . neti*. If you go throughout the length
and breadth of the universe saying of everything you can see and conceive, "not this . . . not this," what remains will be God.[39]

Still, words and concepts cannot be avoided. Being the only equipment at our mind's disposal, any conscious progress toward God must
be made with their aid. Though concepts can never carry the mind to its
destination, they can point in the right direction.

We may begin simply with a name to give our thoughts focus.
The name the Hindus give to the supreme reality is *Brahman*, from
the root *brih* meaning "to be great." The chief attributes to be linked
with this name are *sat*, *chit*, and *ananda*; God is being, awareness, and
bliss. Utter Reality, utterly conscious, and utterly beyond all possibility

of frustration, this is the basic Hindu view of God. Even these words cannot claim to describe him literally, however, for the meanings they carry for us are radically unlike the senses in which they apply to God. What pure being would be like, being infinite with absolutely nothing excluded, of this we have scarcely an inkling. Similarly with awareness and joy. As Spinoza would say, God's nature resembles our words here about as much as the dog star resembles a dog. The most that can be said for these words is that they are pointers; our minds do better to move in their direction than in their opposite. God lies on the further side of being as we understand it, not nothingness; beyond minds as we know them, not mindless clay; beyond ecstasy not agony.

This is as far as some minds need go in their vision of God: infinite being, infinite consciousness, infinite bliss, all else is at best commentary, at worst detraction. There are sages who can live in this austere, conceptually thin atmosphere of the spirit and find it invigorating—with Shankara they can understand that "the sun shines even without objects to shine upon." Most persons, however, cannot be gripped by such high order abstractions. That C. S. Lewis of Oxford University is among their number is proof that their minds are not inferior, only different. Professor Lewis tells us that while he was a child his parents kept admonishing him not to think of God in terms of any form, for these could only limit his infinity. He tried his best to heed their instructions, but the closest he could come to the idea of a formless God was an infinite sea of grey tapioca.

This anecdote, the Hindus would say, points up perfectly the circumstance of the man or woman whose mind must bite into something concrete and representational if it is to find life-sustaining meaning. Most persons find it impossible to conceive, much less be motivated by, anything that is removed very far from what they directly experience. Hinduism advises such persons not to try to think of God as the supreme instance of abstractions like being or consciousness but instead to think of him as the archetype of the noblest reality they actually encounter in this natural world. This means thinking of him as the supreme person (*Ishwara* or *Bhagavan*), for persons are nature's noblest crown. Our discussion of *bhakti yoga*, the path to God through love and devotion, has already introduced us to God conceived in this way. He is, to use Pascal's Western idiom, the God of Abraham, Isaac, and Jacob, not the God of the philosophers. He is God the Father, lovingly merciful, omniscient, almighty, our eternal contemporary, the great companion who understands.

God so conceived is called *Saguna Brahman* or God-with-attributes to distinguish him from the philosophers' more abstract *Nirguna Brahman* or God-without-attributes. *Nirguna Brahman* is the ocean without wave or ripple; *Saguna Brahman* the same ocean cloven with foaming waves. In the language of theology, the distinction is between impersonal and personal conceptions of God. Hinduism has included superb champions of each view, notably Shankara of the impersonal and Ramanuja of the personal, but the conclusion that does most justice to Indian history as a whole and has its own explicit champions like Ramakrishna is that both are equally correct. At first blush this may look like a glaring violation of the law of the excluded middle. God may be either personal or not, we are likely to insist; both he cannot be. But is this so? What the disjunction forgets, India argues, is the distance our rational minds are from God however we define him. As he is in himself, God may not be capable of being two contradictory things—we say may not because logic itself may melt in the full blast of the divine incandescence. But concepts of God contain so much alloy to begin with that two contradictory ones may be true from different points of view, as both waves and particles may be equally accurate heuristic devices for describing the nature of light.[40] On the whole, India has been content to encourage the devotee to conceive of Brahman as either personal or impersonal depending on which carries the most exalted meaning for his particular mind set. The exaltedness is what is true, the symbols through which it comes garbed are but runways that can get the spirit into the air even though they point in different directions. Take care, therefore, in denouncing contradictories: they may be somebody's truth.

God's relation to the world likewise varies with the way in which he is conceived. If he is thought of as personal he will stand in relation to the world as an artist to his handiwork. He will be Creator (*Brahma*), Preserver (*Vishnu*), and Destroyer (*Shiva*) who in the end resolves all finite forms back into the primordial nature from which they emerged. If, on the other hand, he is conceived impersonally, he will stand above the struggle, aloof from the finite in every respect. "As the sun does not tremble, although its image trembles when you shake the cup filled with water in which the sun's light is reflected; thus the Lord also is not affected by pain, although pain be felt by that part of him which is called the individual soul."[41] The world will still depend on him. It will have emerged in some unfathomable way from the plenitude of his being and be sustained by his power. "He shining, the sun, the moon and the stars shine after Him; by His light all is lighted. . . . He is the

Ear of the ear, the Mind of the mind, the Speech of the speech, the Life of life, and the Eye of the eye."[42] But he will not have intentionally willed the world nor be affected by its inherent ambiguity, imperfections, and finitude.

The personalist will see little religious availability in this idea of a God who is so far removed from our predicaments that he is not even aware of us as his children. Is it not religion's death to despoil man's heart of its final treasure, the diamond of God's love? The answer is that for the impersonalist God serves an entirely different function, equally important, equally religious, but different. If one is struggling against a current it is a comfort to have a master swimmer by one's side. It is equally important that there be a bank, solid and serene, that stands beyond the struggle as the terminus of all one's splashings. The impersonalist has become so possessed by the goal that he cannot bring his interest back to himself even to ask if he will make it or if there is a friend cheering him on from the further shore.

COMING OF AGE IN THE UNIVERSE

With God in pivotal position in the Hindu scheme, we can return to man to draw together systematically the Hindu concept of his nature and destiny.

Individual souls, or *jivas*, enter the world mysteriously; by God's power we may be sure, but how or for what reason we are unable fully to explain. Like bubbles that form on the bottom of a boiling teakettle, they make their way through the water (universe) until they break free into the limitless atmosphere of illumination (liberation). They begin as the souls of the simplest forms of life, but they do not vanish with the death of their original bodies. In the Hindu view, spirit no more depends on the body it inhabits than body depends on the clothes it wears or the house it lives in. When we outgrow a suit or find our house too cramped we exchange these for roomier ones that offer our bodies freer play. Souls do the same.

> Worn-out garments
> Are shed by the body:
> Worn-out bodies
> Are shed by the dweller. (*Bhagavad-Gita.*)

This process by which an individual *jiva* passes through a sequence of bodies is known as reincarnation or transmigration of the soul—in Sanskrit *samsara*, a word which means "passing through intensely." On the subhuman level the passage is through a series of increasingly complex bodies until at last a human one is attained. Up to this point the soul's growth is virtually automatic. It is as if the soul were growing as steadily and normally as a plant and receiving at each successive embodiment a body which, being more complex, provides the needed largess for its new attainments.

With the soul's graduation into a human body this automatic, escalator mode of ascent comes to an end. Its assignment to this exalted habitation is evidence that the soul has reached self-consciousness, and with this estate come freedom, responsibility, and effort.

The mechanism that ties these new acquisitions together is the law of *karma*. The literal meaning of *karma* as we encountered it in one of the four *yogas* is work, but as a doctrine *karma* means, roughly, the moral law of cause and effect. Science has alerted the Western world to the importance of causal relationships in the physical world. Every physical event, we are inclined to believe, has its cause, and every cause will have its determinate effects. India extends this concept of universal causation to include man's moral and spiritual life as well. To some extent the West has also. "As a man sows, so shall he reap;" or again, "Sow a thought and reap an act, sow an act and reap a habit, sow a habit and reap a character; sow a character and reap a destiny"—these are ways the West has put the point. The difference is that India tightens up and extends its concept of moral law to see it as absolutely binding and brooking no exceptions. The present condition of each individual's interior life—how happy he is, how confused or serene, how much he can see—is an exact product of what he has wanted and got in the past; and equally, his present thoughts and decisions are determining his future states. Each act he directs upon the world has its equal and opposite reaction on himself. Each thought and deed delivers an unseen chisel blow toward the sculpturing of his destiny.

This idea of *karma* and the completely moral universe it implies carries two important psychological corollaries. First, it commits the Hindu who understands it to complete personal responsibility. Each individual is wholly responsible for his present condition and will have exactly the future he is now creating. Most persons are unwilling to admit this. They prefer, as the psychologists would say, to project—to locate the source of their difficulties outside themselves. They want excuses, someone to blame that they may be exonerated. This, say the Hindus, is simply immature. Everyone gets exactly what he deserves—we have made our beds and we must lie in them. Conversely the idea of a moral universe closes the door to all appeals to chance or accident. Most persons have little idea how much they bank on luck—hard luck to justify past failures, good luck to bring future successes. How many persons drift through life simply waiting for the breaks, for that breathless moment when *his* name will be called to fame and prosperity no more through merit than when a name is selected for a quiz program. If you approach life this way, says Hinduism, you misjudge your position pathetically. Breaks have nothing to do with protracted levels of happiness, and even so do not happen by chance. We live in a world in which there is no chance or accident; the words are simply covers for ignorance.

Because *karma* implies a lawful world, it has often been interpreted as fatalism. However often Hindus may have succumbed to this interpretation, it is untrue to the doctrine itself. *Karma* decrees that every decision must have its determinate consequences, but the decisions themselves are, in the last analysis, freely arrived at. Or, to approach the matter from the other direction, the consequences of a man's past decisions condition his present lot, as a card player finds himself dealt a particular hand, but is left free to play that hand in a number of ways. This means that the career of a soul as it threads its course through innumerable human bodies is guided by its choices, these in turn being decided by what the soul wants at each particular stage of its pilgrimage.

What these wants are and the order in which they appear can be run through quickly here, for they have been considered in detail in previous sections. When it first enters a human body, a *jiva* wants nothing more than to taste widely of the sense delights its new physical equipment makes possible. With repetition, however, even the most ecstatic of these becomes monotonous, whereupon the *jiva* turns to social conquest to keep life from becoming insipid. These conquests—the various modes of wealth, fame, and power—can hold the individual's interest for a considerable time. The stakes are high and their attainment richly gratifying. Eventually, however, this entire program of personal ambition is seen for what it is: a game—a fabulous, exciting, history-making game, but a game none the less.

As long as it holds one's interest, it satisfies. But as there is no other ground on which to recommend it, when its novelty wears off and the winner finds himself stepping forward to accept the same old laurels that have come his way before, he will find himself reaching out again for something new and more deeply satisfying. Duty, the total dedication of one's life to the beloved community,

can step in for awhile to fill the need, but the ironies and anomalies
of history make this object too a revolving door. Lean on it and it gives;
in time one discovers that one is going round and round. After social
dedication the only good that can satisfy is one that is infinite and
eternal whose realization can turn all experience, even the experience
of time and apparent defeat, to splendor, as storm clouds drifting down
a valley look different viewed from the top of a high mountain bathed in
sunshine. The bubble has reached the surface and demands its final
release.

The soul's progress through these ascending strata of human wants
does not take the form of a straight line with an acute upward incidence.
Its course is zigzag as it fumbles its way toward what it really wants. In
the long run, however, the trend of attachments will be upward. By up
here is meant a gradual relaxation of attachment to physical objects and
stimuli, and a gradual movement of interest away from the soul's finite
being toward more durable objects. We can almost visualize the action
of *karma* as it carries through with the consequences of what the soul
asks for. It is as if each desire that aims at the ego's gratification adds a
grain to the wall that surrounds the individual self and insulates it from
the infinite sea of being that surrounds it, whereas each impulse toward
participation in that larger life dislodges a grain from the cramping
dike. Detachment can never be measured externally, however. The fact
that an individual withdraws to a monastery and gives full time to meditation is no proof that he has risen over self and craving, for he may be
catering to them abundantly in the imaginations of his heart. Conversely,
a man may be immersed in the world, busy, holding vast responsibilities,
and surrounded with wealth; but if he is truly detached from these—if,
as the Hindus say, he lives among them as a mudfish lives in the mud,
surrounded by the mud without its sticking to him—he can use these
media as well as any as means for his pilgrimage.

Never during its pilgrimage is the spirit of man completely adrift and
alone. From start to finish its nucleus is the *Atman*. Underlying its whirl-
pool of transient feelings, emotions, and delusions is the self-luminous,
abiding point of God himself. Though he is buried too deep in the soul
to be usually noticed, he is the sole ground of man's being and awareness.
As the sun provides the world's light even while obscured by cloud, "the
Immutable . . . is never seen but is the Witness; It is never heard but
is the Hearer; It is never thought, but is the Thinker; is never known,
but is the Knower. There is no other witness but This, no other hearer
but This, no other thinker but This, no other knower but This."[43]

But God not only energizes the surface self in all that it does; in the end it is his radiance that melts the soul's thick cap that hides his glory almost completely at first but becomes at last a pure capacity for God.

And what happens then? Some say the individual soul passes into complete identification with God and loses every trace of its former separateness. Others, wishing to taste sugar, not be sugar, cherish the hope that some slight differentiation between the soul and God may still remain—a thin line upon the ocean which provides nevertheless the remnant of personal identity some persons consider indispensable for even the beatific vision.

Christopher Isherwood has written a story based on an Indian fable that summarizes this process of the soul's coming of age in the universe. An old man seated on a lawn with a group of children around him tells them of the magic Kalpataru tree that fulfills all wishes. "If you speak to it and tell it a wish; or if you lie down under it and think, or even dream, a wish, then that wish will be granted." The old man proceeds to tell them that he once obtained such a tree and planted it in his garden. "In fact," he tells them, "that is a Kalpataru over there."

With that the children rush to the tree and begin to shower it with requests. Most of these turn out to be unwise, ending in either indigestion or tears. But the Kalpataru grants them indiscriminately. It has no interest in giving advice.

Years pass and the Kalpataru is forgotten. The children have now grown into men and women and are trying to fulfill new wishes that they have found. At first they try to get their wishes fulfilled, but later their aim is just the reverse—to find wishes that can be fulfilled only with ever-increasing difficulty.

The point of the story is that the universe is one gigantic Wishing Tree, with branches that reach into every heart. The cosmic process decrees that sometime or other, in this life or another, each of these wishes will be granted—together, of course, with consequences.

There was one child from the original group, however, so the story concludes, who did not spend his years skipping from desire to desire, from one gratification to another. For from the first he had understood the real nature of the Wishing Tree. "For him, the Kalpataru was not the pretty magic tree of his uncle's story—it did not exist to grant the foolish wishes of children—it was unspeakably terrible and grand. It was his father and his mother. Its roots held the world together, and its branches reached beyond the stars. Before the beginning it had been —and would be, always."[44]

THE WORLD—WELCOME AND FAREWELL

A blueprint of the world as conceived by Hinduism would look something like this: There would be innumerable galaxies comparable to our own, each focusing in an earth from which men wend their ways to God. Ringing each earth would be a number of finer worlds above and inferior ones below to which souls would repair between incarnations depending on the desserts due them.

"Just as the spider pours forth its thread from itself and takes it back again . . . even so the universe grows from the Imperishable."[45] Periodically, however, the thread is taken back; the cosmos collapses into a Night of *Brahma* and all phenomenal being is returned to a state of pure potentiality. Thus like a gigantic accordion the world swells out and is drawn back in. This oscillation is a permanent feature of existence; the universe had no beginning and will have no end. The time scheme of Indian cosmology rocks the imagination and may have something to do with the proverbial Oriental indifference to haste. The Himalayas, it is said, are made of solid granite. Once every thousand years a bird flies over them with a scarf in its beak that brushes the ranges as it passes. When by this process the Himalayas have been worn away, one day of a cosmic cycle will have elapsed.

When we turn from the time-space layout of our world to its philosophical character we find that the first point has already been established in the preceding section. It is a moral world in which everyone gets what he deserves and creates the future into which he will move.

The second thing to be said is that it is a middle world. This is so not only in the sense that it hangs midway between heavens above and hells below; it is also middle in the sense of being middling, a world in which good and evil, pain and pleasure, knowledge and ignorance, meet and blend in about equal proportions. And this is the way it will remain. All talk of social progress, of cleaning up the world, of bringing the kingdom of heaven to earth, in short all dreams of utopianism are not only doomed to disappointment but also misconstrue the world's purpose. The world is the soul's gymnasium, its school, its training field. What we do is important, but ultimately it is important for the discipline it offers our individual spirits; we delude ourselves if we expect it to change the world in any fundamental way. Our work in this world is like bowling in an uphill alley; it can develop nice muscles, but we should not think that by our throws the balls are transported to the other end in any permanent way. They all roll back eventually to confront our children if we happen to have moved along. The world can develop character and teach men to look beyond it—for these it is admirably suited—but it can never be converted into a paradise in which man is fully at home. "Said Jesus, blessed be his name, this world is a bridge: pass over it, but build no house upon it." It is true to Indian thought that this apocryphal saying should have originated on her soil.

If we ask about the world's metaphysical status, we shall have to continue the distinction we have watched divide Hinduism on every major issue thus far; namely, that between the dual and the non-dual points of view. On way of life this distinction divides *jnana yoga* from *bhakti*; on doctrine of God it divides those who conceive God with attributes from those who conceive him without; on doctrine of salvation it divides the advocates of mérger with God from those who aspire to his company. In cosmology an extension of the same line divides those who regard the world as being from the highest perspective unreal from those who think it to be real from every point of view.

All Hindu religious thought denies that the world of nature stands on its own feet. It is grounded in God; if he were removed it would collapse into nothingness. Beyond this point, however, dualist and non-dualist thought parts. For the dualist the natural world is as real as God despite being less exalted; God, individual souls, and nature are distinct kinds of being, none of which can be reduced to the others. Non-dualists on the other hand approach the world by distinguishing three modes of consciousness under which it may appear. The first is hallucination, as when one sees pink elephants, or when a stick in water appears bent when not. Such appearances are marked by not being confirmed by further experience or the experience of others. Second, there is the world as it appears to our normal sense awareness. This world stands up to repeated experience and is common to all possessed of normal human sense receptors. Finally there is the world that comes when man rises through *yoga* to a state of super-consciousness. Strictly speaking this is no world at all, for here every trait that characterizes the natural world— its multiplicity and materiality—disappears. "There is but one reality, like a brimming ocean . . . boundless as the sky, indivisible, absolute. It is like a vast sheet of water, shoreless and calm."

The non-dualist claims that this third perspective is the most accurate disclosure of reality. In relation to this fully accurate point of view the world as it now appears to us is *maya*. This word is often translated "illusion," but this is misleading. For one thing it suggests that the world need not be taken seriously. This the Hindu would deny, pointing out that as long as it appears real and demanding to us we must accept it as such. Moreover, it does have a kind of qualified reality; reality on a provisional level.

Were we to be asked if dreams are real, our answer would have to be qualified. They are real in the sense that we have them, but they are not real in the sense that the things they depict necessarily exist in their own rights. Strictly speaking a dream is a psychological construct, something created by the mind out of its particular state. When the Hindus say the world is *maya*, this too is what they mean. Given the human mind in its normal condition, the world appears as we see it. But we have no right to infer from this that reality is in itself the way it so appears. A child seeing a motion picture for the first time will assume that the objects he sees—lions, kings, canyons—are objectively before him; he does not suspect that they are being projected from a booth in the rear of the theater. It is the same with us; we assume the world we see to be in itself as we see it whereas in actuality it is a correlate of the particular psychophysical condition our minds are currently in. To change the metaphor, our sense receptors pick up only those wave lengths to which they are tuned. With the aid of amplifiers and microscopes we pick up other wave lengths, but it is only when we rise to the condition of super-consciousness that we know reality itself. In this condition our receptors cease to refract, like a prism, the pure light of being into the spectrum of multiplicity. Reality comes to us at last as it actually is: one without a second, infinite, unalloyed.

Maya comes from the same root as magic. In saying the world is *maya*, non-dual Hinduism implies that there is something tricky about it. The trick, we see, lies in the way its materiality and multiplicity pass themselves off for being independently real apart from the state of mind from which they are seen. Reality in itself is actually undifferentiated Brahman throughout, as a rope lying in the dust remains a rope even while it is mistaken for a snake.

But if the world is only provisionally real, will it be taken as seriously as it should? Will not responsibility languish? Hinduism thinks not. In a sketch of the ideal society comparable to Plato's *Republic*, the *Tripura Rahasya* portrays a Prince who achieves this outlook on the world and is freed thereby from "the knots of the heart" and "the identification of the flesh with the Self." The consequences depicted are far from anti-social. Thus liberated he performs his royal duties efficiently but dis-passionately, "like an actor on the stage." Following his example and teachings, his subjects attain a comparable freedom and are no longer motivated by their passions though they still possess them. Worldly affairs continue, but the citizens are no longer torn by past good or evil fortune or pulled by future joys or pains, "in their everyday life laughing, rejoicing, wearied or angered, like men intoxicated and indifferent to their own affairs." Wherefore the sages that visited there called it "the City of Resplendent Wisdom."

If we ask why Reality which is in fact one and perfect is seen by us as many and marred, why the soul which is really united with God throughout sees itself for a while as separate, why the rope appears to be a snake—if we ask these things we are up against the question that has no answer, any more than the comparable Christian question of why God created the world has an answer. The best we can say is that the world is *lila*, God's play. Children playing hide and seek assume various roles that have no validity outside the game. They place themselves in jeopardy and in a condition in which they must make their escape to freedom. Why do they do this when they could become "free" in a twinkling by merely stepping out of the game? The only answer is that the game is its own point; it is fun in itself, a spontaneous overflow of creative, imaginative energy. So too in some mysterious way must it be with the world. Like a child playing alone, God is the lonely cosmic dancer whose routine is all creatures and all worlds. From the tireless stream of his cosmic energy these flow without end as he executes his graceful, repetitious movements.

Those who have seen images of the goddess Kali dancing upon a prostrate body and holding in two of her arms a sword and a severed head; those who have heard that there are more Hindu temples dedicated to Shiva, whose haunt is the crematorium and is God in his aspect of destroyer, than there are temples to God in the form of either creator or preserver; those who know these things will not jump immediately to the conclusion that the Hindu world view is gentle. What they overlook is that what Kali and Shiva destroy is the finite in order to make way for the infinite.

> Because Thou lovest the Burning-ground,
> I have made a Burning-ground of my heart—
> That Thou, Dark One, haunter of the Burning-ground,
> Mayest dance Thy eternal dance (Bengali Hymn).

Seen in perspective the world is ultimately kind. It has no permanent hell and threatens no eternal damnation. It may be loved without fear; its winds, its wide gray skies, its virgin forests, even the poisonous splendor of the lascivious orchid, all may be loved provided they are not lingered over forever. For all is *maya, lila,* the spell-binding dance of the cosmic magician beyond which lies the boundless good which all will achieve in the end. It is no accident that the only art form India failed to produce was tragedy.

In sum: to the question, "What kind of world do we have?" Hinduism answers:

1. A multiple world that includes innumerable galaxies horizontally, innumerable tiers vertically, and innumerable cycles temporally.

2. A moral world in which the law of *karma* never wavers.

3. A middle world that will never in itself replace the supreme as destination for the human spirit.

4. A world that is *maya,* deceptively tricky in that it passes off its multiplicity, materiality and welter of dualities as ultimate whereas these are in fact provisional only.

5. A training ground that can advance man toward the Highest.

6. A world that is *lila,* the play of the divine in its cosmic dance, untiring, unending, resistless but ultimately gentle, with a grace born of infinite vitality.

MANY PATHS TO THE SAME SUMMIT

That Hinduism has shared her land for centuries with Parsees, Buddhists, Muslims, Sikhs, and Christians may help explain a last idea that comes out more clearly through her than through any other leading contemporary religion; namely, her conviction that the various major religions are alternate and relatively equal paths to the same God. To claim salvation as the monopoly of any one religion is like claiming that God can be found in this room but not the next, in this attire but not another. Normally each individual will take the path which leads up life's mountain from his own culture; those who circle the mountain trying to bring others around to their paths are not climbing. In practice India's sects have often been fanatically intolerant, but in principle they have remained notably open. The Vedas early announce Hinduism's classic contention: the various religions are but the different languages through which God has spoken to the human heart. "Truth is one; sages call it by different names."

It is possible to climb life's mountain from any side, but when the top is reached the pathways merge. As long as religions remain in the foothills of theology, ritual, or church organization they may be far apart. Differences in culture, history, geography, and group temperament all make for different starting points. Far from being deplorable, this is good; it adds richness to the totality of man's religious venture. Is life not more interesting for the varied contributions of Confucianists, Taoists, Buddhists, Christians, and Jews? "How artistic," writes a contemporary Hindu, "that there should be room for such variety—how rich the texture is, and how much more interesting than if the Almighty had decreed one antiseptically safe, exclusive, orthodox way. Although he is Unity, God finds, it seems, his recreation in variety!"[46] But the goal beyond these differences is the same goal.

For evidence of this, one of Hinduism's nineteenth century saints sought God successively through the orthodoxies of a number of the world's great religions. In turn he sought him through the person of Christ, the imageless, God-directed teachings of the Koran, and a variety of Hindu God-embodiments. In each instance the result was the same: one God was revealed, now incarnate in Christ, now speaking through his prophet Muhammed, now in the guise of *Vishnu* the Preserver or *Shiva* the Completer. Out of these experiences came a set of teachings on the essential unity of the great religions which comprise Hinduism's finest voice on this matter. As tone is as important as idea here, we shall come closer to the Hindu position if we relinquish the remainder of this section to Ramakrishna's words instead of trying to abstract them in our own.[47]

God has made different religions to suit different aspirants, times, and countries. All doctrines are only so many paths; but a path is by no means God Himself. Indeed, one can reach God if one follows any of the paths with whole hearted devotion. One may eat a cake with icing either straight or sidewise. It will taste sweet either way.

As one and the same material, water, is called by different names by different peoples, one calling it water, another eau, a third aqua, and another pani, so the one Everlasting-Intelligent-Bliss is invoked by some as God, by some as Allah, by some as Jehovah, and by others as Brahman.

As one can ascend to the top of a house by means of a ladder or a bamboo or a staircase or a rope, so diverse are the ways and means to approach God, and every religion in the world shows one of these ways.

As the young wife in a family shows her love and respect to her father-in-law, mother-in-law, and every other member of the family, and at the same time loves her husband more than these; similarly, being firm in thy devotion to the deity of thy own choice, do not despise other deities, but honour them all.

Bow down and worship where others kneel, for where so many have been paying the tribute of adoration the kind Lord must manifest himself, for he is all mercy.

The devotee who has seen God in one aspect only, knows him in that aspect alone. But he who has seen him in manifold aspects is alone in a position to say, 'All these forms are of one God and God is multiform.' He is formless and with form, and many are his forms which no one knows.

The Saviour is the messenger of God. He is like the viceroy of a mighty monarch. As when there is some disturbance in a far-off province, the king sends his viceroy to quell it, so wherever there is a decline of religion in any part of the world, God sends his Saviour there. It is one and the same Saviour that, having plunged into the ocean of life, rises up in one place and is known as Krishna (the leading Hindu incarnation of God), and diving down again rises in another place and is known as Christ.

Every man should follow his own religion. A Christian should follow Christianity, a Mohammedan should follow Mohammedanism, and so on. For the Hindus the ancient path, the path of the Aryan sages, is the best.

People partition off their lands by means of boundaries, but no one can partition off the all-embracing sky overhead. The indivisible sky surrounds all and includes all. So common man in ignorance says, 'My religion is the only one, my religion is the best.' But when his heart is illumined by true knowledge, he knows that above all these wars of sects and sectarians presides the one indivisible, eternal, all-knowing bliss.

As a mother, in nursing her sick children, gives rice and curry to one, and sago arrowroot to another, and bread and butter to a third, so the Lord has laid out different paths for different men suitable to their natures.

Dispute not. As you rest firmly on your own faith and opinion, allow others also the equal liberty to stand by their own faiths and opinions. By mere disputation you will never succeed in convincing another of his error. When the grace of God descends on him, each one will understand his own mistakes.

There was a man who worshipped Shiva but hated all other deities. One day Shiva appeared to him and said, 'I shall never be pleased with thee so long as thou hatest the other gods.' But the man was inexorable. After a few days Shiva again appeared to him and said, 'I shall never be pleased with thee so long as thou hatest.' The man kept silent. After a few days Shiva again appeared to him. This time one side of his body was that of Shiva, and the other side that of Vishnu. The man was half pleased and half displeased. He laid his offerings on the side representing Shiva, and did not offer anything to the side representing Vishnu. Then Shiva said, 'Thy bigotry is unconquerable. I, by assuming this dual aspect, tried to convince thee that all gods and goddesses are but various aspects of the one Absolute Brahman.'

SUGGESTIONS FOR FURTHER READING

The best single book on Indian religion for the Western reader is Heinrich Zimmer's *The Philosophies of India* (New York: Pantheon Books, 1951). Blending as it does superb scholarship with a profound feel for its material, it is a truly great book. Meridian Books has recently reprinted it in a paper-back edition that sells for $1.95. Persons wishing less detailed approaches to the subject will do well to turn to Sir Sarvepalli Radhakrishnan's *The Hindu View of Life* (New York: Macmillan Press, 1927), Swami Nirvedananda's *Hinduism at a Glance* (Vidyamandira, Bengal: S. Mandal, 1946), and Swami Nikhilananda's *The Essence of Hinduism* (Boston: Beacon Press, 1948).

The Hindu scriptures themselves are of enormous scope, but two portions are of worldwide importance. Swami Prabhavananda and Christopher Isherwood have achieved a beautiful translation of the *Bhagavad-Gita* which is available in its Mentor edition for 35¢. The Upanishads require more interpretation, but are readily accessible to Western readers when the texts are accompanied by introductions and commentaries like those found in Swami Nikhilananda's three volume edition *The Upanishads* (New York: Harper & Brothers, 1949, 1952, 1956). Without commentary, *The Upanishads* also appears in Mentor edition.

The life that achieved the finest blend of Hinduism and the West in our time has been well told in Louis Fischer's *Gandhi: His Life and Message for the World*, published in 25¢ edition by The New American Library. Also in the realm of biography, Romain Rolland has given us splendid descriptions of two of modern India's purely religious geniuses in his *Life of Ramakrishna* and *Life of Vivekananda*, both published by the Vedanta Press in Hollywood.

As presentations of the practical teachings of Hinduism, Swami Vivekananda's *Jnana Yoga* and *Karna Yoga and Bhakti Yoga* (New York: Ramakrishna-Vivekananda Center, 1945) are classics. The other volume in this series, his *Raja Yoga*, moves into its material too rapidly for beginners.

Two books edited by Christopher Isherwood, *Vedanta for the Western World* (Hollywood: Vedanta Press, 1952) and *Vedanta for Modern Man* (New York: Harper & Brothers, 1951), present essays half by Indians, half by Westerners like Aldous Huxley, Gerald Heard, and John Van Druten which try to indicate the relevance of key Hindu doctrines for the problems of man in general, be he Easterner or Westerner.

A number of leading cities in the United States—New York, Providence, Boston, Chicago, St. Louis, Seattle, Portland, San Francisco, Berkeley, and Los Angeles—now have Vedanta Societies directed by Hindus who are at once able scholars and deeply religious men. Readers will find them invaluable sources of further information about this religion.

3

Buddhism

The Man Who Woke Up

BUDDHISM begins with a man. In his later years, when India had become electric with his message and kings themselves were bowing before him, people came to him even as they were to come to Jesus asking what he was.[1] How many people have provoked this question: not "Who are you?" with respect to name, origin, or ancestry, but "*What* are you?—what order of being do you belong to, what species do you represent?" Not Caesar, certainly. Not Napoleon, nor even Socrates. Only two, Jesus and Buddha. When the people carried their puzzlement to the Buddha himself, the answer he gave provided a handle for his entire message.

"Are you a god?" they asked. "No." "An angel?" "No." "A saint?" "No." "Then what are you?"

Buddha answered, "I am awake." His answer became his title, for this is what Buddha means. In the Sanskrit root *budh* denotes both to wake up and to know. Buddha, then, means the "Enlightened One" or the "Awakened One." While the rest of the world was wrapped in the womb of sleep, dreaming a dream known as the waking life of mortal men, one man roused himself. Buddhism begins with a man who shook off the daze, the doze, the dream-like inchoateness of ordinary awareness. It begins with the man who woke up.

His life has become encased in loving legend. We are told that the worlds were flooded with light at his birth. The blind so longed to see his coming glory that they received their sight; the deaf and dumb

80

conversed in ecstasy of the things which were to be. Crooked became straight; the lame walked. Prisoners were freed from their chains and the fires of hell were quenched. Even the crimes of the beasts were hushed as peace encircled the earth. Only Mara, the Evil One, rejoiced not.

The historical facts of his life are roughly these: He was born around 560 B.C. in northern India approximately one hundred miles from Benares.[2] His father was a king, but as India was not then united it would be more accurate to think of him as a feudal lord with the environment he provided for his son not unlike that of a Scottish castle in the Middle Ages. His full name was Siddhartha Gautama of the Sakyas; Siddhartha was his given name, Gautama his surname, and Sakya the name of the clan to which his family belonged. By the standards of his day his upbringing was luxurious. "I wore garments of silk and my attendants held a white umbrella over me. . . . My unguents were always from Benares." He appears to have been extremely handsome for there are numerous references to "the perfection of his visible body." At sixteen he married a neighboring princess named Yasodhara who bore him a son whom they called Rahula.

Here, in short, was a man who seemed to have everything: family, "the venerable Gautama is well born on both sides, of pure descent"; appearance, "handsome, inspiring trust, gifted with great beauty of complexion, fair in color, fine in presence, stately to behold"; wealth, "[He] had elephants and silver ornaments for [his] elephants." He had a model wife, "majestic as a queen of heaven, constant ever, cheerful night and day, full of dignity and exceeding grace" who bore him a beautiful son. In addition, as heir to his father's throne, he was destined for power and prestige.

Despite all this, there settled over him in his twenties a discontent which was to lead to a complete break with his worldly estate.

The background of his discontent is embedded in the legend of The Four Passing Sights, one of the most celebrated calls to adventure in the literature of the world. When Siddhartha was born, so this story runs, his father summoned fortunetellers to find out what the future held for his heir. All agreed that this was no usual child. His career, however, was crossed with one basic ambiguity. If he remained with the world he would unify India and become her greatest conqueror, a Cakravartin or Universal King. If, on the other hand, he forsook the world he would become not a king but a world redeemer. Faced with this option, his father determined to steer his son into the former destiny. No effort was spared to keep the prince's mind attached to the world. Three palaces and forty thousand dancing girls were placed at his disposal; strict orders were given that no ugliness intrude upon the courtly pleasures. Specifically the prince was to be shielded from contact with sickness, decrepitude, and death; even when he went riding runners were to clear the roads of these sights. One day, however, an old man was overlooked or, as some versions have it, miraculously incarnated by the gods to effect the needed teaching experience of the moment; a man decrepit, broken-toothed, gray-haired, crooked and bent of body, leaning on a staff, and trembling. That day Siddhartha learned the fact of old age. Though the king extended his guard, on a second ride Siddhartha encountered a body racked with disease lying by the road; and on a third journey, a corpse. Finally on a fourth occasion he saw a monk with shaven head, ochre robe, and bowl; on that day he learned the possibility of withdrawal from the world. It is a legend, this story, but like most legends it embodies an important truth. For the teachings of Buddha show unmistakably that it was the body's inescapable involvement with disease, decrepitude, and death that made him despair of finding fulfillment on the physical plane. "Life is subject to age and death. Where is the realm of life in which there is neither age nor death?"

Once he had perceived the inevitability of bodily pain and passage he could not return to fleshly pleasure. The sing-song of the dancing girls, the lilt of lutes and cymbals, the sumptuous feasts and processions, the elaborate celebration of festivals only mocked his brooding mind. Flowers nodding in the sunshine and snows melting on the Himalayas cried louder of the evanescence of worldly things. He determined to quit the snare of distractions his palace had become and follow the call of a truth-seeker. One night in his twenty-ninth year he made the break, his Great Going Forth. Making his way in the post-midnight hours to where his wife and son were locked in sleep he bade them both a silent goodbye, then ordered the gatekeeper to bridle his great white horse. The two mounted and rode off toward the forest. Reaching its edge by daybreak, Gautama changed clothes with the attendant who returned with the horse to break the news, while Gautama shaved his head and "clothed in ragged raiment" plunged into the forest in search of enlightenment.

Six years followed during which his full energies were concentrated toward this end. "How hard to live the life of the lonely forest-dweller. . . . to rejoice in solitude. Verily, the silent groves must bear heavy

upon the monk who has not yet won to fixity of mind!" The words
bear poignant witness that his search was not easy. In procedure it
appears to have moved through three phases, with no record as to how
long each lasted or how sharply the three were divided. His first act
was to seek out two of the foremost Hindu masters of the day to pick
their minds for the wisdom in their vast tradition. He learned a great
deal, about *raja yoga* especially but about philosophy as well—so much
in fact that Hindus today claim him as their own, holding that his
criticisms of the Hinduism of his day were in the order of reforms
and less sizable than his agreements. In time, however, he concluded
that he had learned all these *yogis* could teach him.

His next step was to join a band of ascetics and give their way full
try. Was it his body that was holding him back? He would break its
power, crush its interference. A man of enormous will power, he out-
did his confreres in every austerity they proposed. He ate so little, one
bean a day during one of his fasts, that "when I thought I would
touch the skin of my stomach, I actually took hold of my spine."
He would clench his teeth and press his tongue to his palate until
"sweat flowed from my armpits." He would hold his breath until it
felt "as if a strong man were to crush one's head with the point of a
sword . . . as if a strap were being twisted round his head . . . as if two
strong men were holding a weaker one over a fire of coals." He would
not wash himself until the dirt grew so thick upon his body "that it
fell off of its own accord."[3] In the end he grew so weak that he fell
into a faint, and if companions had not been around to feed him some
warm rice gruel he might easily have died.

This experience taught him the futility of asceticism. He had given
this experiment all a man could and it had not been successful. It had
not brought enlightenment. But negative experiments are often as rewarding as positive ones, and so in this case the very failure of asceticism
provided the first positive plank in Gautama's philosophy, the principle of the Middle Way between the extremes of asceticism on the
one hand and indulgence on the other. It is the concept of the rationed
life in which the body is given precisely what it needs in the way of
food and rest for optimum functioning but no more.

Having turned his back on mortification, Gautama devoted the final
phase of his quest to a combination of rigorous thought and mystic
concentration along the lines of *raja yoga*. One evening near Gaya in
northeast India, south of the current town of Patna, he sat beneath
a fig tree which has since come to be known popularly as the Bo tree

(short for *Bodhi* or enlightenment). The place was later named the Immovable Spot for tradition reports that the Buddha, sensing that he was on the brink of enlightenment, seated himself that epoch-making evening with the vow not to rise until illumination was his.

The records offer as the first event of the night a temptation scene reminiscent of Jesus' on the eve of his ministry. The Evil One, realizing that his antagonist's success was imminent, rushed to the spot to disrupt his concentrations. He attacked first in the form of Desire, parading three voluptuous goddesses with their tempting retinues. When the Buddha-to-be remained unmoved, the Temptor switched to the guise of Death. His powerful hosts assailed the aspirant with hurricanes, torrential rains, showers of flaming rocks that splashed boiling mud, and finally a great darkness. But the missiles became blossom petals as they entered the field of the yogi's concentration. When, in final desperation Mara challenged his right to be doing what he was, Buddha touched the earth with his right fingertip, whereupon the earth responded, thundering, "I bear you witness" with a hundred, a thousand, and a hundred thousand roars. Mara's army fled in full retreat and the gods of heaven descended in rapture to wait upon the victor with garlands and perfumes.

Thereafter, while the Bo tree rained red blossoms that full-mooned May night, Gautama's meditation deepened through watch after watch until, as the morning star glittered in the transparent skies of the east, his mind pierced at last the bubble of the universe and shattered it to naught only, wonder of wonders, to find it miraculously restored with the effulgence of true being. The Great Awakening had arrived. Gautama's being was transformed, and he emerged the Buddha. The event was of cosmic import. All created things filled the morning air with their rejoicings and the earth quaked six ways with wonder. Ten thousand galaxies shuddered in awe as lotuses bloomed on every tree, turning the entire universe into "a bouquet of flowers sent whirling through the air."[4] The bliss of this vast experience kept the Buddha rooted to the spot for seven entire days. On the eighth he tried to rise but was lost again in bliss. For a total of forty-nine days he was deep in rapture, after which his "glorious glance" opened again onto the world.

Mara was waiting for him with one last temptation. He appealed this time to reason. He did not argue the burden of reentering the banalities and noisy obsessions of life. The challenge he poised was deeper. Who could be expected to understand truth as profound as that the Buddha had laid hold of? How could speech-defying revelation be translated into words? How could visions that shattered definition be rendered in terms of yes and no? In short, how show what can only be found, teach what can only be learned? Why bother to play the idiot before a jury of uncomprehending eyes? Why try to argue the glance of spirit to masses still caught in the whirligig of passion? Why not commit the whole hot world to the devil, be done with the body forever, and slip at once into the cool haven of perpetual Nirvana? The argument contained so much truth that it almost carried the day. At length, however, the Buddha answered, "There will be some who will understand," and Mara was banished from his life forever.

Nearly half a century followed during which Buddha trudged the dusty paths of India until his hair was white, step infirm, and body naught but a burst drum, preaching the ego-shattering, life-redeeming elixir of his message. He founded an order of monks, challenged the deadness of Brahmin society, and accepted in return the resentment, queries, and bewilderment his words provoked. His daily routine was staggering. In addition to training monks, correcting breaches of discipline, and generally directing the affairs of the Order, he maintained an interminable schedule of public preaching and private counseling, advising the perplexed, encouraging the faithful, and comforting the distressed. "To him people come right across the country from distant lands to ask questions, and he bids all men welcome." Underlying his response to these pressures, and enabling him to stand up under them was a pattern which Toynbee has found basic to creativity in all history, the pattern of "withdraw and return." Buddha withdrew for six years, then returned for forty-five. But each year was similarly divided; nine months in the world, the rainy season spent in retreat with his monks. His daily cycle too was patterned to this mold; his public hours were long, but three times a day he withdrew that through meditation he might restore his center of gravity to its sacred inner pivot.

After an arduous ministry of forty-five years, at the age of eighty and around the year 480 B.C., Buddha died upon eating at the home of Cunda the smith some poisoned mushrooms that had gotten into a dish by accident. Even on his deathbed his mind moved toward others. In the midst of his pain it occurred to him that Cunda might feel responsible for his death. His last command, therefore, was that his companions tell Cunda that of all the meals he had eaten during his life only two stood out as exceptional blessings. One was the meal whose strength had enabled him to attain enlightenment under the Bo tree; the other was that which was opening to him the final gates to Nirvana.

"The Silent Sage"

To understand Buddhism it is of utmost importance to gain some sense of the impact of Buddha's life on those who came within its orbit.

It is impossible to read the accounts of Buddha's life without emerging with the impression that one has been in touch with one of the greatest personalities of all time. The obvious veneration felt by almost all who knew him is contagious, and the reader soon finds himself caught up with his disciples in the impression of being in the presence of something very like omniscience incarnate.

Perhaps the most striking thing about him, to use the words of J. B. Pratt, was his combination of a cool head and a warm heart, a blend which shielded him from sentimentality on the one hand and indifference on the other. He was undoubtedly one of the greatest rationalists of all times, resembling in this respect no one as much as Socrates. Every problem that came his way was automatically subjected to the cold, analytical glare of his intellect. First, it would be dissected into its component parts, after which these would be reassembled in logical, architectonic order with their meaning and import laid bare. He was a master of dialogue and dialectic, and calmly confident. "That in disputation with anyone whatsoever I could be thrown into confusion or embarrassment—there is no possibility of such a thing."

The remarkable fact, however, was the way this objective, critical component of his character was balanced by a Franciscan tenderness so strong as to have caused his message to be subtitled "a religion of infinite compassion." Whether he actually risked his life to free a goat that had been caught on a mountain's brambles may be historically uncertain, but such an act would certainly have been in character for his life was one continuous gift to the famished crowds. Indeed his self-giving so impressed his biographers that they could explain it only in terms of a momentum that had been begun as early as the animal level. Assuming reincarnation, the accounts have him sacrificing himself for his herd while a stag, and as a hare hurling himself into a fire to feed a starving Brahmin. Dismiss these *post facto* accounts as we will, there is no question but that in his life as Buddha the springs of tenderness gushed abundant. Intent to draw from all the arrows of sorrow, he gave to each his sympathy, his enlightenment, and that strange power of soul which, even when he did not speak a word, gripped the hearts of his visitors and left them transformed.

The Buddha's royal lineage and upbringing stood him in great advantage socially. "Fine in presence," he moved among kings and potentates with ease, for had he not been one of them? Yet his social sophistication and ready *savoir faire* seem not to have removed him from the simple villagers. Surface distinctions of class and caste meant so little to him that he appears often not even to have noticed them. No matter how far an individual had fallen or been rejected by society, he received from the Buddha an irreducible response of respect arising from the simple fact that he was a fellow creature. Thus many an outcaste and derelict finding himself for the first time understood and accepted found his self-respect returning and was restored to the human community. "The venerable Gautama . . . bids all men welcome, is congenial, conciliatory, not supercilious, accessible to all."[5]

There was indeed an amazing simplicity about this man before whom kings bowed. Even when his reputation stood at its highest point he would be seen, alms-bowl in hand, walking through streets and alleys with the patience of one who knows the illusion of time. Like vine and olive, two of the most symbolic plants which grow nevertheless from the most meager soil, his physical needs were minimal. Once at Alavi during the frost of winter he was found resting in meditation on a few leaves gathered on a cattle path. "Rough is the ground trodden by the hoofs of the cattle; thin is the couch of leaves; light the monk's yellow robe; sharp the cutting winter wind," he admitted. "Yet I live happily, with sublime uniformity."

It is perhaps inaccurate to speak of Buddha as a modest man. John Hay who was secretary to President Lincoln during the entire time he was in the White House said it was absurd to call Lincoln modest, adding that "no great man is ever modest." Certainly Buddha felt that he had risen to a plane of knowledge far beyond that of anyone else in his time. In this respect he simply accepted his superiority and lived in the self-confidence this acceptance bequeathed. But this is different from vanity, conceit, or humorlessness. At an annual final assembly of the monks before they were to resume their wanderings the Exalted One looked round over the silent company and said, "Well, ye disciples, I summon you to say whether you have any fault to find with me, whether in word or in deed." And when a favorite pupil exclaimed, "Such faith have I, Lord, that methinks there never was nor will be nor is now any other greater or wiser than the Blessed One," the Buddha replied:

"Of course, Sariputta, you have known all the Buddhas of the past."

"No, Lord."

"Well then, you know those of the future?"

"No, Lord."

"Then at least you know me and have penetrated my mind thoroughly?"

"Not even that, Lord."

"Then why, Sariputta, are your words so grand and bold?"

Notwithstanding his own objectivity toward himself, there was constant pressure during his lifetime to turn him into a god. He rebuffed all these categorically, insisting that he was human in every respect. He made no attempt to conceal his temptations and weaknesses, how difficult it had been to attain enlightenment, how narrow the margin by which he had won through, how fallible he still remained. He confessed that if there had been another drive as powerful as sex he would never have made the grade. The months when he was first alone in the forest, he admitted, had brought him to the brink of mortal terror. "As I tarried there, a deer came by, a bird caused a twig to fall, and the wind set all the leaves whispering; and I thought: 'Now it is coming— that fear and terror.'" As Paul Dahlke remarks in his Buddhist Essays, "One who thus speaks needs not allure with hopes of heavenly joy. One who speaks like this of himself attracts by that power with which the Truth attracts all who enter her domain."

Buddha's leadership was evidenced not only by the size to which his order grew under his direction but equally by the perfection of the monks' discipline. A king visiting one of their assemblies which was prolonged into a full-moon night burst out at last, "You are playing me no tricks? How can it be that there should be no sound at all, not a sneeze, nor a cough, in so large an Assembly, among 1250 of the Brethren?" Watching the Assembly, seated as silent as a clear lake, he added, "Would that my son might have such calm."

Like other spiritual geniuses—one thinks of Jesus spotting Zacchaeus in a tree—the Buddha was gifted with preternatural insight into character. Able to size up almost at sight the souls of those who approached him, he seemed never to be taken in by fraud and front but would move at once to what was authentic and genuine. One of the most beautiful instances of this was his encounter with Sunita the flower-scavenger, a man so low in the social scale that the only employment he could find was picking over discarded bouquets to find an occasional blossom that was not completely withered and might bring in something to still his hunger. When Buddha arrived one day at the place where he was sorting through refuse, Sunita's heart was filled with awe and joy. Finding no place to hide—for he was an outcaste—he stood as if stuck to the wall, saluting with clasped hands. The Buddha "marked the conditions of Arahantship [sainthood] in the heart of Sunita, shining like a lamp within a jar," and drew near saying, "Sunita, what to you is this wretched mode of living? Can you endure to leave the world?" Sunita, "experiencing the rapture of one who has been sprinkled with ambrosia, said, 'If such as I may become a monk of yours, may the Exalted One suffer me to come forth!'" He became a renowned member of the Order.[6]

Buddha's entire life was saturated with the conviction that he had a cosmic mission to perform. Immediately after his enlightenment he saw in his mind's eye "souls whose eyes were scarcely dimmed by dust and souls whose eyes were sorely dimmed by dust,"[7] the whole world of humanity, milling, lost, desperately in need of help and guidance. He had no alternative but to agree with his followers that he had been "born into the world for the good of the many, for the happiness of the many, for the advantage, the good, the happiness of gods and men, out of compassion for the world."[8] His acceptance of this mission without regard for personal cost won him India's heart as well as her mind. "The monk Gautama has gone forth into the religious life, giving up the great clan of his relatives, giving up much money and gold, treasure both buried and above ground. Truly while he was still a young man without gray hair on his head, in the beauty of his early manhood he went forth from the household life into the homeless state."[9]

Encomia to the Buddha crowd the texts, one reason undoubtedly being that no description ever satisfied his disciples completely. After words had done their best, there remained in their master the essence of mystery—unplumbed depths which their language could not express because their thought could not fathom. What they could understand they revered and loved, but there was more than they could hope to exhaust; to the end he remained half light, half shadow, defying complete intelligibility. So they called him Sakyamuni, "silent sage *(muni)* of the Sakya clan," symbol of something beyond what could be said and thought. And they called him Tathagata, the "Thus-Come," the "Truth-winner," the "Perfectly Enlightened One," for "he alone thoroughly knows and sees, face to face, this universe." "Deep is the Tathagata, unmeasurable, difficult to understand, even like the ocean."[10]

THE REBEL SAINT

In moving from Buddha the man to Buddhism the religion it is imperative that the latter be seen against the background of the Hinduism out of which it grew. Unlike Hinduism, which emerged by slow, largely imperceptible spiritual accretion out of an invisible past, the religion of the Buddha appeared overnight, full formed. In large measure, it was a religion of reaction against Hindu perversions—an Indian protestantism not only in the original meaning of that word which emphasized witnessing (*testis*) for (*pro*) something but equally in its latter-day connotations which emphasize protesting against something else. Buddhism drew its basic vitality from Hinduism, but against her prevailing corruptions she recoiled like a whiplash. She hit back, and hit back hard.

To understand the teachings of the Buddha, then, we shall need a minimal picture of the existing Hinduism that partly provoked it. To lead into this in turn, a few general observations about religion are necessary.

Six aspects of religion appear so regularly as to suggest that their need is rooted in man's very makeup to an extent that no religion which proposes to speak to mankind at large can expect to elude them indefinitely. One of these is authority. By-passing the difficult question of divine authority and confining the problem to its human terms, the point comes down essentially to one of specialization. The problems and solutions of man's religious life are no less complicated than those of health or government. It stands to reason, therefore, that genius and close, continued attention will raise some persons beyond the majority in their capacity to understand and deal effectively with the human spirit. By simple virtue of competence, their advice will win respect and, on the whole, be followed.

A second natural element in religion is ritual; indeed ritual was probably religion's cradle. Ethics and theology did not come first with ritual added later to clothe their coldness. Religion originated in celebration and concern, and when people feel like celebrating or are deeply concerned they get together and act together. Especially in celebrating they act together, compounding their good spirits in happy get-togethers with joy intensified by rhythm, song, and the syncopated, synchronized gesticulations of the dance. The impulse to lose then find oneself in a fluid architecture of form and motion of which one is a significant part runs deeper in life than man: birds fly in formation; and monkeys in high spirits will fall into rhythmic line, draping themselves with rope and banana peels, simian anticipations of the elaborate, needled vestments that will appear at the human level.

Speculation is a third common ingredient of religion. While religion may have had its start in spontaneous, unthinking rites, it was inevitable that the mind eventually enter the act. For man is the animal that wonders and in wondering will sooner or later turn his mind upon everything that enters his field of attention. The objects of religious wonder, however—God, the human spirit, and the way to their alignment—are too deep-lying to admit of easy conceptualization or public, empirical demonstration, which means that they must remain to the end objects of speculation instead of proof—disciplined and responsible speculation, it is to be hoped, yet speculation none the less.[11]

A fourth normal element in religion is tradition. Of all forms of life man is the least ridden by instinct. This places him at great advantage, providing freedom for enormous innovations and advance. At the same time, it makes his position precarious, for the lessons his ancestors learned the hard way, through eons of trial and error experience, are not automatically available to him through his genes but must be transmitted consciously by each generation through the chain of culture. Let one link in this chain fail—let a single generation fall down in its job of passing on to its offspring the wisdom of the fathers —and the human venture will be set back half a million years, which is to say, would have to begin all over again. Of all culture's institutions for transmitting the wisdom of the past, none has proved stronger than religion. Religion has sometimes been prophetic; it has always been conservative. Whether this is good or bad varies, depending in each case on the values it is conserving.

There is a fifth element religion usually includes, namely, the concept of God's sovereignty and grace. When Margaret Fuller announced self-consciously, "I accept the Universe," Carlyle's comment, "Egad, she'd better," was in essence a religious one. Man's finitude, the extent to which his life depends at every point on factors which he neither made nor controls, may well lie at the heart of the religious impulse; Schleiermacher's definition of religion as "the feeling of absolute dependence" is but one statement of the point. This realization that one's existence is completely dependent upon factors beyond one's control—factors unified by the mind's instinctive drive toward simplicity, coherence, and oneness—issues in the theological concept of God's sovereignty. When it is compounded with gratitude for the goodness of this life which God's sovereignty has effected and is continuously sustaining we have the germ of the concept of grace: God's free and unstinted gifts to man which not only have made his life possible but sustain and enable it at every point along the way.

Finally religion brushes with mystery. It is always getting mixed up with magic and mysticism and miracles; with the occult, the esoteric, and the uncanny; with things like spiritualism and the supernatural. Rationalists may complain and all will deplore its credulity and excesses in some of these directions. Yet the connection is understandable. Religion's final business is the infinite, the beyond, the beckoning, and its coin is ecstasy. It will always, therefore, lie tangential to what is mundane, ordinary, and prosaic and move away from these even when it can only grope in the direction of their alternative.

Each of these six things—authority, ritual, speculation, tradition, God's sovereignty and grace, and mystery—has an important function to perform in the religions of man. Yet each can easily get out of hand. They had—all of them—in the Hinduism Buddha faced. Authority, deserved in the beginning, had become a front for the plush privilege of the Brahmin caste. Strict guild regulations had been devised to insure that the religious truth discovered in their culture remain their secret possession. Ritual, instead of providing a warm protecting husk within which the seed of spirit might germinate, had become a confining shell. Endless libations, sacrifices, chants, and musicales were available if one had cash to pay the priest to perform them; but the spirit had largely departed. Speculation was similarly rife—interminable disputes as to whether or not the world had been created, what the upper and nether worlds were like, and what precisely transmigrated after death—but to what end? It was hard to see how such arguments—reminiscent of Western scholastic conundrums as to how many angels could dance on the point of a needle or whether God could create a stone too heavy even for Him to lift—could affect man's ongoing religious life even if they could be settled. Tradition, instead of conserving and transmitting the wealth of the past, had become a drag on progress and obscurantist in its insistence that Sanskrit, no longer intelligible to the people, remain the language of religion. Notions of divine sovereignty and grace had become equally repressive, the latter having been pushed to the false conclusion that nothing needed to be done to effect one's salvation, the former and more prevalent to the even worse conclusion that nothing could be done. Finally mystery had degenerated into mystification with magic and divination having all but taken over. Religion had become a technique for cajoling or coercing innumerable cosmic bellhops to do what you wanted them to.

Onto this religious scene, bleak, corrupt, defeatist, and irrelevant, matted with superstition and burdened with worn-out rituals, Buddha came determined to clear the ground that truth might find purchase and spring again in freshness, strength, and vitality. The consequence was breath-taking. For what we find emerging through the work of this unmistakable genius is a religion almost entirely dissociated from each of the six corollaries of religion without which one would normally suppose it could not survive. The fact is so striking that it calls for documentation.

1. Buddha preached a religion devoid of authority. His attack on authority was double-edged. On the one hand he wanted to break the monopolistic grip of the Brahmins on the religious discoveries to date, and a good part of his reform consisted of no more than making generally known what had hitherto been the property of only a few. Contrasting his own openness with the guild secrecy of the Brahmins, he pointed out that "the Tathagata has no such thing as the closed fist of a teacher." So important did he regard this difference that he returned to it on his deathbed to assure those about him: "I have not kept anything back."[12] But if his first attack on authority was aimed at an institution—the Brahmin caste—his second was directed toward individuals. In a time when the multitudes were passively relying on the Brahmins to tell them what to do, Buddha challenged each individual to do his own religious seeking. "Do not accept what you hear by report, do not accept tradition, do not accept a statement because it is found in our books, nor because it is in accord with your belief, nor because it is the saying of your teacher . . . Be ye lamps unto yourselves. . . . Those who, either now or after I am dead, shall rely upon themselves only and not look for assistance to anyone beside themselves, it is they who shall reach the very topmost height."[13]

2. Buddha preached a religion devoid of ritual. Repeatedly he ridiculed the ancient meticulous observances of Brahmanic rites and prayers to the helpless gods. They are trappings and rigamarole, irrelevant to the hard, practical job of ego-reduction and spiritual release. Indeed they are worse than irrelevant; "Belief in the Efficacy of Rites and Ceremonies" is one of the Ten Fetters that bind man's spirit. Here as apparently everywhere Buddha was consistent; discounting

Hinduism's forms he resisted every temptation, if he felt any, to institute new ones of his own, a fact which had led many writers to characterize his teachings, unfairly, as a rational moralism rather than a religion.

3. Buddha preached a religion devoid of speculation. Ample evidence in the record suggests that he could have been one of the world's great metaphysicians if he had put his mind to the task. Instead he flatly refused to discuss metaphysics. His silence on the subject did not pass unnoticed. "Whether the world is eternal or not eternal, whether the world is finite or not, whether the soul is the same as the body or whether the soul is one thing and the body another, whether a Buddha exists after death or does not exist after death—these things," one of his disciples observed, "the Lord does not explain to me. And that he does not explain them to me does not please me, it does not suit me."[14] There were many it did not suit. Yet despite incessant needling, he continued his "noble silence." His reason was simple. "Greed for views" on questions of this sort "tend not to edification."[15] His practical program was exacting, and he was not going to let his flock be diverted from the hard road of arduous action by the agreeable fields of profitless speculation.

His famous parable of the arrow smeared thickly with poison puts the point with precision.

It is as if a man had been wounded by an arrow thickly smeared with poison, and his friends and kinsmen were to get a surgeon to heal him, and he were to say, I will not have this arrow pulled out until I know by what man I was wounded, whether he is of the warrior caste, or a brahmin, or of the agricultural, or the lowest caste. Or if he were to say, I will not have this arrow pulled out until I know of what name of family the man is;—or whether he is tall, or short, or of middle height; or whether he is black, or dark, or yellowish; or whether he comes from such and such a village, town, or city; or until I know whether the bow with which I was wounded was a chapa or a kodanda, or until I know whether the bow-string was of swallow-wort, or bamboo fiber, or sinew, or hemp, or of milk-sap tree, or until I know whether the shaft was from a wild or cultivated plant; or whether it was feathered from a vulture's wing or a heron's or a hawk's, or a peacock's; or whether it was wrapped round with the sinew of an ox, or of a buffalo, or of a ruru-deer, or of a monkey; or until I know whether it was an ordinary arrow, or a razor-arrow, or an iron arrow, or a calf-tooth arrow. Before knowing all this, that man would die.

Similarly, it is not on the view that the world is eternal, that it is finite, that body and soul are distinct, or that the Buddha exists after death that a religious life depends. Whether these views or their opposites are held, there is still rebirth, there is old age, there is death, and grief, lamentation, suffering, sorrow, and despair. . . . I have not spoken to these views because they do not conduce to absence of passion, tranquillity, and Nirvana.

And what have I explained? Suffering have I explained, the cause of suffering, the destruction of suffering, and the path that leads to the destruction of suffering have I explained. For this is useful.

Therefore, my disciples, consider as unexplained what I have not explained, and consider as explained what I have explained.[16]

4. Buddha preached a religion devoid of tradition. He himself, it is true, stood firmly astride the peaks of the past and his vision was extended enormously by the heights to which they lifted him. But he was convinced that his contemporaries were for the most part not on top of the past but under it, having let it bury them. He encouraged his followers, therefore, to slip free from its burden. "Do not ye go by what is handed down, nor on the authority of your traditional teachings. When you know of yourselves: 'These teachings are not good: these teachings when followed out and put in practice conduce to loss and suffering'—then reject them."[17] His most important personal break with archaism lay in his decision, comparable to Martin Luther's decision to translate the Bible from Latin into German, to quit Sanskrit and do all his teaching in the vernacular of the people.

5. Buddha preached a religion of intense self-effort. We have noted the discouragement and defeat that had settled over the India of Buddha's day. Many had come to accept the round of birth and rebirth as unending, which was like resigning oneself to a nightmarish sentence to hard labor for eternity. Those who still clung to the hope of attaining liberation eventually had resigned themselves to the Brahmin-sponsored notion that the process would take thousands of lifetimes during which they would gradually work their way into the Brahmin caste as the only one from which release was possible.

Nothing struck Buddha as more pernicious than this prevailing fatalism. He denies only one assertion, that of the "fools" who say there is no action, no deed, no power. "Here is a path to the end of suffering. Tread it!" Moreover, every individual must tread this path himself through his own energy and initiative. "Those who, relying upon themselves only, shall not look for assistance to any one besides themselves, it is they who shall reach the topmost height."[18] No god or gods could be counted on, not even the Buddha himself. When I am gone, he told his followers in effect, don't bother to pray to me;

for when I'm gone I'll be really gone. "Buddhas do but point the way—work out your salvation with diligence."[19] Buddha had no patience for the notion that only Brahmins could attain enlightenment. Whatever your caste, he told his followers, you can make it in this very lifetime. "Let a man of intelligence come to me, honest, candid, straightforward; I will instruct him . . . and if he practice according as he is taught then he will come to know for himself and to realize that supreme religion and goal."

6. Buddha preached a religion devoid of the supernatural. He condemned all forms of divination, soothsaying, and forecasting as low arts, and refused to allow his monks to play around with any form of superhuman power. "By this ye shall know that a man is *not* my disciple—that he tries to work a miracle." For all appeal to the supernatural and reliance thereon amounted, he felt, to looking for shortcuts, easy answers, simple solutions that could only divert attention from the hard, practical task of self-advance. "It is because I perceive danger in the practice of mystic wonders that I loathe, and abhor, and am ashamed thereof."

Whether Buddha's religion—without authority, without ritual, without theology, without tradition, without grace, and without the supernatural—was also a religion without God is a key question which must be reserved for later. After his death all the accouterments of religion which Buddha himself labored so carefully to exclude came tumbling into his religion with a vengeance. But as long as he was its leader they remained at bay. As a consequence original Buddhism presents us with an instance of religion which is unique and therefore invaluable, for every new evidence of the forms religion can take furthers our understanding of what religion in its essence really is. Buddha's approach to religion can be summarized in the following terms:

1. It was empirical. Never has a religion set out its case with so complete an appeal to empirical judgment. On every question, direct, personal experience was the final test for truth. "Do not go by reasoning, nor by inferring, nor by argument."[20] A true disciple must "know for himself."

2. It was scientific. Direct experience was final but it was aimed at uncovering the cause and effect relationships that order existence. "That being present, this becomes: that not being present this does not become."[21]

3. It was pragmatic. Call it a transcendental pragmatism if you will to distinguish it from those that are preoccupied with physical problems like plumbing or bridge-building, but pragmatic nonetheless in the generic sense of being exclusively concerned with problem solving. Re-

fusing to be sidetracked by speculation, Buddha kept his attention riveted on predicaments that cried out for solution. Except as his teachings were useful tools, they had no value whatever. They were like rafts, helpful for crossing a stream but of no further value once the other side had been reached.

4. It was therapeutic. Pasteur's words, "I do not ask you either your opinions or your religion; but what is your suffering?" could equally have been his. "One thing I teach," said Buddha: "suffering and the end of suffering. . . . It is just Ill and the ceasing of Ill that I proclaim."[22]

5. It was psychological. The word is used here in contrast to metaphysical. Instead of beginning with the universe and closing in on man's place in it, Buddha invariably began with man, his problems, his nature, and the dynamics of his development.

6. It was democratic. With a breadth of view unparalleled in his age and not frequent in any he attacked the caste system, especially its assumption that aptitudes were hereditary. Born a Kshatrya (warrior, ruler) yet finding himself in fact a Brahmin, he broke caste, opening his order to all regardless of social position.

7. It was directed to individuals. Buddha was not blind to man's social nature. He not only founded an order but also insisted on its importance as an aid to spiritual advance. Yet in the end his appeal was to the individual, that each should make his way toward enlightenment in the silences of confrontation with his own predicament.

Therefore, O Ananda, be ye lamps unto yourselves. Be ye a refuge to yourselves. Betake yourselves to no external refuge. Hold fast to the Truth as a lamp. Hold fast as a refuge to the Truth. . . . Work out your own salvation with diligence.[23]

THE FOUR NOBLE TRUTHS

When Buddha finally managed to break through the spell of rapture that rooted him to the Immovable Spot for the forty-nine days of his enlightenment, he arose and began a walk of over one hundred miles towards India's holy city of Benares. Just before arriving, in a Deer Park at Sarnath, he stopped to preach his first sermon. The congregation was small—only five ascetics who had shared his severe austerities but broke with him in anger when he renounced this approach, only to become now his first disciples. His subject was the Four Noble Truths. The first formal statement after his awakening, it was a declaration of the key discoveries that had come to him as the climax of his six-year quest.

Most persons if asked to list in propositional form their four deepest

and most considered convictions about life would probably find themselves very much at sea. The Four Noble Truths constitute Buddha's
attempt to do just this. Together they constitute the axioms of his system, the basic postulates from which almost everything in his teaching
logically unfolds.

The First Noble Truth is that life is *dukkha*, usually translated "suffering." Though far from its total meaning, this is an important part of it
which deserves to be brought into focus before passing on to the word's
other connotations.

Contrary to the opinion of many interpreters, Buddha's philosophy
was not ultimately pessimistic. An observer's depiction of man's current
condition may be as dark as can be drawn; the question of pessimism
does not arise until he speaks to whether it can be improved. That
Buddha was certain it could causes even his philosophy to back Zimmer's
observation that "everything in Indian thought supports the basic insight that, fundamentally, all is well. A supreme optimism prevails everywhere." That Buddha gave his life to demonstrating how well-being
might be attained is equal proof that this basic optimism was maintained
in the face of the most unromantic recognition that the affairs of men
and society are in the most imperfect state imaginable, a state of misery
bordering on complete chaos.

Buddha did not doubt that it is possible to have a good time in life
and that having a good time is enjoyable. But there are two questions:
First, how much of life is thus enjoyable; and second, at what level does
such enjoyment occur even when it is with us. Buddha thought the level
was superficial, sufficient perhaps for animals but leaving in man a vast
hollowness, vacancy, and frustration. By this understanding, even pleasure is but gilded pain. "Earth's sweetest joy is but disguised pain," as
Drummond wrote, while Shelley speaks of "that unrest which men mis-
call delight." Beneath the neon dazzle is darkness. At the core—not of
reality, we must remember, but of human life—is misery. That is why
we try continuously to distract ourselves with ephemeral pursuits, for
to be distracted is to forget what, in the depths, we are. Some may be
able to forget the darkness for a long time but it is still there diluting
what they think is their happiness.

> Lo! as the wind is, so is mortal life:
> A moan, a sigh, a sob, a storm, a strife.[24]

That such an estimate of the usual condition of human life is prompted
more by realism than by morbidity is suggested by the extent to which

it is shared by thinkers in as wide a spectrum of ideologies as it is possible to find. Existentialists describe life as a "useless passion," "absurd," "too much (*de trop*)." Bertrand Russell, a scientific humanist, finds it difficult to see why people should take unhappily to news that the universe is running down inasmuch as, "I do not see how an unpleasant process can be made less so [by being] indefinitely repeated." Poetry, always one of the human spirit's most sensitive barometers, calls man's forgetful attention to "all the pitiful confusion of life flung in a heap" and "time's slow contraction on the most hopeful heart." Buddha never went further than Robert Penn Warren:

> Oh, it is real. It is the only real thing.
> Pain. So let us name the truth, like men.
> We are born to joy that joy may become pain.
> We are born to hope that hope may become pain.
> We are born to love that love may become pain.
> We are born to pain that pain may become more
> Pain, and from that inexhaustible superflux
> We may give others pain as our prime definition.[25]

Even Schweitzer, who often accused the East of pessimism, echoes Buddha's appraisal almost to idiom when he writes, "Only at quite rare moments have I felt really glad to be alive. I could not but feel with a sympathy full of regret all the pain that I saw around me, not only that of men, but of the whole creation."

Dukkha then means pain that seeps at some level into all finite existence. The word's more constructive overtones suggest themselves when we discover that it is used in Pali to refer to an axle which is off-center with respect to its wheel, also to a bone which has slipped out of its socket. In both cases the picture is clear. To get the exact meaning of the First Noble Truth, we should read it as follows: Life in the condition it has got itself into is dislocated. Something has gone wrong. It has slipped out of joint. As its pivot is no longer true, its condition involves excessive friction (interpersonal conflict), impeded motion (blocked creativity), and pain.

Having an analytical mind, Buddha was not content to leave this first truth in generalized form. He goes on to pinpoint it by citing six occasions when life's dislocation becomes distressingly evident. Rich or poor, average or gifted, all life is subject to the following:

1. The trauma of birth. Psychoanalysts have in our time made a great deal of this point. Though Freud came to deny that the birth trauma was

the source of all later anxiety, he regarded it to the end as anxiety's proto-type. The birth experience "involves just such a concatenation of pain-ful feelings, of discharges and excitation, and of bodily sensations, as have become a prototype for all occasions on which life is endangered, ever after to be reproduced again in us as the dread or 'anxiety' condi-tion."[26] At best ejection from the womb is a shock, else why should the baby's first response be a cry? At worst it can be an experience so severe as to throw the child's life permanently off balance so that it goes through life listing like a ship with a hole in its side.

2. The pathology of sickness.

3. The morbidity of decrepitude. In the early days of flight it was relatively easy to get a plane off the ground. The mischief was to make a good landing. It is not different with man. Life's novelty and sheer physical vitality are enough to make the early years seem good. In the later years the fears come: the fear of being unloved and unwanted; the fear of financial dependence; the fear of protracted illness; the fear of being physically repulsive; the fear of being a nuisance, a care, and a burden. Senile melancholia is only the acute condition of a general prob-lem that in our own time of growing life expectancy has created a new science, the science of gerontology.

4. The phobia of death. On the basis of years of clinical practice, Carl G. Jung reported that he found death the depth terror in every patient he had analyzed who had passed the age of forty. Contemporary exis-tentialists, too, are calling our attention to the extent to which the phobia of death cripples healthy living.

5. To be tied to what one abhors. Sometimes it is possible to break away but not always. An incurable disease, an ineradicable personal weak-ness—for better or for worse there are some martyrdoms to which we are chained for life.

6. To be separated from what one loves.

That the shoe of life does pinch in these six places, few would deny. For Buddha, however, the list is only preliminary. The First Noble Truth concludes with the assertion that the five *skandas* are painful. As these five *skandas* are body, sense, ideas, feelings, and consciousness—in short the sum total of what we regard as human life—his statement amounts to the thesis that the totality of human life in its usual con-dition is steeped in suffering. In some way life has become estranged from reality, and this estrangement precludes real happiness until it be overcome.

Before the estrangement can be healed, however, it is necessary that we understand its cause, and it is to this that the Second Noble Truth speaks. The cause of life's dislocation, Buddha says, is *tanha*—again the imprecision of conventional translations makes it wise to stay close to the original word. *Tanha* is usually translated as "desire." There is a rough accuracy in thus making desire the cause of life's predicament; the kind of adumbrative accuracy that comes in *Heartbreak House* when George Bernard Shaw has Ellie say, "I feel now as if there was nothing I could not do, because I want nothing," and Captain Shotover is drawn to his one enthusiasm of the play: "That's the only real strength. That's genius. That's better than rum." But as soon as we try to come to grips with this hypothesis, it bristles with difficulties. In the first place, if *tanha* is accurately translated as desire Buddha's Second Truth is unhelpful, for to start from where we now are and unequivocally let go of every desire would be to die, and to die is not to solve the problem of living. But beyond this unhelpfulness, the translation is actually wrong, for there are some desires that Buddha deliberately advocated; the desire for liberation, for example, or for the welfare of other beings.

Tanha is a specific kind of desire, the desire to pull apart from the rest of life and seek fulfillment through those bottled-up segments of being we call our selves. When we are selfless we are free—but that is precisely the difficulty, to maintain that state. *Tanha* is the force that ruptures it, the will to private fulfillment, "the ego oozing like a secret sore." It consists of all "those inclinations which tend to continue or increase separateness, the separate existence of the subject of desire; in fact, all forms of selfishness, the essence of which is desire for self at the expense, if necessary, of all other forms of life. Life being one, all that tends to separate one aspect from another must cause suffering to the unit which even unconsciously works against the Law. Man's duty to his brothers is to understand them as extensions, other aspects of himself, as being fellow facets of the same Reality."[27]

This is some distance from the way men normally understand their brothers. The customary human outlook lies a good halfway toward Ibsen's description of a lunatic asylum in which "each shuts himself in a cask of self, the cask stopped with a bung of self and seasoned in a well of self." Given a group photograph, each member of the party looks first to how his face comes through before turning to the effectiveness of the picture as a whole—it is a little point yet a telling symptom of the devouring cancer that lies at the root of all our sorrow. Where is the man who is as concerned that no one go hungry as that he and his own children not go hungry? Rare indeed is the man who is more concerned that the standard of life as a whole be raised than that his own salary be increased. And this, says Buddha, is why we suffer; instead of linking our faith and love and destiny to the eternal we persist in strapping them to the puny burros of our separate selves which are certain to stumble and give out and be gone forever in a twinkling. Prizing our egos, coddling them, we lock ourselves first on their inside and then seek our fulfillment through their intensification and expanse. Fools to suppose that imprisonment can ever bring release, can we not see that " 'tis the self by which we suffer"? Far from being a door to the abundant life, the ego is a strangulated hernia. The more it swells, the tighter it shuts off that circulation of compassion with the rest of life on which man's health depends absolutely, the more pain is bound to rise.

The Third Noble Truth follows logically from the Second. If the cause of life's dislocation is selfish craving, its cure lies in the overcoming of such craving. If we could be released from the narrow limits of self-interest into the vast expanse of universal life, we would be free of our torment. The Fourth Noble Truth advises how this cure can be accomplished. The overcoming of *tanha*, the way out of our captivity, is through the Eightfold Path.

The Eightfold Path

Buddha's approach to the problem of life in the Four Noble Truths was essentially that of a therapist. He begins by observing carefully the symptoms which provoke concern. If everything were going smoothly, so smoothly that we noticed ourselves as little as we notice our digestion when it is normal, there would be nothing to worry about and we would have to attend no further to our way of life. But this is not the case. There is less creativeness, more conflict, and more pain than we feel is right. These symptoms Buddha summarizes in his First Noble Truth with the declaration that life is *dukkha* or out of joint. The next step is diagnosis. Throwing faith and myth and cult to the winds he asks, practically, what is causing these abnormal symptoms? Where is the seat of the infection? What is always present when suffering is present and absent when suffering is absent? The answer is given in the Second Noble Truth; the cause of life's dislocation is *tanha* or the drive for private fulfillment. What, then, of the prognosis? The Third Noble Truth announces hope; the disease can be cured by overcoming the egoistic drive for separate existence. This brings us to prescription. How is this overcoming to be accomplished? The Fourth Noble Truth provides the

answer; the way to the overcoming of self-seeking is through the Eightfold Path.

The Eightfold Path then is a course of treatment. But it is not external
treatment passively accepted by the patient as coming from without; it
is not treatment by pills or cult or grace. It is treatment by training. Men
regularly train for every subsidiary aspect of life—their professions and
avocations—but often, with the exception of individuals like Benjamin
Franklin, assume that it is impossible to train for life itself. Buddha disagreed. He distinguished two ways of life. One, a random, unreflective
way in which the subject is pushed and pulled by circumstance and impulse like a twig in a drain, he called "wandering about." The second, the
way of intentional living, he called the Path. What he is proposing here
is a rigorous system of habit formation designed to release the individual
from the repressions imposed by unwitting impulse, self-ignorance, and
tanha. An entire course from starting line to winning post is mapped,
with mountains, grades, and danger curves carefully marked and resting
places arranged in advance and wisely distributed. By long and patient
discipline the Eightfold Path intends nothing less than to remake the
total man and leave him a different being, a person cured of life's crippling disabilities. "Happiness he who seeks may win," Buddha said,
"*if he practice.*"

What then is the practice Buddha is talking about? He breaks it down
into eight steps. These are preceded, however, by a preliminary step
which Buddha does not include in his list but mentions so often at other
times that we may assume he was presupposing it here. This preliminary
step is right association. No one has recognized more clearly than Buddha
the extent to which we are social animals, influenced at every turn by
the "companioned example" of our associates whose attitudes and values
speak to us more clearly than any others. Asked how one attains illumination, Buddha began, "An arouser of faith appears in the world. One
associates oneself with him." Other injunctions follow; but association
was basic.

When a wild elephant is to be tamed and trained the best way to
begin is by yoking it to one that has already reached that condition. By
contact the wild one gradually perceives that the condition he is asked
to enter is not wholly antithetical to being an elephant, that what is expected of him is not an absolute thwarting of every natural impulse but
a progression that can lead to a condition which though different is also
viable. The constant, immediate, and contagious example of its yoke-
fellow teaches it as nothing else can. Training for the life of the spirit

is no different. The transformation facing the untrained is neither smaller than the elephant's nor less taxing. Without visible evidence that success is possible, without a continuous transfusion of courage from those who have themselves made the grade, discouragement is bound to set in. If, as scientific studies have now shown, anxieties are absorbed from one's associates, cannot trust and devotion be equally? Robert Ingersoll once remarked that had he been God he would have made health contagious instead of disease, to which an Indian contemporary responded, "When shall we come to recognize that health *is* as contagious as disease, virtue as contagious as vice, cheerfulness as contagious as moroseness?" One of the three things for which we should give thanks every day, according to Shankara, is the company of the holy, for as bees cannot make honey save when together neither can man make progress on the way except if he be supported by a field of trust and concern generated by the Truth-winners. Buddha agrees. We should associate with them, converse with them, serve them, observe their ways, and imbibe by osmosis their spirit of love and compassion.

With this preliminary step in place we may proceed to the eight steps of the path proper.

1. Right knowledge. A way of life always involves more than beliefs but it can never by-pass them completely, for man, in addition to being a social animal, is also a rational one. Not entirely, to be sure—Buddha would have been quick to acknowledge this. But life needs some blue-print, some map the mind can trust if it is to move ahead. To return to the elephant for illustration, however great the danger in which it finds itself, it will make no move to escape until it has first assured itself that the track it must take will bear its weight. Unless convinced of this, it will remain trumpeting in agony even in a burning wagon rather than risk a fall. The most vociferous detractors of reason must admit that it plays at least a comparable role in human life. Whether or not man's reason has the power to pull his life in the direction it envisions, it certainly holds the power of veto; let it not believe something and it will be impossible for the individual to move wholeheartedly in that direction. It is as if the mind were to say to the total self, "I don't believe that and you are not going to believe it fully either."

Some convictions, therefore, are necessary if one is to take up the Path. What convictions? They are the Four Noble Truths; that suffering abounds, that it is occasioned by drive for separate existence and fulfillment, that it can be cured, and that the means to its cure is the Eightfold Path.

2. Right aspiration. Whereas the first step called us to make up our minds as to what life's problem basically is, this second advises us to make up our hearts as to what we really want. Is it really enlightenment we seek, or are our affections unsure of their object, turning this way and that and dipping like kites to every current of distraction? If there is to be significant progress on the Path, consistency of intent is indispensable; our determination to transcend our separateness and identify ourselves with the welfare of all must be sure and intense. Men who achieve greatness are almost invariably passionately interested in some one thing. They do a thousand things each day but behind all they do, dominating and influencing their entire lives, is the one thing they count supreme. When men seek liberation with single-mindedness and intensity of this order, when they focus their energies on overcoming life's dislocation, they may expect their steps to turn from a slippery sandbank scramble into strides.

3. Right speech. We begin now to reach down and take hold of the switches that control our lives. Language is the first. Language does two things: it furnishes both an indication of our character and a lever for shifting it. We will do well to begin with language as indicator. Our first move is to become aware of our speech patterns and what they tell us about ourselves. Instead of starting with a resolve to speak nothing but the truth, let us say—a resolve which is likely to prove ineffective anyway at the outset because it is too advanced—we will do well to start further back with a resolve to notice how many times during the day we deviate from the truth and follow this up with an inquiry into why we did so. The same with the lack of charity in our speech; begin not by determining to speak only charitable words but by determining to watch our speech until we are more aware of the motives that prompt the lack of charity in what we say.

After this first step has been reasonably mastered we shall be ready to try some changes. The ground will have been well prepared, for once we have become aware of how we do talk the need for changes will be more evident. In what directions, then, should the changes proceed? First, toward truth. The value of truth in Buddha's eyes was not moral but ontological. Deceit is bad because it reduces one's being. Why do we deceive? Behind the arguments and defenses the motive is almost always a fear of revealing to others or to ourselves what we really are. Each time we give in to the motive we protect the walls of the ego and in so doing remove ourselves further from life and the long-range prospects of happiness (per the Second Noble Truth). To dispense with all protective devices at once might be too radical, but we should at least realize clearly what they are and why lives lived behind them must necessarily be cramped and artificial.

The second direction in which our speech should move is toward charity. False witness, idle chatter, abuse, and slander are to be avoided not only in their obvious forms but also in their covert ones, for the latter—subtle, belittling, "accidental" tactlessness, poisonous wit—are often more vicious precisely because their animus is concealed.

4. Right behavior. Here, too, the admonition as detailed in later discourses involves a call to understand one's behavior more objectively as a prerequisite to improving it. The trainee is to reflect on the things he has done, with special eye to the motives which prompted them. In the end, how much kindliness was involved and how much self-seeking? As to direction in which change should proceed, the answer again is given in terms of selflessness and charity. This general directive is sharpened up in the Five Precepts, the Buddhist variation on the second or ethical half of the Ten Commandments:

Do not kill. Most Buddhists extend this proscription to animals; the strict ones, as a consequence, are vegetarians.

Do not steal.

Do not lie.

Do not be unchaste. For monks and the unmarried this meant continence; for the married it meant restraint in proportion to one's interest in and distance along the Path.

Do not drink intoxicants. It is reported that an early Russian Czar, faced with the prospect of throwing his weight toward Christianity, Islam, or Buddhism, rejected the latter two because both included this last proscription.

5. Right livelihood. Occupation is an exact word, for our work occupies most of our waking attention. Buddha considered spiritual progress to be impossible if one's occupation pulls in the opposite direction. "The hand of the dyer is subdued by the dye in which it works." Christianity has agreed. Luther, for example, while explicitly including the hangman as exercising a tolerable Christian vocation, ruled out the late medieval usurers and speculators.

For those who are so intent upon liberation as to wish to give their complete lives to it, right livelihood demands joining a monastic order and partaking of its discipline. For the layman it means, simply, engaging in occupations that promote life instead of destroying it. But again Buddha was not content to rest the matter with generalization. He named names, the professions of his day he considered incompatible with spiritual advance. Some of these are obvious: poison peddler, slave dealer, prostitute. Others, if taken seriously on a world-wide scale would be revolutionary: butcher, brewer, armament maker, tax collector (different methods were then employed). One continues to be puzzling; why did Buddha condemn the occupation of caravan trader? Merchandising in general was not denounced; why then should this one form be singled out for censure? Perhaps because the caravaner of ancient India was the counterpart of the traveling salesman of the American frontier who had no repeating route and disappeared after each day's stand. Buddha may have felt that under such circumstances the temptations to fleece and put over sharp deals was too great to warrant either confidence or sanction.

While Buddha's actual teachings on occupation were aimed at helping his contemporaries distinguish between those which were conducive and detrimental to spiritual advance, many contemporary Buddhists hold that if Buddha were living today he would be less concerned with which occupations men enter than with the danger that modern man shall forget that earning a living is at best life's means, not its ultimate end.

6. Right effort. Buddha laid tremendous stress on the will. Anyone serious about making the grade will have to exert himself enormously. There are virtues that must be developed, passions to be curbed, and evil mind states to be transcended if love and detachment are to have a chance. " 'He robbed me, he beat me, he abused me'—in the minds of those who think like this, hatred will never cease." But the only way to disperse such crippling sentiments, indeed the only way to overcome life's fetters of any sort, is through effort, what William James called "the slow dull heave of the will." "Those who follow the way," said Buddha, "might well follow the example of an ox that marches through the deep mire carrying a heavy load. He is tired, but his steady gaze, looking forward, will never relax until he comes out of the mire, and it is only then he takes a respite. O monks, remember that passion and sin are more than the filthy mire, and that you can escape misery only by earnestly and steadily thinking of the Way."[28]

In discussing right effort Buddha later added some afterthoughts about timing. Inexperienced climbers out to conquer their first big peak are often impatient with the seemingly absurd saunter at which their veteran guide sets out, but before the day is out the staying pace of the latter has been vindicated. Buddha had more confidence in the steady pull than the quick spurt. A string too taut will snap; a plane nosed up too abruptly will crash. In China, about the same time, the author of the

Tao Teh Ching was making the same point through a different image: "He who takes the longest strides does not walk the fastest."

7. Right mindfulness. No teacher has credited the mind with more influence over life than did Buddha. The best loved of all Buddhist texts, the *Dammapada*, opens with the words, "All we are is the result of what we have thought."

Of all the philosophers of the West, Spinoza stands closest to Buddha on this question of the mind's potential. "To understand something is to be delivered of it"—these words come close to summarizing Spinoza's entire ethic. Buddha would have agreed completely. If we could really understand life, if we could really understand ourselves, we would find neither a problem. Contemporary psychology proceeds in the main on the same assumption. When man's "awareness of experience . . . is fully operating," writes Carl Rogers, "his behaviour is to be trusted." For in these moments the human organism becomes "aware of its delicate and sensitive tenderness towards others." It is ignorance, not sin, that struck Buddha as the offender. More precisely, insofar as sin is at fault it is prompted by a more fundamental ignorance.

To combat this ignorance Buddha counsels such continuous alertness and self-examination as almost to make one weary at the very prospect. But the urgency is not fortuitous; it is occasioned by the importance of the point. The greatness of man is in proportion to his self-knowledge. "You have to churn out butter-fat; then only will it remain unmixed with water"—the authentic and abiding elements in life must be separated from the trivia. To this end Buddha insisted that everything be seen "as it really is." Thoughts and feelings are to be perceived as swimming in and out of our awareness but in no way a permanent part of us; they are to be taken intellectually not emotionally. Everything we witness, especially our moods and emotions, is to be traced to its cause, much as in contemporary psychoanalysis. A miscellany of other practices are also recommended: the aspirant is to keep his mind in control of his senses instead of allowing the latter to become lord; he is to meditate on fearful and disgusting sights until he overcomes his aversion to them; he is to picture vividly his desired goal; and he is to pervade the world with loving thoughts for all creatures.

Out of the longish doze interrupted by fits and starts of semi-alertness which comprises the consciousness of the average man, this seventh step summons the aspirant to steady awareness of what he is about and what is happening to him. Obviously it will take practice. In addition to working at it to some extent all the time, he should set aside special times for undistracted self-analysis and occasionally withdraw for several days—into complete silence and solitude.

On his recent trip around the world to photograph the religions of man Lew Ayres noted Buddhists in Thailand practicing this seventh step,

spending hours slowly walking zombie-fashion about the grounds of the wat in absolute concentration upon the minutest fraction of every action connected with each step. The procedure is also carried into every single physical act of daily life until, theoretically, the conscious mind understands and can control each physiological function of the human body. . . . A fifty-year-old man . . . used to meditate in a small graveyard adjoining his wat, because he'd be undisturbed there. . . . He would be seated, cross-legged and immobile but with eyes open, for hours on end—through the driving rain at midnight or the blistering heat of noonday in Siam. His usual length of stay was two or three hours.[29]

8. Right absorption. It involves substantially the techniques we have already encountered in Hinduism's *raja yoga* and leads to the same goal.

In his later years Buddha told his disciples that his first intimations of deliverance came to him before he left home when, still a boy and sitting one day in the cool shade of an apple tree in deep thought, he was suddenly caught up into the first level of the absorptions. It was his first, faint foretaste of deliverance, and he said to himself, "This is the way to enlightenment." It was nostalgia for the return and deepening of this experience as much as disillusionment with the usual rewards of worldly life that led him finally to his decision to abandon the world and give his life completely to spiritual adventure. The result, as we have seen, was not simply a new philosophy of life: it was a new mode of experience; a transmutation into a different kind of creature with another indescribably wonderful world to live in. Unless this is recognized we shall be unequipped to fathom the power of Buddhism over the souls of men. Something happened to Buddha under that Bo tree, and something has happened to every Buddhist since who has persevered to the final step of the Eightfold Path. Like a camera whose focal length had been out of adjustment, the mind had been ill-focused for reality—until at last the stupendous vision is sharp and distinct. With the final "extirpation of delusion, craving, and hostility" the mind realizes that neither it nor reality is as it thought, for in the fierce combustion of immediate awareness thought itself has been annihilated. In its true state the mind rests.

Basic Buddhist Concepts

Buddha's total outlook on life is as difficult to close in upon with confidence as that of any man in the history of thought. Part of the problem stems from the fact that like most ancient teachers he wrote nothing. There is a gap of almost a century and a half between his spoken words and the first written records, and though the memory in those times appears to have been incredibly faithful, a gap of that length is certain to raise questions. A second problem arises from the wealth of material in the texts themselves. Buddha taught for forty-five years and a staggering amount of his teachings has come down to us in one form or another. While the net result is doubtless a blessing, the sheer quantity of material constitutes in one respect an embarrassment of riches, for though his teachings remained remarkably consistent over the years it was impossible to say things for many minds and in many ways without creating problems of interpretation. These interpretations constitute the third barrier. By the time the texts began to appear, partisan schools had already appeared, some intent on minimizing Buddha's break with Brahmanic Hinduism, others intent on sharpening it. This forces upon scholars the constant question as to how much in what they are reading is Buddha's actual thought and how much is partisan coloring.

Undoubtedly the most serious obstacle to the recovery of Buddha's rounded philosophy, however, is his own silence at crucial points. We have seen that his burning concerns were therapeutic and pragmatic rather than metaphysical. Instead of wanting to construct an abstract blueprint of the universe he wanted to help men change their lives in order to get rid of the pain that was pressing heavily on all. It would be wrong to say he was not interested in metaphysics—his dialogues reveal not only that he had given its problems close attention but also that he had the kind of mind that took to them with relish. He resisted metaphysics on principle, as a man with a mission might turn his back on avocations that would distract him from his central destiny.

His decision is so understandable that it may seem a betrayal to insert a section like this in which we frankly propose to try to dub in the main outlines of Buddha's over-all view of life and the world. In the end, however, the task is unavoidable for the simple reason that metaphysics is unavoidable. Everyone must harbor some notions about ultimate questions and these notions are bound to affect his interpretations of subsidiary issues. Buddha was no exception. Though he refused to initiate philosophical discussions and only occasionally allowed himself to be drawn into them, he unquestionably had his views. Occasionally these come through quite clearly, but for the most part they filter through his teachings ambiguously. In either case, however, they are important. For anyone who would understand the mind of Buddha there is no escape from the hazardous job of trying to work through to some idea of where he stood with respect to life's ultimate character and setting.

We may begin with the concept of Nirvana itself. Etymologically the word means "to blow out," or "to extinguish," not transitively but as a fire ceases to draw. Deprived of fuel the fire goes out. This is Nirvana. From this imagery it has been widely supposed that the extinction to which Buddhism points is total, an absolute annihilation. If this were so, if absolute non-existence were the highest goal to which Buddhism could point for man, there would indeed be grounds for the oft-repeated accusation that Buddhism is life-denying and pessimistic. As it is, scholarship of the last thirty years has exploded this view. Nirvana is the highest destiny of the human spirit and its literal meaning is extinction. But we must be precise as to what is to be extinguished; it is the boundary of the finite self. It does not follow that what is left will be nothing. Negatively Nirvana is the state in which the faggots of private desire have been completely consumed and everything that restricts the boundless life has died. Affirmatively it is that boundless life itself. Buddha parried every request for a positive description of the condition insisting that it was "incomprehensible, indescribable, inconceivable, unutterable," for after we eliminate every aspect of the only consciousness we now know, how can we speak of what is left?[30] An early disciple, Nagasena, preserves his point in the following dialogue. Asked, "What is Nirvana like?" he answered with a counterquestion: "Is there, sir, what is called wind?"

"Yes, revered sir."

"Please, sir, show the wind by its color or configuration or as thin or thick or long or short."

"But it is not possible, revered Nagasena, for the wind to be shown; for the wind cannot be grasped in the hand or touched; but yet there is the wind."

"If, sir, it is not possible for the wind to be shown, well then, there is no wind."

"I, revered Nagasena, know that there is wind; I am convinced of it, but I am not able to show the wind."

"Even so, sir, there is Nirvana; but it is not possible to show Nirvana."[31] Our final ignorance is to imagine that our final destiny is presently conceivable. All we can know is that it is a condition beyond

—beyond the limitations of mind, thought, feelings, and will, all these as well as bodily things being confinements. Buddha would venture only one affirmative characterization: "Bliss, yes bliss, my friends is Nirvana."

Is Nirvana God? When answered in the negative, this question has led to amusingly contrary conclusions. Some concluded that since original Buddhism knew not God it could not be a religion; others, that since Buddhism obviously was a religion, belief in God is not essential to religion. Both conclusions seem so strained as to force a reconsideration of the initial assumption that Nirvana is not God.

The question, "Is Nirvana God?" has no simple answer because the word God has no single meaning. Two meanings at least must be distinguished before any sort of satisfactory answer can be even hoped for.

One accepted meaning of God is that of a personal being who created the universe by a deliberate act of will. If defined in this sense, Nirvana is not God. Buddha did not consider it personal because personality requires definition which is precisely what Nirvana excludes. And while he did not expressly deny creation, he seemed clearly not to have saddled Nirvana with responsibility for it, tracing it instead to primordial ignorance and willfulness which got started no one knows how. If indifference to a personal creator is atheism, Buddha was indeed an atheist.

There is, however, a second meaning of God which to distinguish it from the first we may call the Godhead. The idea of personality is not part of this concept which is strong in the mystical traditions of a number of religions including Christianity. When Buddha comes forward with his decisive declaration, "There is, O monks, an Unborn, neither become nor created nor formed. . . . Were there not there would be no deliverance from the born, the made, the compounded"[32] he seems to be speaking precisely in this tradition. Impressed by the similarities between Nirvana and the Godhead, Edward Conze has compiled from Buddhist texts a series of attributes that apply to both. We are told

that Nirvana is permanent, stable, imperishable, immovable, ageless, deathless, unborn, and unbecome, that it is power, bliss and happiness, the secure refuge, the shelter, and the place of unassailable safety; that it is the real Truth and the supreme Reality; that it is the Good, the supreme goal and the one and only consummation of our life, the eternal, hidden and incomprehensible Peace.[33]

We may conclude with Mr. Conze that Nirvana is not God defined as personal creator but stands sufficiently close to the concept of God as Godhead to warrant the name in this sense.[34]

The most startling thing Buddha said about man was that he has no soul. This *anatta* (no soul) doctrine has again caused Buddhism to look like a peculiar religion, if indeed deserving of the name at all. But once more the word in question must be used with the greatest possible care. What was the *atta* (Pali for the Sanskrit *atman*) or soul which Buddha denied? In Buddha's day it had come to signify (1) a spiritual substance which in accord with the dualistic outlook in Hinduism (2) retained its separateness throughout eternity.

Buddha denied both elements in this concept of soul. His denial of soul as a spiritual substance—a sort of miniature self in the head—appears to have been the chief point that distinguished his concept of transmigration from prevailing Hindu interpretations. Authentic child of India, he never doubted that reincarnation in some sense was a fact, but he was openly uncomfortable over the way his Brahmanic contemporaries were interpreting the concept. The crux of his discontent may be gathered from the clearest description he gave of his own view on the subject. The image he used was a flame being passed from candle to candle. As it is difficult to think of the flame on the last candle as being in any meaningful sense the same as the original flame, the connection would seem instead to be a causal one in which influence was transmitted by chain reaction but not substance.

When to this image of the flame we add Buddha's acceptance of *karma*, we have before us the clearest statements Buddha made on the subject of transmigration. From them, the best summary of his views we can construct would run something like this: (1) There is a chain of causation threading each life to those which have led up to it and others which will follow. That is to say, each life is in the condition it is in because of the way the lives which have led into it were lived. (2) In the midst of this causal sequence, man's will remains free. Though the orderliness of the world sees to it that up to a point acts will be followed by predictable consequences, these consequences never shackle man's will or determine completely what he must do. Man remains a free agent, always at liberty to do something to effect his destiny. (3) Though these points assume the importance of causal connections in life, none of them requires the notion of a lump of mental substance that is passed on from life to life. Impressions, ideas, feelings, "streams of consciousness," "present moments,"—these are all that we find, no underlying spiritual substrata. Hume and James were right; if there be an enduring self, subject always, never object, it cannot be found.

We can repeat these three ingredients in Buddha's combined views of reincarnation and *karma* by way of an analogy. In the realm of ideas, (1) the thoughts that fill my mind have not appeared by accident. They have definite histories. Apart from the conditioning impact which the minds of my teachers, my parents, and the molders of Western civilization have exerted upon me, they could not possibly have come into being. (2) This fact, however, does not mean that I must pass on unchanged the ideas that have thus come my way. By altering and adding to them I can definitely affect the ongoing current of thought which we call civilization. (3) Neither the continuity nor the freedom claimed by the above two points requires that ideas be regarded as entities, things, mental substances that are in any way physically transmitted. Catching the idea of justice from my father did not mean that in the act of transmission some substance, however dematerialized or spiritual, leapt from his mind into mine.

This denial of spiritual substance was only an aspect of Buddha's wider denial of substance of every sort. Substance carries two connotations. In its precise philosophical meaning it refers to something relatively permanent that persists throughout changes in the surface variations of the things in question; in its cruder interpretations it proposes that this more basic feature of things is matter. The psychologist in Buddha rebelled against this second notion, for to him mind was far more basic in man and nature than matter. The empiricist in him, for its part, challenged the implications of permanence contained in the idea of substance. It is impossible to read much Buddhist literature without catching its sense of the transitoriness of all things finite, its profound acknowledgment of the perpetual perishing of every natural object. It is this that gives Buddhist descriptions of the natural world their poignancy and melancholy.

> The waves follow one after another in an eternal pursuit.

Or:

> Life is a journey,
> Death is a return to the earth.
> The universe is like an inn,
> The passing years are like dust.

And again:

> The seaborne traveller seizes a favorable wind,
> He raises anchor and sets sail for distant shores.
> Like a bird flying through innumerable clouds,
> The wake of his ship leaves no memories behind.[85]

So struck was Buddha with impermanence that he listed it as the first of his Three Signs of Being, or characteristics that apply to everything in the natural order, the other two being suffering and the absence of a permanent soul. Nothing in nature is identical with what it was the moment before; in this Buddha was close to modern science which has discovered the problem of identity to be one of the most puzzling. Buddha was concerned to emphasize the ephemeral character of human life that his hearers might be freed from all illusions on this score. So he called the forces holding life together *skandas*—skeins that hang together as loosely as yarn. The body, for its part, was a "heap," its elements no more permanently gathered than the grains of a sandpile. Froth, too, seemed an apposite metaphor, and there were others:

> —a phantom, dew, a bubble,
> A dream, a flash of lightning, and a cloud:
> Thus we should look upon all that was made.[36]

Given this sense of the radical impermanence of all things finite we might expect Buddha's answer to the question "Does man continue to exist after death?" to be a flat "No." Actually his answer turned out to be far more equivocal. Ordinary men when they die leave strands of finite desire that can only be realized in other incarnations; in this sense, at least, these men live on.[37] But what about the *Arhat* who has extinguished all such desires; does he continue to exist? When a wandering ascetic put this question Buddha said,

"The word *reborn* does not apply to him."

"Then he is not reborn."

"The term *not-reborn* does not apply to him."

"To each and all of my questions, Gotama, you have replied in the negative. I am at a loss and bewildered."

"You ought to be at a loss and bewildered, Vaccha. For this doctrine is profound, recondite, hard to comprehend, rare, excellent, beyond dialectic, subtle, only to be understood by the wise. Let me therefore question you. If there were a fire blazing in front of you, would you know it?"

"Yes, Gotama."

"If the fire went out, would you know it had gone out?"

"Yes."

"If now you were asked in what direction the fire had gone, whether to east, west, north, or south, could you give an answer?"

"The question is not rightly put, Gotama."

Whereupon Buddha brought the discussion to a close by pointing out that "just in the same way" the ascetic had not rightly put his question either. "Feelings, perceptions, forces, consciousness—everything by which the Arhat might be denoted, has passed away for him. Profound, measureless, unfathomable, is the Arhat even as the mighty ocean; *reborn* does not apply to him nor *not-reborn*, nor any combination of such terms."[38]

It contributes to the understanding of this conversation to know that the Indians of that day thought that expiring flames do not really go out but return to the pure, invisible condition of fire they shared before they visibly appeared. But the real force of the dialogue lies elsewhere. In asking where the fire, admitted to have gone out, had gone, Buddha was calling attention to the fact that there are some problems which our language poses so clumsily as to admit of no solution in the terms in which they are stated. The question of the illumined soul's existence after death is such a case. If Buddha had said, "Yes, he does live on" his listeners would have assumed a continuation of personal experiencing which Buddha did not intend, for there is nothing in man which entitles him to say, "I am this and you are that" through all eternity. But if he had said, "The enlightened one ceases to exist," his hearers would have assumed that he was consigning him to total extinction, which equally he did not intend. On the basis of this rejection of extremes we cannot say much with certainty but we can venture something. The ultimate destiny of the human spirit is a condition in which all identification with the historical experience of the finite self will disappear while experience itself not only remains but is heightened beyond anticipation. As a minor dream vanishes completely on awakening, as the stars go out in deference to the morning sun, so individual awareness will be eclipsed in the blazing light of total awareness. Some say "the dewdrop slips into the shining Sea." Others say the metaphor would be more accurate if it pictured the ocean as entering the dewdrop itself.

If we try to form a more detailed picture of the state of Nirvana, we shall have to proceed without Buddha's help, not only because he realized almost to despair how far the condition transcends the power of words but also because he did not operate on the device of wheedling his hearers with previews of coming attractions. Still it is possible to form some notion of the logical goal toward which the path of the Buddha points. The universe in the scientific outlook of the Buddha is one of lawful order in which events are governed by pervasive laws of cause and effect. The life of the *Arhat*, however, is one of increasing independence from this causal realm of nature. Its order is not vitiated, but its events hold decreasing power over the *Arhat's* spirit as it increases in autonomy and is less subject to what happens to it from without. In this sense he is increasingly free not only from the passions and worries of the world but also from its happenings in general. With every growth of inwardness, peace and freedom replace the moody bondage of a life more prey to the world. As long as the spirit remains tied to a body its freedom from the particular, the temporal, and the changing cannot be complete. But sever this connection with the *Arhat's* last death, and freedom from the finite will be complete. We cannot imagine what the state would be like, but the direction is discernible.

Paralleling the growth in spiritual freedom, there is a correlative aspect of the *Arhat's* life. Increasing freedom brings an enhancement of his being. Buddha's disciples sensed that he embodied immeasurably more of reality than anyone else they knew, and testified that advance along his path brought an enlargement to their lives as well. Instead of shriveling, theirs expanded; with every step they felt themselves more alive and real than they had ever been. As long as they were limited by their bodies there were limits beyond which they could not go. But let all ties be loosed that the spirit might be free to move indefinitely in the direction begun. We cannot imagine the terminus but we can know the direction. If increased freedom brings increased being, it follows that total freedom should bring total being.

There are a thousand further questions. But the Buddha is silent.

> Others abide our questions. Thou art free.
> We ask and ask; Thou smilest and art still.[39]

BIG RAFT AND LITTLE

Thus far we have been looking at Buddhism as it appears through its earliest records. We turn now to Buddhist history as providing one of the most fascinating evidences anywhere of the irrepressibly varied directions man's religious outreach tends to take.

When we approach Buddhist history with this interest foremost, the thing which strikes us at once is that it splits. Religions are always splitting. In our own tradition the ancient Hebrews split into Israel and Judah, Christendom into the Eastern and Western Churches, the Western Church into Roman Catholicism and Protestantism, and Protestantism has continued to splinter into its many denominations. The same happens in Buddhism. Buddha dies, and before the century is out the seeds of schism have been sown and are beginning to germinate.

One approach to the question of why Buddhism split would be through careful analysis of the events, personalities, and environments that played across the religion during its crucial early centuries. We will probably come as close to the heart of the answer, however, if we cut through all this and say simply that Buddhism divided over the questions people have always divided over.

How many such questions are there? How many questions will divide almost every human group regardless of whether it is assembled in an ancient Indian village or a twentieth century New York apartment? There seem to be at least three.

The first is the question of whether men are independent or interdependent. Some persons are most aware of themselves as individuals; the self as an independent center of freedom and initiative is to them more important than the sum of its ties. The obvious corollary is that men must, in the main, make their own ways through life; that what a man gets will be primarily of his own doing. "I was born in the slums, my father was a drunkard, every one of my brothers and sisters went to the dogs—don't talk to me about environment or influence. I got to where I am all by myself." This is one attitude. On the other side are persons to whom life seems to come in precisely the opposite mode. The separateness of their being seems scarcely real; the impressive thing is the web that binds all life together. Though our visible bodies are separate, on a deeper level, like icebergs grounded in a common floe, we are one. "Send not to ask for whom the bell tolls, it tolls for thee."

A second question concerns the relation in which man stands, not this time to his fellows, but to the universe. Is the universe friendly, on the whole helpful toward man as he reaches out for fulfillment? Or is it indifferent, perhaps even hostile to the human quest? Opinions differ. On bookstore tables one finds a book titled *Man Stands Alone* and right next to it *Man Does Not Stand Alone* and *Man Is Not Alone*. Some people see history as a venture in which man lifts himself by his own bootstraps; others are convinced that from beginning to end it is cradled in "the everlasting arms."

A third dividing question is: What is the best part of man, his head or his heart? A popular parlor pastime used to revolve around the question, "If you had to choose, would you rather be loved or respected?" It was the same point with a different twist. For some, man's crown and glory is his mind, but there are others who put his feelings higher. The first are classicists, the second romanticists; the first seek wisdom above all, the second, if they had to choose, would take compassion. The distinction probably also bears some relation to William James' contrast between the tough-minded and the tender-minded.

Here are three questions that have probably divided men since they became human and certainly continue to do so today. They divided the early Buddhists. One group said man is an individual; whatever progress he makes will be through his own doing, and wisdom above all will carry him to his goal. The other group said the opposite; man's destiny is indissolubly meshed with his fellows, grace is a fact, and love is the greatest thing in the world.

Other differences gathered around these basic ones. The first group insisted that Buddhism was a full-time job. It didn't expect everyone to make Nirvana his central goal, but those who did would have to give up the world and become monks. The second group, perhaps because it did not rest all its hopes on self-effort, was less demanding. It held that its outlook was as relevant for the layman as for the professional, that in its own way it applied as much to the world as to the monastery. This difference left its imprint on the names of the two outlooks. Each called itself a *yana*, a raft or ferry, for each proposed to carry man across the sea of life to the shore of enlightenment. The second group, however, pointing to its doctrine of grace and its ampler provisions for laymen, claimed to be the larger vehicle of the two. It preempted, accordingly, the name *Mahayana*, the Big Raft, *Maha* meaning "great" as in Mahatma (the Great Souled) Gandhi. As the name caught on, the first group came to be known by contrast as *Hinayana* or the Little Raft.

Not exactly pleased with this invidious name, the Hinayanists have preferred to speak of their brand of Buddhism as *Theravada*, or the Way of the Elders. In doing so they voice their claim to represent the original Buddhism as taught by Gautama himself. This claim is justified if we are willing to take our stand on the teachings of Buddha as recorded in the earliest extant texts, those of the Pali Canon, for these do lend themselves on the whole to the Theravada interpretation. But this fact has in no way discouraged the Mahayanists from their counterclaim to represent the true line of succession. They defend their claim by placing their first emphasis on Buddha's life instead of on his teachings as preserved in these earliest accounts. The conspicuous fact about his life, they assert, is that he was not concerned to slip off into Nirvana by himself but to give his life for the help of others. Because he did not dwell publicly on this motive, Theravadins, attending too narrowly to certain of his teachings, have underplayed his great renunciation and thereby missed the most essential and most vital meaning of the religion that goes by his name, for it is through his love and pity more than through his insight into the means of release from suffering that Buddhism is still alive and at work in the world. Only to a select band of intimates whom he felt were capable of understanding the meanings closest to his heart did he reveal the motives that explain his life and teachings. In picking up on these, Mahayanists claim to preserve the true spirit of the Buddha and to stand in the direct line of his inspiration.

We may leave to the two schools their controversy over apostolic succession; our concern is not to judge but to understand the positions they embody. The differences that have come out thus far may be summarized by the following pairs of contrasts if we remember that they are not absolute but speak to emphases.

1. Whereas Theravada Buddhism considers man as basically an individual, his emancipation not contingent upon the salvation of others, Mahayana says the opposite. Life being one, the fate of the individual is linked with the fate of all. This, they maintain, is implicit in Buddha's cardinal doctrine of *anatta* which, as we have seen, means simply that beings and things have no ego entirely of their own. If this is so, how can we escape the corollary that "we are what we are because of what others are?" "As all other beings are sick, so I am sick." Two lines from John Whittier's "The Meeting" summarizes the Mahayanist perspective on this issue.

> He findeth not who seeks his own
> The soul is lost that's saved alone.

2. Theravada holds that man is on his own in this universe. There being no superhuman gods or powers to help him over the humps, every heart should beat in accord with the iron string of self-reliance.

> By ourselves is evil done,
>   By ourselves we pain endure,
> By ourselves we cease from wrong.
>   By ourselves become we pure.
> No one saves us but ourselves,
>   No one can and no one may;
> We ourselves must tread the Path:
>   Buddhas only show the way.

For Mahayana, in contrast, grace is a fact. Peace can be at the heart of all because a boundless power, grounded in Nirvana, regards and dwells without exception in every soul, drawing each in its good time to the goal.

3. In Theravada the key virtue was *bodhi,* wisdom, with the absence of self-seeking emphasized more than the active doing of good. Mahayana moved a different word to the center: *karuna,* compassion. Unless it eventuates in compassion, wisdom is worthless. "A guard I would be to them who have no protection," runs a typical Mahayana invocation; "a guide to the voyager, a ship, a well, a spring, a bridge for the seeker of the other shore." The theme has been beautifully elaborated by Shantideva, a poet-saint who has been called the Thomas à Kempis of Buddhism:

May I be a balm to the sick, their healer and servitor until sickness come never again;
May I quench with rains of food and drink the anguish of hunger and thirst;
May I be in the famine of the age's end their drink and meat;
May I become an unfailing store for the poor, and serve them with manifold things for their need.
My own being and my pleasures, all my righteousness in the past, present and future, I surrender indifferently,
That all creatures may win through to their end.[40]

4. Theravada Buddhism centers on monks. Monasteries are the spiritual focus of the lands where it predominates, reminding all of the higher truth which in the last resort gives life its meaning and is the world's final justification. Renunciation of the world is held in high national esteem, and even men who do not intend to become monks for their entire lives are expected to live as such for a year or two that their lives may take on some of the monastic virtues. Mahayana Buddhism, on the contrary, is primarily a religion for laymen. Even her priests are expected to make the service of laymen their primary concern.

5. It follows from these differences that the ideal type as projected by the two schools will also differ markedly. For the Theravadins the ideal was the *Arhat,* the perfected disciple who, wandering like the lone rhinoceros, strikes out on his own for Nirvana and with prodigious concentration makes his way unswervingly toward that pinpointed goal. The Mahayana ideal, on the contrary, was the *Bodhisattva,* "one whose essence (*sattva*) is perfected wisdom (*bodhi*)," a being who, having brought himself to the brink of Nirvana, voluntarily renounces his prize that he may return to the world to make it accessible to others. He deliberately sentences himself to age-long servitude that others, drawing on his acts of supererogation, may enter Nirvana before him. The difference between the two types is illustrated in the story of four men

who, journeying across an immense desert, come upon a compound surrounded with high walls. One of the four determines to find out what is
inside. He scales the wall and on reaching the top gives a whoop of
delight and jumps over. The second and third do likewise. When the
fourth man gets to the top of the wall, he sees below him an enchanted
garden with sparkling streams, pleasant groves, and delicious fruit.
Though longing to jump over, he resists the impulse. Remembering
other wayfarers who are trudging the burning deserts, he climbs back
down and devotes himself to directing them to the oasis. The first three
men were *Arhats*, the last was a *Bodhisattva*, one who vows not to desert
this world "until the grass itself be enlightened."

6. This difference in ideal naturally works back to color the two schools'
estimates of the Buddha himself. For one he was essentially a saint, for
the other a savior. Though the Theravadins revered him as a supreme
sage who set an incomparable example, he remained for them a man
among men. Upon entering Nirvana his personal influence ceased; he
knows nothing any more of this world of becoming, and is at perfect
peace. The reverence felt by the Mahayanists could not be satisfied with
such prosaic humanness. For them, Buddha is a world savior who continues to draw all creatures toward him "by the rays of his jewel hands."
The bound, the shackled, the suffering on every plane of existence, galaxy
beyond galaxy, worlds beyond worlds coming into being out of the timeless void then bursting like bubbles; all are the recipients of the inexhaustible "gift rays" of the Lord Who Looks Down in Pity.

These differences are the central ones, but several others may be
named to complete the picture. Whereas the Theravadins followed
their founder in looking upon speculation as a useless distraction, Mahayana spawned an elaborate cosmology replete with innumerable heavens,
hells, and descriptions of Nirvana. The only kind of prayer the Theravadins countenanced was meditation, whereas the Mahayanists added
supplication, petition, and calling upon the name of the Buddha. Finally,
whereas Theravada remained conservative to the point of an almost
fundamentalistic adherence to the early Pali texts, Mahayana was liberal
in almost every respect. It accepted later texts as equally authoritative,
was less strict in interpreting disciplinary rules, and held a higher regard
for the spiritual possibilities of women and less gifted monks as well as
laymen generally.

Thus in the end the wheel comes full circle. The religion that began,
according to the evidence of the earliest records, as a revolt against rites,
speculation, grace, and the supernatural, ends with all of these back in

the picture and its founder who was an atheist in respect to belief in a personal God transmogrified into such a God himself. We can schematize the differences which divide the two great branches of Buddhism as follows:

Theravada	Mahayana
Man as an individual	Man as involved with others
Man on his own in the universe (emancipation by self-effort)	Man not alone (salvation by grace)
Key virtue: wisdom	Key virtue: *karuna*, compassion
Religion a full-time job (primarily for monks)	Religion relevant to life in the world (for laymen as well)
Ideal: the *Arhat*	Ideal: the *Bodhisattva*
Buddha a saint	Buddha a savior
Eschews metaphysics	Elaborates metaphysics
Eschews ritual	Includes ritual
Confines prayer to meditation	Includes petitionary prayer
Conservative	Liberal

Which outlook wins? The answer is Mahayana, on the whole. Part of the explanation may lie in the fact that it converted one of the greatest kings the world has ever known. In the history of ancient royalty, the figure of Asoka (c. 272-232 B.C.) stands out like a Himalayan peak, clear and resplendent against a sunlit sky. If we are not all Buddhists today it was not Asoka's fault. Not content to board its Big Raft himself and commend it to his subjects—his Buddhist wheel of the law waves on India's flag today—he strove to extend it over three continents. Thus, finding Buddhism an Indian sect, he left it a world religion. There is a deeper reason, however, for Mahayana's success. Philosophers may argue over which outlook is truer, but there is no doubt as to which is more appealing. Grace, compassion, and mutuality are words against which self-effort, individualism, and even wisdom ring hard and cold. Visitors may be impressed by the strength, pervasiveness, and beneficence of Buddhism in Theravada lands; the fact remains that there is nothing in its outlook which for appeal can rival the lofty spiritual figures of the *Bodhisattvas* who, full of mercy and compassion, evoke an atmosphere of trust and love, a devotional and personal religion to which the Far East could offer no equivalent. China in particular was to find in them a new world of spirit that appealed to all levels of her society. Whether or not, then, we believe that the Big Raft justifies its name by assessing more completely the human situation, there is no doubt but that it has justified its name in geographical spread. It blankets Mongolia, Tibet, China, Korea, and Japan, while the Little Raft remains confined to Ceylon, Burma, Thailand, and Cambodia.

THE SECRET OF THE FLOWER[41]

After Buddhism splits into Theravada and Mahayana, Theravada holds together in a single unified tradition. Mahayana, on the contrary, continues to divide. Its larger territory (Tibet, Mongolia, China, Korea, Japan) may have had something to do with this, but the divisions also reflect Mahayana's more liberal attitude toward variations within her fold. In any event the Big Raft splits into five main schools analogous, we might say, to the major denominational divisions within Protestant Christianity. One stresses faith, another study, another relies on efficacious formulas while a fourth assumes a semi-political tint. We shall by-pass these four and consider only Mahayana's intuitive school which appears in its alivest form today in the Zen Buddhism of Japan. (*Zen* is the Japanese counterpart of the Chinese word *ch'an* which, in turn, is a translation of the Sanskrit word *dhyana* meaning the meditation that leads to insight.) We choose Zen for three reasons. First, many students of religion believe it is the purest form of spirituality in the Far East today. Second, it gives us an opportunity to look at religion as it has appeared among the Japanese. Third, it is the one religion of the Far East which as it is breaking upon the West in descriptions and translations that have become available only in our generation is causing philosophers (Heidegger), psychotherapists (Erich Fromm and Hubert Benoit), writers (Aldous Huxley), and artists (Die Zen Gruppe in Germany) to take notice.

Like other Mahayanists, Zen Buddhists claim to trace their perspective back to Gautama himself. His teachings that found their way into the Pali Canon, they hold, were those the masses seized upon. Those of his followers who were more perceptive, however, caught from their master a higher angle of vision. The classic instance of this is found in Buddha's Flower Sermon. Standing on a mountain with his disciples around him, Buddha did not on this occasion resort to words. He simply held aloft a golden lotus. No one understood the meaning of this eloquent gesture save Mahakasyapa whose quiet smile, indicating that he had gotten the point, caused Buddha to designate him as his successor. The insight that prompted the smile was transmitted in India through Twenty-Eight Patriarchs and carried to China in 520 A. D. by Bodhidharma.

Spreading from there to Japan in the Twelfth Century, it contains the secret of Zen.

Entering the Zen outlook is like stepping through Alice's looking glass. One finds oneself in a topsy-turvy wonderland in which everything seems quite mad—charmingly mad for the most part but mad all the same. It is a world of bewildering dialogues, obscure conundrums, stunning paradoxes, flagrant contradictions, and abrupt non sequiturs, all carried off in the most urbane, cheerful, and innocent style. Here are some examples:

An ancient master, whenever he was asked the meaning of Zen, lifted one of his fingers. That was his entire answer. Another kicked a ball. Still another slapped the inquirer in the face.

A novice who makes a respectful allusion to the Buddha is ordered to rinse his mouth out and never utter that dirty word again.

Someone claiming to understand Buddhism in its purity writes the following stanza:

> The body is the Bodhi-Tree;
> The mind is like the mirror bright.
> Take heed to keep it always clean,
> And let no dust collect upon it.

He is at once corrected by a very different quatrain which becomes accepted as the true Zen position:

> Bodhi (True Wisdom) is not a tree;
> The mind is not a mirror shining.
> As there is nothing from the first,
> Why talk of wiping off the dust?

A monk approaches a master saying, "I have just come to this monastery. Would you kindly give me some instruction?" The master answers, "Have you eaten your breakfast yet?" "I have," is the reply. "Then go wash your bowls." It is said that this conversation accomplished its purpose. The inquirer was brought to the understanding of Zen.

A group of Zen masters, gathered for conversation, have a great time declaring that there is no such thing as Buddhism or Enlightenment or anything even remotely resembling Nirvana. They set traps for one another trying to trick someone into an assertion that might imply, even remotely, that such words refer to real things. Artfully they always elude the shrewdly concealed traps and pitfalls, whereupon the entire company bursts into glorious, room-shaking laughter, for the merest hint that these things exist would have revealed that they were not true masters of their doctrine.

What goes on here? Is it possible to make any sense out of what at first blush looks like nothing so much as some sort of transolympian horseplay? Can they possibly be serious in this kind of spiritual double-talk or are they simply pulling our leg?

The answer is that though they are never solemn, they are completely serious. And though we cannot hope to describe their perspective completely—for it is of the essence of Zen that it cannot be encompassed by words—we can perhaps give some hint as to what they are up to.

Let us admit at the outset that even this much is going to be difficult, for we shall have to proceed through words to talk about a position that is acutely aware of their limitation. Words occupy an ambiguous status in life. They are indispensable to our humanity for without them we would be but howling Yahoos; thus making us human we may assume that they make a positive contribution. On their negative side, however, words can build up a kind of substitute world that dilutes the intensity of direct experience, a world that is warmed over when not downright fraudulent. A man can say the right things about a painting without having the slightest trace of an esthetic experience. A mother can fool herself into thinking she loves her child simply because she addresses it with words of endearment. A nation can assume that the addition of the words "under God" to its pledge of allegiance gives evidence that its citizens actually believe in God whereas all it really proves is that they believe in *believing* in God. With all they contribute, words have three limitations. At worst, they build up a false world in which other people are reduced to stereotypes and our actual feelings are camouflaged in honorific titles. Second, even when their description of experience is in the main accurate it is never adequate; they always dilute the intensity of immediate experience even when they do not distort it. Finally and most important, the highest modes of experience transcend the reach of words entirely.

Every religion that has developed even a modicum of semantic sophistication (and this includes all the religions considered in this book) recognizes to some extent the way words and reason fall short of reality when they do not actually distort it. However much the fact may baffle the intellectualist and utilitarian, supra-rational experience remains the paradox and life blood of religion as well, indeed, as of creative art. The saints of every faith are constantly telling us of contact with another world which dazzles, delights, and transfigures them with its "clear day of eternity which never changes into its contrary." With all this Zen is at one, its uniqueness lying only in the fact that it is so concerned with the limitations of language and reason that it makes their transcendence the central intent of its method.

Only as we keep this fact clearly in mind have we the slightest prospect of understanding this outlook, in many ways the strangest of all contemporary expressions of mature religion. It was Buddha himself, according to Zen tradition, who first made the point in the flower sermon by refusing to identify his discovery with any verbal expression. Bodhidharma reaffirmed the point by defining the treasure he was bringing from India to the Far East as "a special transmission outside the scriptures." This seems so incongruous for a religion as to be almost contradictory. Think of Hinduism with its Vedas, Confucianism with its Classics, Judaism with its Torah, Christianity with its Bible. All would be ready to define themselves as special transmissions *through* their scriptures. Zen, too, has its sacred books. In addition to the Sutras which it shares with Buddhism as a whole, it has its own special texts, the *Hekigan roku,* the *Mumonkan,* and others. But one glance at these will reveal how unlike other scriptures they are. Almost entirely they are given to pressing home the fact that Zen cannot be equated with any verbal formula whatever. Account after account will depict disciples interrogating their masters about Zen, only to have their minds turned back by a roared "Ho!" for answer. For the master sees that through these questions the seekers are trying to fill the lack in their lives with words and concepts instead of experience. Indeed, the students will be lucky if they get off with verbal rebuffs. Often a rain of blows will be the response as the master, totally disinterested in the disciples' physical comfort or what they may think of him personally, resorts to the most forceful way he can find to set their quest on a completely different tack.

As we might expect, this unique stance toward scripture is duplicated in Zen's attitude toward creeds. Whereas most religions have a creed of some sort, Zen refuses to permit itself to be equated with any set of words or theory—"not founded on written words and outside the established teaching," to return to Bodhidharma's putting of the point. Signposts are not the destination, the map is not the fact territory. Life and reality are far too full and integral to be fitted into any scheme of conceptual pigeonholes, much less equated with them. This being so, no Zen affirmation can be more than a finger pointing to the moon. And, lest observers attend to the finger instead of the moon, Zen will point, but only to withdraw its finger at once. Again, whereas blasphemy or disrespect of God's word are regarded as sins in other religions, Zen masters may at times order their disciples to tear their scriptures to shreds and avoid words like Buddha or Nirvana as if they were smut. Actually they intend no disrespect.[42] What they are trying to do with all the force at their disposal is to blast the novices out of the comfortable verbal retreats into which they have settled thinking that these are the destination when in fact they are no more than halfway houses. "Not every one who says to me, 'Lord, Lord,' shall enter the kingdom." Zen is not interested in professions of any sort; it wants living experience. To a person who had never known water, no description could equal being thrown into a lake. Zen is not interested in theories about enlightenment; it wants to plunge its practitioners into enlightenment itself. The shouts, the buffets, the reprimands that figure in Zen training have nothing to do with ill-will. They are designed to help the student crash the word-barrier; to startle his mind out of conventional sluggishness into the heightened, more alert perception that will lead to enlightenment.

We must not infer from this brusqueness that Zen is opposed to words and reason entirely. It is, to be sure, no more impressed with the mind's attempts to mirror ultimate reality than was Kierkegaard with Hegel's metaphysics. The finaglings of reason can no more bring the mind to the point where it can reproduce reality than a brick, however polished, can be brought to reflect the sun. But this does not mean that reason has no value. Obviously it can help us to make our way in this physical and social world, a fact which leads Zennists, in the main, to be staunch advocates of education. But more. Working in special ways, reason can actually help awareness toward its goal. If the way it is employed to do this seems somewhat like the way poison is used in small amounts as antidote for disease, we may add that reason can also play an interpretive role, serving as a bridge to join the newly discovered world to the common sense world to which the mind is accustomed. For there is not a Zen problem whose answer, once discovered, does not make good sense within its own frame of reference, not an experience which the masters are unwilling to try to describe or explain, given the proper circumstances. The point regarding Zen's relation to reason is simply a double one: first, Zen logic and description make sense only from an experiential perspective radically different from the ordinary; and second, Zen masters are determined that their students attain the experience itself, not allow talk to take its place.

Nowhere is Zen's determination on this latter point more evident than in the method it has adopted for its own perpetuation. Whereas other religions have answered the difficult problem of historical continuity by institutional organization, papal succession, or resort to the authority of a fixed creed or scripture, Zen has rested its survival on the transmission of a specific state of awareness directly from mind to mind, like flame passed from candle to candle, or water poured from bucket to bucket. It is this "transmission of Budda-mind to Budda-mind" that constitutes the 'special transmission' Bodhidharma cited as Zen's essence. For a number of centuries this inward transmission was symbolized by the handing down of Budda's robe and bowl from patriarch to patriarch, but in the Eighth Century A.D. the Sixth Patriarch in China considered even this simple gesture a step toward confusing form with essence and ordered it discontinued.[43] The point is that here is a tradition that claims to center in a succession of enlightened men, each of whom right down to the Zen masters of today has received from his master the exact mind-state that Buddha succeeded in awakening in his disciple Mahakasyapa. How strict has been the effort to preserve the purity of this lineage the following figures will suggest. The master of the teacher under whom I studied estimated that he gave personal instruction to about nine hundred aspirants. Of these, thirteen completed their Zen training, and four were given the *inka*, that is to say, stamped as *roshis* (Zen masters) and given permission to teach.

And what is the training by which aspirants are brought to or toward the Budda-mind that has been thus preserved? We can approach it by way of three key terms: *zazen, koan,* and *sanzen.*

Zazen means literally 'seated meditation.' The bulk of Zen training takes place in a large meditation hall. Visitors to these will be struck by the seemingly endless hours the monks devote to sitting silently on two long, raised platforms extending the length of the hall on either side, their faces toward the center. Their position is the lotus posture, taken over from India. Their eyes are half open, their gaze falls unfocused to the floor a few feet before them.

So they sit, hour after hour, day after day, year after year, seeking first to develop their intuitive powers (thought to center physiologically in the abdomen) and later to relate their intuitive discoveries to the immediacy of their daily lives. The most intriguing element in the process, however, is the use made of one of the strangest devices for spiritual training to be encountered anywhere in the religions of man. We refer to the *koan.*[44]

In a general way *koan* means problem, but from man's normal perspective the problems the koans pose seem fantastic. At first glance they look like nothing so much as a cross between a riddle and a shaggy dog story. Here are some examples:

A master, Wu Tsu, says, "Let me take an illustration from a fable. A cow passes by a window. Its head, horns, and the four legs all pass by. Why did not the tail pass by?"

Another: What was the appearance of your face before your ancestors were born?

Another: We are all familiar with the sound of two hands clapping. What is the sound of one hand? (If you protest that one hand can't clap, you go back to the foot of the class. Such a remark simply shows you haven't even begun to get the point.)

One more: Li-ku, a high government officer of the T'ang dynasty, asked a famous Ch'an master: "A long time ago a man kept a goose in a bottle. It grew larger and larger until it could not get out of the bottle any more. He did not want to break the bottle, nor did he wish to hurt the goose; how would you get it out?"
The master called out, "O Officer!"
"Yes," was the response.
"There, it's out!"

Our first impulse is to dismiss these puzzles as absurd, but this is precisely what the Zen trainee is not permitted to do. He is commanded to bring the full impact of his mind to bear upon them, sometimes locking logic with them, sometimes plunging them into the mind's deeper, intuitive well, until he comes up with an answer his master considers acceptable, a task that on a single *koan* may take as long as writing a doctoral dissertation.

During this time the mind is intently at work. But it is working in a very special way. We in the West rely on reason so fully that we must remind ourselves that in Zen we are dealing with a perspective that is convinced above everything else that reason is inherently limited and in the end must yield to, or at least be supplemented by, another mode of knowing that can grasp reality far more accurately.

For Zen, if reason is not a ball and chain anchoring the mind to earth it is at least a ladder too short to reach to the full heights of truth. It must, therefore, be transcended, and it is just this transcendence that *koans* are designed to assist. If they appear to contain ingredients that are a scandal to ordinary reason, we must remember that Zen is not trying to make peace with man's ordinary, cooped-up perspective. Its first job must be just the opposite: by agitation to stir the mind to impatience; to loosen the mind into discontent with the conventional canons of reason in which the mind has been locked up to that point. But this puts the matter too mildly. By forcing reason to wrestle with what, from its normal point of view, is flat absurdity, by compelling it to conjoin incompatibles, Zen tries to reduce it to the frantic condition of throwing itself against its walls with the desperation of a cornered rat. By paradox and puzzle it will provoke, excite, baffle, and exhaust the mind until it sees that thinking is never more than thinking *about*, or feeling more than feeling *about*. Then having brought the subject to an intellectual and emotional impasse, it counts on a flash of sudden insight to bridge the gap between second- and firsthand experience. The *koans'* contradictions increase pressure in the trainee's mind until the structures of ordinary reason collapse completely, clearing the way for sudden intuition.

> Light breaks on secret lots . . .
> When logics die
> The secret grows through the eye.[45]

Before we dismiss this strange method as completely foreign, it is well to remember that Kierkegaard regarded meditation on the paradox of the Incarnation—the rational absurdity of the divine becoming human, of the infinite becoming finite—as the most rewarding of all Christian exercises. The *koan* appears illogical because reason operates within its own constructs—a structured framework of reference. But seen from another and quite opposite perspective than that of the reasoning mind trapped in its own operation, the *koan* has its own inexorable and transcendental "logic." With the breakthrough of the mental barrier its puzzle is annihilated. Thus the *koan* is a kind of alarm clock to awaken the sleeping mind locked in the dreams of its reasoning. It contains as it were the enlightenment of the Master who constructed it, and by answering it the same enlightenment is realized by the student.

As he struggles with his *koan* the Zen monk is alone, yet not alone. Books will not help him, and he does not discuss his problem with his fellow monks, for these avenues could only lead to second-hand answers. But he does, twice daily on the average, confront his master in private audience known as *sanzen*, or consultation concerning meditation. These meetings are always brief. The trainee states his *koan* and follows it with the answer to which he has come. The role of the master is then three-fold. On the happy occasions when the answer is correct he validates this fact. This, however, is his least important service, for when the right answer comes, it usually does so with a force the student can recognize on his own. A greater service is rendered in slapping down the inadequate answers the student produces, for nothing so helps the student to put these permanently behind him as his master's categorical rejection. This aspect of *sanzen* is fittingly described in the Ninth Century *Rules of Hyakujo* as affording "the opportunity for the teacher to make a close personal examination of the student, to arouse him from his immaturity, to beat down his false conceptions and to rid him of his prejudices, just as the [smelter] removes the lead and quicksilver from the gold [in the] smelting-pot, and as the jade-cutter, in polishing the jade, discards every possible flaw."[46] The master's other service is, like that of any exacting examiner, to keep the student's energies roused over the years to total and at times almost frantic application.

And to what does this *zazen, koan* study, and *sanzen* lead? The first important step is an intuitive experience called *satori*. Though its preparation may take years, the experience itself comes in a flash, exploding like a silent rocket deep within the experiencer and making everything look different thereafter.

Ever fearful of being sucked into the wave of words, Zennists waste little breath in trying to depict *satori*. Occasionally, however, descriptions do appear.

Ztt! I entered. I lost the boundary of my physical body. I had my skin, of course, but I felt I was standing in the center of the cosmos. . . . I saw people coming toward me, but all were the same man. All were myself. I had never known this world before. I had believed that I was created, but now I must change my opinion: I was never created; I was the cosmos; no individual . . . existed.[47]

From this and similar descriptions we can infer that *satori* is Zen's counterpart of the mystical experience which, wherever it appears, in Zen or any other religion, brings joy, a feeling of· oneness with all things and a heightened sense of reality which cannot be adequately translated into the language of the everyday world. But whereas most religions regard such experiences as the acme of at least the earthly phase of man's religious quest, for Zen it is only the point of departure. In a very real sense, Zen training begins in earnest after *satori* has been achieved. For one thing there must be further *satoris* as the trainee learns to move with greater range and freedom in this noumenal realm.[48] But the important point is that Zen, drawing half its inspiration from the practical, commonsense, this-worldly orientation of the Far East to balance the mystical other-worldly half it derived from India, refuses to permit man's spirit to withdraw—shall we say retreat?—into the mystical state completely. Once we achieve *satori*, we must

get out of the sticky morass in which we have been floundering, and return to the unfettered freedom of the open fields. Some people may say: "If I have [achieved *satori*] that is enough. Why should I go further?" . . . The old masters lashed out at such persons, calling them "earthworms living in the slime of self-accredited enlightenment."[49]

The genius of Zen lies in the fact that it neither leaves the world in the less-than-ideal state in which the unregenerated awareness encounters it nor withdraws from the world in increasing aloofness, indifference, and lack of differentiation. The heart of Zen training lies in introducing the eternal into the now, in widening the doors of perception to the point where the delight and wonder that characterize the *satori* experience can carry over to the ordinary events of man's day-to-day life. "What," asks the student, "is the meaning of Bodhidharma's coming from the West?" The master answers, "The cypress tree standing in the garden." The indescribable wonder of being must be sensed: to bring one to the first dramatic awareness of it is the function of *satori*. But until, through experiencing the interpenetration and interconvertability of all phenomena, this wonder is seen to spread until it envelops an object as common and natural as the tree in your backyard, until you can perform your daily duties however large or small with the perception that each is equally a manifestation of the infinite in its particular time and place, the business of Zen remains unfinished.

With the possible exception of Buddha himself, in no individual life is it ever completely finished. Yet by extrapolating hints taken from Zen writing as a whole we can form an idea of what the "man who has nothing further to do" would be like. This in turn will draw together the points that have been made in the course of this section and furnish a summary suggestion of the condition of life Zen seeks to attain.

First, it is a condition in which life and the awareness that forms its core are experienced to be distinctly good. In answer to the question, To what does Zen training lead? a Western student who had been training in Kyoto for seven years answered, "No parapsychic experiences, as far as I am aware. But you wake up in the morning, and the world seems so beautiful you can hardly stand it."

With this perception of life's goodness there comes, secondly, an objective outlook on the relation of oneself to others, their welfare appearing as important as one's own. Looking at a dollar bill one's gaze may be possessive; looking at a sunset it can't be. Between these two, Zen attainment is like looking at the sunset. Involving as it does the utilization of the full powers of awareness, the questions "whose awareness?" or "awareness of what?" become secondary. The dualisms of self and object, of self and other, are transcended. And as they fade, there grows upon one a feeling of infinite gratitude to all things past and infinite responsibility to all things present and future.

Third, the life of Zen (as we have sought to emphasize) does not draw the individual away from the world but returns him to it with things in new perspective. We are not called to seek oblivion to temporal things or identity with something beyond time. Life's purpose is not to get the soul out of the body as a piston out of its syringe, but instead to discover the satisfaction of full awareness even as it proceeds from a bodily base. "What is the most miraculous of all miracles?" asks the Zennist. "That I sit quietly by myself." Simply to see things as they are, as they truly are in themselves, is joy enough. Zen does, it is true, bring an experience of oneness, but it is a oneness which is at once empty because it dismisses all distinctions as inconsequential, and completely full because it spills over to include everything. As the Zennist puts the matter, "All is one, one in none, none is all." The infinite is not something that stands apart from the world of flux; if you seek it as such, you will cut yourself off from the world of relativity where you belong as much as anywhere. We find in Zen, as a consequence, a sense of what might be called "divine ordinariness." "Have you eaten? Then wash your bowls." If you cannot find the ultimate justification of existence in an act as simple as that of doing the dishes, you will find it nowhere.

> My daily activities are not different,
> Only I am naturally in harmony with them.
> Taking nothing, renouncing nothing,
> In every circumstance no hindrance, no conflict . . .
> Drawing water, carrying firewood,
> This is supernatural power, this marvelous activity.[50]

With this perception of the infinite in the finite there comes, fourthly, an attitude of total agreeableness. "Yesterday was fair, today it is raining"—the experiencer has passed beyond the opposites of good and evil, pleasure and pain, preference and rejection. As both kinds of pull are needed to supply the dynamic for this relative world, each is welcomed in its place.

There is a poem by Seng Ts'an on "Trust in the Heart," which is the finest expression of this ideal of total acceptance.

> The Perfect Way is only difficult for those who pick and choose;
> Do not like, do not dislike; all will then be clear.
> Make a hairbreadth difference, and Heaven and Earth are set apart;
> If you want the truth to stand clear before you, never be for or against.
> The struggle between "for" and "against" is the mind's worst disease. . . .
> Do not try to drive pain away by pretending that it is not real;
> Pain, if you seek serenity in Oneness, will vanish of its own accord. . . .
> Thoughts that are fettered turn from Truth,
> Sink into the unwise habit of "not liking."
> "Not liking" brings weariness of spirit; estrangements serve no purpose . . .
> The One is none other than the All, the All none other than the One.
> Take your stand on this, and the rest will follow of its accord;
> To trust in the Heart is the "Not Two," the "Not Two" is to trust in the Heart.
> I have spoken, but in vain; for what can words tell
> Of things that have no yesterday, tomorrow, or today?[51]

Even truth and falsity are brought into new perspective. "Do not seek after truth," we are advised, "merely cease to hold opinions."

Fifth, as the dichotomies between self and other, finite and infinite, and acceptance and rejection are transcended, the dichotomy between life and death, too, disappears.

When this realization is completely achieved, never again can one feel that one's individual death brings an end to life. One has lived from an endless past and will live into an endless future . . . At this very moment one partakes of Eternal Life—blissful, luminous, pure.[52]

As we leave Zen to its future we may note that its influence on the total cultural life of Japan has been enormous. Though its greatest influence has been on pervasive life attitudes, four specific aspects of Japanese culture carry its imprint indelibly. In *sumi* or black ink landscape painting, Zen monks, living their simple lives close to the earth, have rivaled the skill and depth of feeling of their Chinese masters. In landscape gardening, Zen temple gardens surpassed those of their Chinese teachers and raised the art to a perfection unrivaled anywhere else in the world. Flower arrangement began by placing floral offerings before the Buddha, but developed into an art which today is a part of the training of every refined Japanese girl. Finally there is the celebrated tea ceremony in which an austere but beautiful setting, a few fine pieces of old pottery, a slow, graceful ritual and a spirit of utter tranquility combine to epitomize the harmony, respect, clairty, and calm that characterize Zen at its best.

THE IMAGE OF THE CROSSING

We have looked at three angles within Buddhism: the Little Raft, the Big Raft, and (most unique perspective within the latter) Zen. These angles are so different that we must ask in closing whether, on any grounds other than historical accident, they deserve to be considered aspects of a single religion.

There are two respects in which the various branches of Buddhism must be regarded as variations within a single religion. They all root back to a single founder from whom they claim to derive their teachings. Beyond this, they can all be subsumed—not to be sure under some all-inclusive meta-philosophy, but within a metaphor, a single image. This—we are taking our cue here from Heinrich Zimmer—is the image of the crossing, the simple everyday experience of crossing a river on a ferryboat.

To appreciate the force of this image we must remember the indispensable role the ferry plays in Eastern life. In lands laced with un-bridged rivers and canals, almost any journey will require a ferry. This commonplace fact underlies and inspires every school of Buddhism, as the use of the word *yana* by all of them clearly indicates. Buddhism is a voyage across the river of life, a transport from the common-sense shore of nonenlightenment, spiritual ignorance, desire, and death, to the far-flung bank of wisdom which brings liberation from this prevailing bondage. Compared with this agreed fact, the differences within Buddhism are no more than variations in the kind of vehicle one boards or the stage one has reached on the journey.

What are these stages? While we are on the first bank it is almost the world to us. Its earth underfoot is solid and reassuring. The rewards and disappointments of its social life are vivid and compelling. The opposite shore is barely visible and has no impact on our world of affairs.

But if something prompts us to see what the other side is like we may decide to attempt a crossing. If we are of independent bent, we may decide to make it on our own. In this case we are Theravadins or Hina-yanists; we shall make ourselves a little raft and push off. Most of us, however, have neither the time nor the inclination for this kind of feat. Mahayanists, we move down the bank to where a ferryboat is expected. As the group of explorers clamber aboard at the landing there is an air of excitement. Attention is focused on the distant bank, still indistinct, but the voyagers are still very much like citizens of this side of the river. The ferry pushes off and moves across the water. The bank we are leaving behind is losing its substance. The shops and streets and antlike figures are blending together and releasing their myriad pulls upon us. Meanwhile the shore toward which we are headed is not in focus either; it seems almost as far away as it ever was. There is an interval in the crossing when the only tangible realities are the water with its treacherous currents and the boat which is stoutly but precariously contending with them. This is the moment for Buddhism's Three Vows: I take refuge in the *Buddha*—the fact that there was an explorer who made this trip and proved to us that it is possible. I take refuge in the *dharma*, the vehicle of transport, this boat to which we have committed our lives in the conviction that it is seaworthy. I take refuge in the *sangha*, the Order, the crew that is navigating this trip and in whom we have confidence. The shoreline of the world has been left behind; until we set foot on the further bank, these are the only things in which we can trust.

The further shore draws near, becomes real. The raft jolts onto the sand and we step out upon solid ground. The land which had been misty and unsubstantial as a dream is now fact. And the shore that we left behind, which was so tangible and real, is now only a slender horizontal line, a visual patch or a memory without any hold on us.

Impatient to explore our new surroundings, we nevertheless remember our gratitude for the splendid ship and crew who have brought us safely to what promises to be a fascinating land. It will be no act of gratitude, however, to insist on packing the boat with us as we plunge into the woods. "Would he be a clever man," Buddha asks, "if out of gratitude for the raft that has carried him across the stream to safety he, having reached the other shore, should cling to it, take it on his back, and walk about with the weight of it? Would not the clever man be the one who left the raft (of no use to him any longer) to the current of the stream, and walked ahead without turning back to look at it? Is it not simply a tool to be cast away and forsaken once it has served the purpose for which it was made? In the same way the vehicle of the doctrine is to be cast away and forsaken once the other shore of Enlightenment has been attained."[53]

Here we come to Zen. The rules of Buddhism, the Eightfold Path;

the technical terminology of *dukkha, karuna*, Nirvana, and the rest; the sacred Order; the person of Buddha himself—all are vitally important to the individual in the act of making the crossing. They lose their relevance for those who have arrived. Indeed, if the traveler not merely reaches the shore of this promised land but keeps moving into its interior, there comes a time when not only the raft but the river itself drops out of view. When such a one turns around to look for the land that has been left behind, what does he see? What *can* one see who has crossed a horizon line beyond which the river dividing this shore from that has faded? He looks—and there is no "other shore"; there is no torrential separating river; there is no raft; there is no ferryman. These things are no longer a part of his world.

Before the river has been crossed, the two shores, human and divine, can appear only distinct from each other, different as life and death, as day and night. But once the crossing has been made and left behind, no such dichotomy remains. The realm of the gods is no distant place; it is where the traveler stands, and if his stance be still in this world, that world itself has become perfected. In this sense we are to read Buddhist assertions that "this our worldly life is an activity of Nirvana itself, not the slightest distinction exists between them."[54] Turning his gaze back from his introspection which has brought a condition described positively as Nirvana and negatively as emptiness because it transcends all forms, the Buddhist now perceives without the same ocean of being he has found within. "Form is emptiness, emptiness indeed is form. Emptiness is no different from form, form is not different from emptiness." Having stepped out of the delusions of his former self-assertive, self-defensive ego, he loses the disjunction between acceptance and rejection as well. Every moment becomes accepted completely. Like a net of perfect jewels each of which gathers into itself and throws back to the viewer the living splendor of all, every experience becomes a reflex of a power that endures, untouched by pain. From such a perspective the tragic view of life becomes Byronic, adolescent, and self-conscious. Even the categories of good and evil are thrown back into solution. "That which is sin is also Wisdom," we read; "the realm of Becoming is also Nirvana."[55]

From this new shore we are in a position to understand the profound intuition that underlies the *Bodhisattva*'s vow of renunciation. He has paused on the brink of Nirvana, resolved to forego entering the untroubled pool of eternity "until the grass itself be enlightened," which, as grass keeps coming, means until the end of time. Does this mean that he may never, himself, reach total fulfillment? It means, rather, that he has risen to the point where the distinction between time and eternity has lost its force, having been made by the rational mind but dissolved in the perfect knowledge of the lightning-and-thunder insight that has transcended the pairs of opposites. Time and eternity are now two aspects of the same experience-whole, two sides of the same unsliceable completeness. "The jewel of eternity is in the lotus of birth and death."

From the standpoint of normal, worldly consciousness there must always remain a baffling inconsistency between this climactic insight and worldly prudence. But the world will always look different to those who have not been portered across the ocean of ignorance and to those who have. Only the latter can see through the delusory distinctions between time and eternity. The river separating the two shores has faded from view. Or if to one with eagle vision it still remains, it is seen now as connecting the two banks. We have come home to Zen.

THE CONFLUX OF BUDDHISM AND HINDUISM IN INDIA

Among the surface paradoxes of Buddhism—this religion which began as a sharp revolt against ritual, speculation, grace, mystery, and a personal God and ended with all of these brought back in abundance—among these paradoxes there is a final one. Today Buddhists abound in every Asian land except India. Buddhism wins impressively in the world at large only, it would seem, to lose in the land of her birth.

This is the way it looks on the surface. The deeper fact is that in India Buddhism came to be not so much defeated by Hinduism as accommodated within it. Up to around 1000 A.D. Buddhism continued in India as a distinct movement. As these 1500 years of her history wore on, however, her differences with Hinduism softened—Hinduism admitting the need for the reforms Buddha championed and Buddhism becoming more like Hinduism as it widened into Mahayana—until in the end Buddhism merged back into the historical stream from which it had arisen. It is as if Catholics and Protestants were to work out their differences and there were again to be in the West one all-embracing family of Christians.

Only if one assumes that Buddhist principles were excluded from post-Buddhist Hinduism can the merger be considered a Buddhist defeat. Actually almost all of Buddhism's affirmative doctrines found their place or parallel. Its contributions, accepted by Hinduism in principle if not always by Hindus in practice, included its renewed emphasis on kindness to all living things, on non-killing of animals, on the elimination of caste barriers in matters religious and their reduction in matters social, and its strong ethical emphasis in general. Its *Bodhisattva* ideal seems to have left its mark in prayers like the following by Ranti Deva in the great Hindu devotional classic, the *Bhagavatam:* "I desire not of the Lord the greatness which comes by the attainment of the eightfold powers, nor do I pray him that I may not be born again; my one prayer to him is that I may feel the pain of others, as if I were residing within their bodies, and that I may have the power of relieving their pain and making them happy." On all these points Buddha was affectionately reclaimed as "a rebel child of Hinduism," her great reformer, and an actual incarnation of God. As to parallels, the basic outlook and goal of Theravada Buddhism were acknowledged to be substantially those of non-dual Hinduism. Even Zen's *tour de force,* her thesis that to eternity itself there is no other handle than the present moment and her consequent crashing of the spirit barrier until Nirvana be found in this very world of time and flux—this too was found to have its Hindu counterpart:

> This very world is a mansion of mirth;
> Here I can eat, here drink and make merry (Ramakrishna).

Especially in Tantric schools, which are old and somewhat esoteric, the disciple is brought to the point where he can see even sex, meat, and wine, things which had formerly appeared as the most formidable barriers to the divine, as but varying forms of God. "The Mother is present in every house. Need I break the news as one breaks an earthen pot on the floor."[55]

SUGGESTIONS FOR FURTHER READING

J. B. Pratt's *The Pilgrimage of Buddhism and A Buddhist Pilgrimage* (New York: Macmillan, 1928) remains perhaps the best general book on Buddhism in English. Edward Conze's *Buddhism: Its Essence and Development* (New York: Philosophical Library, 1951), is an excellent recent study. A nice collection of some of the most important Buddhist texts laced together with useful introductions is available for 50 cents in the Mentor publication of E. A. Burtt's *The Teachings of the Compassionate Buddha.* Paul Carus' *The Gospel of the Buddha* (Chicago: Open Court) furnishes the best study of Buddha the man. Christmas Humphrey's 65 cent Pelican book titled *Buddhism* is uneven but contains some good chapters.

In the realm of Zen, the writings of Professor D. T. Suzuki tower so incomparably above all others that one is tempted to confine mention to these. Because of the special angles from which they approach the subject, however, three supplementary items may be noted. Eugen Herrigel's *Zen in the Art of Archery* (New York: Pantheon, 1953) makes a unique contribution by taking the reader vicariously but vividly through a Westerner's six years training under an authentic Zen Master. Readers with a love for literature who would like to approach Zen through characters like Don Quixote and the poets' vision will be rewarded by R. H. Blyth's *Zen in English Literature and Oriental Classics* (Tokyo: Hokuseido Press, 1948). Akihisa Kondo's "Morita Therapy: A Japanese Therapy for Neurosis," *The American Journal of Psychoanalysis*, Vol. XIII (1953), develops some of Zen's implications concerning human personality and mental health.

As for Professor Suzuki's writings, the titles are too numerous to be appropriately listed, yet one is at a loss as to which to omit. Fortunately, this dilemma has been resolved by the recent appearance of a book that gathers within one pair of covers some of the most important products of his lifelong scholarship. Edited by William Barrett and published as an Anchor Book for 95 cents, it is titled *Zen Buddhism*.

For those who live in the United States or Canada, The First Zen Institute of America, 156 Waverly Place, and the Zen Study Society, Room 1500, 26 Broadway, both in New York City, are the best sources of further information.

4

Confucianism

THE FIRST TEACHER

IF THERE is one name with which Chinese culture has been associated it is Confucius'—Kung Fu-tzu or Kung the Master. Chinese reverently speak of him as The First Teacher—not that there were no teachers before him but because he stands above them all in rank. No one claims that he molded Chinese culture single-handed; he himself expressly depreciated his innovations, preferring to regard himself simply as "a lover of the ancients."[1] This characterization gives him less than his due; it stands as an excellent example of the modesty and reticence he advocated. For though Confucius did not author Chinese culture, he remains its supreme editor. Winnowing the past, underscoring here, playing down or discarding there, reordering and annotating throughout, he brought his culture to a focus which has remained remarkably distinct for twenty-five centuries.

If the reader supposes that such an achievement could come only from a dramatic life, he will be disappointed. Confucius was born around 551 B.C. in the principality of Lu (in what is now Shantung province). We know nothing for certain about his ancestors but it is clear that his early home life was modest. "When young, I was without rank and in humble circumstances." His father died before Confucius was three, leaving his upbringing to a wonderful but impoverished mother. Financially, therefore, he was forced to make his own way, at first through menial tasks. The hardship and poverty of these early years gave him a tie with the common people which was to be reflected in the democratic tenor of his entire philosophy.

Though reminiscences of his boyhood contain nostalgic references to hunting, fishing, and archery, thereby suggesting that he was anything but a bookworm, he took early to his studies and did well in them. "On reaching the age of fifteen, I bent my mind to learning." In his early twenties, having held several insignificant government posts and contracted a not too successful marriage, he established himself as a tutor. This was obviously his vocation. The reputation of his personality and practical wisdom spread rapidly, attracting a circle of ardent disciples.

Despite these disciples' conviction that "since the beginning of the human race there has never been a man like our Master," Confucius' career was in terms of his own ambitions a failure. His goal was public office, for he believed—how wrongly we shall see!—that his theories would not take hold unless they were channeled into the world of affairs through administration. He had supreme confidence in his ability to reorder society if given a chance. Being told of the growth of population in the state of Wei and asked what should be done, he answered, "Enrich them." "And what after that?" "Educate them," was his famous reply, adding with a sigh, "Were a prince to employ me, in a twelve-month something could be done, but in three years the work could be completed!" Doting biographers, unable to conceive that a man so gifted could remain permanently blocked in his life's ambition, credit him with five years of brilliant administration in his early fifties, years in which he is pictured as advancing rapidly from Minister of Public Works through Minister of Justice to Prime Minister and in which Lu became a model state. Dissoluteness and dishonesty hid their heads, the romanticized account continues. "A thing dropped in the streets was not picked up." Loyalty and good faith became standard in men, and chastity and docility in women. The truth is that contemporary rulers were much too afraid of Confucius' candor and integrity to appoint him to any position involving power. When his reputation rose to the point where the ruler of his own state, who had achieved his power through usurpation, felt obliged to ask him perfunctorily for advice on how to rule, Confucius replied tartly that he had better learn to govern himself before trying to govern others. The ruler did not have him cut into small pieces as he might have done save for Confucius' reputation, but neither did he appoint him Prime Minister. Instead he tossed him an honorific post with an exalted title but no authority, hoping thus to keep him quiet. Needless to say, once Confucius discovered the ruse he resigned in disgust.

Prompted as if by call—"At fifty I perceived the divine mission"—
he gave his next thirteen years with many a backward look and "resisting footstep" to "the long trek" in which he wandered from state
to state proffering unsolicited advice to rulers on how to improve their
governing, and seeking a real opportunity to put his ideas into practice. The opportunity never came; a bystander's prediction as he set
out that "Heaven is going to use the Master as a bell to rouse the
people" turned as the years slipped by to mockery. Once he was invited to office in the state of Chen, but finding that the official who
issued the invitation was in rebellion against his chief refused to become a party to the intrigue. The dignity and saving humor with
which he carried himself during these anomalous years does great
credit to his person. Taunted once by a bystander: "Great indeed is
Confucius! He knows about everything and has made no name in
anything," Confucius pursued the point with his disciples in mock
dismay: "Now what shall I take up? Charioteering? Archery?" As state
after state disregarded his counsels of peace and concern for the people, recluses and hermits sneered at his efforts to reform society and
advised him to join their quest for a self-mastery sufficient to offset
the ills of a society beyond redemption. Even peasants criticized him
as "a man who knows he cannot succeed and keeps on trying." Only
a small band of faithful disciples stood by him through rebuff, discouragement, and near starvation. Once the records give us a picture
of them together: Confucius' heart swelling with pride and happiness
as he looked at them; Ming Tzu so calm in reserved strength, Tzu Lu
so full of energy, Jan Ch'iu and Tzu Kung so frank and fearless.

In time, with a change of administration in his own state, he was
invited to return. There, recognizing that he was now too old for
office anyway, he spent his last five years quietly teaching and editing
the classics. In 479 B.C., at the age of 73, he died .

A failure as a politician, Confucius was undoubtedly one of the
world's greatest teachers. Prepared to instruct in history, poetry, government, propriety, mathematics, music, divination, and sports, he was, in
the manner of Socrates, a one-man university. His method of teaching
was likewise Socratic. Always informal, he seems not to have lectured
but instead to have conversed on problems his students posed, cited
readings, and asked questions. He was particularly skilled at the latter:
"The Master's way of asking,—how different it is from that of others!"
He expected much of his students, especially able ones, for he saw the

cause in which he was enrolling them as nothing less than the redressing of the entire social order.

This conviction made him a zealot, but humor and a sense of proportion preserved him from being a fanatic. When the skeptic Tsai Wo proposed derisively, "If someone said there is a man in the well the altruist, I suppose, would go after him," Confucius corrected him by remarking that "even an altruist would first make certain there really was a man down the well!" When someone was recommended to him as "thinking thrice before he took action," Confucius replied dryly, "Twice is sufficient." Confident as he was, he was ready to admit always that he might be wrong and at times that he definitely had been.

There was nothing other-worldly about him. He loved to be with people, to dine out, to join in the chorus of a good song, and to drink though not in excess. His disciples reported that "When at leisure the Master's manner was informal and cheerful. . . . He was affable, yet firm; dignified yet pleasant." His democratic attitudes have already been remarked upon. Not only was he always ready to champion the cause of common people against the oppressive nobility of his day, but in his personal relations cut "scandalously" across class lines and never slighted his poorer students even when they could pay him nothing. He was kind though capable of acid sarcasm when he felt a student needed it. Of one who had taken to criticizing his companions Confucius observed, "Obviously Tzu-kung must have become quite perfect himself, to have time to spare for this; I do not have this much leisure."

It was true; he remained to the end more exacting of himself than of anyone else. "How dare I allow myself to be taken as sage and humane!" he said. "It may rather be said of me that I strive to become such without satiety."[2] He remained faithful to the quest. Power and wealth could have been his for the asking if he had been willing to compromise with those in authority. He preferred, instead, his integrity. He never regretted the choice. "With coarse food to eat, water to drink, and my bended arm for a pillow, I still have joy in the midst of these things. Riches and honors acquired by unrighteousness mean no more to me than the floating clouds."

With his death began his glorification. Among his disciples the move was immediate. Said Tzu Kung, "He is the sun, the moon, which there is no way of climbing over. The impossibility of equalling our Master is like the impossibility of scaling a ladder and ascending to the skies." Others came to agree; within a few generations he was regarded throughout China as "the mentor and model of ten thousand generations." What would have pleased him more was the attention given to his ideas. For the past two thousand years every Chinese school child until recently has raised his clasped hands each morning to a tablet in the corner bearing Confucius' name. Virtually every Chinese student has pored over his sayings for hours with the result that these have become a part of the Chinese mind, trickling down to the illiterate in spoken proverbs. Chinese government, too, has been influenced more deeply by Confucius than by any other figure. Since the start of the Christian era a large number of governmental offices, including some of the highest, have presupposed a knowledge of the Confucian classics. There have been a number of moves, some of them quasi-official, to elevate him to the stature of divinity.

What produced this influence, so great that as recently as 1938 careful observers were still regarding Confucianism as "the greatest single intellectual force" among one-fifth of the world's population? It could hardly have been his personality. Exemplary as this was it contained too little dramatic force to explain his historical impact. If we turn instead to his sayings our puzzle only deepens. As a series of homey anecdotes and moral maxims they too are completely commendable. But how a collection of sayings so patently didactic, so pedantically unexciting and commonplace, could have rallied a civilization looks at first glance to be one of the real mysteries of history. Here are some examples:

Is not he a true philosopher who, though he be unrecognized of men, cherishes no resentment?

What you do not wish done to yourself, do not do to others.

I will not grieve that men do not know me; I will grieve that I do not know men.

Do not wish for quick results, nor look for small advantages. If you seek quick results, you will not attain the ultimate goal. If you are led astray by small advantages, you will never accomplish great things.

The nobler man first practices what he preaches and afterwards preaches according to his practice.

If, when you look into your own heart, you find nothing wrong there, what is there to worry about, what is there to fear?

When you know a thing to recognize that you know it; and when you do not, to know that you do not know—that is knowledge.

To go too far is as bad as to fall short.

A man without virtue cannot long abide in adversity, nor can he long abide in happiness.

When you see a man of worth, think of how you may emulate him. When you see one who is unworthy, examine your own character.

Wealth and rank are what men desire, but unless they be obtained in the right way they may not be possessed.

Feel kindly toward everyone, but be intimate only with the virtuous.

Maids and servants are hardest to keep in your house. If you are friendly with them, they lose their deference; if you are reserved with them, they resent it.[3]

There is certainly nothing to take exception to in such sayings. But where is their power?

THE PROBLEM CONFUCIUS FACED

For the clue to Confucius' power and influence we must see both his life and his teaching against the background of the problem he faced. This was the problem of social anarchy.

Early China had been neither more nor less turbulent than other lands. The eighth to the third centuries B.C., however, witnessed a collapse of the Chou Dynasty's ordering power. Rival baronies were left to their own devices, creating a precise parallel to conditions in Palestine in the period of the Judges: "In those days there was no king in Israel; every man did what was right in his own eyes."

The almost continuous warfare of the age began in the pattern of chivalry. The chariot was its noble weapon, courtesy its code, and acts of generosity were accorded its highest honor. Confronted with invasion a baron would send, in an act of bravado, a convoy of provisions to the invading army. Or, to prove that his men were beyond fear or intimidation, he would send as messengers to his invader braves who would cut their throats in his presence. As in the Homeric age, warriors of opposing armies, recognizing each other, would exchange haughty compliments from their chariots, drink together, and even trade weapons before doing battle.

By Confucius' day, however, the interminable warfare had degenerated a long way from this code of chivalrous honor toward the undiluted horror of the Period of the Warring States. The horror reached its height in the century following Confucius' death. The chariot, arm of the tournament, gave way to the cavalry with its surprise attacks and sudden raids. Instead of nobly holding their prisoners for ransom, conquerors put them to death in mass executions. Soldiers were paid upon presenting the severed heads of their enemies. Whole populations unlucky enough to be captured were beheaded, including women, children, and the aged. We read of mass slaughters of 60,000, 80,000, 82,000, and even 400,000. There are accounts of the conquered being thrown into boiling caldrons and their relatives forced to drink the human soup.

In the midst of such an age the one question that eclipsed all others was: How can we learn to live together? Answers differed but the question was always the same. It is a question that with the invention of the multimegaton hydrogen bomb has returned to haunt contemporary man with peculiar force.

As the heart of Confucianism lies in its answer to this problem of social cohesion, we need to see that problem in perspective. Confucius lived at a time when social cohesion had deteriorated to a critical point. The glue was no longer holding. What had held society together up to then?

Up to the human level the answer is obvious. The glue that holds the pack, the herd, the hive together is instinct. The cooperation it produces among ants and bees is particularly impressive, but throughout the animal world generally, except for man, it can be relied on to insure reasonable peace and cooperation. Violence in nature there has been aplenty but not as a rule within species themselves. Within the species an inbuilt gregariousness, the "herd instinct," has kept life whole.

With the emergence of man, this automatic source of social cohesion is turned off. Man being "the animal without instincts," no inbuilt mechanism can be counted on to keep him in harmony with his fellows. What now is to keep anarchy in check? During the eons of man's infancy as a species the answer was spontaneous tradition or, in the anthropologists' phrase, "the cake of custom." Through trial and error over the generations certain behavioral patterns come to be accepted as conducive to the well-being of the tribe. No council sets out consciously to decide what values the tribe wants and what rules will promote them; the pattern emerges over centuries in which the generations feel their way toward satisfying mores and away from destructive ones. Once the pattern becomes set—and societies that fail to evolve a viable one read themselves out of existence, simply vanish from the face of the earth—it is transmitted from generation to generation unthinkingly, passed on to the young *cum lacte*, as the Romans would say, "with the mother's milk."

Contemporary Western life has moved so far from the tradition-dominated life of early man as to make it difficult for us to imagine how completely it is possible for human life to be controlled by mores. In one area only does custom continue to reach into our lives to control the switches, the area of dress and attire. If in dressing a businessman were to overlook his tie he could not get through the day. The predicament has nothing to do with indecent exposure; it is purely a matter of convention. He would be laughed at for forgetfulness. If it should be suspected that he had omitted his tie by intent, the reaction would be more serious. All day long he would be regarded out of the corner of his associates' eyes as queer, peculiar, different. And this he cannot stand—which is why custom and tradition as long as they are alive have such power. There is in a woman's certitude that she is wearing precisely the right thing for the occasion, as someone has observed, a peace which religion can neither give nor take away.

If we generalize to all areas of life this power of tradition which we feel only in matters of dress, we shall have a picture of the tradition-oriented life of early man. There are two things about this life that interest us here. The first is its phenomenal capacity to keep asocial acts in check. There are tribes among the Eskimos and Australian aborigines that do not even have a word for disobedience, so unknown is the phenomenon among them. The second impressive thing is the spontaneous, unthinking way in which at this level socialization is accomplished. No laws are formulated with penalties attached, no careful plans for the moral education of the child devised. Group expectations are so solid and unvarying that the young internalize them unquestioningly and unconsciously. The Greenlanders have no conscious program of education, nevertheless anthropologists report that their children are universally obedient, good-natured, and ready to help. Recently Ruth Benedict found American Indians who remembered back to a time when social controls were internal: "In the old days there were no fights about hunting grounds or fishing territories," they repeated. "There was no law then . . . everybody did what was right."

In pre-Confucian China, likewise, custom and tradition may have automatically provided sufficient cohesion to keep the community reasonably intact. Vivid evidence of its power has come down to us. There is, for example, the recorded case of a noble lady who was burned to death in a palace fire because she refused to violate convention and leave the house without a chaperon to escort her. The comment of the historian in relating this incident—he was writing as Confucius' contemporary—shows that in his own thinking convention had lost its absolute character but was still, from our point of view, incredibly alive.

Had the lady been a young girl, he observes, her conduct would have been beyond question. But as she was a married woman, and an elderly one at that, it would have been "fitting under the circumstances" for her to leave the burning mansion on her own.[4]

The historian's sensitivity to the past is stronger than most. Not everyone in Confucius' day gave even this much ear to tradition. China had reached a new point in her social development, a point marked by the emergence of large numbers of individuals in the full sense of that word. Self-conscious rather than group-conscious, these individuals had ceased to think of themselves primarily in the first person plural and were thinking in the first person singular instead. Reason was replacing social habit, and self-interest outdistancing the expectations of the group. The fact that others were behaving in a given way or that their ancestors had done so from time immemorial could not be automatically counted on as sufficient reason for individuals to follow suit. Each call to action had now to answer the question, "What's in it for me?"

The old mortar that had held society together was chipping and flaking. In working their way out of the "cake of custom" individuals had cracked it beyond repair. The rupture did not occur overnight. In history nothing begins or ends on time's knife-edge, least of all cultural change. The first individualists were probably wild mutants, lonely eccentrics who raised strange questions and resisted complete group identification not from wish but from simple inability to feel themselves completely one with the gang. But individualism and self-consciousness are contagious. Once they appear they spread like epidemic and the unreflecting oneness of the group is gone forever.

RIVAL ANSWERS

When tradition is no longer adequate to hold society together man faces the gravest crisis that has beset him. It is a crisis that the West should have no difficulty in understanding, for in recent years it has returned to face her in an acute form. America provides the clearest example. A genius for absorbing peoples of varying nationalities and traditions has earned for her the reputation of being a melting pot. But in reducing these distinctive patterns of life without replacing them with a clear alternative of her own, America has become one of the most traditionless societies in history. As substitute she has proposed reason. Educate everyone and provide them with facts on which they can build reasoned decisions and people can be counted on to behave sensibly and well—this has been the Jeffersonian-Enlightenment faith on which she has proceeded. But has this proved so? With more education than almost any other nation, America leads the world in rising crime, divorce, and delinquency rates.

With the contemporary Western answer to the problem of human coherence having still to prove its adequacy, it is of more than antiquarian interest to look at the alternatives that were proposed in ancient China. One was the answer of the so-called Realists.[5] What do you do when people don't behave? Hit them. It is a classic answer to a classic question. What people understand best is force. Once they emerge from the chrysalis of tradition and start to steer their lives by individual reason, the pull of passion and self-interest is so strong that only the threat of heavy reprisal will keep them in line. Prate as you please of reason and morality; in the last analysis it is brute force that commands obedience. The only way to avoid universal violence in a society composed of self-seeking individuals is to maintain a large militia and effective police force poised to bat the people back in line when they misbehave. There must be laws that allow people to know what is and is not permitted; the penalties for violation must be so heavy that no one will dare incur them. In short, the Realists' answer to the problem of social order was: laws with teeth in them. It was essentially the answer Hobbes was to propose in the West. Left to individual devices, without an absolute hand to restrain the encroachments of self-interest, life is "nasty, brutish, and above all, short."

The application of the Realists' philosophy of social order proceeded by way of an elaborate mechanism of "punishments and rewards." Those who did what the state commanded were to be rewarded; those who did not were to be punished. Given this approach, the list of laws obviously had to be long and detailed—no few pious generalities which could be bent to individual interpretation would do. "If a law is too concise," said Han Fei Tzu, the leading spokesman for the Realists, "the common people dispute its intentions. . . . An enlightened ruler, when he makes his laws, sees to it that every contingency is provided for in detail."[6] Not only must the requirements of law be spelled out in detail but penalties for infractions should also be clearly fixed. And they should be heavy. "Idealists," Han Fei Tzu continues, "are always telling us that punishments should be light. This is the way to bring about confusion and ruin. The object of rewards is to encourage; that of punishments, to prevent. If rewards are high, then what the ruler wants will be quickly effected; if punishments are heavy, what he does not want will be swiftly prevented."

The estimate of human nature from which this political philosophy proceeded was obviously low. It was low in two ways. The Realists saw man's lower impulses dominating him. He is born lustful, greedy, and jealous, with goodness needing to be imposed on him as wood is straightened in a press. "Ordinary people are lazy; it is natural to them to shirk hard work and to delight in idleness."[7] Many may simulate moral attitudes if they think these will enable them to get ahead; indeed, a country may reek with pseudo-morality and pseudo-benevolence. But when the pinch is on, self-interest will out. The Realists saw man as short-sighted. Herein lay the second need for force. A ruler must envision the long-run good of his people; they themselves are incapable of doing so. Consequently, they will not voluntarily accept the present sacrifices that are needed to produce future results.

Suppose a baby has a scalp disease. "If the baby's head is not shaved, there is a return of its malady; if a boil is not lanced, it will go on growing. But while such things are being done to it, though someone holds it close and soothes it and its own mother lovingly performs these operations, the child will nevertheless scream and howl the whole while, not understanding at all that the small pain to which it is being subjected will result in a great gain."[8]

Similarly, the masses "want security, but hate the means that produce security." If they are allowed to follow the promptings of immediate pleasure they will soon be victims of the pains they most dread, whereas if they are made to accept some things they currently dislike and have no illusions—with the masses this requires force—they will in the end be brought to the pleasures they want.

This low estimate of human nature in general did not lead the Realists to deny man's higher impulses. They simply doubted that these were sufficiently widespread to keep the average state in order. Occasional geniuses appear who are able to draw perfect circles without compasses, but can wheel-making wait on these? One person in a thousand may be scrupulously honest, but of what use are these few when millions are in question? For the millions, accounts and tallies are indispensable. One ruler in a thousand might be able to inspire a people to live cooperatively without invoking laws and the police, but to tell Chinese caught in the Period of the Warring States to wait for another model ruler of the order of the legendary heroes of the past is like telling a man who is drowning in Middle China to wait till an expert swimmer arrives from a border province. Though exceptional persons might be ruled by exceptional monarchs through kindness, the average man could be ruled only through law and force.

Life is hard. We may wish it were not, but wishing does not alter the fact.

> No lake so still but that it has its wave;
> No circle so perfect but that it has its blur.
> I would change things for you if I could;
> As I can't, you must take them as they are.[9]

The harsh facts of existence call for unwavering realism, for compromise cancels by trying to move two ways at once. "Ice and embers cannot lie in the same bowl."

Actually, side by side with the Realists' approach to the social problem, there did exist another view, as different from it as fire from ice. Known as Mohism, after its principal spokesman Mo Tzu or Mo Ti, it proposed as the solution to China's social problem not force but love. The only hope of peace lay in brotherly kindness and good will toward all. One should "feel towards all people under heaven exactly as one feels towards one's own people, regard other States exactly as one regards one's own State."[10] Nearly five hundred years before Christ, Mo Tzu proclaimed this thesis so unequivocally that his words deserve quoting at length:

Mutual attacks among states, mutual usurpation among houses, mutual injuries among individuals . . . these are [among] the major calamities in the world.

But whence did these calamities arise? . . .

They arise out of want of mutual love. At present feudal lords have learned only to love their own states and not those of others. Therefore they do not scruple about attacking other states. The heads of houses have learned only to love their own houses and not those of others. Therefore they do not scruple about usurping other houses. And individuals have learned only to love themselves and not others. . . . Therefore they do not scruple about injuring others. . . . Therefore all the calamities, strifes, complaints, and hatred in the world have arisen out of want of mutual love. . . .

How can we have the condition altered?

It is to be altered by the way of universal love and mutual aid.

But what is the way of universal love and mutual aid?

It is to regard the state of others as one's own, the houses of others as one's own, the persons of others as one's self. . . . When all the people in the world love one another, then the strong will not overpower the weak, the many will not oppress the few, the wealthy will not mock the poor, the honored will not disdain the humble, and the cunning will not deceive the simple. And it is all due to mutual love that calamities, strifes, complaints, and hatred are prevented from arising.[11]

Mo Tzu simply disagreed with the Realists' charges that such emphasis on love was sentimental and impractical. "If it were not useful, even I would disapprove of it. But how can there be anything that is good but not useful."[12] The Mohists drew their confidence in love ultimately from their estimate of a universe they believed to be wonderfully good. They saw it as ruled over by Shang Ti, the Sovereign on High, a personal god who "loves men dearly . . . ordered the sun, the moon, and the stars . . . sent down snow, frost, rain, and dew . . . established the hills and rivers, ravines and valleys . . . appointed dukes and lords to reward the virtuous and punish the wicked. . . . Heaven loves the whole world universally. Everything is prepared for the good of man."[13]

As love is obviously good, and the god who made and orders the world also good, it is inconceivable that he would have made a world in which love does not pay. The case for love need not rest on speculation or inference; in the long run it is the only way that pays. For "whoever loves others is loved by others; whoever benefits others is benefited by others; whoever hates others is hated by others; whoever injures others is injured by others."[14]

Confucius' Answer

None of the rival answers to the problem of social coherence looked promising to Confucius. He rejected the Realists' answer of force because it was clumsy and external. Force defined by law can regulate the grosser dealings between men but is too crude to enter the subtleties of the day-to-day, face-to-face exchanges that constitute life's substance. With regard to the family, for example, law and the power that backs it up can establish the conditions of marriage and divorce but the heart of the marriage relationship—love itself—it can neither elicit nor destroy. So it is in general. Police can inhibit theft and assault; they cannot compel people to be friendly and enjoy one another's company. Society, Confucius was convinced, needs more than the long arm of the state to make it good.

As for the Mohists' reliance on love, Confucius agreed with the Realists in dismissing this answer as utopian.[15] Love has a key part to play in human relationships and we shall soon be watching Confucius himself advocating it in its proper place. But love requires arrangements and social structures to come into being. To call for it alone was to call for the end without indicating the means that might bring it into being. There was also a secondary objection. Different situations require different responses; to propose meeting them all with an identical emotion is to propose that life be played in monotone. When Confucius was asked, "Should one . . . love one's enemy, those who do us harm?" he replied, "By no means. Answer hatred with justice and love with benevolence. Otherwise you would waste your benevolence." Mencius objected to Mo Tzu's call "to love all equally" on similar grounds; in ignoring the peculiar affection due to members of one's own family it condemned itself as deficient in discrimination.

The contemporary West's approach to the social problem—through the cultivation of reason—may not have suggested itself to Confucius at all. If it did he certainly dismissed it forthwith. Those who hold an evolutionary view of intelligence, seeing it as increasing with the centuries, may argue that this was because he was dealing with a society in its immaturity—when like an adolescent it was too old to spank but too young to reason with. It is more probable that Confucius, insofar as he raised the question to consciousness at all, assumed that the mind must always operate in a context of attitudes and emotions that are conditioned by the individual's relationships with his group, and that unless his experiences in this latter area dispose him to cooperation, reason however strengthened and refined is likely to prove no more than an instrument for rationalized self-interest. In this respect Confucius was no child of the Enlightenment. He was closer to contemporary anthropologists who are pointing out that it has taken our present condition of value-uncertainty to show us how little emotional commitment straight intellectual and verbal instruction can impart.[16]

Confucius found himself intrigued by tradition, man's original answer to the social problem. With others of his day, he believed that there had been in China's past a period of Grand Harmony. It was tradition that had effected this golden age; because the traditions had been powerful, people lived by them; because they had been finely wrought, in living by them the people lived well. Confucius may have idealized, even romanticized, China's past; he unquestionably envied it and wished to duplicate it as nearly as possible in his own time. As tradition held the secret then, so must it in some way now. The art of social life, writes one of today's distinguished social analysts,

has to be transmitted from the old to the young, and the habits and the ideas must be maintained as a seamless web of memory among the bearers of the tradition, generation after generation. . . . When the continuity of the traditions of civility is ruptured, the community is threatened. Unless the rupture is repaired, the community will break down into factional . . . wars. For when the continuity is interrupted, the cultural heritage is not being transmitted. The new generation is faced with the task of rediscovering and reinventing and relearning by trial and error most of what [it] needs to know. . . . No one generation can do this.[17]

Though Confucius would not have put the matter in these words, he would have concurred emphatically.

This in no way implies that he was an antiquarian. He was a contemporary man alert to the new features which made his time unlike any before and so precluded all hope that a simple duplication of measures effective in the past would be equally effective in the present. The decisive difference that set off his age from that of the Grand Harmony was that men had become individuals, self-conscious and reflective. This being so, spontaneous tradition—a tradition that had emerged unconsciously out of the trial and error of innumerable generations and that held its power because men felt completely identified with the tribe—could not be expected to command their assent. The alternative was deliberate tradition. When tradition can no longer hold its own in the face of the eroding wash of critical self-consciousness, shore it up by giving it deliberate attention and reenforcement.

The answer held the appositeness of social genius. In times of transition an effective answer to the social problem must meet two conditions. It must preserve true continuity with the past, for only by tying in with what men have known and are accustomed to can it be widely accepted. "Think not that I came to destroy; I came not to destroy but to fulfill" must be the standard here. The answer must also take sufficient account of new factors that now render the old answers inapplicable. Confucius' answer met both requirements superbly. Continuity was preserved by keeping tradition in the center of the picture. Don't rush, Confucius seemed to be saying. Let's see how it was done in the past. "Myself, I am simply a lover of the ancients." With the regularity of a politician taking his stand on the Constitution, he appeals to the Classics as the sole basis for his proposal. And yet it wasn't the old answer. All the way through Confucius was reinterpreting, modifying. Unknown to his people, he was effecting a momentous reorientation by shifting tradition from an unconscious to a conscious base.

Unknown to his people—and for the most part unknown to himself we should add, for it would be a mistake to suppose that Confucius was fully aware of what he was doing. But genius does not depend upon full, self-conscious understanding of its acts. A poet may have less than a critic's awareness of why he chooses the words he does; the lack in no way precludes his words from being right. Probably all radical origination proceeds more by feel than by conscious design. It was clearly so with Confucius. He would not, he could not have justified or even described his answer in the frame of reference we have used. He merely conceived the answer in the first place, leaving to posterity the secondary task of trying to understand precisely what he had done and why it proved effective among the sons of the Middle Kingdom.

The shift from spontaneous to deliberate tradition requires that the powers of critical intelligence be turned both to continuing the force of tradition intact and to determining what ends tradition shall henceforth serve. A people must first decide what values are important to their collective well-being; this is why "among the Confucians the study of the correct attitudes was a matter of prime importance."[18] Then every device of education, formal and informal, should be turned to seeing that these values are internalized as far as possible by everyone. As one Chinese describes the process: "Moral ideas were driven into the people by every possible means—temples, theatres, homes, toys, proverbs, schools, history, and stories—until they became habits in daily life. . . . Even festivals and parades were always religious in character."[19] By these means even a society composed of individuals can, if it puts itself to the task, spin a web of enveloping tradition, a power of suggestion, which its members will internalize and which will prompt them to behave socially even when out of sight of the law.

The technique pivots around what sociologists today are calling "patterns of prestige." Every group, the sociologists tell us, has such patterns. In a teen-age gang in Brooklyn it may include the pose of toughness in preference to any trace of tenderness, a "sissy" trait; violence may be exalted above reasonableness, and everything resembling culture disdained. Among monks in a monastery the pattern might be precisely the reverse. Whatever its content, a "pattern of prestige" consists of those values that the leaders of a group admire. The followers, taking their cue from the leaders whom *they* admire, come to respect these values and are inclined to enact them, partly because they, too, now admire them and partly to win their leaders' approval.

It is a powerful routine, perhaps the only one by which distinctively human values ever permeate large groups. For nearly two thousand years the first sentence a Chinese child, living in the direct light of Confucius, learned to read was not "Look, look; look and see," but "Man is by nature good." It is easy to smile at such straightforward preachment but no civilization has been able to manage without it. American children have George Washington and his cherry tree and the simple moralisms of the McGuffy Reader. The Roman's renown for discipline and obedience was not unrelated to his legend of the father who condemned his son to death for winning a victory against orders. Did Nelson actually say, "England expects every man to do his duty"? Did Francis I really exclaim, "All is lost save honor"? It doesn't much matter. The stories express national character and form it. Similarly, the interminable anecdotes and maxims of Confucius' *Analects* were designed to create the prototype of what the Chinese character could achieve and be.

The Master said: "The true gentleman is friendly but not familiar; the inferior man is familiar but not friendly."

Tzu King asked: "What would you say of the man who is liked by all his fellow townsmen?" "That is not sufficient," was the reply. "What is better is that the good among his fellow townsmen like him, and the bad hate him."

The Master said: "The well-bred are dignified but not pompous. The ill-bred are pompous, but not dignified."

Once when Fan Ch'ih was rambling along with the Master under the trees at the Rain Altars, he remarked: "May I venture to ask how one may improve one's character, correct one's personal faults, and discriminate in what is irrational?"

"An excellent question," rejoined the Master. "If a man put duty first and success after, will not that improve his character? If he attacks his own failings instead of those of others, will he not remedy his personal faults? For a morning's anger to forget his own safety and involve that of his relatives, is not this irrational?"

Confucius was creating for his countrymen their second nature which, to return to Lippmann's words, is what a man receives when he becomes civilized.

This second nature is made in the image of what he is and is living for and should become. . . . Full allegiance to the community can be given only by a man's second nature, ruling over his first and primitive nature, and treating it as not finally himself. Then the disciplines and the necessities and the constraints of a civilized life have ceased to be alien to him, and imposed from without. They have become his own inner imperatives.[20]

No longer is it necessary to remember the rules of the game, for the habit of the art of life has become engrained.

THE CONTENT OF DELIBERATE TRADITION

Deliberate tradition differs from spontaneous tradition in requiring attention. It requires attention first to maintain its force in the face of the increased individualism confronting it. This Confucius regarded as the main responsibility of education in its broadest terms. But, second, it requires that attention be given to the ends it is to serve.

What were Confucius' proposals on this second score? What was to be the content of deliberate tradition and what were the goals of character and social life it was to serve? The main outlines of his answer can be gathered under five key Confucian terms.

1. *Jen*, etymologically a combination of the character for "man" and for "two," names the ideal relationship which should pertain between people. Variously translated as goodness, man-to-man-ness, benevolence, and love, it is perhaps best rendered as human-heartedness. *Jen* was the virtue of virtues in Confucius' view of life. It was a sublime even transcendental perfection that he confessed he had never seen fully incarnated. Involving as it does the display of human capacities at their best, it is a virtue so exalted that one "cannot but be chary in speaking of it."[21] To the noble it is dearer than life itself. "The determined scholar and the man of *Jen* ... will even sacrifice their lives to preserve their *Jen* complete."

Jen involves simultaneously a feeling of humanity toward others and respect for oneself, an indivisible sense of the dignity of human life wherever it appears. Subsidiary attitudes follow automatically; magnanimity, good faith, and charity. In the direction of *Jen* lies the perfection of everything that separates man from the beasts and makes him distinctively human. In public life the man of *Jen* is untiringly diligent. In private life he is courteous, unselfish, and gifted with empathy, "able to measure the feelings of others by his own." Stated negatively, this empathy leads to what the West, contrasting it with Jesus' parallel statement, has called the Silver Rule: "What you do not want done to yourself, do not do to others." There is no reason, however, to rest with this negative formulation, for Confucius puts the point positively as well: "The man who possesses *Jen*, wishing to be established himself, seeks also to enlarge others." Such largeness of heart knows no national boundaries for the man of *Jen* knows that "within the four seas all men are brothers."

2. The second concept is *Chun-tzu*. If *Jen* is the ideal relationship between human beings, *Chun-tzu* refers to the ideal term of such relations. It has been translated True Manhood, the Superior Man, and Manhood-at-its-Best. The word gentleman has declined to the point where it now denotes little but matters of etiquette—tipping the hat, pushing in ladies' chairs, and the like. But if we understand etiquette in its original French meaning as "the ticket on the outside of a package that indicates what's on the inside" we shall not be wrong in thinking of the *Chun-tzu* as a gentleman in the most significant sense.

The *Chun-tzu* is the opposite of the petty man, the mean man, the little man. Fully adequate, poised, he has toward life as a whole the approach of the ideal host who is so at home in his surroundings that he is completely relaxed and being so can turn his full attention to putting others at their ease. As he needs nothing himself, he is wholly at the disposal of others. Having come to the point where he is at home in the universe at large, the *Chun-tzu* carries these qualities of the ideal host with him through life generally. His approach to others is in terms not of what he can get but of what he can do to accommodate.

With the gentleman's adequacy go a pleasant air and good grace. Poised, confident, and competent, he is a man of perfect address. His movements are free of brusqueness and violence; his expression is open, his speech free of lewdness and vulgarity. The gentleman does not talk too much. He does not boast, push himself forward, or in any way display his superiority save perhaps at sports. Holding always to his own standards however others may forget theirs, he is never at a loss as to how to behave and can keep a gracious initiative where others are at sea. Schooled to meet any contingency "without fret or fear," his head is not turned by success nor his temper soured by adversity.

"It is only the man who is entirely real," Confucius thought, "who can establish the great foundations of civilized society." Only as the persons who make up society are transformed into *Chun-tzus* can the world move toward peace.

> If there be righteousness in the heart, there will be beauty in the character.
> If there be beauty in the character, there will be harmony in the home.
> If there be harmony in the home, there will be order in the nation.
> If there be order in the nation, there will be peace in the world.[22]

3. The third concept, *Li*, has two meanings.

Its first meaning is propriety, the way things should be done. Confucius thought individuals were not likely to achieve much in their search for beauty and goodness if starting from scratch. They needed precedent. Confucius wanted to lift to the collective attention of the community the finest precedents for social life that had been discovered, that everyone might gaze and memorize and duplicate. The French, whose culture not only in its love of cooking but in its attention to the art of life in general is China's nearest counterpart in the West, have several phrases that capture this idea so exactly that they have made their way into every Western vocabulary: *savoir faire*, the knowledge of how to comport oneself with grace and urbanity whatever the circumstance; *comme il faut*, the way things are done; *apropos*, that which is appropriate; and *esprit*, the right feel for things. Confucius wanted to cultivate the Chinese character in precisely the direction pointed by these idioms. Through maxims (burlesqued in the West by parodies of "Confucius say . . ."), anecdote (*The Analects* are full of them), and his own example ("Confucius, in his village, looked simple and sincere; . . . when in court he spoke minutely but cautiously . . ."), he sought to order an entire way of life so that no one properly raised need ever be left to improvise his responses on momentary impulse because he is at a loss as to how to behave. "Manners maketh man" said a wise medieval bishop. To the extent that this is true, *Li* was to be the making of the Chinese character.

Propriety covers a wide range, but we can get the gist of what Confucius was concerned with if we look at his teachings on the Rectification of Names, the Mean, the Five Key Relationships, the Family, and Age. Confucius said:

If names be not correct, language is not in accordance with the truth of things. If language be not in accordance with the truth of things, affairs cannot be carried on to success. . . . Therefore a superior man considers it necessary that the names he uses may be spoken appropriately, and also that what he speaks may be carried out appropriately. What the superior man requires is just that in his words there may be nothing incorrect.

This may sound like undue concern with words. But Confucius was grappling with a problem that in our time has spawned a whole new discipline, semantics; the inquiry into the relation between words, thought, and objective reality. All human thought proceeds through words. As long as words are askew, thought cannot be straight. When Confucius says that nothing is more important than that a father *be* a father, that a ruler *be* a ruler, this implies first that we know what we mean when we use the words father and ruler and that we mean the right things. Behind the concept of *Li*, therefore, stands the presumption that the various roles and relationships of life will have been normatively delineated and defined.

So important was the Doctrine of the Mean in Confucius' vision of the good life that an entire book by that title is an important part of the Confucian canon. The two Chinese words for Mean are *chung yung*, literally "middle" and "constant." The Mean, therefore, is the way that is "constantly in the middle" between life's extremes. With "nothing in excess" its guiding principle, its closest Western equivalent is the Golden Mean of Aristotle. The Mean balances a sensitive temperament against overdose and indulgence and checks depravity before it occurs. "Pride," admonishes the *Book of Li*, "should not be allowed to grow. The desires should not be indulged. The will should not be gratified to the full. Pleasure should not be carried to excess." Following the Mean brings harmony and balance. It disposes men to compromise, and issues in a becoming reserve. Never plunging to extremes, toward pure values "equally removed from enthusiasm as from indifference," China's regard for the Mean has come out in her recoil from everything approaching fanaticism.

The Five Relationships that make up the warp and woof of social life are in the Confucian scheme those between father and son, elder brother and junior brother, husband and wife, elder friend and junior friend, and ruler and subject. It is, therefore, vital to the health of society that they be rightly constituted. None of these relationships are transitive; in each case different responses are appropriate to the two terms. A father should be loving, a son reverential; an elder brother gentle, a younger brother respectful; a husband good, a wife "listening"; an elder friend considerate, a younger friend deferential; a ruler benevolent, a subject loyal. In effect Confucius is saying: You are never alone when you act. Every action affects someone else. Here in these five relationships is a frame within which you may achieve as much as is possible of individuality without doing damage or creating a bitter conflict with any other individual in the pattern of life.

That three of the Five Relationships pertain within the family is indicative of how important Confucius believed this institution to be. He was not inventing but continuing the Chinese assumption that the family is the basic unit of society, an assumption graphically embedded in Chinese legend which credits the hero who "invented" the family with bringing the Chinese from animal to human level by the discovery. Within the family, in turn, it is the children's respect for their parents that holds the key; hence the concept of filial piety. When the meanings of the father are no longer meaningful to the son, someone has recently written, civilization is in danger. Confucius could not have agreed more. "The duty of children to their parents is the fountain from whence all virtues spring." Accounts of devoted children pepper Confucian literature. They are simple stories, many of them, as for example that of the woman whose aged mother-in-law was pining for fish to eat in the depth of winter. The young woman prostrated herself on the ice of a pond and bared her bosom to melt the ice so she might catch the fish which immediately swam up to the hole.

Finally in this elaborate Confucian pattern of propriety that constituted *Li* there was respect for age. The West, accenting the physical, has eulogized youth as the best years of our lives. For the Chinese there is a wonder that only time can bestow. Age gives to all things, objects, institutions, and individual lives, their value, their dignity, their worth. As a consequence, esteem should always turn upward to those who have gone ahead and stand before us. Three of the Five Relationships prescribe that the bulk of respect flow from young to the old.

In the Rectification of Names, the Doctrine of the Mean, the Five Relationships, and attitudes toward Age and the Family we have sketched the main ingredients of Confucius' concept of *Li* in its first meaning, namely propriety. The other meaning of the word is ritual. When appropriate response is detailed to Confucian lengths, the individual's entire life becomes stylized into a vast, intricate, ceremonial rite. Life has become ordered completely. Every step of life's procession has been worked out leaving neither need nor room for improvisation. There is a pattern for every act, from the way thrice-yearly the Emperor renders to heaven an account of his mandate right down to the way you entertain the humblest guest in your home and serve him his tea.

Alfred North Whitehead's wife reported a Cambridge vicar who concluded his sermon by saying "Finally, my brethren, for well-conducted people life presents no problems."[23] *Li* was Confucius' blueprint for the well-conducted life.

4. The fourth pivotal concept Confucius sought to devise for his countrymen was *Te*.

Literally this word meant power, specifically the power by which men are ruled. But this is only the beginning of its definition. What is this power? Confucius disagreed with the Realists' thesis that the only effective rule is by physical might. How right he was in this dispute, history demonstrated through the one dynasty, Ch'in, that attempted to base its policy squarely on Realist principles. Fantastically successful in its early years, it conquered all of existing China within nine years and was the first dynasty to unite the nation only to collapse before the generation was out—vivid witness to Talleyrand's dictum that "You can do everything with bayonets except sit on them." One of the best known of all the stories of Confucius is how on the lonely side of Mount T'ai he heard the mourning wail of a woman. Asked why she wept, she replied, "My husband's father was killed here by a tiger, my husband also, and now my son has met the same fate."

"Then why," Confucius asked, "do you dwell in so dreadful a place?"

"Because here," she answered, "there is no oppressive ruler."

"Scholars," he said to his disciples, "remember this: oppressive rule is more cruel than a tiger."[24]

No state, Confucius was convinced, can constrain all its citizens all the time nor even any large fraction of them a large part of the time. It must depend on widespread acceptance of its will, which in turn requires a certain positive fund of faith in its total character. Observing that the three essentials of government were economic sufficiency, military sufficiency, and the confidence of the people, he added that popular trust is by far the most important since "if the people have no confidence in their government, it cannot stand."

This spontaneous consent from its citizens, this morale without which the community cannot live, arises only when a people sense their leaders to be men of capacity, sincerely devoted to the common good and possessed of the kind of character which compels respect. Real *Te*, therefore, lies in the power of moral example. In the final analysis, goodness becomes embodied in society neither through might nor through law but through the impress of a great personality. Everything depends on the character of the man at the top. If he is crafty or worthless there is no hope for the social order. But if one can get as head of state a true King of Consent, the sanction of whose rule lies in his inherent righteousness, such a man will gather around him a cabinet of "unpurchaseable men." Their complete devotion to the public welfare will quicken in turn the public conscience of leaders in local communities and seep down from there to leaven the lives of the masses. In short, the imitation of the leader provides a new destination for society and a new set of values and purposes which start it moving on a new path. But men of this order are completely beyond personal ambition, which is why as the Confucians say "only those are worthy to govern who would rather be excused."

The following statements epitomize Confucius' idea of *Te*:

He who exercises government by means of his virtue [*te*] may be compared to the north polar star which keeps its place and all the stars turn toward it.

Asked by the Baron of Lu how to rule, Confucius replied: "To govern is to keep straight. If you, Sir, lead the people straight, which of your subjects will venture to fall out of line?"

When on another occasion the same ruler asked him whether the lawless should be executed, Confucius answered: "What need is there of the death penalty in government? If you showed a sincere desire to be good, your people would likewise be good. The virtue of the prince is like unto wind; that of the people like unto grass. For it is the nature of grass to bend when the wind blows upon it."

Justice Holmes used to say that he liked to pay taxes because he felt he was buying civilization. As long as there can be this kind of affirmative attitude toward the state, Confucius would have thought things were all right. But how is this positive attitude to be elicited? Among thinkers of the West, Confucius would have found his spokesman in Plato:

Then tell me, O Critias, how will a man choose the ruler that shall rule over him? Will he not choose a man who has first established order in himself, knowing that any decision that has its spring from anger or pride or vanity can be multiplied a thousandfold in its effects upon the citizens?

The words of Thomas Jefferson would also have awakened in him a warm response: "The whole art of government consists in the art of being honest."

5. The final concept in the Confucian gestalt is *Wen*. This refers to "the arts of peace" as contrasted to "the arts of war"; to music, art, poetry, the sum of culture in its esthetic mode.

Confucius valued the arts tremendously. A simple piece of music once cast such a spell over him that for three months he was unable to distinguish the taste of meat. If there is anyone who is totally immune to the power of art, he taught that such a one has no place in human society. Nevertheless Confucius was not on the whole an advocate of "art for art's sake." He cherished it primarily as an instrument for moral education.

By poetry the mind is aroused; from music the finish is received.
The odes stimulate the mind. They induce self-contemplation. They teach

the art of sensibility. They help to regulate resentment. They bring home the duty of serving one's father and one's prince.[25]

The intriguing aspect of Confucius' doctrine of *Wen*, however, is neither his esteem for the arts in their own right nor his confidence in their didactic power but his insight into their relevance for international relations. What succeeds in interstate affairs? Here again the Realists answered in terms of physical might, victory goes to the state with the largest army. Confucius on the contrary contended that the ultimate victory goes to the state that develops the highest *Wen*, the most exalted culture—the state that has the finest art, the noblest philosophy, the grandest poetry, and gives evidence of realizing that "it is the moral character of a neighborhood that constitutes its excellence." For in the end it is these things that elicit the spontaneous admiration of men and women everywhere. The Gauls were fierce fighters and so crude of culture that they were considered barbarians; but once they experienced what Roman civilization meant, its superiority was so evident they never, after Caesar's conquest, had any general uprising against Roman rule. Confucius would not have been surprised.

Jen, Chun Tzu, Li, Te, and *Wen*—goodness, the gentleman, propriety, government by virtue, and the arts of peace—such were the values to which Confucius had given his heart. His entire life was lived under their spell. They, then, together were to comprise the content of deliberate tradition. Held before the individual from birth to death, they would furnish that "habitual vision of greatness" which Whitehead has called the essence of all true education—a continuum of public aspiration which alone can tie men together for good and in so doing initiate the individual into the mystery of true community.

ETHICS OR RELIGION?

Is Confucianism a religion, or is it an ethic? The question obviously depends on how one defines religion. With its close attention to personal conduct and the moral order, Confucianism hits life from a different angle than do other religions. But this does not deny it the dignity of being considered a religion. If religion is taken in its widest sense as a way of life woven around a people's ultimate concerns, Confucianism clearly qualifies. Even if religion be taken in a narrower sense as the concern to align man to the trans-human ground of his existence, Confucianism is still a religion albeit a muted one. For though we have thus far spoken only of Confucius' social concerns, these while definitely the focus were not the whole of his outlook.

To see the trans-human dimension of Confucianism in perspective we need to set it against the religious background of the ancient China in which Confucius lived. Until the first millenium B.C. the unquestioned outlook was a compound of three related ingredients:

First, Heaven and Earth were considered a continuum. The terms referred not primarily to places but to people who lived in those places, as the House of Lords refers to the persons who sit in that House. The people who comprised Heaven were the ancestors (*Ti*) who were ruled over by a supreme ancestor (*Shang Ti*). They were the forefathers who had gone ahead and soon would be joined by the present retinue of Earth—the whole was one unbroken procession in which death spelled no more than promotion to a more honorable estate. The two realms were mutually implicated and in constant touch. Heaven held control of earth's welfare—the weather for example was "Heaven's mood"—while depending on the current inhabitants of Earth to supply some of her needs through sacrifice. Of the two realms, Heaven was by far the more important. Her inhabitants were more venerable and august and their authority was greater. Consequently, they commanded Earth's reverence and dominated her imaginings.

Being mutually dependent, communication between Earth and Heaven would have been dictated by need even if not by affection. The most concrete way by which Earth spoke to heaven was through sacrifice. It was not only wise but natural to wish to share with those who had preceded the goods of Earth whose essences were borne to them on the ascending smoke of the sacrificial fire. A mound for such offerings was the focus of every ancient village. When a nation arose the ruler, the "Son of Heaven," affirmed his right to that proud title by maintaining the collective sacrifices to the ancestors. Even as late as Confucius' day an administration that lapsed in its worship of the ancestors was considered to have lost its right to exist.

If sacrifice was the principal way Earth spoke to Heaven, augury was the means by which she listened. As the ancestors knew the entire past of the tribe they were equipped to calculate its entire future. Augury was the device by which Earth might tap this store of knowledge. Being pleasantly disposed toward their descendants, the ancestors would naturally want to share with them their knowledge of things to come. Denied the ordinary means of communication, however, they were forced to resort to sign language. It followed that everything that happened on earth had to be divided into two classes. Things men did on purpose were without numinous significance but things that "happen of themselves" were to be watched with care. They were ominous, for one could never tell when the ancestors might be using them to alert their children to things that were to come. Some of these omens occurred within the body: itchings, sneezings, twitchings, stumblings, buzzings in the ears, tremblings of the eyelids. Others were external: thunder, lightning, the courses of the stars, the doings of insects, birds, and animals. It was also possible for man to take the initiative toward Heaven in the search for signs. He could throw yarrow stalks on the ground and observe their pattern; he could apply a hot iron to a tortoise shell and watch the direction of the cracks. Whatever the occasion—a trip, a war, a birth, a marriage—it was prudent to consult the signs of Heaven. An ancient record tells of a visitor who was asked by his host to prolong his stay into the evening. He answered, "I have divined about the day. I have not divined about the night. I dare not."

In each of these three great features of early Chinese religion—its sense of continuity with the ancestors, its sacrifice, and its augury—there was a common emphasis. The emphasis was on Heaven instead of Earth. To understand the total dimensions of Confucianism as a religion it is important to see Confucius (a) shifting the emphasis from Heaven to Earth (b) without dropping Heaven out of the picture entirely.

The first of these twin aspects of Confucianism can be documented easily. On a much debated issue of his day—which should come first, the claims of the people or those of the spirit world through lavish sacrifices?—he answered that though the spirits should not be neglected completely the people should come first. The worldliness and practical concern by which the Chinese were later to be known was coming to the fore, and Confucius crystallized it in a distinctly this-worldly orientation.

"I do not say that the social as we know it *is* the whole," wrote John Dewey, "but I do emphatically suggest that it is the widest and richest manifestation of the whole accessible to our observation." The statement would have suited Confucius perfectly. His philosophy was an incarnation of common sense and practical wisdom. It contained no depth of metaphysical thought, no flights of speculation, no soul-stirring emotions of cosmic piety. Normally he "did not talk about spirits." "Recognize that you know what you know, and that you are ignorant of what you do not know," he said.[26] "Hear much, leave to one side that which is doubtful, and speak with due caution concerning the remainder. See much, leave to one side that of which the meaning is not clear, and act carefully with regard to the rest." Consequently, whenever he was questioned about other-worldly matters he drew the focus back to man. Asked about serving the spirits of the dead he answered, "While you are not able to serve men, how can you serve their spirits?" Asked about death itself, he replied, "While you do not know life, how can you know about death."[27] In short: one world at a time.

One specific illustration of the way in which Confucius shifted the focus from Heaven to Earth is seen in his change of emphasis from ancestor worship to filial piety. In ancient China the dead were actually worshipped. True to the conservative component in his nature, Confucius did nothing to interrupt the ancestral rites themselves. He does not deny that the spirits of the dead exist; on the contrary he advises treating them "as if they were present." At the same time his own emphasis was directed toward the living family. He stressed that the most sacred tie is the tie among blood relatives. For him the obligations of present members of a family to one another were more important than their duties to the departed.

The extent to which Confucius shifted emphasis from Heaven to Earth should not blind us, however, to the balancing point; namely, that he did not sunder man from heaven altogether. He never repudiated the main outlines of the world view of his time—Heaven and Earth, the divine creative pair, half physical and half more-than-physical, ruled over by the supreme *Shang Ti*. Reticent as he was about the supernatural, he was not without it. Somewhere in the universe there was a power that was on the side of right. The spread of righteousness was, therefore, a cosmic demand, and "the will of Heaven" the first thing a gentleman would fear. Confucius believed he had a personal commission to spread his teachings. When during the "long trek" he was attacked at the town of Kwang he reassured his followers by saying, "Heaven has appointed me to teach this doctrine, and until I have done so, what can the people of Kwang do to me?"[28] Feeling neglected of men, he consoled himself with the thought: "There is Heaven—that knows me!" One of the most quoted religious sayings of all time came from his pen, "He who offends the gods has no one to whom he can pray."[29]

Following his master's restrained but affirmative theism, even the most rationalistically trained Confucianist of today will be inclined to say that the foundation of all true humanism is the fact that behind the visible and material world is a spiritual power which in some mysterious way has decreed the ordering laws of the universe. If, therefore, we are to condense Confucianism into a single sentence, we must describe it as a social order in communion and collaboration with a cosmic order. As a contemporary Chinese describing his feeling as he stood by the Confucian Temple of Heaven in Peiping has written, "I felt as if heaven, earth and myself merged in one vastness. Nature and man are one and inseparable."[30]

IMPACT ON CHINA

In his book *The Next Million Years*, Charles Galton Darwin notes that anyone who wishes to make a sizeable impact on human history has the choice of three levels at which to work. He may choose direct political action; he may create a creed; or he may attempt to change man's genetic nature by working through the laws of biological heredity. The first method is the weakest because as a rule the effects of political action barely outlast their agent. The third is not feasible for even if we knew all about man's genes a genetic policy would be almost impossible to enforce even for a short time and would almost certainly be dropped long before any perceptible effects were achieved. "That is why," Darwin concludes, "a creed gives . . . the best practical hope that man can have for really controlling his future fate."[31]

History to date affords no clearer support for this thesis than the work of Confucius. For over two thousand years his teachings have profoundly affected a quarter of the population of this globe. Their advance reads like a success story of the spirit. During the Han Dynasty (206 B.C.–A.D. 220) Confucianism became in effect China's state religion. In 130 B.C. it was made the basic discipline for the training of government officials, a pattern which continued in the main until the establishment of the Republic in 1912. In 59 A.D. sacrifices were ordered for Confucius in all urban schools, and in the seventh and eighth centuries temples were erected in every prefecture of the empire as shrines to him and his principal disciples. To the second half of the twelfth century his *Analects* remained one of the classics. But in the Sung Dynasty it became not merely a school book but the school book, the basis of all education.[32] In 1934 his birthday was proclaimed a national holiday.

The real testament to Confucius' influence, however, is the character of the civilization he so largely molded. A cross section of Chinese life through the centuries reveals his imprint at almost every point.

Nowhere has family solidarity been greater. "A single family may embrace eight generations, including brothers, uncles, great-uncles, sons, nephews and nephews' sons. . . . As many as thirty male parents with their offspring, each with their ancestors and offspring even unto grand-parents and grandchildren, may live in a single joint family home comprising but one single family."[33] The Chinese vocabulary for family relationships reflects the close attention constantly given this institution. A single word for brother is too clumsy; there must be two words to designate whether he is older or younger than the person in question. Likewise with sister; and with aunt, uncle, and grandparent where different words are required to indicate whether these relations are on the father's side or the mother's.

Age in China has uniformly been accorded respect, even veneration. In the West when someone confesses to being fifty the response is likely to be, "You don't look a year over forty." In China if the same fact were disclosed the response would very likely be, "Why you look every bit of sixty." In each culture the intent is courtesy. The difference is in its direction.

In social prestige the scholar has traditionally ranked at the top of the scale, the soldier at the bottom—clear reflection of the doctrine of *Wen*.

The Doctrine of the Mean lives on in the Chinese preference for negotiation, mediation, and the "middle man" as against applying rigid, inflexible statutes of positive law. As a consequence, legal action is regarded as something of a disgrace, reflecting (as is assumed) an incapacity to work things out by sensitive compromise.

Acute social sensitivity, which Confucius cultivated as the prime device for ingraining deliberate tradition, is reflected in the peculiarly Oriental factor of "face." The importance of "saving face," in turn, has led to a completely different attitude toward suicide from that in the West. In the West suicide is taken as a symptom of mental or moral lapse; the Roman Catholic Church, for example, will bury no one who has fallen by his own hand. In Oriental eyes, to forfeit voluntarily what one holds most dear in order to prove the depth of one's regret is a noble deed. The provocation tends to be equally different. In the West we think of a person in the death throes of a fatal disease as perhaps having a supportable argument for saving himself from further pointless agony. In the Orient, suicide is invoked to escape loss of self-respect, to recompense for falling seriously short of the expectations of one's peers and thereby to enable one's relatives again to face society without humiliation.

As it has turned out, not all of Confucius' impact on China has been for the good. Though Confucius himself was, as we have seen, a contemporary man, bent upon devising original methods to meet the new that had entered history in his day, Confucianism has often been content to duplicate the exact content of his message to the neglect of his pioneering spirit. The result often has been the fossilization of what was once a living tradition into a lifeless traditionalism. Thus while Harvey, Kepler, Galileo, Huyghens, Boyle, and Newton were breaking through to fresh and important knowledge in the West, the scholars of China were still memorizing the past. Obviously patterns that fit former conditions can create problems for a later age. To cite one example only, the special ties which in the past have characterized large interlocking families must be watched with extraordinary care when processes of democratic government on a massive scale are at stake; otherwise they are likely to spawn intolerable nepotism. Confucius would have been the first to see this; the interlocking families that headed the Kuo Ming Tang—the Changs, the Sungs, and the Kungs—did not, with the result that they lost their *Te* over the Chinese people and created a vacuum of confidence into which the Communists could move in the end without resistance.

These, however, are perversions. The authentic spirit of Confucius moves through Chinese history in different directions. In the direction of *Wen*, for example—"the arts of peace." There have been golden ages in China when the arts have flourished as nowhere else on earth and deep learning has been achieved. Four centuries before Gutenberg movable type was discovered. A fifteenth century encyclopedia, climax of the research of 2000 scholars, reached a total of 11,095 volumes. There has been great poetry, magnificent painting, and ceramics which "because of the fineness of their material and decoration, and because of the elegance of their shapes . . . may be considered the best pottery of all countries and of all times."[34] Blending into the Confucian art of life itself, these objects of *Wen* have produced a culture with a flavor all its own. It is a compound of subtlety, brilliance, and reticence that produces an effect that can only be described as good taste. We must remember China's reputation for having the most pacific people in the world. She has exalted the life of reasonable enjoyment and despised the destructive. As a consequence she has been able to unite an immense area of fertility and preserve the longest continuous civilization man has ever achieved, one which at its height united one-third of the human race. The political structure of this civilization alone, the Chinese Empire, lasted under various dynasties for 2133 years (from 221 B.C. to

A.D. 1912)—a stretch that makes the empires of Alexander the Great and Caesar look ephemeral.

Her power of assimilation has been equally impressive. Having the most open frontier of all great civilizations, China was subject to wave after wave of invasions by cavalried barbarians who were always ready to fall on the earth-bound agriculturalists. To their gates came the Tartars whose one long-range raid inflicted a mortal wound on the Roman Empire. But what the Chinese could not exclude they absorbed. Each wave of invaders tends to lose its identity through an assimilation which is completely voluntary. Time after time a barbarian conqueror, coming in for plunder, succumbs within twenty years to the point where his chief desire is to write a copy of Chinese verse which his teacher, who is likewise his conquered slave, might acknowledge as not altogether unworthy of a gentleman; and already he is hoping to be mistaken for Chinese. Kublai Khan is the most striking instance. He conquered China but was himself conquered by Chinese civilization, for his victory enabled him to realize his lasting ambition to become a real son of Heaven.

Here, then, has been a cultural furnace with heat sufficient to effect a true melting pot. We are not surprised to encounter the judgment that "the Chinese civilization is to be accepted as the model type . . . to a greater degree than any of the other civilizations of the world."[35]

The force of the Confucian impact is not spent. At the turn of the century, during the Boxer Rebellion, the Empress Dowager issued an edict that all foreigners be slain. Five of her ministers schooled in Confucian principles of *Jen* and the *Chun-tzu* changed her word "slain" to "protected," knowing well that the act would cost them their lives. Confucian principles concerning the family live on in Chinese-Americans whose juvenile delinquency is the lowest of any immigrant group. And the art of life continues: an old gentleman boards a train for his Sunday outing, a bird cage in one hand and in the other an ounce of choice tea which he is taking to a small village where the water is soft enough for his fastidious taste. In all, Toynbee can still write that, "In A.D. 1956 it could be surmised that, under a veneer of Communism, Confucianism was still decisively moulding the lives of a Chinese people who, at that date, amounted to something between a fifth and a quarter of the whole living generation of Mankind."[36]

And yet one cannot but wonder: What is the future of this religion? This we must frankly admit is a question to which nobody has the answer. It may be that we are looking here at a religion that is dying.

It may be that we should close this chapter with words Confucius applied to himself when on his deathbed his eyes rested for the last time on the majestic dome of T'ai Shan, China's sacred mountain and he murmured:

> The Sacred Mountain is falling,
> The beam is breaking,
> The wise man is withering away.

On the other hand, prophets have a strange way of outlasting politicians and even revolutions. Gandhi will outlast Nehru and Confucius will outlast Mao Tze-tung. Already there are intimations that the Confucianism that received such rough treatment during the early years of the Communists is making some comeback. Whereas in his early writings Mao Tze-tung blasted Confucianism as semi-feudal, he has recently advised his countrymen to study Confucius as well as Marx and Lenin. It is possible, therefore, that today even Communists are pondering Confucius' basic formula:

> If there be righteousness in the heart, there will be beauty in the character.
> If there be beauty in the character, there will be harmony in the home.
> If there be harmony in the home, there will be order in the nation.
> If there be order in the nation, there will be peace in the world.

SUGGESTIONS FOR FURTHER READING

Arthur Waley's *The Analects of Confucius* (London: George Allen & Unwin, 1938) remains the best book on Confucianism that has appeared in English. The third of his *Three Ways of Thought in Ancient China*—a Doubleday Anchor Book available for 85 cents—that is devoted to Mencius' thought is a delightful study of Confucius' foremost disciple.

An able, inexpensive translation of the *Analects* is available in James R. Ware's *The Sayings of Confucius*, published by The New American Library as a Mentor Religious Classic for 35 cents.

5

Taoism

No CIVILIZATION is monochrome. In China the classical tones of Confucianism have been balanced not only by the spiritual shades of Buddhism but also by the romantic hues of Taoism.

THE OLD MASTER

According to tradition, Taoism (pronounced Dowism) originated with a man named Lao Tzu, said to have been born about 604 B.C. Some scholars date his life as much as three centuries later than this; some doubt that he ever lived. If he did we know almost nothing about him. We don't even know his name, Lao Tzu—which can be translated "the Old Boy," "the Old Fellow," or "the Grand Old Master"—being obviously a title of endearment and respect. All we really have is a mosaic of legends. Some of these are fantastic: that he was immaculately conceived by a shooting star; carried in his mother's womb for eighty-two years; and born already a wise old man with white hair. Other parts of the story have the ring of authenticity: that his occupation was that of keeper of the archives in his native western state; and that around this occupation he lived a simple and undemanding life. Estimates of his personality have been based almost entirely on one slim volume attributed to him. From this it has been surmised by some that he must have been a solitary recluse wound up in his personal occult meditations; others picture him as "the everlasting neighbor," as natural, genial, and homely as Lincoln with Lincoln's sense of humor and proportion as well. The one purportedly contemporary portrait speaks only of the enigmatic impression he left—the sense that here were depths that defied ready comprehension. Confucius, intrigued by what he had heard of Lao Tzu, once visited him. His description suggests that he was baffled by the strange man yet came away respecting him. "Of birds," he told his disciples, "I know that they have wings to fly with, of fish that they have fins to swim with, of wild beasts that they have feet to run with. For feet there are traps, for fins nets, for wings arrows. But who knows how dragons surmount wind and cloud into heaven. This day I have seen Lao Tzu. Today I have seen a dragon."

Saddened by men's disinclination to cultivate the natural goodness he advocated, and seeking greater personal solitude for his closing years, Lao Tzu is said at length to have climbed on a water buffalo and ridden westward toward what is now Tibet. At the Hankao Pass a gate-keeper sensing the unusual character of the truant tried to persuade him to turn back. Failing this, he asked the "Old Boy" if he would not at least leave a record of his beliefs to the civilization he was deserting. This Lao Tzu consented to do. He retired for three days and returned with a slim volume of 5000 characters titled *Tao Te Ching*, or "The Way and Its Power." A testament to man's at-home-ness in the universe, it can be read, as one chooses, in half an hour or a lifetime and remains to this day the basic text of all Taoist thought.[1]

What a curious life this was for the supposed founder of a religion. He didn't preach; he didn't organize a church. He wrote a few pages, rode off on a water buffalo, and that (as far as he was concerned) was the end of the matter. How unlike Buddha who trudged the dusty roads of India for forty-five years to make his point. How unlike Confucius who hit the capitols for thirteen years trying to gain an administrative foothold for his philosophy. Here was a man so little concerned with the success of his own ideas, to say nothing of fame and fortune, that he didn't even stay around to answer questions. And yet, whether the story of this life be fact or fiction, it is so true to Taoist values that it will remain a part of the religion forever.

THE THREE MEANINGS OF TAO

On opening Taoism's bible, the *Tao Te Ching*, we sense at once that everything revolves around the pivotal concept of *Tao* itself. Literally this word means "path" or "way." There are three senses, however, in which this "way" can be understood.

First, *Tao* is the *way of ultimate reality*. This *Tao* cannot be perceived for it exceeds the reach of the senses. If it were to reveal itself in all its sharpness, fullness, and glory, mortal man would not be able to bear the vision. Not only does it exceed the senses, however; it exceeds all thoughts and imaginings as well. Hence words cannot describe nor define it. The *Tao Te Ching* opens by stating this point categorically: "The Tao which can be conceived is not the real Tao." Ineffable and transcendent, this ultimate *Tao* is the ground of all existence. It is behind all and beneath all, the womb from which all life springs and to which it again returns. Overawed by the very thought of it, the author of the *Tao Te Ching* bursts recurrently into hymns of praise, for he is face to face with life's "basic mystery, the mystery of mysteries, the entrance into the mystery of all life." "How clear and quiet it is! It must be something eternally existing!" "Of all great things, surely Tao is the greatest." *Tao* in this first and basic sense can be known, but only through mystical insight which cannot be translated into words—hence Taoism's teasing epigram, "Those who know don't say, and those who say don't know."

Though *Tao* ultimately is transcendent, it is also immanent. In this secondary sense it is *the way of the universe*; the norm, the rhythm, the driving power in all nature, the ordering principle behind all life. Behind, but likewise in the midst of, for when *Tao* enters this second form it "assumes flesh" and informs all things. It "adapts its vivid essence, clarifies its manifold fullness, subdues its resplendent lustre, and assumes the likeness of dust." Basically spirit rather than matter it cannot be exhausted; the more it is drawn upon the richer the fountain will gush. There are about it the marks of inevitability; when autumn comes "no leaf is spared because of its beauty, no flower because of its fragrance." Yet ultimately it is benign. Graceful instead of abrupt, flowing rather than hesitant, it is infinitely generous. Giving as it does without stint to nature and man, "it may be called the Mother of the World." As nature's agent, *Tao* bears a resemblance to Bergson's *élan vital*; as her orderer, it parallels to some extent the *lex aeterna* of the Classical West, the eternal law of nature in accord with which the universe operates. Darwin's colleague Roames could have been speaking of it when he referred to "the integrating principle of the whole—the Spirit, as it were, of the universe—instinct with contrivance, which flows with purpose."

In its third sense *Tao* refers to *the way man should order his life* to gear in with the way the universe operates. Most of what follows in this chapter will detail what Taoism suggests this way of life should be. First, however, it is necessary to point out that there have been in China not one Taoism but three.

THREE INTERPRETATIONS OF POWER AND THE
DIFFERENT TAOISMS TO WHICH THEY LED

Tao Te Ching, the title of Taoism's basic text, may be translated
The Way and Its Power. We have seen that the first of these substan-
tive terms, the Way, can be taken in three senses. We must now
add that this is also true of the second. According to the three
ways *Te* or "power" can be conceived, there have arisen in China three
species of Taoism so dissimilar that it is an anomaly that a common
name and handbook should link them even formally.

One way to approach the basic power of the universe is through magic.
From this approach to the power of *Tao* comes Popular Taoism, the
Taoism of the masses. Popular Taoism is not a pretty sight. We have
already said enough about the original doctrine of *Tao* to indicate that
it was a concept too subtle to be grasped by the average mind or spirit.
It was perhaps inevitable that when the concept was translated to make
contact with the average villager and institutionalized around this translation it would be rendered in cruder and eventually perverted terms. To
pass from the lofty heights of the *Tao Te Ching* to the priestcraft of
Popular Taoism is like passing from a crystal mountain spring to the
thick, fetid waters of a stagnant canal. Mysticism becomes mystification
and religion is perverted into necromancy and sorcery. There have been
long epochs in China's history when Taoism in its popular form could be
characterized as little more than a funeral racket.

A second approach to the power of the universe is mystical. From this
approach to *Tao's* power came a second form of Taoism which, because
it was more or less a covert doctrine, we may label Esoteric Taoism.
Though it barely survived into the Christian era and left little mark on
Chinese culture as a whole, it deserves mention for its instrinsic interest.

Originating at about the same time, Esoteric Taoism like Confucius
was concerned with *Te,* the power that holds society together. Instead of granting Confucius' contention that such power was generated
by moral example, however, the Esoteric Taoists maintained that it was
basically psychic in nature. By cultivating "stillness" through yogic
practices paralleling if not actually derived from India—"sitting with a
blank mind," practicing "the dawn breath"—a few key individuals in each
community could become perfect receptacles for *Tao,* the basic power of
the universe. Thereafter these persons would radiate a kind of healing,
harmonious psychic influence over the communities in which they lived.
Though they would do nothing overt or dramatic and hence remain com-

pletely anonymous, the social health of the community would depend entirely on their presence.

Behind Esoteric Taoism lay a fascination with the inner as contrasted with the outer man. Every human being can be considered either externally according to what he says and does and the surface emotions he displays, or from within in which case he is approached as a subjective center of self-consciousness. As a child is not aware of this second internal aspect of his being, neither is early man. Esoteric Taoism arose as the Chinese mind was first discovering its inward dimension and was captivated by it. So wonderful was spirit that matter suffered by comparison; so sublime was the interior life that the exterior was dismissed as shell and accretion. Successive deposits of toil and worry had so silted up the soul that it was necessary to work back through their layers until "man as he was meant to be" was reached. Pure consciousness would then be struck; at last the individual would see not merely "things perceived" but "that by which we perceive."

To arrive at this inwardness it was necessary to reverse all self-seeking and cultivate perfect cleanliness of thought and body. Pure spirit can be known only in a life that is "garnished and swept." "Only where all is clean" will it reveal itself, therefore "put self aside." Perturbing emotions must likewise be quelled. Ruffling the surface of the mind they prevent introspection from seeing past them to the springs of consciousness beneath. Desire and revulsion, grief and joy, delight and annoyance —each must subside if the mind is to return to its original purity, for in the end only peace and stillness are good for it. Let anxiety be dispelled and harmony between the mind and its cosmic source will come unsought.

It is close at hand, stands indeed at our very side; yet is intangible, a thing that by reaching for cannot be got. Remote it seems as the furthest limits of the Infinite. Yet it is not far off; every day we use its power. For . . . the Way of the Vital Spirit . . . fills our whole frames, yet man cannot keep track of it. It goes, yet has not departed. It comes, yet is not here. It is muted, makes no note that can be heard, yet of a sudden we find that it is there in the mind. It is dim and dark, showing no outward form, yet in a great stream it flowed into us at our birth.[2]

Selflessness, cleanliness, and emotional calm are the preliminaries to arriving at full self-knowledge, but they must be climaxed by deep meditation. "Bide in silence, and the radiance of the spirit shall come in and make its home." For this to happen, all outward impressions must be stilled and the senses withdrawn to a completely interior point of focus.

Postures paralleling the Indian *asanas* are recommended and the breath must be similarly controlled—it must be as soft and light as that of an infant, or even an embryo in the womb. The result will be a condition of alert waiting known as "sitting with a blank mind."

And when the realization comes, what then? With it come truth, joy, and power. The climactic insight of Esoteric Taoism came with the impact of finality, everything at last having fallen into place. The condition could not be described as merely pleasurable. The direct perception of the source of one's awareness as "serene and immovable, like a monarch on a throne" brought an absolute joy completely unlike any that hitherto had been experienced. The social utility of the condition, however, lay in the extraordinary power it provided over people and things, a power in fact which "could shift Heaven and Earth." "To the mind that is still the whole universe surrenders." As Waley points out this concept of psychic power has not been confined to the East. St. John of the Cross offers an identical promise: "Without labor you shall subject the peoples, and things shall be subject to you." Without lifting a finger overtly, a ruler who was adept in "stillness" could order a whole people with his mystical-moral power. A ruler who is desireless himself and has this much psychic power automatically turns his subjects from their unruly desires. He rules without even being known to rule.

> The Sage relies on actionless activity, . . .
> Puts himself in the background; but is always to the fore.
> Remains outside; but is always there.
> Is it not just because he does not strive for any personal end
> That all his personal ends are fulfilled?[3]

The Esoteric Taoists recognized that they could not hope for their abstruse and demanding perspective to take hold among the populace as a whole, and they made no attempt to publicize their position. When they did write, their words tended to be veiled and cryptic, open to one interpretation by initiates and another by the general public. Doubtless they wrote this way because they were sensitive to the lampooning to which mysticism so readily lends itself when the uncongenial get wind of it. So Chuang Tzu, burlesquing their breathing exercises reported that these people "expel the used air with great energy and inhale the fresh air. Like bears, they climb trees in order to breathe with greater ease." Mencius joined the fun by likening psychic short-cuts to social order to the impatient farmer who, grieved that his crops grew so slowly, went out nightly to help them along by pulling at the stalks. Despite such ridicule from outsiders, Esoteric Taoism had an appreciable core of devotees during the first five centuries before Christ. Arthur Waley considers it the basic perspective from which the *Tao Te Ching* was written.

This may be true. If so, it is proof of its veiled language. For the *Tao Te Ching* lends itself to a third reading in which the *Tao's* power is interpreted as neither magical (as in Popular Taoism) nor mystical (as in Esoteric Taoism) but philosophical.[4] In this third sense, the power of *Tao* is the power that enters a life that has reflectively and intuitively geared itself in with the Way of the Universe. More a perspective than an organized movement, a point of view which has had a profound influence on Chinese life, Philosophical Taoism will be the focus of the remainder of this chapter. Esoteric Taoism has vanished; Popular Taoism is corrupt; but Philosophical Taoism continues to shape Chinese character in the direction of serenity and grace.

CREATIVE QUIETUDE

The basic quality of life in tune with the universe is *wu wei*. This concept is often translated as a do-nothingness or inaction, but this (suggesting as it does a vacant attitude of passive abstention) misses the point. A better rendering is "creative quietude."

Creative quietude combines within a single individual two seemingly incompatible conditions—supreme activity and supreme relaxation. These seeming incompatibles can coexist because man is not a self-enclosed entity. He rides on an unbounded sea of *Tao* which feeds him, as we would say, through his subliminal mind. One way to create is through following the calculated directives of the conscious mind. The results of this mode of action, however, are seldom impressive; they tend to smack more of sorting and arranging than of genuine creation. Genuine creation, as every artist has discovered, comes when the more abundant resources of the subliminal self are somehow released. But for this to happen a certain dissociation from the surface self is needed. The conscious mind must relax, stop standing in its own light, let go. Only so is it possible to break through the law of reversed effort in which the more we try the more our efforts boomerang.

Wu wei is the supreme action, the precious suppleness, simplicity, and freedom that flows from us, or rather through us, when our private egos and conscious efforts yield to a power not their own. In a way it is virtue approached from a direction diametrically opposite to that of Confucius. With Confucius every effort was turned to building up a complete pattern of ideal responses which might thereafter be consciously imitated.

Taoism's approach is the opposite—to get the foundations of the self in tune with *Tao* and let behavior flow spontaneously. Action follows being; new action, wiser action, stronger action will follow new being, wiser being, stronger being. The *Tao Te Ching* puts this point without wasting a single word. "The way to do," it says simply, "is to be."

How are we to describe the action that flows from a life that is grounded directly in *Tao*? Nurtured by a force that is infinitely subtle, infinitely intricate, it is a consummate gracefulness born from an abundant vitality that has no need for abruptness or violence. One simply lets *Tao* flow in and flow out again until all life becomes an even dance in which there is neither imbalance nor feverishness. *Wu wei* is life lived above tension:

> Keep stretching a bow
> You repent of the pull,
> A whetted saw
> Goes thin and dull. (Ch. 9)[5]

Far from inaction, however, it is the pure embodiment of suppleness, simplicity, and freedom—a kind of pure effectiveness in which no motion is wasted on outward show.

> One may move so well that a foot-print never shows,
> Speak so well that the tongue never slips,
> Reckon so well that no counter is needed. (Ch. 27)

Effectiveness of this order obviously requires an extraordinary skill, a point conveyed in the Taoist story of the fisherman who was able to land enormous fish with a thread because it was so delicately made that it had no weakest point at which to break. But Taoist skill is seldom noticed, for viewed externally *wu wei*—never forcing, never under strain—seems quite without effort. The secret here lies in the way it seeks out the empty spaces in life and nature and moves through these. Chuang Tzu, the greatest popularizer of Philosophical Taoism, makes this point with his story of a butcher whose cleaver did not get dull for twenty years. Pressed for his secret the butcher replied, "Between the bones of every joint there is always some space, otherwise there could be no movement. By seeking out this space and passing through it my cleaver lays wide the bones without touching them."

The natural phenomenon which the Taoists saw as bearing the closest resemblance to *Tao* itself was water. They were struck by the way it would support objects and carry them effortlessly on its tide. The Chinese characters for swimmer, deciphered, mean literally "one who

knows the nature of water." Similarly one who knows the nature of
the basic life-force knows that it will sustain him if he will only stop
his thrashing and flailing and trust it to buoy him and carry him gently
forward.

> Those who flow as life flows know
> They need no other force:
> They feel no wear, they feel no tear,
> They need no mending, no repair. (Ch. 15)

Water, then, was the closest parallel to *Tao* in the natural world. But it
was also the prototype of *wu wei*.

The Taoists were struck by the way it adapts itself to its surroundings
and seeks out the lowest places. So too,

> Man at his best, like water,
> Serves as he goes along:
> Like water he seeks his own level,
> The common level of life. (Ch. 8)

Yet despite its accommodation, water holds a power unknown to hard and
brittle things. In a stream it follows the stones' sharp edges only to turn
them in the end into pebbles, rounded to conform to its streamlined
flow. It works its way past frontiers and under dividing walls. Its gentle
current melts rock and carries away the proud hills we call eternal.

> What is more fluid, more yielding than water?
> Yet back it comes again, wearing down the tough strength
> Which cannot move to withstand it.
> So it is that the strong yield to the weak,
> The haughty to the humble.
> This we know
> But never learn. (Ch. 78)

Infinitely supple yet incomparably strong—these virtues of water are
precisely those of *wu wei* as well. The man who embodies this condition,
says the *Tao Te Ching*, "works without working." He acts without strain,
persuades without argument, is eloquent without flourish, and makes his
point without violence, coercion, or pressure. Though as an individual he
may be scarcely noticed, his influence is in fact decisive.

> A leader is best
> When people barely know that he exists.
> . . . Of a good leader, who talks little,
> When his work is done, his aim fulfilled,
> They will all say, "We did this ourselves." (Ch. 17)

A final characteristic of water that makes it an appropriate analogue to *wu wei* is the clarity it attains through being still. "Muddy water let stand," says the *Tao Te Ching*, "will clear." If you want to study the stars after being in a brightly lit room, you have to wait twenty minutes for your eyes to dilate for their new assignment. There must be similar periods of waiting if the focal length of the mind is to be readjusted from the world's external glare to the internal recesses of the soul.

> The five colors can blind,
> The five tones deafen,
> The five tastes cloy.
> The race, the hunt, can drive men mad
> And their booty leave them no peace.
> Therefore a sensible man
> Prefers the inner to the outer eye. (Ch. 12)

Clarity can come to the inner eye, however, only in so far as man's life attains a quiet equaling that of a deep and silent pool.

OTHER TAOIST VALUES

Still following the analogy of water, the Taoists rejected all forms of self-assertiveness and competition. The world is full of people who are determined to be somebody or give trouble. They want to get ahead, to stand out. Taoism has little use for such ambition. "The ax falls first on the tallest tree."

> Standing tiptoe a man loses balance,
> Admiring himself he does so alone. . . .
> At no time in the world will a man who is sane
> Over-reach himself,
> Over-spend himself,
> Over-rate himself. (Ch. 24, 29)

Their almost reverential attitude toward humility led the Taoists to honor hunchbacks and cripples because of the way they typified meekness and self-effacement. They were fond of pointing out that the value of cups, windows, and doorways lies precisely in the parts of them that are empty. "Selfless as melting ice" is one of their descriptive figures.

The Taoists' refusal to clamber for position sprang from a profound disinterest in the things the world prizes. The point comes out in the story of Chuang Tzu's visit to the minister of a neighboring state. Someone told the minister that Chuang Tzu was coming in the hope of replacing him. The minister was severely alarmed. But when Chuang Tzu heard of the rumor he said to the minister: "In the South there is a bird. It is called *yuan-ch'u*. Have you hear of it? This *yuan-ch'u* starts from the southern ocean and flies to the northern ocean. During its whole journey it perches on no tree save the sacred Wo-tung, eats no fruit save that of the Persian Lilac, drinks only at the Magic Well. It happened that an owl that had got hold of the rotting carcass of a rat looked up as this bird flew by, and terrified lest the *yuan-ch'u* should stop and snatch at the succulent morsel, it screamed, 'Shoo! Shoo!' And now I am told that you are trying to 'Shoo' me off from this precious Ministry of yours."⁶

So it is with most of the world's prides. They are not the true values they are thought to be.

> Surrounded with treasure
> You lie ill at ease,
> Proud beyond measure
> You come to your knees:
> Do enough, without vieing,
> Be living, not dying. (Ch. 9)

What is the point of competition or assertiveness? *Tao* seems to get along very well without them.

> Nature does not have to insist,
> Can blow for only half a morning,
> Rain for only half a day. (Ch. 23)

Man should avoid being strident and aggressive not only toward other men but also toward nature. How should man relate himself to nature? On the whole the modern Western attitude has been to regard nature as an antagonist, something to be squared off against, dominated, controlled, conquered. Taoism's attitude toward nature tends to be the precise opposite of this. There is a profound naturalism in Taoist thought, but it is the naturalism of Rousseau, Wordsworth, Thoreau rather than that of Galileo or Bacon.

> Those who would take over the earth
> And shape it to their will
> Never, I notice, succeed.
> The earth is like a vessel so sacred
> That at the mere approach of the profane
> It is marred
> And when they reach out their fingers it is gone. (Ch. 29)

Nature is to be befriended. When Mount Everest was scaled the phrase commonly used in the West to describe the feat was "the conquest of Everest." An Oriental whose writings have been deeply influenced by Taoism remarked, "We would put the matter differently. We would speak of 'the befriending of Everest.'" Taoism seeks to be in tune with nature. Its approach is basically ecological, a characteristic that has led Joseph Needham to point out that despite China's backwardness in scientific theory she early developed "an organic philosophy of nature ... closely resembling that which modern science has been forced to adopt after three centuries of mechanical materialism." This ecological approach of Taoism has made it one of the inspirations of Frank Lloyd Wright. Taoist temples do not stand out from the landscape. They are nestled against the hills, back under the trees, blending in with the environment. At best man too blends in with nature. His highest achievement is to identify himself with the *Tao* and let it work through him.

This Taoist approach to nature has made a deep impression on Chinese art. It is no accident that the seventeenth century "Great Period" of Chinese art coincided with a great surge of Taoist influence on the Chinese sentiment and imagination. Painters took nature as their subject, and before assuming brush and silk would go out to nature, lose themselves in it, and become one with it. They would sit for half a day or fourteen years before making a stroke. The Chinese word for landscape painting is composed of the radicals for mountain and water, one of which suggests vastness and solitude, the other pliability, endurance, and continuous movement. Man's part in that vastness is small, so we have to look closely for him in the paintings if we find him at all. Usually he is climbing with his bundle, riding a buffalo, or poling a boat—man with his journey to make, his burden to carry, his hill to climb, his glimpse of beauty through the parting mists. He is not as formidable as a mountain; he does not live as long as a pine; yet he too belongs in the scheme of things as surely as the birds and the clouds. And through him as through the rest of the world flows the rhythmic movement of *Tao*.

Taoist naturalism was combined with a propensity for naturalness as well. Pomp and extravagance were regarded as pointless accretions. When Chuang Tzu's followers asked permission to give him a grand funeral he replied: "Heaven and earth are my inner and outer coffins. The sun, moon, and stars are my drapery, and the whole creation my funeral procession. What more do I want?" As with Rousseau, civilization tended to be condemned and the simplicity of primitive society idealized. "Let us have a small country with few inhabitants," said Lao Tzu. "Let the people return to the use of knotted cords [for keeping records]. Let them obtain their food sweet, their clothing beautiful, their homes comfortable, their rustic tasks pleasurable." Travel should be discouraged as pointless and conducive to idle curiosity. "The neighboring state might be so near at hand that one could hear the cocks crowing in it and dogs barking. But the people would grow old and die without ever having been there."[7]

This drive toward simplicity most separated the Taoists from the Confucianists. The basic values of the two schools did not differ widely, but the Taoists had small patience with the Confucian approach to securing them. All formalism, show, and ceremony left them cold. What could be hoped from punctiliousness or the meticulous observance of propriety? The whole approach was artificial, a lacquered surface which was bound to prove brittle and repressive. Confucianism here was but one instance of man's general tendency to approach life in the wrong mode. All calculated systems, every attempt to arrange life in neat apple-pie order, is pointless. Different ways of slicing the same reality, in the end none of them comes to more than Three in the Morning. And what is Three in the Morning? Once in the state of Sung hard times forced a keeper of monkeys to reduce the ration of nuts he could give his charges. "From now on," he announced, "it will be three in the morning and four in the evening." At once the monkeys howled a furious protest. The keeper agreed to reconsider. When he returned he said to them, "I see your point and have revised my proposal to accommodate it. It will be four in the morning and three in the evening." The monkeys accepted with delight.[8]

Another feature of Taoism is its notion of the relativity of all values and, as the correlate of this principle, the identity of contraries. Here Taoism tied in with the traditional Chinese symbolism of *yang* and *yin*, pictured as follows:

This polarity sums up all life's basic oppositions: good-evil, active-passive, positive-negative, light-dark, summer-winter, male-female, etc. But though its principles are in tension, they are not flatly opposed. They complement and counterbalance each other. Each invades the other's hemisphere and establishes itself in the very center of its opposite's territory. In the end both are resolved in an all-embracing circle, symbol of the final unity of *Tao*. Constantly turning and interchanging places, the opposites are but phases of a revolving wheel. Life does not move onward and upward towards a fixed pinnacle or pole. It turns and bends back upon itself until the self comes full-circle and knows that at center all things are one.

Those who meditate upon this profoundly symbolic figure, Taoists maintain, will find that it affords better access to the world's secrets than any length of words or philosophies. Faithful to it, Taoism eschews all clean-cut dichotomies. No perspective in this relative world can be considered as absolute. Who knows when the longest way around will prove the shortest way home? Or consider the relativity of dream and wakefulness. Chuang Tzu dreamed that he was a butterfly, and during the dream had no notion that he had ever been anything else. When he awoke, however, he was astonished to find that he was Chuang Tzu. But this left him with a question. Was he really Chuang Tzu who had dreamed he was a butterfly, or was he a butterfly now dreaming he was Chuang Tzu?

All values and concepts, then, are ultimately relative to the mind that entertains them. When it was suggested to the wren and cicada that there are birds that fly hundreds of miles without alighting, both quickly agreed that such a thing was impossible. "You and I know very well," they said, "that the furthest one can ever get even by the most tremendous effort is that elm-tree over there; and even this one can not be sure of reaching every time. Often one finds oneself dragged back to earth long before one gets there. All these stories about flying hundreds of miles at a stretch are sheer nonsense."[9]

In Taoist perspective even good and evil lose their absolute character. The West, encouraged in the last few centuries by puritanism, has tended to draw categorical distinctions between the two. Taoists are seldom this positive. They buttress their reticence with the story about a farmer whose horse ran away. His neighbor commiserated only to be told, "Who knows what's good or bad?" It was true. The next day the horse returned, bringing with it a drove of wild horses it had befriended in its wanderings. The neighbor came over again, this time to congratulate the farmer on his windfall. He was met with the same observation: "Who knows what is good or bad?" True this time too; the next day the farmer's son tried to mount one of the wild horses and fell off breaking his leg. Back came the neighbor, this time with more commiserations, only to encounter for the third time the same response, "Who knows what is good or bad?" And once again the farmer's point was well taken, for the following day soldiers came by commandeering for the army and because of his injury the son was not drafted. If this all sounds very much like Zen, it should; for Indian Buddhism processed through Chinese Taoism becomes Japanese Zen.

Taoism follows its principle of relativity to its logical limit, life and death themselves being regarded as relative phases of the Tao's embracing continuum. When Chuang Tzu's wife died, a friend came to join in the rites of mourning. He was surprised to find Chuang Tzu drumming upon an inverted rice bowl and singing a song.

"After all," said his friend, "she lived with you, brought up your children, grew old along with you. That you should not mourn for her is bad enough; but to let your friends find you drumming and singing—that is going too far!"

"You misjudge me," said Chuang Tzu. "When she died I was in despair, as any man well might be. But soon, pondering on what had happened, I told myself that in death no strange new fate befalls us. . . . If some one is tired and has gone to lie down, we do not pursue him with hooting and bawling. She whom I have lost has lain down to sleep for awhile in the Great Inner Room. To break in upon her rest with the noise of lamentation would but show that I know nothing of nature's Sovereign Law. That is why I ceased to mourn."[10]

Elsewhere Chuang Tzu expressed his confidence in the face of death directly:

> There is the globe,
> The foundation of my bodily existence.
> It wears me out with work and duties,
> It gives me rest in old age,
> It gives me peace in death.
> For the one who supplied me with what I needed in life
> Will also give me what I need in death.[11]

It is no surprise to find an outlook as averse to violence as Taoism verging on strict pacifism in its attitude toward war. There are passages in the *Tao Te Ching* that read almost like the *Sermon on the Mount*.

> One who would guide a leader of men in the uses of life
> Will warn him against the use of arms for conquest.
> Even the finest arms are an instrument of evil:
> An army's harvest is a waste of thorns.
>
> In time of war men civilized in peace
> Turn from their higher to their lower nature.
> But triumph is not beautiful.
> He who thinks triumph beautiful
> Is one with a will to kill.
> The death of a multitude is cause for mourning:
> Conduct your triumph as a funeral. (Chs. 30, 31, rearranged.)

That in traditional China the scholar ranked at the top of the social scale may be the doing of Confucius, but Taoism is fully as responsible for placing the soldier at the bottom. "The way for a vital man to go is not the way of a soldier." Only the man "who recognizes all men as members of his own body is a sound man to guard them. . . . Heaven arms with compassion those whom she would not see destroyed."

War is a solemn matter, and Taoism spoke to life's solemn issues. Yet it always retained in its approach to every problem a quality of lightness verging on gaiety. There is a sophistication, an urbanity, a charm about the perspective which is infectious. "He who feels punctured," observes the *Tao Te Ching*, "must once have been a bubble." The economy, directness, and fundamental good humor of such a statement is typical of its entire outlook. In its freedom from the tortured, heavy-booted approach to life it is at one with the rest of China; but it is also, as we have seen, free of the Confucian tendency toward rigidity and formalism. Taoist literature is full of dialogues with Confucianists in which the latter are shown up as stuffy and pompous. An instance is the story of Chuang Tzu (the Taoist) and Hui Tzu (the Confucianist) who were strolling one day on a bridge over the Hao river. Observed Chuang Tzu:

"Look how the minnows dart hither and thither at will. Such is the pleasure fish enjoy."

"You are not a fish," responded Hui Tzu. "How do you know what gives pleasure to fish?"

"You are not I," said Chuang Tzu. "How do you know I do not know what gives pleasure to fish?"[12]

CONCLUSION

Blending like *yang* and *yin* themselves, Taoism and Confucianism represent the two indigenous poles of the Chinese outlook. Confucius represents the classical, Lao Tzu the romantic. Confucius stresses social responsibility, Lao Tzu sings the glories of spontaneity and naturalness. Confucius' focus is always on man, Lao Tzu's beyond man. As the Chinese themselves say, Confucius roams within society, Lao Tzu wanders beyond. Something in life reaches out in each of these directions, and Chinese civilization would certainly have been poorer if either had not emerged.

There are books whose first reading casts a spell never quite undone, the reason being that they speak to the deepest "me" in the reader. For all who quicken to the thought that anywhere, anytime, *Tao* can dwell within us, the *Tao Te Ching* is such a book. Mostly it has been so for the Chinese, but a contemporary American poet equally can find it "the straightest, most logical explanation as yet advanced for the continuance of life, the most logical use yet advised for enjoying it."[13] Though obviously never practiced to perfection, its lessons of simplicity and openness have been for millions of Chinese a joyful guide.

There is a being, wonderful, perfect;
It existed before heaven and earth.
How quiet it is!
How spiritual it is!
It stands alone and it does not change.
It moves around and around, but does not on this account suffer.
All life comes from it.
It wraps everything with its love as in a garment, and yet it claims no honor,
    it does not demand to be Lord.
I do not know its name, and so I call it Tao, the Way, and I rejoice in its
    power.[14]

SUGGESTIONS FOR FURTHER READING

The best single volume dealing with the Taoist movement as a whole has reached me too late to be utilized in the present chapter but in time, happily, for mention. It is Holmes Welch's *The Parting of the Way: Lao Tzu and the Taoist Movement* (Boston: Beacon Press, 1957).

Paul Carus' *The Canon of Reason and Virtue* (LaSalle: Open Court

Publishing Co.) continues as probably the best general translation of the *Tao Te Ching* in English.

The finest introductions to Esoteric Taoism are Chung-Yuan Chang's "An Introduction to Taoist Yoga," which appeared in the March, 1956, issue of *The Review of Religion*, and Arthur Waley's *The Way and Its Power* (London: George Allen & Unwin, 1934). As an interesting and suggestive sequel to these, the reader may wish to look at *The Secret of the Golden Flower* (London: Routledge & Kegan Paul, 1931) in which Richard Wilhelm and Carl Jung relate this ancient Taoist yoga to some themes in contemporary analytic psychology.

I personally consider Witter Bynner's translation of the *Tao Te Ching* —*The Way of Life According to Lao Tzu* (New York: John Day, 1944) on which I have drawn heavily for quotations—the best English rendition of Philosophical Taoism. Some scholars feel that it sacrifices literal accuracy for poetic beauty, but the Chinese text is in itself so cryptic as scarcely to support the claim of any translation to be literal. My own view is that if Waley's translation gives us the perspective that went into the *Tao Te Ching*, Bynner's gives us the perspective that has come out of it; if Waley's translation gives us the *Tao Te Ching* as it was written, Bynner's gives us the *Tao Te Ching* as it has been read.

The first third of Arthur Waley's *Three Ways of Thought in Ancient China* (recently made available as an 85 cent Doubleday Anchor Book) consists of a delightful presentation of the best of Chuang Tzu, the foremost popularizer of a Taoism that is largely Philosophical but not without occasional Esoteric breakthroughs.

An inexpensive translation of the *Tao Te Ching* is R. B. Blakney's 35 cent Mentor Edition titled *The Way of Life: Lao Tzu*.

6

Islam

MISUNDERSTANDINGS begin with the very name of this religion. It is often
referred to in the West as Mohammedanism, after the prophet who gave
it definite form. From the Muslim perspective, this is inaccurate and
offensive. It is inaccurate, they say, because Muhammed didn't shape
this religion, God did. Muhammed merely transmitted it from God to
his people. The title is offensive because it gives the impression that
Islam focuses around Muhammed the man instead of God. To name
Christianity after Christ, they say, is fitting, for Christians believe that
Christ was God. But to call Islam Muhammedanism is like calling
Christianity St. Paulism. The proper name of this religion is Islam. Derived from the word *salam* which means primarily "peace" but in a secondary sense "surrender," its full connotation is "the perfect peace that
comes when one's life is surrendered to God." The corresponding adjec-
tive is *Muslim*.

BACKGROUND

"Around the name of the Arabs," writes Philip Hitti, "gleams that
halo which belongs to the world-conquerors. Within a century after their
rise this people became the masters of an empire extending from the
shores of the Atlantic Ocean to the confines of China, an empire greater
than that of Rome at its zenith. In this period of unprecedented expansion they 'assimilated to their creed, speech, and even physical type,
more aliens than any stock before or since, not excepting the Hellenic,
the Roman, the Anglo-Saxon, or the Russian.' "[1]

Central in this Arab rise to greatness was their religion, Islam. If we ask how this religion came into being, an external answer would begin by noting the economic and political currents playing over Arabia in the sixth and seventh centuries A.D. when Muhammed lived, and would then develop a picture of the environmental factors that brought this outlook into being. Viewed through Muslim eyes the question assumes a different cast. From the Muslim point of view the story of Islam begins not with Muhammed in sixth century Arabia but with God. "In the beginning God . . ." opens the book of Genesis. The Koran agrees. It differs only in using the word *Allah*. Allah is formed by joining the definite article *al* (meaning "the") with *Illah* (God). Literally, Allah means "the God." Not *a* God for there is only one. *The* God.

Allah then created the world, and after it man. The name of this first man? Adam. The descendants of Adam lead to Noah who has a son named Shem. This is where the word Semite comes from; a Semite, literally, is a descendant of Shem. Like the Jews the Arabs regard themselves as a Semitic people. The descendants of Shem are traced to Abraham and still we are within a common tradition. Indeed, it was the submission of Abraham in the supreme test, the attempted sacrifice of his son described in the Koran by the verb *aslama*, that appears to have provided Islam with its name. Abraham marries Sarah. Sarah has no son and Abraham, wanting to continue his line, takes Hagar for his wife as well. Hagar bears him a son, Ishmael, whereupon Sarah also has a son named Isaac. Sarah then demands that Abraham banish Ishmael and Hagar from the tribe. Here we come to the first divergence between the Koranic and Biblical accounts. According to the Koran, Ishmael goes to Mecca. His descendants, growing up in Arabia, are Muslims whereas those of Isaac, who remains in Palestine, are Jews.

The Seal of the Prophets

Following the line from Ishmael in Arabia we come eventually in the latter half of the sixth century A.D. to Muhammed, the prophet through whom Islam emerged, orthodox Muslims would say, in its full and final focus. There had been true prophets of God before him but he was their culmination; hence he is called "The Seal of the Prophets"—there will be no more after him.

The world into which Muhammed was born is described by subsequent Muslims in a single word: barbaric. Life under the conditions of the desert had never been serene. The Bedouin felt almost no obligation to anyone outside his tribe. Scarcity of material goods and a fighting mood chronically inflamed by the blazing sun had made brigandage a regional institution and the proof of virility. In the sixth century A.D. political deadlock and the collapse of the magistrate in the leading city of Mecca made this generally chaotic situation even worse. Drunken orgies often ending in brawls and bloodshed were commonplace. The gaming impulse, always strong among nomads, was uncontrolled, with Meccan gambling tables busy the night through. Dancing girls moved from tent to tent inflaming the passions of the impetuous sons of the desert. Meanwhile the prevailing religion was providing no check whatever. Best described as an animistic polytheism, it peopled the desert with beastly sprites called *jinn* or demons. Fantastic personifications of the terrors of the desert, there is no evidence that they inspired anything in the way of genuine religious enthusiasm much less moral conduct. On the whole, conditions could hardly have been better calculated to produce a smoldering undercurrent which erupted in sudden affrays and blood feuds some of which stretched on for half a century. The time was ripe for a deliverer.

He was born into the leading tribe of Mecca, the Koreish, in approximately 571 A.D. He came to be called Muhammed or "highly praised," a name that has since been borne by more male children than any other in the world. His early life was cradled in tragedy, for his father died a few days before he was born, his mother when he was six, and his grandfather, who cared for him after his mother's death, when he was nine. Thereafter he was taken into his uncle's home. Though the latter's declining fortunes forced the young orphan to work hard minding his uncle's flocks, he was warmly accepted in his new home. The angels of God, we are told, were opening out Muhammed's heart and filling it with light.

The description epitomizes his early character as this comes down to us by tradition. Pure-hearted and beloved in his circle, he was, it is said, of sweet and gentle disposition. His bereavements having made him sensitive to human suffering in every form, he was always ready to help others, especially the poor and the weak. His sense of honor, duty, and fidelity won him as he grew older the high and enviable titles of "The True," "The Upright," "The Trustworthy One." Yet despite his concern for others he remained removed from them in outlook and ways, isolated in the midst of an effete and chaotic society. As he grew from childhood to youth and from youth to manhood the lawless strife of his contemporaries, the repeated outbursts of pointless quarrels among the tribes frequenting the Meccan fairs, and the general immorality and cynicism of the day combined to produce in the prophet-to-be a sustained reaction of horror and disgust. Silently, broodingly, his thoughts turned inward.

Upon reaching maturity he took up the caravan business and at the age of twenty-five entered the service of a wealthy widow named Khadija. His prudence and integrity impressed her greatly, and gradually their relation deepened into affection and love. Though she was fifteen years his senior they were married. The match proved happy in every respect. During the long periods that lay ahead in which the world was to turn desolate before Muhammed's eyes and no one was to believe in him, not even himself, Khadija was to remain steadfast at his side, consoling him and keeping alive hope's thin flame. "God," tradition was to say, "comforted him through her, for she made his burden light."

There were, however, fifteen years of preparation and spiritual communion after his marriage before his ministry was to begin. There was a huge, barren rock on the outskirts of Mecca known as Mount Hira, torn by cleft and ravine, erupting unshadowed and flowerless from the desert sands. In this rock was a cave which Muhammed, in need of deep solitude, began to frequent. Peering into the mysteries of good and evil, unable to accept the crudeness, superstition, and fratricide that were accepted as normal, "this great fiery heart, seething, simmering like a great furnace of thoughts," was reaching out for God.[2]

The desert *jinn* were irrelevant to this quest but one deity was not. Named Allah, he was worshipped by the Meccans not as the only God but as an impressive one nonetheless. Creator, supreme provider, and determiner of man's destiny, he was capable of inspiring authentic religious feeling and genuine devotion. Through vigils often lasting the entire night, Allah's reality gradually became for Muhammed increasingly evident and impressive. Fearful and wonderful, real as life, real as death, real as the universe he had ordained, Allah, Muhammed became convinced, was far greater than his countrymen had supposed. This God whose majesty overflowed a desert cave to fill all heaven and earth was surely not a god or even the greatest of gods. He was what his name literally claimed: the God, One and only, One without rival. Soon from this mountain cave was to sound the greatest phrase of the Arabic language; the deep, electrifying cry which was to rally a people and explode their power to the limits of the known world: *La ilaha illa Allah!* There is no God but Allah!

But first the prophet must receive his commission. Gradually as Muhammed's visits to the cave became more compelling, the command which in retrospect appeared predestined took form. It was the same command that had fallen earlier on Abraham, Moses, Samuel, Isaiah, and Jesus. Wherever, whenever this call comes its form may differ but its essence is the same. A voice falls from heaven saying, "Thou art the man." On the Night of Power and Excellence, as a strange peace pervaded creation and all nature was turned towards its Lord, in the middle of that night, say the Muslims, the Book was opened to a ready soul. As he lay on the floor of the cave, his mind locked in deepest contemplation, a voice commanded Muhammed to cry. Twice the voice commanded and Muhammed resisted, wishing nothing so much as to escape from the overwhelming Presence. "Cry!" commanded the voice for the third time.

"What shall I cry?" answered Muhammed in terror. The answer came back:

> Cry—in the name of thy Lord!
> Who created man from blood coagulated.
> Cry! Thy Lord is wondrous kind
> Who by the pen has taught mankind
> Things they knew not (being blind).[3]

Arousing from his trance, Muhammed felt as if the words he had heard had been branded on his soul. Terrified, he rushed home and fell into paroxysms. Coming to himself, he told Khadija that he had become either a prophet or "one possessed—mad." At first she resisted this disjunction but on hearing his full story she became his first convert—which, Muslims often remark, in itself speaks well for his authenticity for if anyone knows a man thoroughly it is his wife. "Rejoice, O dear husband, and be of good cheer," she said, "Thou wilt be the Prophet of this people."[4]

We can imagine the spiritual anguish, the mental doubts, the waves of misgivings which followed in the wake of this experience. Was the voice really God's? Would it come again? Above all, what would it require?

It returned again and again and its command was always the same— to preach. "O thou, inwrapped in thy mantle, arise and warn, and glorify thy Lord." Muhammed's life was no more his own. From that time forth it was given to God and to man, preaching with unswerving purpose in the face of relentless persecution, insult, and outrage, the words which God was to transmit for twenty-three years.

The content of this revelation may be reserved for later sections. Here we need only speak of the response it drew and note that its appeal throughout was to man's reason.

In an age charged with supernaturalism, when miracles were accepted as the stock-in-trade of the most ordinary saint, Muhammed refused to traffic with human weakness and credulity. To miracle-hungry idolators seeking signs and portents he cut the issue clean: "God has not sent me to work wonders; He has sent me to preach to you. My Lord be praised! Am I more than a man sent as an apostle?"[5] From first to last he resisted every impulse to glamorize his own person. "I never said that Allah's treasures are in my hand, that I knew the hidden things, or that I was an angel. . . . I am only a preacher of God's words, the bringer of God's message to mankind."[6] If signs be sought, let them be not of Muhammed's greatness but of God's, and for these one need only open one's eyes. The heavenly bodies holding their swift silent course in the vault of heaven, the incredible order of the universe, the rain that falls to relieve the parched earth, palms bending with golden fruit, ships that glide across the seas laden with goodness for man—can these be the handwork of gods of stone? What fools to cry for signs when creation harbors nothing else! In an age of credulity, Muhammed taught respect for the world's incontrovertible order which was to awaken Muslim science before Christian. Only one miracle he claimed, that of the Koran itself. That he by his own devices could have produced such truth—this was the one naturalistic hypothesis he could not accept.

As for the reaction to his message, it was violently hostile. The reasons for this hostility can be reduced to three: its uncompromising monotheism threatened the considerable revenue that was coming to Mecca from Bedouin pilgrimages to its three hundred sixty shrines (one for every day of the lunar year); its moral teachings demanded an end to the licentiousness which citizens were disinclined to give up; and its social content was dynamite to an effete and unjust economic order. In a society riven with class distinctions, the new Prophet was preaching a message intensely democratic, insisting that in the sight of his Lord all men were equal.

As such a teaching suited neither their taste nor their privilege, the Meccan leaders were determined to have none of it. They began their attack with ridicule: pin-pricks of laughter, petty insults, and hoots of derision. When these proved ineffective their words took a fiercer turn in abuse, calumny, vilification, and threat. When these, too, failed they turned from taunts to open persecution. They covered Muhammed and his followers with dirt and filth while they were engaged in their devotions. They pelted them with stones, beat them with sticks, threw them in prison, and tried to starve them out by refusing to sell to them. A favorite form of torture was to expose them to the burning heat of the desert where reduced by thirst they would be offered the alternative of adoring idols or death. The first *muezzin* to call the faithful to prayer, being a slave, was taken by his master to the desert, forced to lie shirtless on his back on the burning sand with a large stone on his chest on which were inscribed the words, "There shalt thou remain until thou art dead or thou hast abjured Islam." The slave refused to surrender. As he lay dying of thirst his only word, which he kept repeating over and over, was "*ahadun, ahadun,*" "One [God], one," until his master seeing that he would never recant sold him to another Muslim.

His heroism was typical. At the sacrifice of all their worldly interests and hopes, and at repeated risks of death itself, followers adhered to the new prophet with a loyalty and devotion seldom paralleled in the world's history. "Never since the days when primitive Christianity startled the world from its sleep and waged a mortal conflict with hea-thenism," wrote a scholar whose words assume added weight because he was on the whole a severe critic of Islam, "had men seen the like arousing of spiritual life—the like faith that suffered sacrifices, and took joyfully the spoiling of goods for conscience' sake."[7] Muhammed himself set the pattern for their fidelity. Standing with his band, as it were, in the lion's mouth, his heart never flinched nor wavered. On the contrary, persecution only caused him to throw his heart and soul more fervently into his preaching. By the wondrous sights of nature—her noonday brightness, the night when she spread her veil, the dawn when she appeared in glory—he adjured his listeners to turn from their false gods, abandon their evil ways, and prepare for the day of reckoning when the earth would be folded up and none would be near but Allah.

At first the odds were so heavily against him that he made few con-verts; three long years of heartbreaking effort yielded less than forty. But his enemies could do nothing to seal the hearts of the Meccans against his burning words forever. Slowly but steadily men of energy, talent, and worth became convinced of the truth of his message until by the end of a decade several hundred families were acclaiming him as God's authen-tic spokesman.

The Flight that Led to Victory

By this time the Meccan nobility was thoroughly alarmed. What had begun, seemingly, as a pretentious claim on the part of a half-crazed camel driver to be God's prophet had turned into a serious revolutionary movement that was threatening their very existence. They were determined to silence the fiery troublemaker forever.

As he faced this severest crisis of his career, Muhammed was suddenly waited on by a delegation of about seventy-five of the leading citizens of Yathrib, a city some two hundred miles to Mecca's north. Through pilgrims and other visitors to Mecca, Muhammed's teachings had won a firm hold in Yathrib. The city was facing internal rivalries that put it in need of a strong leader from without and Muhammed looked like the man. After due thought and upon receiving his delegates' pledge that they would worship none but God, that they would observe the precepts of Islam, that they would obey him in all that was right, and defend him and his as they would their women and children, Muhammed agreed to come. About a hundred of his followers' families preceded him. When the Meccan leaders got wind of the exodus they did everything in their power to prevent his going, but he eluded their watch and hid with a companion in a crevice south of the city. Horsemen scouring the countryside came so close to discovering them that Muhammed's companion was moved to despair. "We are but two," he cried. "Nay, we are three," Muhammed answered, "for God is with us." The Koran agrees. "He was with them," it observes, for they were not discovered. After three days when the search had slackened, they managed to procure two camels and make their hazardous way by unfrequented paths to the city of their destination.

The year was 622 A.D. The migration—known in Arabic as the *Hijrah* or *Hegira* and translated the "flight"—is regarded by Muslims as the turning point in world history and is the year from which they date their calendar. Yathrib soon changed its name to Medinat un-Nabi, the City of the Prophet, and then by contraction simply to Medina, "the city."

From the moment of his arrival at Medina, Muhammed assumes a different role. From prophecy he is rocketed into administration. The despised preacher becomes a masterful politician; the prophet is transformed into statesman. We see him now as the king not merely of the hearts of a handful of devotees but of the collective life of a city, its judge and general as well as its teacher.

Even his enemies concede that he plays his new role brilliantly. Faced with problems of extraordinary complexity, he turns out to be extraordinarily endowed as a statesman. Supreme magistrate, he continues to lead as he had in the days of his obscurity, an unpretentious life. Scorning palaces, he continues to live in an ordinary clay house, milks his own goats, and is accessible day or night to the humblest of his subjects. Often seen mending his own clothes, "no emperor with his tiaras was obeyed as this man in a cloak of his own clouting."⁸ God, say Muslim historians, had indeed put before him the key to the treasures of this world but he refused it.

Tradition depicts his administration as an ideal blend of justice and mercy. As chief of state and trustee of the life and liberty of his people, he exercised the justice necessary for order, unflinchingly meting out punishment to those who were guilty. When the injury was toward himself, on the other hand, he was gentle and merciful even to his enemies. In all, the Medinese found him a master whom it was as difficult not to love as not to obey for he had, as one biographer has written, "the gift of influencing men, and he had the nobility only to influence them for good."⁹

For the remaining ten years of his life, his personal history merged with that of the Medinese commonwealth of which he was the center. Exercising superb statecraft, he welded the five heterogeneous and conflicting tribes of the city, two of which were Jewish, into an orderly confederation. The task was not an easy one and despite the freedom he permitted the Jews considerable blood was spilt in the process. But in the end he succeeded in awakening in the citizens a spirit of union unknown in the city's history. His reputation spread and people began to flock from every part of Arabia to see the man who had wrought this achievement.

There followed the struggle with the Meccans for the mind of Arabia as a whole. In the second year of the *Hijrah*, the Medinese won a spectacular victory over a Meccan army that many times outmanned and outspeared them, and interpreted the victory as a clear sign that the angels of heaven were battling on their side. The following year, however, witnessed a reversal during which Muhammed himself was wounded. The Meccans failed to follow up their victory until two years later when they laid siege to Medina in a last desperate effort to force the Muslims to capitulate. The failure of this effort turned the tide permanently in Muhammed's favor and within three years, or eight years after his Flight from Mecca, he who had left a fugitive returned almost unopposed as a conqueror. The city that had treated him cruelly now lay at his feet with his old persecutors at his mercy. He refused, however, to press his victory; in the hour of his triumph the past was forgotten. Making his way to the famous Kaaba stone which had been the religious focus of Mecca since time immemorial and which he now rededicated to

Allah, he accepted the almost mass conversion of the city but returned himself to Medina.

Two years later, in 632 A.D. (10 A.H.), Muhammed died with virtually all of Arabia under his control. With all the power of armies, police, and civil service, no other Arab had ever succeeded in uniting his countrymen as he had. By the time a century had passed, his followers had conquered Armenia, Persia, Syria, Palestine, Iraq, Egypt, and Spain, and had crossed the Pyrenees into France. But for their defeat by Charles Martel in the Battle of Tours in 732 A.D., the entire Western world might today be Muslim. Within a brief span of mortal life, Muhammed had "called forth out of unpromising material a nation never united before, in a country that was hitherto but a geographical expression; established a religion which in vast areas superseded Christianity and Judaism and still claims the adherence of a goodly portion of the human race; and laid the basis of an empire that was soon to embrace within its far-flung boundaries the fairest provinces of the then civilized world."[10]

Muslims have a simple explanation. "The entire work," they say, "was the work of God."

The Standing Miracle

The blend of admiration, respect, and affection which the devout Muslim feels for Muhammed is an impressive fact of religious history. Rarely will he mention the Prophet's name without the benediction "Peace be upon him!" And today as for thirteen centuries the faithful will be found praying, "Salam upon you, O Prophet of God."

Despite their fervor for the Prophet, however, Muslims never mistake him for the earthly cornerstone of their faith. This place is reserved for Islam's bible, the Koran. So great was Muhammed's personal regard for it that he considered it the only miracle God worked through him—his "standing miracle" as he called it. Meaning "to read" or "to recite," the purposes for which it was intended, the Koran is perhaps the most read book in the world. Certainly it is the most often memorized and possibly it exerts the most influence on those who read it.

The Koran is four-fifths the length of the New Testament. It is divided into one hundred fourteen chapters or *surahs* which with the exception of the short first chapter that figures in the Muslim's daily prayers are arranged in almost exact order of decreasing length. Thus, Surah Two has 286 verses, Surah Three 200, down to Surah One Hundred Fourteen which has only six.

Muslim attitudes toward the Koran run the full gamut one finds in

Christian approaches to the Bible but tend to be fundamentalistic. According to the strictly orthodox view, the Koran's every letter was directly dictated by God. Its words came to Muhammed in manageable segments over twenty-three years through voices that seemed at first to vary and sometimes sounded like "the reverberating of bells" but gradually focused in a single voice that became identified as Gabriel's. Some Muslims take the references to this angelic intermediary literally; others say he may have been raised by Muhammed's mind in the hours of its greatest fervor. In either case no orthodox Muslim doubts the divine origin of the words themselves. Emblazoned on Muhammed's mind, they were recorded by his followers on bones and bark and leaves and scraps of parchment with God preserving their literal accuracy throughout.

Islam assumes that the Bibles of the Jews and Christians too were originally authentic revelations from God, which fact entitles those who hold them sacred to be classed with Muslims as "People of the Book." Nevertheless, the Old and New Testaments share two defects from which the Koran is free. Having been revealed at earlier stages in man's spiritual development when, as with a child, he was incapable of receiving the full truth, they are incomplete. Beyond this, the Jewish and Christian Bibles have in the process of transmission become partially corrupted, a fact that explains the discrepancies that occasionally appear between their accounts and parallel ones in the Koran. Exemption from these two limitations makes the Koran the final and infallible revelation of God's will. Its second chapter caps the latter point categorically: "There is no doubt in this book."

No book in the religious heritage of any other culture is as inaccessible to Western appreciation as the Koran. Carlyle said of it, "It is as toilsome reading as I ever undertook, a wearisome, confused jumble, crude, incondite. Nothing but a sense of duty could carry any European through the Koran." Muslims, by contrast, consider it an incontrovertible miracle. As we have seen, the only miracle Muhammed claimed was that he, unschooled to the extent that he could barely write his own name, should have produced a book embodying all wisdom and theology essential to human life which in addition is grammatically perfect and without poetic equal. "Ask you a greater miracle than this, O unbelieving people! than to have your vulgar tongue chosen as the language of that incomparable Book, one piece of which puts to shame all your golden poesy and suspended songs?"

We cannot hope to bridge this discrepancy between a Muslim's feeling for the Koran and that of an outsider, but it may help toward explaining it to suggest that the difference stems in part from language as an aspect of racial psychology. "No people in the world," writes Philip Hitti, "are so moved by the word, spoken or written, as the Arabs. Hardly any language seems capable of exercising over the minds of its users such irresistible influence as Arabic." Even today, crowds in Cairo, Damascus, or Baghdad can be stirred to the highest emotional pitch by statements which when translated seem banal. The music, the rhyme, the rhythm produce a powerfully hypnotic effect.

It is not difficult to surmise why this is so. Nomads are prohibited by their transient way of life from developing visual art. Their architecture is restricted to flapping tents, their crafts to the few pots and fabrics they can carry with them. With life one long process of packing and unpacking, one is not likely to accumulate a museum. Blocked on the visual side by the need to keep gear light, the nomad's art took a verbal turn. "Wisdom," says a famous adage, "has alighted on three things: the brain of the Franks, the hands of the Chinese, and the tongue of the Arabs."[11]

Grant that the Arabs channeled their esthetic talents into words; grant their unique susceptibility to the language they developed; grant finally that no one else has played on Arabic's deep-toned instrument with Muhammed's power, and we can begin to appreciate the insistence of many Muslims that the Koran cannot be translated. While Christian Bible Societies have been busy translating God's Word into every known tongue, Muslims have turned their primary efforts to teaching the people of other tongues the language in which God spoke for all time with incomparable force and directness.[12]

Face to face with this unique language barrier we will gain little by speaking further of the Koran itself. We must turn to its ideas insofar as these can be transposed into a foreign tongue.

BASIC THEOLOGICAL CONCEPTS

The basic theological concepts of Islam as outlined in the sweeping strokes of the Koran are at most points identical with those of Judaism and Christianity, its neighbors. We shall confine our attention in this section to the most important four: Allah, Creation, Man, and the Day of Judgment.

As in other high religions, everything in Islam centers in the primal fact of God or Allah. To begin with, Allah is immaterial and hence invisible. For the Arabs this cast no doubt on his reality for they had never learned the art of ignoring everything but what could be seen. As desert dwellers, the notion of invisible hands that drove the blasts that swept the desert and formed the deceptive mirages that lured the traveler to his destruction was always with them.

The Koran did not introduce the Arab to the unseen world of the spirit. What it did by way of innovation was to focus the divine in a single God, a unified Personal Will who overshadows the entire universe with his power and grace. The indelible contribution of Islam to Arabic religion was monotheism.

To the Muslim, we must add, monotheism is Islam's contribution not simply to Arabic religion but to the religion of man in its entirety. Hinduism's prolific images he takes as obvious proof that this religion has never really approached the worship of one God only. Judaism, standing in the tradition the Koran culminates, was correctly instructed in its great *Shema*: "Hear O Israel, the Lord our God, the Lord is One." Alas, from the Muslim perspective the Jews prior to Muhammed's reminder departed tragically from this truth. They reverted to the worship of household gods and golden calves, episodes that figure far more frequently in the Koran than in the Old Testament; in the persons of the Scribes and Pharisees they approached idolatry in their worship of the Law. Christians, for their part, have in Islam's eyes compromised their monotheism by deifying Christ. Islam honors Jesus as a true prophet of God. It even accepts the Christian doctrine of his virgin birth.[13] But at the doctrine of the Incarnation and Trinity it draws the line, seeing these as concessions to man's inclination to seek a compromise between the human and the divine. In the words of the Koran: "They say the God of mercy hath gotten to himself a son. Now have ye uttered a grievous thing. . . . It is not meet for God to have children" (iii:78, xix: 93). When Jesus claimed to be the Son of God, He was thinking of God's Fatherhood as embracing all mankind. Every human being was to him a child of God. The accretions of councils and theologies have carried Christian doctrine a long way from the simple purity of the Nazarene.

Against all these apostasies the Muslim sees the Koran taking its stand as the grand advocate of God's unity. The strength of the Arab's arms was to wax and wane but again and again the Prophet's vision of a single God triumphed over peoples like the Mongols and the Turks who would subdue his followers in physical combat. Almost every page of the Koran cries out with burning fervor: "Your God is one God. . . . There is no God but He—the Living, the Eternal" (ii:158, 255).

Islam is so well known for its recognition of the majesty and might of its one God that this point needs little documentation. Allah is almighty, omnipotent, Lord of the worlds, the Author of heaven and earth, the Creator of life and death in whose hand is dominion and irresistible power. Where the outsider has often misjudged Allah is in picturing him as domineering and ruthless; "a pitiless tyrant, who plays with humanity as on a chess-board, and works out His game without regard to the sacrifice of the pieces" is one not atypical Western characterization. Muslims see him otherwise. He who is Lord of the worlds is also

the Holy, the Peaceful, the Faithful, the Guardian over His servants, the Shelterer of the orphan, the Guide of the erring, the Deliverer from every affliction, the Friend of the bereaved, the Consoler of the afflicted; in His hand is good, and He is the generous Lord, the Gracious, the Hearer, the Near-at-Hand, the Compassionate, the Merciful, the Very-forgiving, whose love for man is more tender than that of the mother-bird for her young.[14]

Because of Allah's grace the world of the Koran, despite its heavy warnings to the unrighteous, is a world of joy. There is air and sun and a confidence not only in ultimate justice but also in help along the way and pardon for the contrite.

By the noonday brightness, and by the night when it darkeneth, thy Lord hath not forsaken thee, neither hath He been displeased. Surely the future shall be better for thee than the past; and in the end He shall be bounteous to thee, and thou shalt be satisfied. Did He not find thee an orphan, and give thee a home; erring, and guided thee; needy, and enriched thee? (xciii).

Standing beneath God's gracious skies, the Muslim can at any moment lift his heart directly into the divine presence, there to receive both strength and guidance for the living of his days. He has such ready access to the divine because between man and Allah stands nothing.

Is He not closer than the vein of thy neck? Thou needest not raise thy voice, for He knoweth the secret whisper, and what is yet more hidden. . . . He knows what is in the land and in the sea; no leaf falleth but He knoweth it; nor is there a grain in the darkness under the earth, nor a thing, green or sere, but it is recorded (vi: 12, 59).

Allah, then, is one, immaterial, all-powerful, all-pervading, and benevolent. He is also creator, which brings us to the second basic concept in Islam. In the Islamic conception the world did not emerge, as the Hindus would have it, by some process of unconscious emanation from the divine. It was created by a deliberate act of God's will: "He hath created the heavens and the earth" (xvi:3). This fact carries two important consequences. First, the world of matter is completely real. It is dependent to be sure on God as its creator, but once originated it is as real as anything there is. Herein lies the basis of Muslim science which during Europe's Dark Age flourished in the Near East as nowhere else. Second, being the handiwork of a God who is both great and good, the world of matter must likewise be basically good. "No defect canst thou see in the creation of the God of mercy; repeat the gaze, seest thou a single flaw" (lxvii:4). Here we meet a confidence in the material aspects of life and existence which we shall find pervading the other two semitically originated religions, Judaism and Christianity, as well.

Wonderful as is Allah's material creation—and the Koran abounds in lyric descriptions of the majesties of heaven and earth—God's supreme accomplishment lies in the fact that "He hath created man" (xvi:3). Coming to Islam as we do after surveying Indic and Far Eastern religions, the most important thing to note about the Muslim view of man is its appreciation of both the ultimacy and value of individuality. In the religions of the Far East, the indivisible, all-encompassing cosmic spirit is the primary fact and the fleeting expressions of individuality have no permanence or value. But for Islam individuality is not only fully real but also good in principle. As expressed in the human soul it is also eternal, for once created the soul lives forever. Value, virtue, goodness, and spiritual fulfillment come by expressing one's unique self by virtue of which one is different from anyone or anything else. As a great Muslim philosopher has written, "This inexplicable finite centre of experience is the fundamental fact of the universe. All life is individual; there is no such thing as universal life. God Himself is an individual: He is the most unique individual."[15]

So intense and vivid is the Koran's feel for Allah's power and sovereign will that some interpreters have concluded that it eclipses man's freedom. That there is in Islam a problem of reconciling man's free will with God's omnipotence no Muslim will deny. What he does deny is, first, that the problem is more acute in Islam than in any other developed theology, and second, that it lands the Muslim in fatalism. In the final analysis man is master of his conduct and completely responsible for the decisions he makes. "Whoever gets to himself a sin, gets it solely on his own responsibility" (iv:111). "Whoever goes astray, he himself bears the whole responsibility of wandering" (x:103).

This belief in man's freedom and responsibility leads directly to Islam's doctrine of the afterlife. For the Muslim life on earth is the seedbed of an eternal future. It will be followed by a day of reckoning which is foreshadowed in the most awesome terms. "When the sun shall be folded up, and the stars shall fall, and when the mountains shall be set in motion. . . . and the seas shall boil. . . . then shall every soul know what it hath done" (lxxxi). On that day of judgment each individual will be accountable for the way he has lived. "Every man's actions have we hung round his neck, and on the last day shall be laid before him a wide-open Book" (xvii:13).

Depending on how it fares in this accounting the soul will then repair either to Heaven or Hell. In the Koran these conditions are described with all the vividness of Eastern imagery. Heaven abounds in deep rivers of cool, crystal water, lush fruit and vegetation, boundless fertility, and beautiful mansions with gracious attendants. Hell's portrayal is at times equally graphic with its account of molten metal, boiling liquids, and the fire that splits everything to pieces. Conservative Muslims take these descriptions literally; others as symbolically as modernist Christians read New Testament passages about pearly gates and streets of gold. In defense of their allegorical interpretation, these liberal Muslims quote the Koran itself: "Some of the signs are firm— these are the basis of the book—and others are figurative" (iii:5). Also supporting the non-materialistic interpretation of paradise is Muhammed's statement that for the favored of God, to "see his Lord's face night and morning [is] a felicity which will surpass all the pleasures of the body, as the ocean surpasses a drop of sweat."[16] From this view, the joy of joys consists in the beatific vision in which the veil which divides man from Allah will be rent forever and his heavenly glory disclosed to the soul untrammeled by its earthly raiments. In the midst of these subtleties of interpretation, the belief that unites all Muslims concerning the afterlife is that each soul will be held accountable for his actions on earth with his happiness or misery thereafter dependent upon how well he has observed God's laws.

God, Creation, Man, and the Day of Judgment—these are the chief theological pegs on which all the Koran's teachings are hung. In spite of their crucial importance, however, the Koran, as Muhammad Iqbal tells us, is "a book which emphasizes deed rather than idea." It is to these deeds that we turn in the next two sections.

THE FIVE PILLARS OF ISLAM

If a Muslim were asked to summarize the way his religion counsels man to live, he might answer: Islam teaches man to walk in the straight path. The phrase comes from the opening surah of the Koran itself which is recited by every Muslim five times each day:

Praise belongs to God, Lord of the Worlds,
The Compassionate, the Merciful.
King of the day of Judgment.
'Tis Thee we worship and Thee we ask for help.
Guide us in the straight path,
The path of those whom Thou hast favored,
Not the path of those who incur Thine anger nor of those who go astray.

Why the straight path? One meaning is obvious; a straight path is undevious, neither crooked nor corrupt. The phrase contains another meaning, however, which speaks to something distinctive in Islam. The straight path is one that is straightforward, direct and explicit. Compared with other religions, Islam spells out the way of life it proposes; it pinpoints it, nailing it down through explicit injunctions. The consequence is a definiteness about this religion that gives it a flavor all its own. A Muslim knows where he stands. He knows who he is and who God is. He knows what his obligations are and if he transgresses these he knows what to do about it. The world of Islam is the exact opposite of a Kafkaesque world in which man is separated from his destination, he can't get through, the lines are jammed, he doesn't know who he's talking to or who's inside the castle; he knows only that he has done something terrible though he can't find out what it is. Islam has a clarity, an order, a precision which is in sharp contrast to the shifting, relative, uncertain, at-sea quality of much of modern life. Muslims explicitly claim this as one of Islam's strengths. God's revelation to man, they say, has proceeded through four great stages. First, through Abraham God revealed the truth of monotheism, God's oneness. Second, through Moses he revealed the Ten Commandments. Third, through Jesus he revealed the Golden Rule, that we are to love our neighbors as ourselves. All these men were authentic prophets; each nailed down indispensable planks in the platform of the God-directed life. One question only remained unanswered. How should we love our neighbor? What does the love of neighbor require in this complicated world in which human interests can cross and tangle like pressure hoses on the loose? A final prophet was needed to answer that question and he was Muhammed. Because God answered this final question through him he deserves the title, the Seal of the Prophets. "The glory of Islam consists in having embodied the beautiful sentiment of Jesus into definite laws."[17]

What, then, is the content of this straight path that spells out the duties of man? We shall divide our presentation into two parts. In this section we shall consider the Five Pillars of Islam, the principles that regulate on the whole the private life of Muslims in their direct relationships with God. In the next section we shall consider the Koran's social teachings.

The first pillar is Islam's creed. Every religion contains convictions that orient its adherents' lives in some way. In some religions these premises are simply assumed; in most religions they are condensed and articulated in some sort of creed. The creed of Islam wastes no words. Brief, simple, explicit, it consists of a single sentence: "There is no God but Allah, and Muhammed is His Prophet." At least once during his lifetime a Muslim must say this creed correctly, slowly, thoughtfully, aloud, with full understanding, and with heartfelt conviction in its truth. In actuality, practicing Muslims repeat it many times each day, but at least once during one's lifetime is mandatory.

The creed contains only two phrases. The first announces the cardinal principle of monotheism. Islam entered the world as a desert religion—stretches of sand as far as the eye could reach, and above, only the blazing sun. This makes a difference. The austerity of the setting as well as its purity carries over into theology. "There is no God but Allah." There is no God but *The* God. More directly still, there is no God but *God*—for the word is not a common noun embracing a class of objects; it is a proper name designating a unique being, a single individual and Him only. In a single stroke, this affirmation demolishes forever God's rivals for man's loyalty. Once for all, it toppled the innumerable idols the Bedouin had worshipped since the dawn of history, and in the Muslim's view sounded toward Judaism and Christianity as well a recall from their near-idolatry of the Torah and Christ.

The second affirmation in Islam's creed—that "Muhammed is [God's] prophet"—speaks at once to the Muslim's faith in the authenticity of Muhammed and in the validity of the book he transmitted. So highly has the Prophet been regarded that his status has at times come near to threatening the monotheism he preached. Come near but not more than that. When Muhammed died there were some who attempted to deify him, but his appointed successor killed the thought with one of the most famous speeches in religious history. "If there are any among you who worshipped Muhammed, he is dead. But if it is God you worship, He lives forever."[18]

The second pillar of Islam is prayer in which the Koran adjures the faithful to "be constant." (xxix:45).

If we ask why the Muslim is admonished to "be constant" in prayer, the basic reason implied by all the Koran's direct statements is to keep man's life in perspective. The most important and difficult lesson man must learn and continually relearn, the Koran assumes, is that he is not God. Creature rather than creator, man has nevertheless an inveterate tendency to place himself at the center of his universe and live as a law to himself. When he does so, however, when he tries to play God, everything goes wrong. Man is creature; his life slips into place and stays in proper perspective only when he recognizes this fact. When one asks, therefore, why the Muslim prays, a partial answer is doubtless: in response to the natural yearning of the human heart to pour forth its love and gratitude toward its Creator. But accompanying this desire is a need to keep his life in its proper perspective; to see it in its objective setting; to acknowledge his creatureliness before his creator, and to submit himself to the will of God as rightfully sovereign over his life.

When should a Muslim pray? Five times daily—upon rising, at noon, in mid-afternoon, after sunset, and before retiring. The schedule is not absolutely binding. The Koran says explicitly, for example, that "When ye journey about the earth it is no crime to you that ye come short in prayer if ye fear that those that disbelieve will set upon you." Under normal conditions, however, the five-fold pattern should be maintained. While in Islam no day of the week is as sharply set apart from others as is the Sabbath for the Jews or Sunday for the Christians, Friday most nearly approximates a holy day. Formality is not a pronounced features in Islam but the closest that Muslims come to a formal service of worship is when they gather on Fridays for noon prayers and collective recital of the Koran. These gatherings are usually in mosques, and visitors to Muslim lands testify that one of the most impressive sights in the religions of man occurs when, in a dimly lighted mosque, hundreds of men stand shoulder to shoulder, then kneel and prostrate themselves toward Mecca. The exact answer to *where* the Muslim should pray, however, is anywhere. "It is one of the glories of Islam," writes an Englishman, "that its temples are not made with hands, and that its ceremonies can be performed anywhere upon God's earth or under His Heaven."[19] Every corner of Allah's universe being equally pure, the faithful are encouraged to spread their prayer rug wherever they find themselves at the appointed hour.

As to *how* the Muslim is to pray, the Koran mentions almost nothing in the way of specifics. Muhammed's personal teachings and practices, however, have crystallized into traditions that, in keeping with Islam's explicitness on almost every point, move in to structure the void. To keep alive the memory of the glorious center where Islam first entered the world in its fullness, Muhammed directed that Muslims should pray facing Mecca. The realization that his brothers are doing likewise creates a sense of participating in a world-wide fellowship even when the Muslim is physically isolated. Paralleling the Christian's purifying rite of Baptism, the Muslim washes himself and spreads his prayer rug before him. Standing erect with hands open on either side of his face and his thumbs touching the lobes of his ears, he recites, "*Allahu akbar*" (God is most great). Still standing he recites the opening *surah* of the Koran (quoted above) followed by other optional selections. Bowing from his hips and placing his hands on his knees, he says, "I extol the perfection of my Lord the Great." He returns to upright position, again repeating, "*Allahu akbar.*" Gliding gently to his knees, he places his hands and his face to the ground. He rises to his knees, sits on his heels, and again returns his hands and his face to the ground. The entire process is repeated several times, with the Muslim creed and optional prayers interpolated between each pair of prostrations. The entire routine is designed to give form to the prayer while allowing ample scope for the most heartful outpouring of devotion before the Almighty Presence.

This brings us to the content of Muslim prayer. Its two great themes are the expression of praise and gratitude on the one hand, and supplication on the other. There is a Muslim saying that every time a bird drinks a drop of water it lifts its eyes in gratitude toward heaven. "All who are in the heavens and the earth celebrate His praises, and the birds, too, spreading out their wings; each one knows its prayer and its praise." Ideally every micro-second of man's life should also be lifted to God in gratitude. In point of fact we repeatedly fall away from this grateful attitude. Five times a day, however, we should bring ourselves back to it. Here is a typical prayer through which the Muslim attempts to do so:

Thanks be to my Lord; He the Adorable, and only to be adored. My Lord, the Eternal, the Ever-existing, the Cherisher, the True Sovereign whose mercy and might overshadow the universe; the Regulator of the world, and Light of the creation. His is our worship; to Him belongs all worship; He existed before all things, and will exist after all that is living has ceased. Thou art the adored, my Lord; Thou art the Master, the Loving and Forgiving. . . . O my Lord, Thou art the Helper of the afflicted, the Reliever of all distress, the Consoler of the broken-hearted; Thou art present everywhere to help Thy servants . . . O my Lord, Thou art the Creator, I am only created; Thou art my Sovereign, I am only Thy servant; Thou art the Helper, I am the beseecher; Thou art the Forgiver, I am the sinner; Thou, my Lord, art the Merciful, All-knowing, All-loving.

Turning then to supplication, the devout might combine two traditional prayers as follows:

O Lord, grant to me the love of Thee. Grant that I may love those that love Thee. Grant that I may do the deeds that win Thy love. Make Thy love to be dearer to me than self, family or than wealth.

O Lord! Grant me firmness in faith and direction. Assist me in being grateful to Thee and in adoring Thee in every good way. I ask Thee for an innocent heart, which shall not incline to wickedness. I ask Thee for a true tongue. I pray Thee to defend me from that vice which Thou knowest, and for forgiveness of those faults which Thou knowest. O my Defender! assist me in remembering Thee and being grateful to Thee, and in worshipping Thee with the excess of my strength. Forgive me out of Thy loving kindness, and have mercy on me; for verily Thou art the forgiver of offences and the bestower of blessings on Thy servants.

The third pillar of Islam is charity. Material things are important in life, but some people have more than others. Why? Islam is not concerned with this theoretical problem. Instead, it turns to the practical question of what should be done about the situation. Its answer is simple. Those who have much should help lift the burden of those who are less fortunate. It is a principle twentieth century democracy has reached in its concept of the welfare state. Muhammed instituted it in the seventh by prescribing a graduated tax on the haves to relieve the circumstance of the have-nots.

The figure he set was two and one-half per cent. Compared with the tithe of Judaism and Christianity (which being directed more to the maintenance of religious institutions than to the direct relief of human need is not strictly comparable), this looks modest until we discover that it refers not just to income but to holdings. Poorer people owe nothing, but those in the middle and upper-income brackets must annually distribute among the poor one-fortieth of the value of all they possess.

And to whom among the poor should this money be given? This too, characteristically, is prescribed: to those in direst need; to slaves in the process of buying their freedom; to debtors unable to meet their obligations; to strangers and wayfarers; and to those who collect and distribute the alms.

The fourth pillar of Islam is the observance of *Ramadan*. *Ramadan* is a month in the Arabian calendar, Islam's holy month because during it Muhammed received his initial commission as a prophet and ten years later made his historic *Hijrah* from Mecca to Medina. To commemorate these two great occasions, able-bodied Muslims not involved in crises like war or unavoidable journey fast during *Ramadan*. From daybreak to the setting of the sun neither food nor drink passes their lips; after sundown they may partake in moderation. Being a month in a lunar calendar, *Ramadan* rotates around the year. When it falls in the winter its demands are not excessive. When, on the other hand, it falls during the scorching summers, to remain active during the long days without so much as a drop of water is an ordeal.

Why, then, does the Koran require it? For one thing, fasting makes one think, as every Jew who has watched through the long fasts of Yom Kippur will testify. For another thing, fasting teaches self-discipline; he who can endure its demands will have less difficulty controlling his appetites at other times. Fasting underscores man's dependence upon God. Man, says the Koran, is as frail as the rose petal; nevertheless he assumes airs and pretensions. Fasting reminds him vividly of his essential frailty and dependence. Finally, fasting sensitizes compassion. Only those who have been hungry can know what hunger means. If a man has himself fasted for thirty days within the year he will be apt to listen more carefully the next time he is approached by someone in need.

Islam's fifth pillar is pilgrimage. Once during his lifetime every Muslim who is physically and economically in a position to do so is expected to journey to Mecca where God's climactic revelation was first disclosed. The basic purpose of the pilgrimage is to heighten the pilgrim's devotion to God and to his revealed will, but the practice has some beneficial ancillary effects as well. It is, for example, a reminder of the equality between man and man. Upon reaching Mecca pilgrims remove their usual clothes, which tend to carry clear indications of their social status, and don two simple sheet-like garments. Everyone as he nears Islam's earthly focus wears the same thing. All distinctions of rank and hierarchy are removed; prince and pauper stand before God in their undivided humanity. Pilgrimage also provides a useful service in international relations. It brings together people from various countries demonstrating that they have in common a loyalty that transcends the loyalties of the warring kingdoms of man. Pilgrims pick up information about their brothers in other lands and return to their own with better understanding of one another.

Such are the five basic supports of the Muslim's faith. Traditionally he was also expected to abstain from gambling, drinking, and pork. The proscription against gambling continues in force but liberal Muslims tend to relax the other two. The rule against drinking, they say, was directed against the orgiastic excesses of Muhammed's day; not drinking but intoxication is the true target of this rule. The prohibition against pork was for hygienic reasons which need continue only as long as the disease connected with that meat remains.

With the exception of charity, the precepts we have considered in this section pertain to the Muslim's personal life. We must now turn explicitly to the social teachings of Islam.

THE BROTHERHOOD OF ISLAM

"O ye men! harken unto my words and take ye them to heart! Know ye that every Muslim is a brother to every other Muslim, and that ye are now one brotherhood."[20] These notable words, spoken by the Prophet during his "farewell pilgrimage" to Mecca shortly before his death, epitomize one of Islam's loftiest ideals and strongest emphases. The brotherhood of Islam is a reality.

Looking at the difference between pre- and post-Islamic Arabia we are forced to ask whether history has ever witnessed a comparable ethical advance among so many people in so short a time. Before Muhammed there was virtually no restraint on inter-tribal violence. Glaring inequities in wealth and possession were accepted without conscience. Women were regarded more as possessions than as human beings. Rather than say that a man could marry an unlimited number of wives, it would be more accurate to say that his relations with women were so casual that beyond the first wife or two they scarcely approximated marriage at all. Child infanticide was common especially among girls. Drunkenness and large-scale gambling have already been alluded to. Within a half century there was effected a remarkable change in the moral climate on each of these counts.

If we ask what it was in Islam that enabled it to accomplish this near-miracle, we are brought back to a point we have already remarked, namely, Islam's explicitness. Its basic objective in interpersonal relations, Muslims will say, is precisely that of Jesus and the other prophets: brotherly love.

The distinctive thing about Islam is not its ideal but the detailed proposals it sets forth for achieving it. We have already encountered its theory on this point. If Jesus had had a longer career, or if mankind had been sufficiently advanced to absorb more in the way of refinements, he would have placed his ideas on a more systematic basis. As it was, "the work of Jesus was left unfinished. It was reserved for another Teacher to systematize the laws of morality."[21] The Koran in addition to being a manual of spiritual exercise is an immense body of moral and legal ordinance. When its innumerable laws are supplemented with only slightly less authoritative *Hadith* or tradition based on what Muhammed did or said informally (in large part during the decade he was involved in administering the collective life of Medina), we are not surprised to find Islam the most socially vocal of man's enduring religions. Westerners who define religion in terms of personal experience would never be understood by Muslims whose religion calls them to establish a very explicit kind of social order. Faith and politics, religion and society are inseparable in Islam.

No useful purpose would be served here in trying to detail Muslim law or social theory in full. It will be enough if we consider its main teachings in four important areas of man's collective life.

1. Economic regulations. Islam is acutely aware of the physical basis of man's life. Far from being irrelevant to his well-being, the needs of his body are of crucial importance for until they are met his higher concerns cannot flower. When one of Muhammed's followers ran up to him crying, "My mother is dead; what is the best alms I can give away for the good of her soul?" the Prophet, thinking of the panting heat of the desert, answered instantly, "Water! Dig a well for her, and give water to the thirsty."

If an individual's health requires that his physical needs be reasonably met, a society's health requires that material goods be widely distributed and wealth be in easy circulation. These are the basic principles of Muslim economics and nowhere did Muhammed's democratic thunder speak with greater force or clarity than in this area. Finding men ground under the tyranny of vested interests, he propounded measures that broke the barriers of economic caste and enormously reduced the injustices of special privilege.

The main points of Muslim economics cluster around her concern that the wealth of her people be widely shared. Islam does not oppose the profit motive or economic competition. It does not discourage a man from working harder than his neighbor nor object to his being rewarded with a larger income. It simply insists that acquisitiveness and competition be balanced by fair play and compassion. Since human nature automatically takes care of the former, it falls to social laws to safeguard the latter. The Poor Due which provides for the annual distribution of one-fortieth of what one possesses to the poor is Islam's basic device for institutionalizing regard for others, but it is supplemented by a number of other important measures.

A glaring economic curse in Muhammed's day was primogeniture. By restricting inheritance to the eldest son this worked an obvious hardship on the other children and concentrated wealth in a limited number of enormous estates. The Koran reversed this system. By requiring that inheritance be divided among all children—daughters as well as sons— it insured a more even distribution of economic opportunity among descendants and saw to it that whatever financial concentrations may have accumulated in a lifetime would be dispersed thereafter instead of accruing more and more. F. S. C. Northrop tells of a chance glimpse into the settlement of a Muslim's estate. The application of Islamic law that afternoon resulted in the dividing of some $53,000 among no less than seventy heirs.

One verse in the Koran prohibits the taking of interest. Up to the last century this verse was taken as binding for all loans though often there were informal understandings about gifts which the borrower would make to the lender as an expression of his appreciation. Gradually with the advance of capitalism throughout Muslim countries in the nineteenth century this verse came to be reinterpreted to mean that interest should not be charged on loans used for the relief of human needs but that this restriction did not apply to loans for business purposes. As the latter were designed to bring profit to the borrower, it was felt that the Koran could not have intended that the lender be excluded from this profit. With this interpretation it is the prevailing Muslim view that there is no incompatibility between Islam and capitalism, though it is assumed that in view of the Koran's vehement denunciations of usury Muslims will keep their interest rates on business loans low.

As a final point deserving mention in the economic area, Islam lays down the principle that unearned money is not one's own. This is aimed at sleeping partners and all who live on inheritance without themselves contributing to society. Every time a Muslim lifts a morsel of food to his mouth he should be able to answer affirmatively the question, "Have I contributed to the human enterprise sufficiently to deserve what I am now receiving?"

2. The status of women. Chiefly because it has permitted a plurality of wives Islam has been accused of degrading women.

If we approach the question timewise, comparing the status of Arabian women before and after Muhammed, the charge is patently false. In the pre-Islamic "Days of Ignorance," marriage arrangements were so loose as to be scarcely recognizable. Conditional and temporary contracts were commonplace. Women were regarded as little more than chattel to be done with as their fathers or husbands pleased. Daughters had no inheritance rights and were often buried alive in their infancy.

In the face of these conditions, under which the very birth of a daughter was regarded as a calamity, Muhammed's reforms improved the status of women enormously. He forbade infanticide. He required that daughters be included in inheritance—not equally it is true but to half the proportion of sons, which seemed to Muhammed just in view of the fact that unlike the sons they would not carry economic responsibility for their households. In her rights as citizen—education, suffrage, and vocation—the Koran opens the way to woman's full equality with man, an equality which is being steadily approximated as the customs of Muslim nations become modernized. If in another century woman under Islam does not attain the social position of her European sister, a position to which the latter has been brought by industrialism and democracy rather than religion, there will then be time, says the Muslim, to hold Islam accountable.

In the institution of marriage, however, Islam made its greatest contribution to women. It sanctified marriage, first, by making it the sole locus of the sexual act. To the adherents of a religion in which the punishment for adultery is death by stoning and even today the young will dance facing but not touching each other because the body of a girl is not to be touched by a boy before marriage, Western imprecations of Islam as a lascivious religion sound ill-directed indeed. Second, Islam demands a woman's full consent before she is wed; not even a Sultan may marry her without her express approval. Third, Islam tightened the wedding bond enormously. Though Muhammed did not forbid divorce categorically, he countenanced it only as a last resort. Asserting repeatedly that nothing displeased God more than the disruption of marital vows, he instituted legal provisions to keep the marriage bond intact. Husbands are required in advance of marriage to set up a sizeable trust in a wife's name; in the event of divorce the entire sum goes to her. Divorce proceedings call for three distinct and separate periods, in each of which arbiters drawn from both families try to reconcile the two parties. Though such devices are intended to keep divorces to a minimum, wives no less than husbands are permitted to initiate them.

There remains, however, the question of polygamy or more precisely polygyny, the number of wives a Muslim is permitted to marry. Opinion differs on this point, but the growing consensus is that the ideal toward which Koranic law pressures man is monogamy. Supporting this view is the Koran's statement that "if you cannot deal equitably and justly with [more than one wife], you shall marry only one." As the word equitably is used in the Koran to signify not merely equality in material disbursements but also complete equity in love, affection, and esteem, the impossibility of equally dividing the latter causes this verse to preclude polygyny under normal circumstances. This interpretation has been in the Muslim picture as early as the third century of the *Hijrah,* and is gaining increasing acceptance. To avoid any possible misunderstanding, many Muslims now insert in the marriage deed a clause by which the husband formally renounces his supposed right to a second concurrent spouse.

But what of the other verse in the Koran which says "You may marry two, three, or four wives, but not more." And what of Muhammed's own multiple marriages? Some Muslims argue that this verse justifies polygyny even under normal circumstances. The growing number, however, see in it another instance of Islam's flexible capacity to speak with wise relevance to diverse situations.

There are circumstances in this imperfect state of human existence when polygyny is morally preferable to its alternative. Individually such a condition might arise, for example, if a partner were early in marriage to contract paralysis or another disability which would debar her from sexual union. Collectively a war which reduced the number of men to half the number of women would be an example. Idealists may call for the exercise of heroic continence under such circumstances, but heroism cannot be mass-produced. The actual choice is between a recognized and moral polygyny in which sex is kept linked with responsibility, equality in material goods, and affection—remember the requirement of equal love and esteem—and, on the other hand, a system of monogamy which being unrealistic fosters prostitution in which sex is disjoined from affection and responsibility for women and their offspring. It is this, ultimately, that leads a Western student of Islam, Bosworth Smith, to write: "By his severe laws at first, and by the strong moral sentiment aroused by these laws afterwards, [Muhammed] has succeeded, down to this very day and to a greater extent than has ever been the case elsewhere, in freeing all Mohammedan countries from those professional outcasts who live by their own misery, and, by their existence as a recognized class, are a standing reproach to every member of the society of which they form a part."[22]

Concerning *purdah,* woman's practice of secluding herself generally and veiling her face when abroad, Muhammed perceived its advantage as a check on the widespread promiscuity of his day. But that he ever intended his admonitions concerning modesty or privacy to assume the rigid extremes into which they have hardened is to the modernist Muslim inconceivable. "O Prophet!" they quote from the Koran, "Speak to thy wives and to thy daughters, and to the wives of the Faithful, that they let their wrappers fall low. Thus will they more easily be known, and they will not be affronted" (xxxiii:59).

3. Race relations. Islam stresses absolute racial equality. As the ultimate test of this is willingness to intermarry, the prophets have deliberately intermarried to demonstrate to mankind the unequivocal character of this ideal. According to the Muslim view, Abraham's second wife, Hagar, was a Negro. Muhammed himself was probably of the same skin coloring as Jesus—a sun-tanned white—but he married a Negro as one of his wives and gave his daughter in marriage to a Negro. Today his followers are drawn from all colors—black men from Africa, brown men from Malaya, yellow men from China, white men from Turkey. The spectacular advances Islam is making in colorconscious Asia and Africa today is not unrelated to the explicit way in which the principle of absolute racial equality is embedded in its teachings.

4. The use of force. The Western stereotype of a Muslim, it has been claimed on good ground, is a man marching with sword aloft and followed by a long train of wives. Next to their attitude toward women, Muslims feel that they have been most misrepresented in their attitude toward the use of force.

Admit, they say, that the Koran does not counsel turning the other cheek or pacifism. It teaches forgiveness and the return of good for evil when the circumstances warrant,[23] but these are very different from not resisting evil. Far from requiring the Muslim to turn himself into a doormat for the ruthless, the Koran allows punishment of wanton wrong doers to the full extent of the injury they do (xxii: 39-40). Refuse to permit this and morality evaporates into impractical idealism or sheer sentimentality. Extend this provision for justice to man's social life and you have the *jihad*, the Muslim concept of a holy war in which the martyrs who die are assured of heaven. All this the Muslim will affirm as integral to Islam. But we are still a far cry from the traditional charge that as a religion of the sword Islam spread by the sword and was upheld by the sword.

As an outstandingly successful general, Muhammed left many traditions regarding the decent conduct of war. Agreements are to be fulfilled; treachery avoided; the wounded are not to be mutilated, nor the dead disfigured. Women, children, and the old are not to be slain; orchards, crops, and sacred objects are to be spared. These, however, are not to the point. The important question is the definition of a righteous war. According to prevailing interpretations of the Koran, a righteous war must either be defensive or to right a wrong. "Defend yourself against your enemies; but attack them not first: God hateth the aggressor" (ii:190). The aggressive and unrelenting hostility of the idolaters forced Muhammed to seize the sword in self-defense or, together with his entire community and his God-entrusted faith, be wiped from the face of the earth. That other teachers succumbed under force and became martyrs was to Muhammed no argument that he need do the same. Having seized the sword in self-defense he held it with unsleeping vigilance to the end. This much is acknowledged, but not that he used the sword as an instrument of conversion.

The crucial verses in the Koran bearing on the point in question read as follows:

Let there be no compulsion in religion (ii:257).

To every one have we given a law and a way. . . . And if God had pleased, he would have made you all [all mankind] one people [people of one religion]. But He hath done otherwise, that He might try you in that which He hath severally given unto you: wherefore press forward in good works. Unto God shall ye return, and He will tell you that concerning which ye disagree (v:48).

Unto you your religion, and unto me my religion (cix:6).

Muslims point out that Muhammed incorporated the principle of religious toleration announced in these verses in his charter to the people of Medina, a document which is at once the first charter of freedom of conscience in human history and the authoritative model for those of every subsequent Muslim state: "The Jews who attach themselves to our commonwealth [similar rights were later mentioned for Christians, these two being the only non-Muslim religions on the scene] shall be protected from all insults and vexations; they shall have an equal right with our own people to our assistance and good offices: the Jews . . . and all others domiciled in Yathrib, shall . . . practice their religion as freely as the Muslims." Even conquered nations are to be permitted freedom of worship contingent only on the payment of a special tax in lieu of the Poor Due from which they are exempt; thereafter every interference with their liberty of conscience was regarded as a direct contravention of Islamic law. If clearer indication than this of Islam's stand on religious tolerance be asked, we have the direct words of

Muhammed: "Wilt thou then force men to believe when belief can come only from God?"[24] Once when a deputy of Christians visited him, Muhammed invited them to conduct their service in his mosque, adding, "It is a place consecrated to God."

This much for theory and Muhammed's personal practice. When we ask how well Muslims have lived up to his principles of toleration, we are into a question of history far too complex to admit of either simple or objective answer. On the positive side, Muslims point to the long centuries during which in India, Spain, and the Near East, Christians, Jews, and Hindus lived quietly and in freedom under Muslim rule. Even under the worst caliphs, Christians and Jews held positions of influence and in general retained their religious freedom. The Christians, not Muslims, we are reminded, expelled the Jews in the fifteenth century from Spain where they had lived in freedom while the Muslims were in power. Indeed if the wish is to enter into comparisons, Muslims see the record of Christianity as much darker than their own. Who was it, they ask, who preached the Crusades in the name of the Prince of Peace. Who instituted the Inquisition, invented the rack and the stake as instruments of religion, and plunged Europe into its devastating wars of religion?

Laying aside countercharge, the Muslim will admit that his own record in the area of force is far from pure. Every religion at some stages in its career has been used by its professors to mask aggressions and Islam is no exception. Time and again it has furnished to designing chieftains or caliphs a pretext for gratifying their ambitions. What Muslims deny in this area can be summarized in three points: First, they deny that Islam's record of intolerance is greater than that of other major religions. Second, they deny that Western histories have been fair to Islam in their accounts of its resorts to force. A growing number of Western historians including H. G. Wells and Arnold Toynbee are with them in this denial. Third, Muslims deny that those blots which have marred their history are due to the principles of their faith. However poorly one may conclude that the music of Islam has been played, the Koranic score itself is perfect. In the area of human relations its ideal is epitomized in the traditional Muslim greeting: *"Salam alakum,"* ("Peace be upon you").

WHITHER ISLAM?

For long periods since Muhammed first called his people to the unrivaled oneness of Allah, Muslim nations have wandered from the spirit of the Prophet. Muslim leaders are the first to admit that practice has often been replaced by mere profession, that routine observance has counterfeited for authentic action, that fervor has waned and devotion to Allah and his Prophet have dwindled into meaningless verbiage.

Viewed as a whole, however, Islam unrolls before us one of the most remarkable panoramas in all history. We have spoken of its early greatness. Had we pursued its history instead of its essence there would have been sections on the Muslim empire which, a century after Muhammed's death, stretched from the Bay of Biscay to the Indus and the frontiers of China, from the Aral Sea to the upper Nile. More important would have been the sections describing the march of Muslim ideas, the development of a fabulous culture, the rise of literature, science, medicine, art and architecture, the glory of Baghdad and Damascus, the splendor of Spain under the Moors. There would have been the heartening story of how during the long centuries of Europe's Dark Ages Muslim philosophers and scientists kept the lamp of learning bright, ready to rekindle the Western mind when it roused from its long sleep.

Nor would the story be set entirely in the past, for there are strong indications that at precisely the present, when history seems to be focusing around the Near and Middle East, Islam is emerging from the partial stagnation which followed in the wake of its once mighty empire. Of some of the religions considered in this book, we have had to admit that they may be dying and on their way out. Not so Islam. Youngest of the major religions of the world, it is again stirring with some of the strength and vigor of youth. From Morocco, opposing Gibraltar on the Atlantic, eastward by way of Egypt through the entire Middle East, Pakistan and Indonesia to the Philippines in the Pacific, Islam is a vital force in the contemporary world. Numbering in the vicinity of 350,000,000 followers, one out of every seven persons in today's world belongs to this religion which guides both thought and deed to a detail not often paralleled in the West. Nor is Islam merely consolidating its position; it is expanding and expanding rapidly. As early as 1773, Goethe wrote a poem in which he compared Muhammed to a stream which moves onward always increasing, carrying his brothers with him to the eternal Father. Today Islam is spreading not only in Africa and Southeast Asia but even to some extent in China, England, and the United States. Some claim it to be the fastest growing religion in the world. As recently as 1947, a new Muslim state has been born, Pakistan, with a population of 70 millions. In some areas where Islam and Christianity are competing for converts, Islam is gaining at a rate of ten to one.

As we lower the curtain on Islam, then, we leave a religion that encircles the larger part of the warm areas of the globe and is still on the move. Read these words at any hour of day or night and somewhere from minaret or now by way of radio tower a *muezzin* will be calling the faithful to prayer, crying:

> God is most great!
> God is most great!
> I testify that there is no God but Allah.
> I testify that Muhammed is the prophet of Allah.
> Arise and pray; arise and pray.
> God is great;
> There is no God but Allah!

SUGGESTIONS FOR FURTHER READING

Granting the Muslim's contention that the Koran suffers incomparably in translation, Mohammed Pickthall's 75¢ Mentor *The Meaning of the Glorious Koran* may be recommended as being as serviceable as any.

Standard and easily accessible factual surveys of Islam are to be found in H. A. R. Gibb's 35¢ Mentor *Mohammedanism* and Alfred Guillaume's 50¢ Pelican *Islam*. Both of these authors are great scholars. Unfortunately, however, each writes so obviously from the outside looking in that he sometimes puts his point in a condescending manner which dismays the Muslim reader. For this reason it is important that these factual Westernized descriptions be balanced by an account written from inside the religion even if it be frankly apologetic. Muhammed Iqbal's *The Reconstruction of Religious Thought in Islam* (London: Oxford University Press, 1934) does this balancing job for the philosopher, and is notable for being perhaps the most serious attempt to reconcile Islam with Western philosophic and scientific thought. In addition to being abstract, however, Mr. Iqbal takes such personal liberties in his interpretation of Islam that a better book for presenting Islam to the general Western reader from the inside is Ameer Ali's *The Spirit of Islam* (London: Christophers, 1922). Philip Hitti's *The Arabs: A Short History* (Princeton; Princeton University Press, 1949) provides a nice summary of the sweep and achievements of Muslim civilization as a whole. In addition to standing as a model of the spirit in which an author can deal with a religion other than his own, the first half of Kenneth Cragg's *The Call of the Minaret* (New York: Oxford University Press, 1956) furnishes the most discerning statement of the unresolved issues confronting Islam in the contemporary world.

7

Judaism

IT HAS been estimated that one-third of our Western civilization bears
the marks of its Jewish ancestry. We feel its force in the names we give
our children: *Adam* Smith, *Noah* Webster, *Abraham* Lincoln, *Isaac*
Newton, *Rebecca* West, *Sarah* Teasdale, Grandma *Moses*. Michaelangelo
felt it when he chiseled his David and painted the Sistine Ceiling; Dante
when he wrote the *Divine Comedy* and Milton, *Paradise Lost*. The
United States carries the indelible stamp of its Jewish heritage in its
collective life: the phrase "by their Creator" in the Declaration of Independence; the words "Proclaim Liberty throughout the land" on the
Liberty Bell. The real impact of the ancient Jews, however, lies in the
extent to which Western civilization took over their angle of vision on
the deepest questions life poses.

When, mindful of the impact the Jewish perspective has had on
Western culture, we go back to the land, the people, and the history
that made this impact, we are in for a shock. We might expect these to
be as impressive as their influence but they are not. In time span the
Jews were latecomers on the stage of history. By 3000 B.C. Egypt already
had her pyramids and Sumer and Akad were world empires. By 1400
Phoenicia was colonizing. And where were the Jews in the midst of these
mighty eddies? They were overlooked. A tiny band of nomads milling
around the upper regions of the Arabian desert, they were too incon-
spicuous even to be noticed.

When they finally settled down, the land they chose was equally
unimpressive. One hundred and fifty miles in length from Dan to

Beersheba, about fifty miles across at Jerusalem but much less at most places, Palestine is a postage stamp of a country, about one-eighth the size of Illinois. Nor does the terrain make up for what the region lacks in size. Visitors to Greece who climb Mount Olympus find it easy to imagine that the gods chose to live there. Palestine, by contrast, was a "mild and monotonous land. Did the Prophets, in their gloom of foreboding, flash their lightning of conviction from these quiet hills, where everything is open to the sky?" asks Edmund Wilson on one of his visits. "Were the savage wars of Scripture fought here? Did its paeans first sound from these pastures? . . . How very unlikely it seems that they sprouted from the history of these calm little hills, dotted with stones and flocks, under pale and transparent skies."[1] Even Jewish history when viewed from without amounts to little. It is certainly not dull history but by external standards it is very much like the histories of countless other little peoples, the people of the Balkans, say, or possibly our own Indian tribes in pre-Columbian times. Small peoples are always getting pushed around. They get shoved out of their land and try desperately to scramble back into it. Compared with the history of Assyria, Babylon, Egypt, and Syria, Jewish history is strictly minor league.

If the key to the achievement of the Jews lies neither in their antiquity nor the proportions of their land or history, where does it lie? There are a number of ways that this question, which has been one of the greatest puzzles of history, might be approached. At least a partial clue to the mystery, however, and the one whose lead we shall follow throughout this chapter, is this: What lifted the Jews from obscurity to permanent religious greatness was their passion for meaning.

MEANING IN GOD

"In the beginning God. . . ." From beginning to end the Jewish quest for meaning was rooted in their understanding of God.

Whatever a man's philosophy, it must take account of the "other." There are two reasons for this. First, no man seriously supposes that he brought himself into being; and as he did not, other men (being like him human) could not have brought themselves into being either. From this it follows that mankind has issued from something other than itself. Second, every man at some point finds his power limited. It may be a rock too large for him to lift, a tidal wave that sweeps away his village because he cannot stem it. Added to the "other" from which he has *issued*, therefore, is the "other" by which he is *confronted*.

Faced by this inescapable "other," man wonders if it is meaningful.

Four characteristics could keep it from being so; if it were prosaic, chaotic, amoral, or hostile. The triumph of Jewish thought lies in its refusal to surrender meaning for any of these alternatives.

The Jews resisted the prosaic in their thought of the "other" by personifying it. In this they were at one with their ancient contemporaries. The concept of the inanimate—senseless dead matter governed by blind, impersonal laws—is a late invention. For early man the sun which could bless or scorch, the earth which gave of its fertility, the gentle rains and the terrible storms, the mystery of birth and the reality of death were not to be explained as clots of matter regulated by mechanical laws. They were parts of a world that was heavy with feeling and purpose to its very core.

It is easy to smile at the anthropomorphism of the early Jew who could imagine ultimate reality as a person walking in the Garden of Eden in the cool of the morning. But when we make our way through the poetic concreteness of his perspective to its underlying claim—that in the final analysis reality is more like a person than like a machine— we must ask ourselves two questions. First, what is the evidence against this hypothesis? It seems to be so completely lacking that as knowledgeable a philosopher-scientist as Alfred North Whitehead could embrace it without reservation in our own generation. Second, is the concept intrinsically less exalted than its alternative? The Jews were reaching out for the most exalted concept of the "other" they could conceive, an "other" which embodied such inexhaustible worth that in all his history man would never begin to encompass its fullness. The Jews found a greater depth and mystery in persons than in any of the other wonders at hand. How could they be true to this conviction of the "other's" worth except by extending and deepening the category of the personal to include it?

Where the Jews differed from their neighbors was not in conceiving the "other" as personal but in focusing its personalism in a single, supreme, nature-transcending will. For Egyptians, Babylonians, Syrians, and the lesser Mediterranean peoples of the day each major power of nature was a distinct deity. The storm was the storm-god, the sun the sun-god, the rain the rain-god. When we turn to the Old Testament we find ourselves in a completely different atmosphere. Nature here is an expression of a single Lord of all being. As an authority on polytheism in the ancient Middle East has written:

When we read in Psalm 19 that 'the heavens declare the glory of God; and the firmament sheweth his handiwork,' we hear a voice which mocks the beliefs of Egyptians and Babylonians. The heavens, which were to the psalmist but a witness of God's greatness, were to the Mesopotamians the very majesty of godhead, the highest ruler, Anu. To the Egyptians the heavens signified the mystery of the divine mother through whom man was reborn. In Egypt and Mesopotamia the divine was comprehended as immanent: the gods were in nature. The Egyptians saw in the sun all that a man may know of the Creator; the Mesopotamians viewed the sun as the god Shamash, the guarantor of justice. But to the psalmist the sun was God's devoted servant who is as a bridegroom coming out of his chamber, and 'rejoiceth as a strong man to run a race. The God of the psalmists and the prophets was not in nature. He transcended nature. . . . It would seem that the Hebrews, no less than the Greeks, broke with the mode of speculation which had prevailed up to their time.[2]

Though the Old Testament contains references to gods other than Yahweh (misspelled Jehovah in the King James Version), this does not upset the familiar claim that the basic contribution of Judaism to the religious thought of ancient Mediterranean man was monotheism. For a close reading of the text shows that these other gods differed from Yahweh in two respects. First, they owed their origin to him—"Gods are ye, the children of the Most High, all of ye" (Ps. 82:6). Second, unlike Yahweh, they were mortal—"Like men ye shall die" (Ps. 82:7). These differences are clearly of sufficient importance to place the God of Israel in a category that differs from that of the other gods not merely in degree but in kind. They are not his rivals; they are his subordinates. From a very early date, possibly from the very beginning of the Biblical record, the Jews were monotheists.

The significance of this achievement in religious thought lies ultimately in the focus it introduces into life. If a man's God be that to which he gives himself completely, to have more than one God is to have more than one life—to be drawn literally toward becoming a split personality. If man's life is not to be scattered, if he is not to spend his days darting from one cosmic bureaucrat to another to discover who is setting the standards today, if, in short, there is a consistent way in which life is to be lived if it is to move toward fulfillment, a way that can be searched out and approximated, there must be a singleness to the Other that supports this way. That there is, has been the central affirmation of the Jews: "Hear, O Israel, the Lord our God, the Lord is One."

There remains the question of whether the Other, now seen as personal and ultimately one, was either amoral or hostile. If it were either, this too could frustrate meaning. Man's life with his fellows obviously goes more smoothly if he behaves morally, but if ultimate reality does not support such conduct, if man's world is such that morality does not pay, man faces an impasse in how to live. As to the Other's disposition toward man, its power so obviously outweighs man's that if its intents run counter to his well-being, man's life, far from being fully meaningful, can be nothing but a game of cat-and-mouse. This insight caused Lucretius, a short distance around the Mediterranean in Rome, to preach atheism on grounds that are actually religious. If the gods are as the Romans believed them to be—immoral, vindictive, and capricious—meaningful existence requires that they be denied.

The God of the Jews possessed none of these traits which, in greater or lesser degree, characterized the gods of their neighbors. It is here that we come to the supreme achievement of Jewish thought; not in its monotheism as such, but in the character it ascribed to the God it discovered to be One. The Greeks, the Romans, the Syrians, and most of the other Mediterranean peoples would have said two things about their gods' characters. First, the gods tend to be amoral; second, toward man they are preponderantly indifferent. The Jews reversed the thinking of their contemporaries on both points. Whereas the gods of Olympus tirelessly pursued beautiful women, the God of Sinai watches over widows and orphans. While Mesopotamia's Anu and Canaan's El were going their aloof ways, Yahweh is speaking the name of Abraham, lifting his people out of slavery, and (in Ezekiel's vision) seeking his lonely, heartsick exiles in Babylon. God is a God of righteousness whose loving kindness is from everlasting to everlasting and whose tender mercies are over all his works.

Such, then, was the Jewish view of the Other with which man is confronted. It is not prosaic, for at its center sits enthroned a Being of unutterable greatness and holiness. It is not chaotic, for it coheres in a divine unity. The reverse of amoral or indifferent, it centers in a God of righteousness and love. Are we surprised, then, to find the Jew exclaiming with the exultation that accompanies all frontier discovery: "Who is like unto thee among the Gods, O Yahweh?" "What great nation hath a God like the Lord?"

MEANING IN CREATION

In *The Brothers Karamazov* Dostoyevsky has Ivan blurt out: "I don't accept this world of God's, and although I know it exists, I don't accept it at all. It's not that I don't accept God, you must understand, it's the world created by Him I don't and cannot accept."

Ivan is not alone in finding God, perhaps, good, but the world not. Entire philosophies (such as Cynicism among the Greeks) and even religions (like Jainism in India) have done likewise. Against all such forms of world pessimism, the chronicle of the Jewish perspective opens with the statement: "In the beginning God created the heavens and the earth."

What does it mean to say that the universe, the entire realm of natural existence as we know it, is God-created? Philosophers might look to such a statement as an explanation for the means by whch the world got started. This, however, is a purely academic question with no bearing whatever on the living of our lives. What difference does it make to us how the world was created, whether it is eternal or came into being in time?

There is another angle to the affirmation that the universe is God-created. In this second sense the statement speaks not to the mode by which the universe and life within it originated but to their worth. This, unlike the first question, is a matter that concerns us profoundly. Everyone at times finds himself asking whether life is worthwhile, which is the same as asking whether, when the going gets rough, it is worthwhile to try. Those who conclude it isn't give up, if not once and for all by suicide then piecemeal by retreating inch by inch into defeatism and despair. Now, whatever else the word God may mean, it means a being in whom power and value converge, a being who can do what he wants to do and who wants to do what is good. In this sense to affirm that existence is God-created is to affirm its enduring worth.

There is a passage in T. S. Eliot's *The Cocktail Party* that speaks precisely to this point. Celia, who has been disappointed and disillusioned in love, goes to a psychiatrist for help. And this is the way she begins her notable interview:

> I must tell you
> That I should really *like* to think there's something wrong with me—
> Because, if there isn't, then there's something wrong . . .
> With the world itself—and that's much more frightening!
> That would be terrible. So I'd rather believe
> There is something wrong with me, that could be put right.

Celia in these lines is speaking to the most basic decision man has to make. Things repeatedly go wrong in human life. When they do, what are we to conclude? Ultimately our options come down to two. One possibility is that the fault lies in the stars, dear Brutus. Many have so concluded. They range all the way from quipsters who propose that the only truly educational toy we might give our children is a jigsaw puzzle no two pieces of which fit together, to a Thomas Hardy who infers that the power that spawned a universe so inherently tragic must be some sort of dumb vegetable. In Somerset Maugham's *Of Human Bondage*, the principal character, Philip, was given a Persian rug by a Bohemian roué who assured him that by studying the carpet he would be able to comprehend life's meaning. The donor died, and Philip was still puzzled. How could the involved pattern of a Persian rug solve the problem of life's meaning? When the answer finally came to him it seemed obvious: life had no meaning. "For nothing was there a why and a wherefore."

This is one possibility. The other possibility is that when things go wrong the fault lies not in the stars but in ourselves. Neither answer can be objectively validated, but there is no doubt which one elicits the more creative response. In the one case man is helpless, for his troubles stem from the botched character of existence itself, which is obviously beyond his power to revise. If, on the contrary, man resists the temptation to force the blame on the way life has been made, his alternative is to assume that the source of his troubles lies closer home where he can do something about it. In this sense the Jewish affirmation that the world was God-created laid a central plank in their outlook. Thenceforth, however desperate their lot, however deep the valley of the shadow of death, they never despaired of life itself. Meaning was always latent and the opportunity for creative response always at hand. For the setting had been fashioned by the God who meted out the heavens with a span and whose goodness was from everlasting to everlasting.

Thus far we have been speaking of the Jewish estimate of creation as a whole. One specific element in the Biblical account, however, deserves special notice; namely, its estimate of nature, the physical component of things.

Much of Greek thought, notably that dominated by Plato and Plotinus, takes a dim view of matter. In Hinduism and Theravada Buddhism the basic outlook is optimistic in spite of the material world rather than because of it. In India matter tends to be regarded as a barbarian, spoiling everything she touches. Liberation lies ultimately in extricating spirit from its material involvement.

How different the first chapter of Genesis, which opens, "In the beginning God created the heavens and the earth" and builds from there to its climax in which "God saw everything that he had made, and behold it was *very* good." Let the reader dwell for a moment on the wonderful little word "very." It gives a lilt to the entire religion. Pressing for meaning in every direction, the Jews refused to abandon the physical aspects of existence as illusory, defective, or unimportant. Fresh as the morning of Creation, they were to be relished with zest. The abundance of food made the Promised Land "a good land, a land of wheat and vines and figs and pomegranates, a land of olive trees and honey; a land in which thou shalt eat bread without scarceness" (Deut. 8:7-8). Sex, too, was good. An occasional minority movement like the Essenes might exalt celibacy; Jews as a whole, honoring God's instructions to "be fruitful and multiply," have had a high opinion of marriage. The entire assumption behind the prophets' denunciation of the extreme inequalities of wealth they saw was the reverse of the notion that material possessions are bad; they are so good that more persons should have more of them.

Such an affirmative and buoyant attitude toward nature does seem to set Judaism off from India's basic outlook. It does not, however, distinguish it from the Far East where the appreciation of nature is profound. What divides the Hebraic from the Chinese view of nature does not come out until we note a third verse in this crucial first chapter of Genesis. In verse twenty-six, God speaks of the men he intends to create. "Let them," he says, "have dominion . . . over all the earth." How much this differs from the Chinese attitude toward nature can be seen by recalling its opposite statement in the *Tao Te Ching*:

> Those who would take over the earth
> And shape it to their will
> Never, I notice, succeed.

Indeed if propositions are made of the three key assertions about nature in the opening chapter of Genesis:

> God created . . . the earth;
> God said: Let [man] have dominion . . . over all the earth;
> And behold, it was very good;

we find an appreciation of nature, blended with confidence in man's power to transform nature for the good, that is unique in any literature of the age. It was, as we well know, an attitude destined to bring results, for it is no accident that modern science first jumped to life in the Western world. Archbishop Temple used to say that Judaism and its descendant, Christianity, are the most materialistic religions in the world. Islam should probably be added to the list. But if we take the three

Semitically oriented religions together, it does seem that no other insists so strongly that man is ineradicably body as well as spirit and that this coupling is no liability. From this basic premise three corollaries follow: that the material aspects of life are important (hence the strong emphasis in the West on humanitarianism and social service); that matter can participate in the condition of salvation itself (as affirmed in the doctrine of the Resurrection of the Body); that nature can become host to the divine (the doctrine of the Kingdom of God on Earth and, later in Christianity, the Incarnation).

MEANING IN MAN

The most crucial element in man's thinking tends to be his thinking about himself. Here, too, the Jews were looking for meaning. Early Jews were profoundly interested in man but they were not looking for bare facts about him. They wanted truth-for-life; they wanted to make sense of the human situation in order to release the most creative response of which man is capable.

Of man's limitations, the Jews were acutely aware. Compared with the splendors of heaven, he is "as dust" (Ps. 103:14); compared with the forces of nature that surround him, he is frail. Haunted even in his proudest moments by the realization of his insufficiency, he is weak as those "crushed before the moth!" (Job 4:19). His span upon the earth is swiftly spent. Like grass that in the morning groweth up and flourish-eth, "in the evening it is cut down and withereth" (Ps. 90:7). Even this brief span is interlocked with pain that causes us to "spend our years as a sigh" (Ps. 90:9). Not once but repeatedly the Jews were forced to the rhetorical question: "What is man" that God should give him a second thought? (Ps. 8:4).

Considering the freedom of Israel's thought and the openness with which she voiced her skepticism when she felt it, it is not surprising to find some Jews concluding that man is no more than animal. "The sons of men . . . are in their nature but beasts, the fate of the sons of men and the fate of beasts is one: as this dies, so dies that; they have all the same spirit, and man has no superiority above the beasts" (Eccles. 3:18-20). Here is a biological interpretation of man as uncompromising as any the nineteenth century ever produced. The significant point, however, is that this is not the view that prevailed. The epochal fact in the Hebraic view of man is that without in the least blinking man's frailty it went on to affirm in the same breath his unspeakable grandeur.

The word unspeakable in the preceding sentence is not mere rhetoric.

The King James Version translates the central Jewish claim concerning man as follows: "For thou hast made him a little lower than the angels" (Ps. 8:5). The last word is a straight mistranslation, for the original Hebrew plainly reads "a little lower than the gods [or God]"—the number of the Hebrew word *'elohim* is indeterminate. Why did the translators tone down this word for deity to angels? The answer seems obvious: it was not erudition they lacked but rather the boldness—one is tempted to say nerve—of the ancient Jews. We can appreciate their reserve. It is one thing to write a Hollywood scenario in which everyone seems wonderful; it is another thing to make these people seem real. The one charge that has never been leveled against the Bible is that its characters are not real people. Even its greatest heroes like David are presented so unvarnished that the Book of Samuel has been called the greatest historical writing of the ancient world. Yet no amount of realism could repress Jewish aspiration. Man who on occasion so justly deserves the epithets "maggot and worm" (Job 25:6) is equally the being whom God hath "crowned with glory and honor" (Ps. 8:6).

In speaking of Jewish realism we have noted only its awareness of man's physical limitations: his weakness, his susceptibility to pain, the briefness of his days. We shall not have its full extent, however, until we add that man's basic limitation is something in his spirit rather than his physique. Man is not only frail, he is a sinner: "For I was shaped in iniquity and in sin did my mother conceive me" (Ps. 51:5). It is totally false to claim this verse for the defense of either the doctrine of man's total depravity or the notion that sex is evil. Both these notions are completely un-Jewish. The verse does, however, contribute something of great importance to the Jewish doctrine of man. The word sin comes from a root meaning "to miss the mark," and this despite his high origin and nature, man continually does. Meant to be noble, he is ordinarily less than such; meant to be generous, he seeks his own. Created more than animal, he often sinks to be nothing else.

Yet never in these "missings" is man's misstep required. Freedom has always been for the Jews unquestioned. The first recorded act of man was an act of free choice. In eating Eden's forbidden fruit, Adam and Eve were, it is true, seduced by the snake, but they had the power to refuse. The snake merely tempted them; it is clearly a story of human freedom. Inanimate objects cannot be other than they are; they do what their natures determine them to do. Man once created makes or breaks himself. He creates his own destiny through his choices. "Cease to do evil, learn to do good" (Isa. 1:16-17)—for man only does this injunction hold. "I have set before you life and death . . . therefore choose life" (Deut. 30:19).

Finally, it followed from the Jewish conception of God as a God of love that man is his beloved child. In one of the tenderest metaphors of the entire Bible, Hosea pictures God yearning over his people as though they were toddling infants:

> I taught Ephraim to walk,
>   I took them up in my arms . . . ;
> I led them with cords of compassion,
>   with the bands of love. . . .
> How can I give you up, O Ephraim!
>   How can I hand you over, O Israel!
> My heart recoils within me,
>   my compassion grows warm and tender (Hos. 11:3-4, 8).

Even in this world, immense and ringed by the mighty powers of nature, man can walk with the confidence of a child in a home in which he is fully accepted.

What are the ingredients of the most creatively meaningful image of man that the mind can conceive? Remove his frailty—as grass, as a sigh, as dust, as they that are crushed before the moth—and the estimate becomes romantic. Remove his grandeur—a little lower than God—and aspiration declines. Remove sin—his tendency to miss the mark—and the picture grows sentimental. Remove freedom—choose ye this day! —and man becomes a puppet. Remove, finally, his sonship to God and man becomes estranged, cut loose and adrift on a sea of blind forces for which he is no match. With all that has been discovered about man in the intervening 2500 years it is difficult to find the flaw.

MEANING IN HISTORY

Let us begin with a contrast. "According to most classical philosophies and religions," writes Bernhard Anderson, "ultimate reality is disclosed when man, either by rational contemplation or mystic ascent, goes beyond the flow of events which we call 'history.' The goal is the apprehension of an order of reality unaffected by the fleeting days or by the unpredictable fortunes of mankind. In Hinduism, for instance, the world of sense experience is regarded as *maya*, illusion; the religious man, therefore, seeks release from the wheel of life in order that his individuality may fade out into the World-Soul, Brahma. Or, Greek philosophers looked upon the world as a natural process which, like the rotation of the seasons, always follows the same rational scheme. The philosopher, however, could soar above the recurring cycles of history by fixing his mind upon the unchanging absolutes which belong to the eternal order. Both of these views are vastly different from the Biblical claim that God is found within the limitations of the world of change and struggle, and especially that he reveals himself in events which are unique, particular, and unrepeatable. For the Bible, history is neither *maya* nor a circular process of nature; it is the arena of God's purposive activity."[3]

What is at stake when we ask if there is meaning in history? At stake is our whole attitude toward the social order and man's collective life. If we decide that history is meaningless, it follows that the social, political, and cultural contexts of life are unimportant and matters for indifference. This does not mean that if we so regard them we must also regard *life* as unimportant. But it does mean that we would regard life's problems, opportunities, and solutions as having little to do with the outward circumstances under which life is lived. To the extent that we believe this we will naturally take little interest in, and feel little responsibility for, the various collective enterprises, cultures, and civilizations which make up the stuff of history.

The Jewish estimate of history was the exact opposite of this attitude of indifference. To the Jews history was of towering significance. It was important, first, because they were convinced that the context in which life is lived affects that life in every way, setting up its problems, delineating its opportunities, conditioning its fulfillment. It is impossible to talk about Adam and Noah (the same may be said of almost every Biblical character) apart from the particular circumstances—in this case Eden and Flood—that surrounded them and in response to which their lives took shape.

Second, if contexts are crucial for life so is group action—social action as we usually call it—for there are times when it takes group action to change contexts to the needed extent. The destiny of the individual Hebrew slave in bondage in Egypt is not depicted as depending on the extent to which he "rose above" his slavery by praising God with his spirit while his body was in chains; he had to rise with his people and break for the desert.

Third, history was important for the Jews because they saw it, always, as a field of opportunity. God was the ruler of history; nothing, therefore, happened by accident. His hand was at work in every event—in Eden, the Flood, the Tower of Babel, the years in the wilderness—shaping each sequence into a teaching experience for those who had the wit to learn.

Finally, history was important because its opportunities did not stream forth on an even plateau. Events, all of them important, were nevertheless not of equal importance. It was not the case that anyone, anywhere, at any time could turn to history and find awaiting him an opportunity equivalent to any other. Each opportunity was unique but some were decisive. "There is a tide in the affairs of men which, taken at the flood, leads on to fortune."[4] One must, therefore, attend to history carefully, for when opportunities pass they are gone.

This uniqueness in events is epitomized in the Hebraic notions (a) of God's direct intervention in history at certain critical points and (b) of a chosen people as recipients of his unique challenges. Both are vividly illustrated in the epic of Abraham. This epic is introduced by a remarkable prologue, Genesis 1-11, which describes the steady deterioration of the world from its original goodness. Disobedience (eating the forbidden fruit) is followed by murder (Cain of Abel), promiscuity (the sons of God and the daughters of men), incest and homosexuality (the sons of Noah) until a flood is needed to sluice out the mess. In the midst of this corruption God is not inactive. Against its backdrop, in the last days of the Sumeric universal state, God calls Abraham. He is to go forth into a new land to establish a new people. The moment is decisive. Because Abraham seizes it, he ceases to be anonymous. He becomes the first Hebrew, the first of "the chosen people."

We shall have to pursue this notion of a chosen people at a later point, but for the present we must ask what gave the Jews their insight into history's significance. We have noted the kind of meaning they found in history. What enabled them to see it as embodying this meaning?

For India, man's destination is beyond history altogether. The world in which he currently lives is, as we have seen, the "middle world;" it will always contain approximately the same amount of good and evil, pleasure and pain, right and wrong. This being its inherent and intended condition, all thought of cleaning it up, of changing it appreciably, is in principle misguided. The nature religions of Egypt, Mesopotamia, and the other Mediterranean folk reached the same conclusion by a different route. For these, man's destination was not beyond history; it was in history all right but in history as it was currently manifesting itself, not in history as amenable to improvement. We can see why not. If one's attention is on nature, as the nature polytheist's always was, one does not look beyond nature for fulfillment. But neither—and this is the point —does one look for improvement in the natural order. The idea of an improved nature scarcely suggests itself to man, for the matter seems completely out of his hands. The Egyptian no more asked whether the sun god Ra was shining as he should than the modern astronomer asks whether sunlight travels at a proper speed. In nature the emphasis is on what is rather than on what ought to be.

Israel's historical outlook differed from that of India and her polytheistic neighbors because she had a different idea of God. Against India (if the issue had been raised to the level of conscious debate) she would have argued that God would not have deliberately created man as a material being and intentionally placed him in the historical order if these conditions were adventitious to his destiny. Against the nature polytheists she would have argued that as God transcends nature and uses it to his purposes he should not be thought of exclusively in terms of what "is"—the "ought" also concerns him profoundly. By the double stroke of involving man's destiny in the natural order and making moral categories relevant to this order, Judaism simultaneously establishes history as both important and subject to criticism. Man is an historical being, but because he has misused his freedom he has corrupted history and denied himself the full range of its potential rewards.

The nature polytheisms that surrounded Judaism all buttressed the status quo. Conditions might not be all the heart would wish, but what impressed the polytheist was that they might be a great deal worse. For if the powers of nature reside in many gods—in Mesopotamia their number was in the thousands—there was always the danger that these gods might fall out among themselves and universal chaos result. As a consequence, religion's attention was directed toward keeping things as they were. Egyptian religion, for example, repeatedly contrasted the "passionate man" to the "silent man," exalting the latter because he never disturbs the established order. Small wonder that no nature polytheism has ever produced a major social revolution fired by a high concept of social justice. India's religion has likewise lacked social emphasis, for whereas the existing order in polytheism should not be changed, in Hinduism it cannot be, not, certainly, to any appreciable extent.

In Judaism, by contrast, history is in tension between its divine potentialities and its present frustrations. There is a profound disharmony between God's will and the existing social order. As a consequence, more than any other religion of the time Judaism laid the groundwork for social protest. As things are not as they should be, revolution in some form is to be expected. The idea bore fruit. It is in the countries that have been affected by the Jewish perspective on history, which was taken over by Christianity and to some extent by Islam, that the most intensive movements for social reform have occurred. The prophets set the pattern. "Protected by religious sanctions," Professor William Albright has written, "the prophets of Judah were a reforming political force which has never been surpassed and perhaps never equalled in subsequent world history." Passionately convinced that things were not as they ought to be, they created in the name of the God for whom they spoke an atmosphere of reform that "put Hyde Park and the best days of muckraking newspapers to shame."[5]

MEANING IN MORALITY

Man is a social animal. Permanently separated from others of his kind he would not even be human; with them, however, both wisdom and attention are needed to keep his relationships from becoming seriously tangled. The need for morality stems from this double fact. Nobody likes moral codes any more than they like stop lights or "no left turn" signs. But without them wills collide, lives get wrecked, and emotions snarl as hopelessly as would five o'clock traffic in the Chicago loop if every car disregarded every other.

The Jewish formulation of "those wise restraints that make men free" is contained in her Law. This Law contains ritualistic as well as ethical prescriptions as we shall have occasion to see, but for the present we are concerned with the latter. According to the Rabbinic view, there are no less than 613 commandments in the Old Testament regulating human behavior. We shall be content to look at four, the four ethical injunctions of the Ten Commandments. For it is through the Ten Commandments that Hebraic morality has made its greatest impact upon the world. Taken over by Christianity and Islam, the Ten Commandments constitute the moral foundation of half the world's present population.

There are four danger areas in man's life which can cause unlimited trouble if they get out of hand: force, wealth, sex, and the spoken word. On the animal level these do not raise nearly as many problems as they do in human life. Two scarcely emerge as problems at all. The spoken word does not, for animals cannot communicate enough to deceive. Neither, really, does wealth, for to become a serious social problem the drive for possessions calls for foresight and sustained greed unknown in the animal kingdom. As for sex and force, while animals are definitely involved with them, instinct keeps them amazingly within bounds. Periodicity keeps sex from becoming the obsessive force it can be in man, while the herd instinct holds down violence within the species to an amazing degree. With the strange exception of the ants, intraspecial warfare has seldom broken out below the human level; where it has, the species has almost invariably destroyed itself.

With man the situation is critically different. Jealousies, hatred, vengeance can lead to violence which unless checked will rip a community to pieces. Murder can set going blood feuds that drag on indefinitely. Sex, if it breaks out of appropriate channels, can rouse passions so intense as to upset entire tribes. Similarly with theft and prevarication. Theoretically we can imagine a society in which everyone does exactly as he pleases with these things. Actually no such society exists; at least anthropologists who by now have pretty well covered the globe have discovered none. Apparently if there are societies that try the experiment of leaving these areas completely unregulated, they do not stay around long enough to be observed. Here perhaps more than anywhere else man is universal. Parisian man is brother to the Bongolanders, twentieth century man is one with the aborigines in that each must regulate his appetites in some way if society is to continue.

What the Ten Commandments prescribe in these areas is the minimum standard by which man's collective life becomes an enduring possibility. In this sense the Ten Commandments are to man's social order what the opening chapter of Genesis is to the natural order; without each there is formlessness and the void. Just as Genesis is an explosive denial of the randomness of the physical universe, so the Ten Commandments take their stand against chaos in the social order. Regarding force they say in effect: You can bicker and fight but one thing is out; namely killing within the ingroup. For this, we have found, sets going that awful social cancer the blood feud which can rip the community to shreds. Therefore, *thou shalt not murder*. Similarly with sex. You can be a rounder, flirtatious, even promiscuous, and although such behavior is not commendable we shall not get the law after you. But at one point we draw the line; you are not to play around with another man's wife, for this rouses passions the community cannot endure. Catch you at this and we will string you up. *Thou shalt not commit adultery*. As to possessions, you may make your pile as big as you please and in so doing you may use your shrewdness and cunning. But there is one thing you may not do and that is pilfer directly off the other fellow's pile. For this outrages the most minimal sense of fair play and builds up animosities that become ungovernable. *Thou shalt not steal*. Finally, regarding the spoken word you can be as cagey and cunning, as deceptive and round about as you wish, but there is one time when we require of you the truth. If a dispute reaches such proportions as to be brought before the tribal court, on such occasions the judges must know what happened. Catch you lying then, when you are under oath to tell the truth, and the penalty will be heavy. *Thou shalt not bear false witness.*

The importance of the Ten Commandments in their ethical dimension lies not in their uniqueness but in their universality, not in their finality but in their inescapable priority. They do not speak the final word in any area they touch; they speak instead the first word which must be spoken if other words are to follow. This is why, over three thousand years after their formulation, they remain the moral cornerstone of half the world. It is what led Heine to exclaim of the man who transmitted them, "How little does Sinai appear when Moses stands upon it"; and the Biblical writers to assert categorically, "There arose not in Israel [another] prophet like Moses." (Deut. 34:10.)

MEANING IN JUSTICE

It is to a remarkable group of men whom we call the Prophets more than to anyone else that Western civilization owes its double conviction (1) that the future of any people depends in large part on the justice of their social order, and (2) that individuals are responsible for the condition of their society as well as for the tidiness of their personal lives.

When someone today is referred to as a prophet or said to prophesy, we think of him as foretelling the future. This was not the original meaning of the word. "Prophet" comes from the Greek word *prophetes* in which *pro* means "for" and *phetes* means "to speak." In the Greek, then, a prophet is someone who "speaks for" someone else. This meaning is faithful to the original Hebrew. When God commissions Moses to demand from Pharaoh the release of his people and Moses protests that he cannot speak, God says, "Aaron, thy brother, shall be thy prophet" (Ex. 7:1).

If for the Jews the general meaning of the word prophet was "one who speaks on the authority of another," its special meaning as used to refer to a distinctive group of persons in the Biblical period was "one who speaks for God." A prophet differed from other men in that his mind, his speech, and even at times his body could become a conduit through which God could speak to man.

The ways in which the divine laid hold of the prophets differed as the history of the prophetic movement clearly indicates. Moses, as we saw in the last section, stands to one side in a class by himself, but when we come to prophecy as a historical movement, we find it developing through three stages.

The first is the stage of the Prophetic Guilds, of which the Ninth and Tenth Chapters of First Samuel provide one of the best glimpses. In this stage, prophecy is a group phenomenon. At this stage the prophets are not mentioned by name because their talent does not inhere in them as individuals. Traveling in schools or bands, their prophecy was a "field phenomenon" which could occur only when the group was together. In contemporary psychological terms, it might be described as a form of collective, self-induced ecstasy. With the help of music and dancing the band would work itself up to a state in which it was possessed. Its individuals would lose their self-consciousness in a collective sea of divine intoxication.

There was no ethical dimension to prophecy in this guild stage. The prophets assumed that they were possessed by the divine only because the experience brought an inrush of ecstasy and power. In the second stage ethics entered. This was the stage of the Individual Pre-Writing Prophets. Being alive and in movement, prophecy now began to shoot up individuals like rockets out of its bands. Their names have come down to us—Elijah, Elisha, Nathan, Micaiah, Ahijah, and others—but as they were still in the pre-writing stage no books of the Bible carry their names. Ecstasy still figured large in their prophetic experience, and power, too: when "the hand of the Lord" is on these men they outrun chariots for thirty miles and get caught up from the plains and cast on mountain tops.[6] But two things were different. Though these prophets, too, had a guild base, they could receive the divine visitation while they were by themselves. And second, the divine came through more clearly. No longer did it manifest itself as an overpowering emotion only; it was emotion backing God's demand for justice.

Two episodes from the Bible may be drawn from many to make this unmistakably clear. One is the story of Naboth who, because he refused to turn over his family vineyard to King Ahab, was framed on false charges of blasphemy and subversion and stoned. When news of the incident reached Elijah, the word of the Lord came to him, saying, "Arise, go down to meet Ahab king of Israel. . . . And you shall say to him, 'Thus says the Lord: "In the place where dogs licked up the blood of Naboth shall dogs lick your own blood." ' "

The story carries revolutionary significance for human history for it is the story of how a man without official position of any sort took the side of a wronged man and denounced a king to his very face on grounds of injustice. One will search in vain in the literature of other religions of the time to find its parallel. Elijah is not a priest. He had no formal authority for the terrible judgment he delivered. The normal pattern of the times would have called for him to be struck down by the king's guard on the spot. But the fact that he was "speaking for" an authority not himself is so transparent that the king accepted this verdict of the moral conscience as divine and hence ultimate.

The same striking sequence recurred in the incident of David and Bathsheba. From the top of his roof David glimpsed Bathsheba bathing and wanted her for his wife. One obstacle stood in the way; she was already married. To the royalty of those days, however, this was a small matter. David simply ordered Uriah to the front lines with instructions to his commanding officer that he be placed in the thick of the fighting and support withdrawn so he would be killed. Everything went as planned, indeed the entire procedure seemed routine, until Nathan the prophet got wind of it. Sensing instinctively that "the thing that David had done displeased the Lord," he went straight to his king who had absolute power over his life and said to him:

Thus says the Lord, the God of Israel: 'You have smitten Uriah the Hittite with the sword, and have taken his wife to be your wife. . . . Behold, I will raise up evil against you out of your own house; and I will take your wives before your eyes, and give them to your neighbor, and he shall lie with your wives in the sight of this sun. For you did it secretly; but I will do this thing before all Israel, and before the sun' (II Samuel 12:7, 9, 11-12).

The surprising point in each of these accounts is not what the kings do, for they were merely exercising the universally accepted prerogatives of royalty in their day. The revolutionary and unprecedented fact is the way the prophets challenged their behavior.

We have spoken of the Prophetic Guilds and the Individual Pre-Writing Prophets. The third and climactic phase of the prophetic movement came with the great Writing Prophets: Amos, Hosea, Micah, Jeremiah, Isaiah, and the rest. Again at this stage, ecstasy was not absent from the prophetic experience; Ezekiel 1-3, Jeremiah 1, and Isaiah 6 in which the prophet "saw the Lord, high and lifted up," are some of the most impressive theophanies on record. The ethical emphasis of the Pre-Writing Prophets likewise carried over into this third stage. But in this area there was an important development. Whereas a Nathan or an Elijah sensed God's condemnation of flagrant, *individual* acts of injustice, an

Amos or an Isaiah could sense God's equal revulsion against injustices less personal because they were embedded in the entire social order. Whereas the Pre-Writing Prophets challenged individuals, the Writing Prophets challenged the entire structure of existing *society*.

The Writing Prophets found themselves in a time that was shot through with inequities, special privilege, and injustice of the most flagrant sort. Wealth was concentrated in the hands of rich grandees, the poor were branded like cattle and sold as slaves, persons in debt were traded for a pair of shoes. It was a world in which masters punished and tortured their slaves as they pleased; in which women were subjugated to men and unwanted children were abandoned in lonely places to die.

This moral delinquency was one important fact of Jewish political life of the time, but there was another. Danger within was matched by danger from without, for sandwiched between the colossal empires of Assyria and Babylonia to the east, Egypt to the south, and Phoenicia and Syria to the north, Israel and Judah were in danger of being crushed. In similar situations, the other peoples of the region would have assumed that the outcome rested on the relative strength of the national gods in question—in other words on a simple calculus of power in which questions of morality were irrelevant. Such an interpretation, however, reduces opportunity, and hence meaning in the situation, drastically. If what happens is simply a function of power there is little a small nation can do. This is precisely the conclusion the Jews refused to draw. The most remarkable trait of the Jews as we have contended throughout has been their passion for meaning. Even where it seemed almost impossible to do otherwise, they refused to concede that any event was meaningless in the sense of making no demands or leaving them without significant choice. Thus what other nations would have interpreted as simply a power squeeze, they saw as God's warning to clean up their national life, to establish justice throughout the land, or be destroyed.

Stated abstractly, the Prophetic Principle can be put as follows: The prerequisite to political stability is social justice; it is ingrained in the nature of things that injustice breeds its own demise. In theological terms, God's standards are high; he will not put up forever with exploitation, corruption, and mediocrity. This principle does not contradict what has been said previously about Yahweh's love. On the whole the prophets, like the psalmists, speak more of God's love than of his justice, more of his mercy than of his demands for righteousness. In this section our attention is on justice, but in the prophets' full message God's balancing tenderness figures fully as prominently. A Rabbi later put the relationship between the two thus: Commenting on Genesis 2:4, "In the day that the Lord God made earth and heaven," he said:

This may be compared to a king who had some empty glasses. The king said: "If I pour hot water into them they will crack; if I pour ice-cold water into them they will also crack!" What did the king do? He mixed the hot and the cold water together and poured it into them and they did not crack. Even so did the Holy One, blessed be He, say: "If I create the world on the basis of the attribute of mercy alone, the world's sins will greatly multiply. If I create it on the basis of the attribute of justice alone, how could the world endure? I will therefore create it with both the attributes of mercy and justice, and may it endure!"[7]

The prophets of Israel and Judah are one of the most amazing groups of individuals in all history. In the midst of the moral desert in which they found themselves, they spoke words the world has been unable to forget. Amos, a simple shepherd, but no straw blown north by accident; instead, a man with a mission, stern and rugged as the desert from which he came, a man with all his wits about him and every faculty alert crying in the putrid marketplace of Bethel, "Let justice roll down like waters and righteousness like a mighty stream." Isaiah, city-bred, stately, urbane, cultivated, but no less aflame with moral passion, crying out for one "who will bring forth justice in the land, who will not fail nor be discouraged until he hath set justice in all the earth." Hosea, Micah, Isaiah, Jeremiah —what a company they make! The prophets come from both sides of the track. Some are sophisticated, others as plain and natural as the hillsides from which they come. Some hear God roaring like a lion, others hear him in the ghostly stillness that precedes the storm.

Yet, one thing is common to them all; the conviction that every man simply by virtue of the fact that he is a human being, a child of God, has rights that even kings cannot erase. The prophets come upon the stage of history like a strange, elemental, explosive force. They live in a vaster world than those about them, a world in which pomp and ceremony, wealth and splendor count for nothing, where kings seem small and the power of the mighty is as nothing compared with purity, justice, and mercy. So it is that whenever men and women have gone to history for encouragement and inspiration in the age-long struggle for justice they have found it, more than anywhere else in the prophets.

MEANING IN SUFFERING

From the eighth to the sixth centuries B.C.E. (Before the Common Era as the Jews prefer to render the period B.C.), during which Israel and Judah tottered before the aggressive power of Syria, Assyria, Egypt, and Babylon, the prophets found meaning in their predicament by seeing it as God's way of underscoring his demand for righteousness. God was engaged in a great controversy with his people, a controversy involving moral issues not evident to the secular observer. To correct a wayward child a parent may coax and cajole, but if words fail he will eventually be forced to act. Similarly, in the face of Israel's indifference to his commands and pleadings, God had no alternative but to let his people know who was God—whose will must be done! It was to make this point that God was using Israel's enemies against her.

> Thus saith the Lord:
> For three transgressions of Israel,
>   and for four, I will not revoke the punishment;
> Because they sell the righteous for silver,
>   and the needy for a pair of shoes. . . .
> Therefore an adversary shall surround the land,
>   and bring down your defences from you
> And your strongholds shall be plundered (Amos 2:6; 3:11).

Jeremiah takes up the refrain. Because the Jews had forsaken righteousness,

> Thus saith the Lord: . . .
> Surely I will make you a desert,
> An uninhabited city.
> I will prepare destroyers against you (Jer. 22:6, 7).

We can appreciate the moral energy required to come up with this interpretation of danger. How much easier it is for a people who face danger either to assume complacently that "God and uranium are on their side," or else to give up completely in hopeless resignation.

The climax, however, is yet to come. Defeat was not averted. In 721 B.C.E., Assyria "came down like a wolf on the fold," wiping the Jews' Northern Kingdom from the map forever and converting its people into "the Ten Lost Tribes of Israel." In 586 B.C. Judah, the Southern Kingdom, was conquered too, though in this case its leadership remained intact as Nebuchadnezzar marched it collectively into captivity in Babylonia.

If ever there was a time when the possibility of meaning seemed to have played out completely, this was it. The Jews had had their chance. They had muffed it and, as a consequence, had been brought to their nadir. Surely now the prophets might be expected to concede their people's doom with a self-vindicating "I told you so."

This phrase, however, being a blend of vindictiveness and despair, was not in the prophetic vocabulary. The most staggering fact in the Jewish quest for meaning is the way in which in this zero hour, when meaning had given out in the deepest strata the Jews had yet mined, the prophets dug deeper to uncover an entirely new vein, the vein of meaning in suffering. It was Second Isaiah's thesis, writing in Babylonia in the sixth century where his people were being held captives, that their suffering was not simply chastisement. As long as punishment looms as a conditional possibility, it has enormous meaning, for it warns man of directions in which not to proceed. Once the blow falls, however, there is little further meaning to be found in pain by viewing it retrospectively as punishment for past misdoings. If suffering is to be fully meaningful, it must hold out better or worse ways of responding to it in the present. The *prospect* of national destruction had had tremendous meaning, for it warned the Jews to mend their ways. The *actuality* of destruction was another matter. It was not enough for the prophets to represent its meaning as "Don't ever do that again!" for at the time it seemed unlikely that they would be given another chance. If there was meaning in their defeat it would have to lie in another direction.

The thesis the prophets offered was that the suffering that had come to the Jews was not simply a *punishing* experience. It was a *teaching* experience for them and a *redemptive* experience for the world.

On the teaching side there are lessons and insights which suffering illumines as nothing else can. In this case the experience of defeat and exile was teaching the Jews the true worth of freedom which, despite their early Egyptian captivity, they had come to hold too lightly. Lines have come down to us that lay bare the spiritual agony of these early displaced persons—how heavily they felt the yoke of captivity, how fervently they longed for release.

By the rivers of Babylon, there we sat down.
  Yea, we wept, when we remembered Zion.
We hanged our harps upon the willows in the midst thereof.
For there they that carried us away captive required of us a song; and they
  that wasted us required of us mirth, saying,
  Sing us one of the songs of Zion.

How shall we sing the Lord's song in a strange land.
If I forget thee, O Jerusalem, let my right hand forget her cunning.
If I do not remember thee, let my tongue cleave to the roof of my mouth
    (Ps. 137).

Sometimes a single phrase is enough to convey the poignancy and pathos of their plight: "Is it nothing to you, oh ye who pass by"; or, "How long, O Lord, how long?" When Cyrus, King of Persia, conquered Babylon in 538 B.C.E. and permitted the Jews to return to Palestine the prophets saw another lesson that only suffering can fully teach, the lesson that those who in the midst of adversity do not despair but remain faithful to the best that has been made known to them will be vindicated. The remnant that remains true to God will be restored.

> Go forth from Babylon, flee from Chaldea,
>   declare this with a shout of joy,
>   proclaim it,
> send it forth to the end of the earth;
>   say, "The Lord has redeemed His servant Jacob" (Is. 48:20-22).

But what the Jews might learn from their captivity personally was not the only meaning of their ordeal. God was using the occasion to funnel into history insights every nation needs but which the ease and consequent superficiality of other peoples' experience was keeping them from discovering at first hand. Through their suffering God was burning indelibly into the hearts of the Jews a passion for freedom and justice, counting on these to spread from them to all mankind:

> I have given you as . . . a light to the nations,
>   to open the eyes that are blind,
> to bring out the prisoners from the dungeon,
>   from the prison those who sit in darkness (Isa. 42:7).

In short: stated in a general way, the deepest meaning the Jews found in the Exile was the meaning of vicarious suffering, the meaning that comes to a life that is willing to accept pain in order that others might be spared it. Second Isaiah related this general principle to the experience of his people by envisioning a day when the nations of the earth would see that the tiny nation they once scorned (and whom Isaiah here personifies as an individual) had actually been suffering in their behalf:

> It was our pains that he bore,
> Our sorrows that he carried;
> While we accounted him stricken,
> Smitten by God, and afflicted.

He was wounded for our transgressions,
He was crushed for our iniquities;
The chastisement of our welfare was upon him,
And through his stripes we were healed.
All we like sheep had gone astray,
We had turned everyone to his own way;
And the Lord made to light upon him
The guilt of us all (Isa. 53:4-6).

THE HALLOWING OF LIFE

Up to this point in our effort to enter the Jewish perspective we have been dealing with ideas as these occurred to the Jews in their endeavor to make sense out of life. As an entrance to Judaism this has been advisable, for ideas have a universality which makes them intelligible even to those who stand in a different tradition. We have reached a point, however, where if we are to move deeper into Judaism we must hold further consideration of Jewish ideas and look at Jewish ceremony and observance. For ideas are only one part of Judaism. How far they are from being central is evidenced by the fact that Judaism has never promulgated an official creed, a doctrine which must be intellectually accepted if one is to be regarded as Jew. Observance, on the other hand, has been repeatedly stressed. In this respect Judaism has an Oriental rather than a Western flavor. Whereas the West, following the Greek partiality for abstract reason, has tended to focus religion in creed and theology, the East has approached religion through ritual and narrative. The difference is between the abstract and the concrete. It is the difference between regarding Plato's or Dostoyevsky's writings as closer to reality; between expressing love through words or an embrace.

Before plunging into Jewish ritual as such, it will be well to speak briefly of ritual in general, for despite its place in every major religion we have thus far not taken the occasion to consider it directly. From a narrowly rational or utilitarian point of view, ritual is nonsense, a waste any way you look at it. All the money that goes into cathedrals and prayer books and candles; all the time that goes into worship and prayer and sacrament; all the energy that goes into kneeling and prostration, rising up and sitting down and singing—all of this, to what end? Ritual bakes no bread. In addition it has about it an arbitrariness which makes it almost impossible to be appreciated from the outside. Several years ago a leading picture magazine carried a photograph of Eleanor Roosevelt rubbing noses with Eskimos. To Eskimos rubbing noses is a ritual; to us it is simply funny.

Yet with all its arbitrariness and seeming waste, ritual plays a part in life which nothing else can fill, a part which is by no means confined to religion. For one thing, ritual eases us over tense situations. Some of these are trivial—the matter of introductions, for example. I am introduced to a stranger. Not knowing how he will respond, I don't know how I should approach him. What should I say? What should I do? Ritual covers my uncertainty. It tells me to extend my hand and say "How do you do?" And in so doing it brings form out of chaos. It provides the moment I need in which to get my bearings. The awkwardness is over; I have recovered my balance and am ready for reason to take over and guide my actions.

If we need ritual to help us through situations as inconsequential as a casual introduction, how much more when we find ourselves faced by a situation in which we are really at a loss. Death is a crucial example. Stunned by tragic bereavement, we would flounder completely if we had to think out how to respond. This is why death with its wakes and funerals, its memorial services, and its sitting *shiva* is the most prescribed and ritualized event in all life. Ritual steps in to direct us. It channels our feelings at a time when solitary emotion falters and sustains us until we are able to rely on our independent selves again. In the process it also softens tragedy's blow by making it less. "Ashes to ashes, dust to dust"— the words don't say whose ashes, for this is everybody, all of us. Ritual also counters tragedy with courage: "The Lord giveth and the Lord taketh away; blessed be the name of the Lord!" Finally ritual provides perspective so that the death in question is not seen as an isolated, solitary event. It is a part of the agelong march of life into death, and then into life and death again, with the continuum stretching both ways toward eternity.

From the triviality of an introduction to the shock of death, ritual can smooth life's transition as can perhaps nothing else. But it also serves another function; namely, to intensify appreciation and crown man's joy with celebration. Here an example would be an anniversary, a marriage ceremony, or, most simply, a family's evening meal. Here in this best meal of the day, when perhaps for the only time during the day the entire family is together, a blessing can become something more than a time device for getting the children into their seats so that, like horses, all may begin the race together. It can hallow the occasion. Far from being dead weight, ritual on such an occasion is a celebration of life in its unspeakable goodness.

Against the background of these observations concerning the place of ritual in life generally, we may turn to its place in Judaism. Its basic aim is precisely the hallowing of all life. The Nineteenth Chapter of Leviticus capsules the point when God says to Moses, "You shall say to the congregations of the people of Israel, 'You shall be holy for I, your God, am holy!'" What does holiness involve? To many in the modern world the word has lost its meaning entirely. But those who feel the stir of basic wonder and sense the ineffable pressing their lives from every side will recognize Plato's experience when he writes, "First a shudder runs through you, and then the old awe creeps over you." Those who have had such experiences will know the blend of mystery, ecstasy, and the numinous which has received its finest discursive description in Rudolph Otto's *The Idea of the Holy.*

To speak of the hallowing of life in Judaism is to refer to its conviction that all life down to its smallest element can, if rightly approached, be seen as a reflection of the infinite source of holiness which is God himself. The name for this right approach to life and the world is piety, carefully distinguished from its counterfeit, piosity. In Judaism, piety prepares the way for the coming of God's kingdom on earth: the time when everything will be redeemed and sanctified and the holiness of all God's creation will be fully evident.

The secret of piety consists in seeing the whole world as belonging to God and reflecting his glory. To rise in the morning on seeing the light of a new day, to eat a simple meal, to see a stream running between the mossy stones, to watch the day slowly turn into evening—even small things like these can brim with meaning when seen as allusive of God's majesty. "To the religious man," writes Abraham Heschel, "it is as if things stood with *their backs to him, their faces turned to God.*" To accept the good things of life, most of which come to us quite apart from our own efforts, as if they were matters of course without relating them to God is quite wrong. In the Talmud, to eat or drink without first making a blessing over the meal is compared to robbing God of his property. Through all Judaism runs this double theme: we should enjoy life's goodness, and at the same time we should augment this joy by sharing it with God, just as any joy we feel is augmented when shared with our human friends. Jewish law sanctions all the good things of life —eating, marriage, children, nature, while elevating them all to holiness. It teaches that man should eat, that he should prepare his table in the presence of the Lord; it teaches that man should drink, that he should use wine to consecrate the Sabbath; it teaches that man should be merry, that he should dance around the Torah.

If we ask how this sense of the sanctity of all things is to be preserved against the backwash of the world's routine, the Jew's chief answer is: through tradition. Without attention, man's sense of wonder and the holy will stir occasionally, but to become a steady flame it must be deliberately fed. One of the best means of doing this is to be steeped in a history that cries aloud of God's superb acts of providence and mercy in every generation. Against those who would throw the past away with both hands that they may grasp the present more readily, Judaism accounts the memory of the past a priceless treasure. Most historically minded of all the religions, it finds holiness and history inseparable. In sinking the roots of his life deep into the past, the Jew draws nourishment from events in which God's acts were clearly visible and in doing so keeps the deadly prosaicness of the God-eclipsed perspective at bay. The Sabbath eve with its candles and cup of sanctification, the Passover feast with its many symbols, the austere solemnity of the Day of Atonement, the ram's horn sounding the New Year, the scroll of the Torah adorned with breastplate and crown—the Jew finds nothing less than the meaning of life in these things, a meaning which spans the centuries in affirming God's great goodness to man. Even when he recalls the tragedy of his people and the price of their survival he is made vividly aware of God's sustaining hand. "To live the Law," writes a contemporary Jewish philosopher, "is to live within time the life of eternity."[8]

The basic manual for the hallowing of life is this Law, the first five books of the Bible, the Torah. When in the traditional synagogue service the time comes for returning the Torah to the Ark, the people recite a line from the Book of Proverbs: "It is a tree of life to those who grasp it." There is meaning in this simile, for a tree is symbolic of life itself, of the miracle whereby inert elements in sun and rain and soil are taken up and transformed in the mystery of growth. So, too, for the Jews, the Torah: it too is a creative power which can elicit and sustain holiness in the lives of those whose flowering world would otherwise become a wasteland of dry stones. "It is a tree of life to those who grasp it."

REVELATION

We have followed the Jews in their interpretation of the major areas of human experience and found them coming up with a profounder grasp on meaning than any of their Mediterranean neighbors; indeed, a grasp which in essential respects remains unsurpassed to this very day. The question this raises is: What produced this achievement? Was it an accident? Did the Jews simply stumble by chance on this cache of insight? If they had struck profundity in only one or two areas this thesis might be acceptable, but as they rose to genius on every basic question of human existence it seems inadequate. Is the alternative, then, that the Jews were innately wiser than other people? The Jewish doctrine that all men are members of a single family—symbolically portrayed in the story of Adam and Eve—expressly precludes such a notion. The Jews' own answer is that they did not achieve these insights at all. They were revealed to them.

Revelation means disclosure. When someone says, "It came as a revelation to me," he means that something hitherto obscure is suddenly lit; a veil has lifted, and that which previously had been concealed has now been made known. As a theological concept revelation shares this basic meaning of disclosure but focuses it in the disclosure of a specific object; namely God, his nature, and his will for man.

As the record of these disclosures is in a book, there has been a tendency to approach revelation as if it were primarily a matter of words; to think of it as what God said either to the prophets or through those who otherwise wrote the Bible. This, however, puts the cart before the horse. For the Jews, God revealed himself first and foremost in what he did; not in words but in deeds. This comes out clearly in Moses' instruction to his people and their descendants: "When your son asks you in time to come, 'What is the meaning of the testimonies and the statutes and the ordinances which the Lord our God has commanded you?' then you shall say to your son, 'We were Pharaoh's slaves in Egypt; and the Lord brought us out of Egypt with a mighty hand.'" The Exodus, that incredible incident in which God liberated an unorganized, enslaved people from the mightiest power of the age, was not only the event which launched the Jews as a nation. It was also the first clear act by which God made known to the Jews the fullness of his nature.

It is true that Genesis describes a number of occasions on which God disclosed himself before the Exodus, but these accounts were all written later in the light of this decisive experience. That God was a direct party to their escape from Pharaoh the Jews had no doubt. "By every known sociological law," writes Carl Mayer, "the Jews should have perished long ago." The Biblical writers would have placed the emphasis differently: by every known sociological law the Jews should never have begun to exist at all. Yet here was the fact: a tiny, loosely-related group of people who had no real collective life of their own and who were in servitude to the great power of the day had succeeded in making their get-away and in eluding the chariots of the pursuers. Knowing their own weakness as vividly as Egypt's strength, it seemed to the Jews flatly impossible that the liberation was of their own doing. It was a clear miracle. "By the grace of God, Israel was saved from death and delivered from the power of the Egyptians" (Ex. 12:50).

Having been made vividly aware of God's saving power in the Exodus, the Jews proceeded to review their earlier history in the light of this revealing experience. As their liberation had obviously been engineered by God, what of the sequence leading up to it? Had this been mere chance? Looking back it seemed to the Jews that God's initiative had been involved in every decisive step of their corporate existence. No vagabond impulse had prompted Abraham to leave his home in Ur and assume the long, uncharted trek toward Canaan. Yahweh had called him to father a people to destiny. So it had been throughout: Isaac and Jacob had been kept providentially and Joseph exalted in Egypt for the express purpose of preserving his people from famine. From the perspective of the Exodus everything fell into place: from the very beginning God had been leading, protecting, and shaping his people for this climactic event which gave birth to their nation.

The Exodus, we are saying, was more than an historical divide which turned a people into a nation. It was an episode in which this people became overwhelmingly aware of God and for the first time perceived his character clearly. But to put it this way—to say that the Jews perceived God—is to put the matter quite backward from the way they saw it. As the initiative had obviously come from God, he should be the subject of the assertion, not its object. Strictly speaking, the Jews had not perceived God; God had disclosed himself to them, inescapably and overwhelmingly.

And what was the nature of the God who thus vividly revealed himself in the Exodus? First, he was a God of power—power enough to outdo the mightiest empire, Egypt, with whatever gods might be backing it. But equally, a God of goodness and love. Though this might be less obvious to outsiders, it was overwhelmingly evident to the Jews who were its immediate recipients. Repeatedly their gratitude burst forth into song: "Happy art thou, O Israel; who is like unto thee—a people saved by Yahweh" (Deut. 33:29). Had they as Jews done anything to deserve this miraculous release? Not as far as they could see. Freedom had come to them as an act of sheer, spontaneous, unmerited grace, a clear instance of Yahweh's unanticipated and astonishing love. It is of small moment whether the Jews recognized at once that this love was for all men, not just for themselves. Once the realization of God's love had taken root, it would spread quickly to encompass everyone. By the eighth century B.C.E., the Jews would be hearing God saying, "Are ye not as the Ethiopians to me?" But before the question of the range of God's love could become meaningful the *fact* of that love had first to be grasped, and it was in the Exodus that this fact first dawned upon the Jews with clarity.

Besides God's power and love, the Exodus disclosed a God who is intensely concerned with man and his doings. Whereas the gods of the other peoples of the region were primarily nature gods, deifying the numinous awe men felt for the natural powers of the universe, Israel's God had revealed himself not primarily in sun or storm or fertility but in an historical event. The difference this made to Jewish religion cannot be exaggerated. Disclosing to them as it did a God who cared enough about man's historical situation to intervene directly in it, it turned Judaism from the prevailing preoccupation of the surrounding religions —which was to keep the forces of nature operating beneficially—and directed its primary concern toward achieving God's will in the affairs of men.

Given these three basic disclosures by God in the Exodus—his power, his goodness, and his concern with the happenings of history—the Jews' other insights into his nature followed readily enough. If God is himself good, there can be little question concerning his will for men: he will want them to be good as well. Hence Sinai. It was no accident that the Ten Commandments, as the Jews' understanding of God's will for his people, followed the Exodus immediately. God's goodness calls for an answering goodness from men. The prophetic demand for justice, in turn, was simply an extension of Sinai's moral expectations to the entire structure of society, while suffering was plumbed for significance because the Jews found it unthinkable that a God so good to his people at their start ever would abandon them utterly.

The entire gestalt when it burst upon the Jews took shape around the idea of the covenant. A covenant is a contract, but more. Whereas a contract (to build a house for example) concerns only a part of the lives of those who enter it, a covenant (such as marriage) involves the pledging of total selves. Another difference is that a contract usually has a terminus, a completion date, whereas a covenant carries through to death. To the Jews, God's singular disclosure of himself in the Exodus was invitation to a covenant of these proportions. Yahweh would continue to give himself in goodness to his people if they in their turn would pledge themselves to keep his commandments.

You have seen what I did to the Egyptians,
  and how I bore you on Eagle's wings
  and brought you to Myself.
Now, therefore, if you will obey My voice
  and keep My covenant,

You shall be My own possession
  among all peoples;
  for all the earth is Mine,
And you shall be to Me a kingdom of priests
  and a holy nation (Ex. 19:4-6).

Once the covenant relation was clearly formulated at Sinai, those who wrote the Bible saw the Abraham epic in its light as well. In the last days of the Sumeric universal state, from all the peoples of the mighty Euphrates region God called Abraham and entered into compact with him. If Abraham would be faithful to God's will, God would not only give him a goodly land as his inheritance but would cause his descendants to number as the sands of the sea.

We began this chapter by taking as our key to Judaism its promulgator's passion for meaning. Having advanced in our understanding of the religion, however, we now see that the key must be recast. Meaning is here, it is true, but from the Jewish perspective it was not gotten because the Jews sought it with exceptional diligence. It was revealed to them; by which we do not mean that it was told to them but that it was shown to them through decisive events. The sequence began with the startling disclosure of Yahweh's goodness, might, and concern in the incredible act of the Exodus; from this we can understand how the rest might flow.

But why was this disclosure made to the Jews? Their own answer has been: because we were chosen. The answer is so simple it sounds ingenuous. Whether or not it actually is, we must now see.

THE CHOSEN PEOPLE

There is a familiar quatrain that runs:

> How odd
> Of God
> To choose
> The Jews.

Certainly the doctrine that a universal God of all peoples chose to reveal himself uniquely and incomparably to one is among the most awkward doctrines to take seriously in the entire study of religion.

It is awkward not only because it seems to violate all principles of impartiality and fair play, but because first and last so many people have made similar and thereby incompatible claims. One thinks, for example, of Japanese Shintoism with its conviction that the Land of the Sun and its people were created by special fiat for the express glory and beatitude of the Sungod himself. Considering the regularity with which this kind of claim is repeated in early religions, is there any reason to think we are in the presence of anything other than conventional religious chauvinism when we find Moses saying to his fellow Jews: "The Lord God has chosen you to be a people for His own possession, out of all the peoples that are on the face of the earth" (Deut. 7:6)?

It is true that the Jewish doctrine of the election begins in conventional mold. But almost at once it produces a sharp surprise. For unlike other people, the Jews did not take themselves to have been chosen primarily as recipients of special privilege; they were chosen to serve and to suffer the ordeals such service entails. By requiring that they "do and obey all that the Lord hath spoken," their election imposed on them a far more exacting morality than that of their contemporaries. The point has been nicely embodied in a Rabbinic theory that God initially offered the Torah to every other nation on earth but found only the Jews willing to accept the rigor of its demands; and even they, so this theory ends whimsically, did so in a moment of impulse without realizing what they were getting into. For acceptance of the lofty demands of the Torah opened the Jews to penalties for its violation.

> You only have I known of all the families of the earth;
> Therefore I will visit upon you all your iniquities (Amos 3:2).

Nor was this all. Second Isaiah's doctrine of vicarious suffering meant that the Jews were elected to shoulder a suffering which would otherwise have been distributed among the nations of the earth generally:

> It was our pains that he bore,
> Our sorrows that he carried. . . .
> He was wounded for our transgressions. . .
> And the Lord made to light upon him
> The guilt of us all (Isa. 53:4, 5, 6).

How different from the routine variety this Jewish doctrine of election turns out to be; how much more demanding, how unenviable to man's normal inclinations! Still, the problem is not resolved. For grant that

God called the Jews to heroic ordeal instead of to sinecure, the fact that he singled them out for any role of special partnership in the redemption of the world is still indication that he held them in special regard and even love. The Bible states the fact openly: "It was not because you were more in number than other people. . . . but . . . because the Lord loves you [that he] has chosen you to be a people for his own" (Deut. 7:6-8).

This rankles. Flying as it does in the face of all democratic sentiments, it has provoked a special theological phrase to accommodate it: "the scandal of particularity," the doctrine that God's saving action in addition to enveloping history as a whole has focused at special times, in specific places, and upon particular people.

We shall not be able to prove the validity of this doctrine, but three things we can do. We can understand (1) what led the Jews to adopt it, (2) what it did for their history, and (3) why God's revelation to man might require something of the sort.

Search for what inclined the Jews to the conviction that they were God's chosen will carry us past an obvious possibility—national arrogance —to the facts of history we noted in part in the preceding section. Israel was brought into being as a nation by an extraordinary occurrence in which a nondescript group of slaves broke the bonds of the mightiest power of their day and were lifted to the status of a free and self-respecting people. Almost immediately thereafter they had been brought to an understanding of God that was immeasurably above that of their contemporaries and had deduced from it standards of morality and justice that still indict the world. Through the more than three thousand years that have followed they have continued their existence in the face of fantastic odds, and have contributed to civilization out of all proportion to their numbers.

From beginning to end—this is the point that lies at the heart of the matter—the story of the Jews has been a story contrary to expectation. According to expectation they should not have escaped from Pharaoh in the first place; they should have been recaptured. Why their God, Yahweh, becomes in their eyes a God of righteousness whereas Chemosh, the god of the Moabites, or any of the other surrounding deities do not, is, as even such a protagonist of natural explanation for Biblical matters as Wellhausen admits, "a question to which one can give no satisfactory answer." The prophetic protest against social injustice is universally conceded to be "without close parallel in the ancient world."[9] We have already quoted the judgment of a sociologist that "by every sociological law the Jews should have perished long ago"; to which we may now add that of a noted philosopher, Nicholas Berdyaev: "The continued existence of Jewry down the centuries is rationally inexplicable."

If what these facts and judgments attest is true and Jewish history and achievement *have* been atypical, there are two possibilities. Either the credit belongs to the Jews themselves, or it belongs to God. Given this alternative the Jews instinctively turned the credit Godward. One of the striking features of this exceptional people has been their refusal to see anything intrinsically exceptional in themselves *as people*. According to a Midrashic legend, when God took clay for the making of Adam he gathered it from every part of the world and from every color of earth to insure the universality and basic homogeneity of the human race. Whatever special had come to the Jews could not have been by their own doing. The only alternative was that it had come from God's special grace. Thus it is that a concept which looks at first to have been prompted by national arrogance turns out to be the humblest interpretation they could give of the facts they found coming their way.

When we turn to the question of what the conviction of their election did for the Jews once they became convinced of it, the answer is obvious. Nothing awakens response from people so much as the demonstration of interest in them; whether it be a child flowering under its mother's love, a student coming to life in response to a teacher's expectations and interest, or a girl blossoming from a suitor's attentions, no principle of human relations is better documented than this. It worked for the Jews as well. Nothing does more to explain the extraordinary response the Jews have made to the diverse and severe challenges that have befallen them than the conviction that God loved them uniquely and was counting on them to make his will known and bring healing to the nations.

Both the preceding points have been psychological. With a little thought we can understand quite readily why the Jews felt themselves to be chosen and how such a conviction would catalyze their history. But the most important question remains. Was it true? Did God *really* choose them?

This is the point no one can establish objectively, but two observations are in order. First, against the assumption that election outrages the principles of impartiality and fair play it must be noted that the heart of the doctrine is not the issue of favoritism. In the realm of theory, Judaism expressly affirms that the righteous of every nation shall have a part in the world to come; in the realm of historical fact no people have suffered as much as the Jews. The central claim of the election is not that God objectively favored the Jews above all other people but that he revealed himself most clearly through them.

It is possible, of course, to resent particularism even here, but one must ask whether those who do so are not in actuality resenting the kind of world we have. For like it or not, this is a world of particulars, with human minds adjusted to respond thereto. Nothing can register on man's attention unless it stands in some contrast to the rest of the world. Carry this point into theology and what do we have? God doubtless blesses us through the air we breathe as much as through anything, but if piety had had to wait for man to infer God's goodness from the availability of oxygen, it would have been long in coming. Air is too common to provoke a vivid sense of wonder and gratitude. The same holds for history. If God had freed every little people from their oppressors, the Jews would have taken their liberation for granted; the incident would have been routine. Chalk it to man's obtuseness if you will, the fact remains that God's favors could surround man like the sea surrounds fish; if they were standard they would be regarded as commonplace. This being so, is it possible that the only medium through which God *could* have disclosed himself vividly at the start was the particular, the unique, the individual?

Today Jewish opinion itself stands divided on the doctrine of the election. Some Jews believe that it has outgrown whatever usefulness or objective validity it may have had in Biblical times. Playing as it does to invidious comparisons, and no longer factually defensible in any case, it should be dropped without equivocation. Other Jews believe that until the day when the world's redemption is complete God continues in need of a people apart, peculiar in the sense of being God's special task force in history. For these the words of Isaiah speak not only of the past but with continued and contemporary meaning:

> Listen to me, O coastlands,
> 　and harken, you peoples from afar.
> The Lord called me from the womb,
> 　from the body of my mother he named my name.
> He made my mouth like a sharp sword,
> 　in the shadow of his hand he hid me;
> He made me a polished arrow,
> 　in his quiver he hid me away.
> And he said to me, "You are my servant,
> 　Israel, in whom I will be glorified" (49:1-3).

ISRAEL

Judaism is the faith *of* a people. As such it contains, as one of its features, faith *in* a people—in the significance of the role the Jews have played in human history, are playing today, and will continue to play in the future.

This faith calls for the preservation of the identity of the Jews as a distinct and distinguishable people. In the past, Jewish self-identity posed no problem for theory. During the Biblical period, the Jews *needed* to be separate, for intimate cultural fraternization would inevitably have diluted their superior moral and religious outlook. This is clearly the basis of the constant prophetic demand that the Jews remain a "peculiar" people. Later, especially in post-mediæval Europe up to the French Revolution, the Jews were *forced* to be separate. Required to live in ghettos surrounded with walls whose gates were locked at night, they had no alternative but to live a life that was almost entirely their own.

Since the French Revolution the issue of Jewish integrity in the sense of integralness—strong coherence in a life pattern clearly distinguishable from that of others—has become more of a problem. With the emancipation of the Jews and their entry into the political, professional, and cultural life of the nations in which they live, it is no longer required from without. Nor is there the clear ethical discrepancy that once compelled the Jews to remain aloof from their neighbors on moral grounds. Today Jewish separatism stands in need of argument.

Within Judaism itself the arguments differ. Some Jews follow the religious argument of the preceding section: as God has chosen Israel to be the unique instrument of his will, it is imperative that this instrument retain its form and edge. Other Jews find the rationale for distinctiveness more in philosophy than in religion, in a thesis which has come to be known as cultural pluralism. According to this doctrine, man's life together, if it is to be creative, requires both unity and variety. Unity is obviously needed if man's energies are not to be wasted in brute conflict. But variety is equally essential, for monotony, sameness, and conformity threaten man's spirit as surely as head-on antagonism. As great orchestral music calls not only for many instruments but for many kinds of instruments, so great culture requires the presence of multiple convictions and virile differences. These group differences and loyalties need not threaten the unity of mankind as a whole. The organs of a body are very different, but a body's unity far exceeds a sandpile's whose grains are nearly identical.

The implications of this doctrine of cultural pluralism for Judaism are plain. In retaining his distinctiveness, the Jew is in no way betraying the human race or the nation in which he happens to live. Quite the contrary: living as he does in a time when democracy's greatest threat is man's shakedown into an undifferentiated, agglomerated herd or mass, to absorb and be absorbed in a great and distinctive tradition is the most hopeful contribution a Jew could seem to make. This is not an abstract hypothesis. Since their emancipation from the ghettos, the contribution of the Jews to almost every aspect of culture has been far out of keeping with their numbers. One thinks immediately of Marx, Freud, and Einstein. Agree or disagree with their views, is it possible to name three men of the last century who have had greater influence? And their names would be just the beginning, for though the Jews comprise less than two per cent of Western man, in field after field they have ranked the contributors of their day.

If the argument thus far has carried weight and we have been able to catch some of the Jew's sense of the importance of maintaining his separate identity, of what is this identity to consist?

Not doctrine, we must answer at once. There is nothing one *has* to believe in order to be a Jew. Jews run the entire gamut from those who are convinced that every syllable of the Torah was dictated by God to those who do not believe in God at all. Indeed, it is impossible to name any one thing which of itself suffices to make a person a Jew. Judaism is a complex. It is like a circle: a whole, yet divisible into sections all of which converge toward a common center. There is no law or authority which says that a Jew must incarnate all of these areas—or any of them —or face excommunication from his people. At the same time, the more a Jew does embody these features, the more completely will he be a Jew.

Generally speaking, the four great sectors of Judaism which converge to define the spiritual anatomy of the complete Jew are faith, observance, culture, and nation. The character and content of Jewish faith need not be repeated here, for it has been outlined in the first seven sections of this chapter. In the intellectual stance from which they approach this faith, Jews run the entire range from extreme fundamentalists to ultra-liberals, but the direction their faith takes thereafter is remarkably uniform and substantially as we have described it. The same may be said of Jewish observance. Orthodox Jews steep an amazing portion of their lives in Sabbath, dietary, home, and other rituals; Reform Jews observe very few, while Conservative Jews fall midway between. Yet however great the difference in extent of observance, its intent is the same: the hallowing of life as we have described it. What remains is to say a few words about the other two components of total Judaism; namely, culture and nation.

Culture, denoting as it does a total way of life, is by definition an all-inclusive term which defies exhaustive description. It includes folk-ways, art forms, styles of humor, philosophy, and who can say precisely what else? All of these are to be found in that subtle yet definite complex called Jewish culture. In fact, they are present so richly that we shall have to limit ourselves to three specific items. Jewish culture involves a language, a lore, and an affinity for a land.

Its lore is apparent, for much of it has spilled over into Western culture generally. There is an aura that surrounds Old Testament characters and events that dwarfs Olympus. But for Judaism this is only the beginning. The Torah is followed by the Talmud, a vast com-pendium of law, commentary, history, and folklore which is the basis of post-Biblical Judaism. This in turn is supplemented by the Midrashim, an almost equal collection of legend, exegesis, and homily which began to develop before the Biblical canon was fixed and was not completed until the late Middle Ages. The whole provides an inexhaustible mine for scholarship, anecdote, and general cultural enrichment.

In addition to its lore, every people has its language and its land. For the Jews, these are, respectively, Hebrew and the land of Israel. Both are sacred for their associations. It was in Hebrew and in the Holy Land, together with Sinai, that revelation came to the Jews. Reverence for this revelation led naturally by transference to reverence for the idiom through which it grew and the land from which it sprang. It is in Hebrew that a Jew conducts all or part of his prayer and worship, while consciousness of the Holy Land pervades the Torah he reads, the prayers he recites, and the Rabbinic literature he studies. It is one of the para-doxes of Judaism that during the two thousand years in which it jumped every national boundary and required no habitation other than the souls of men, it retained its passion for the land of its birth. At every public service, morning, afternoon, and evening, and in each private devotion whether in grace after meals or after retiring at night, Jews prayed for their return to Zion.

In the opening pages of this chapter we quoted Edmund Wilson as describing Palestine as "mild and monotonous." To the Jew this descrip-tion seems incredible, for it is a wonderful land, even physically. Much of its terrain is spectacular: the course from Jerusalem to the Dead Sea that falls 3481 feet in thirty-five miles, the Jordan that cuts deeply through rock as it winds south from Mount Hermon, the spiny ridge that runs southward from Mount Carmel by the sea, the rough wilderness of Tekoah that runs off southward into the deeper desolation of Negev, sharp contrast to the lush greenness along the south Jordan. There are the pinnacles of cypress reaching up like dark spires, the Fields of Esdraelon that slope up toward Galilee in a broad checkerboard of brown and green, the harbors deep with the blue of the Mediterranean, all bathed in a brilliant sunlight and limpid air that lifts the expectant spirit. History cries out from every city and hillside storied in the past. A brooding sense of the ages is present everywhere, now as when the ancient Hebrew seer beheld, enthroned, the "Ancient of Days."

But to speak of this land is to lead to the fourth component of total Judaism, the nation. For we live in a generation when, for the first time since their compulsory dispersion in 70 C.E., Palestine has been returned to the Jews.

The reasons leading to the establishment in 1948 of the modern state of Israel are complex. Beyond the powerful religious pull toward return, the chief contributing motifs can be catalogued as four.

1. The argument from security. The savage anti-semitism of the Nazis in which 6,000,000 Jews—one-third their total number at the time—were obliterated, convinced many Jews that their security in the face of latent anti-semitism in other lands was more apparent than real, and that complete safety could be realized only in a land of their own.

2. The psychological argument. Some were convinced that it was psychologically unhealthy for the Jews to be everywhere in minority status, that this was breeding in them a subservience and self-repudiation which only the having of a nation of their own would cure.

3. The cultural argument. The stuff of Judaism was running thin and its tradition was bleeding to death. Somewhere in the world there needed to be a place where Judaism could be the primary culture of the Jews.

4. The argument from idealism. Somewhere in the world there ought to be a nation dedicated to the complete historical realization of prophetic ideals and ethics.

Whatever the reasons that have gone into her creation, however, Israel is here. Already her achievements have been spectacular. Her land reclamation—land creation might almost be a more accurate phrase— her provisions for the laboring class, her new patterns of group living, her intellectual and cultural vitality, have all combined to make this new nation one of the most exciting social experiments in contemporary history.

There is a striking point that runs through Jewish history as a whole. Western civilization was born in the Middle East, and the Jews were at its crossroads. In the heyday of Rome, the Jews were close to the Empire's center. When power shifted eastward, the Jewish center was in Babylon; when it skipped to Spain, there again were the Jews. When in the Middle Ages the center of civilization moved into central Europe, the Jews were waiting for it in Germany and Poland. The rise of the United States to the leading world power found Judaism focused there. And now, today, when the pendulum seems to be swinging back toward the old world and the East rises to renewed importance, there again are the Jews in Israel. As the Star of David waves over their spiritual home for the first time in history and Israel stands again on its feet, the dominant thought in the minds of the Jews is: How wonderful to be alive today when all this is happening!

SUGGESTIONS FOR FURTHER READING

Milton Steinberg's *Basic Judaism* (New York: Harcourt, Brace & Co., 1947) is as nice a brief statement concerning this religion as a whole as can be found. For Jewish history, A. L. Sachar's *History of the Jews* (New York: Knopf, 1953) and Solomon Grayzel's *A History of the Jews* (Philadelphia: Jewish Publication Society of America, 1947) are excellent. William Irwin's *The Old Testament: Keystone of Human Culture* New York: Schuman, 1952) provides an admirable summary of the basic ideas of Biblical Judaism, while Joseph H. Hertz's *An Authorized Daily Prayer Book* (New York: Bloch, 1953) will introduce the reader to the world of Jewish piety and observance.

A noteworthy book showing how Judaism has stood out from the ancient religions that have surrounded it is G. Ernest Wright's *The Old Testament Against its Environment* (Chicago: Allenson, 1951).

Of all contemporary writers, Abraham Heschel deals most sensitively with the hallowing of life in Judaism. See especially *The Earth is the Lord's* (New York: Abelard, 1949) and *The Sabbath* (New York: Farrar, Straus, 1951).

Milton Steinberg's *A Partisan Guide to the Jewish Problem* (Indianapolis: Bobbs-Merrill Co., 1945) offers an excellent analysis of the issues confronting contemporary Judaism.

8

Christianity

Of all the religions of man, Christianity is the most widespread and has the largest number of adherents. Almost one out of every three persons today is a Christian, bringing the total number into the neighborhood of 800 million.

Nearly two thousand years of history have brought an astonishing diversity to this religion. From the glittering scene of a pontifical High Mass in St. Peter's to the quiet simplicity of a Quaker meeting, from the intellectual sophistication of Thomas Aquinas to Negroes in Georgia singing "Lord, I want to be a Christian," from St. Paul's, the Parish Church of the British Empire, to Kagawa in the slums of Tokyo or thousands pressing forward in Madison Square Garden at the appeal of Billy Graham—all this is Christianity. From this dazzling and often bewildering complex it will be our task to indicate first the central strain that unites it and then the three major divisions—Roman Catholicism, Eastern Orthodoxy, and Protestantism—that make up contemporary Christendom.

THE ANOINTED

Christianity is basically an historical religion. That is to say, it is not founded primarily in universal principles, but in concrete events, actual historical happenings. The most important of these is the life of a little-known Jewish carpenter who, as has often been pointed out, was born in a stable, died at the age of thirty-three as a criminal rather than a hero, never traveled more than ninety miles from his birthplace, owned

266

nothing, attended no college, marshaled no army, and instead of producing books did his only writing in the sand. Nevertheless, as George Buttrick has added, his birthday is kept across the world and his death-day sets a gallows against every skyline. Who then, was he?

When we try to pin down the biographical details of Jesus' life we are immediately struck—and disappointed—by how little definite information is available. We do not know what he looked like, for though the New Testament is about Jesus, nowhere in it is there a physical description of him.[1] Carlyle once said that though he was a poor man he would gladly give a third of everything he had for an accurate representation of Jesus' physical appearance. "Had these carvers of marble chiseled a faithful statue of the Son of Man . . . and shown us what manner of man he was like, what his height, what his build and what the features of his . . . face were, I . . . would have thanked the sculptor with all the gratitude of my heart for that portrait as the most precious heirloom of the ages." Countless others have yearned to know the human form in which Jesus walked among men those nineteen hundred years ago, but their wishes will have to remain unfulfilled. Those who long for a time machine that would roll back the centuries and set us down in his midst must forever be disappointed. As a consequence, people will continue to visualize him differently. To some he will remain the gentle Jesus, meek and mild, surrounded by children and lambs, who adorns nursery walls. Others will visualize him as a rugged, red-bearded prophet swinging over the hills of Palestine toward Jerusalem.

When we pass from physiognomy to biography, solid information is again surprisingly scant, so much so that the early years of this century produced a small flurry of literature dedicated to the proposition that Jesus never lived at all. The hypothesis was too flimsy to last, but the fact remains that it is impossible to produce a biography of Jesus in the conventional sense of that word—we know too little. We know that he was born in Palestine during the reign of Herod the Great, probably around 4 B.C.—our reckoning of the centuries that purports to date from his birth is almost certainly off by a few years. He grew up in or near Nazareth, presumably after the fashion of the normal Jew of the times. He was baptized by John, a dedicated prophet who was electrifying the region with his proclamation of God's coming judgment. In his early thirties he had a teaching-healing career which lasted between one and three years and was focused largely in Galilee. In time he incurred the hostility of some of his own compatriots and the suspicion of Rome, which led to his crucifixion in the outskirts of Jerusalem.

These come close to being all the undisputed facts of Jesus' career that we have. One cannot relate them without sensing how unimportant such facts really are when taken by themselves. Statistics, as someone has said, are rarely vital. To see the stature of the life and its historical moment we must turn to the *kind* of person he was, the quality and power of his life.

Here, fortunately, we are on much firmer ground. For though, as John Knox has aptly said, the Gospels do not succeed in fully revealing Jesus, they are utterly unable to conceal him. "No critical reader, unless he be entirely devoid of imagination, can miss the might and distinctive force of the personality which moves through their pages. . . . Whatever may be lacking in our picture of Jesus, we know more than enough to characterize him as a person of strange and incomparable greatness." Out of obscurity, he steps forth in heroic dimensions. He belonged to first-century Palestine as Shakespeare belonged to Elizabethan England. It produced him; but it cannot explain him.

Those who were closest to him found themselves gradually induced by what they saw to hold the conviction that he was God. The first acknowledgment of his Messiahship came not from claims he made about himself but from the total impression he made upon his disciples. No man in history has been more exalted since his death, but it is important to remember that no later generation has exalted Jesus more than did his own, the generation of Peter, James, and Paul.

What was there in this life that forced those who knew it best to come to the conclusion that it was divine? The answer takes three parts: what he did, what he said, and what he was.

"He Went About Doing Good"

Let us begin with what he did. The Gospel accounts are filled with praise for his actions. Their pages, especially those of Mark, are crowded with miracles. There is no question but that these impressed the people tremendously. We err, however, if this is where we place our emphasis. For one thing, it was not where Jesus placed his. He never used miracles as a means to convince. Not once did he try to ·amaze, overrule, or bludgeon people into believing in him by waving a magic wand—part of the meaning of his Temptation in the Wilderness lies precisely in his rejection of such approaches as devices of the devil. Almost all his extraordinary deeds were performed quietly, apart from the crowds and as a demonstration of the power of faith. Moreover, other writings of the times contain accounts of miracles in profusion. The fact that we may not believe these other accounts does not affect the fact that the people of the time certainly believed them; but this did not cause them to consider those who worked these other miracles to be divine. They simply assumed that they possessed occult powers, which is not the same thing at all.

We get a better perspective on Jesus' actions if we place the emphasis where one of his disciples did. Once, while addressing a group, Peter found it necessary to compress into short compass what Jesus did during his lifetime. He put the matter in five short words: "He went about doing good." What a simple epitaph, yet it is difficult to imagine a better one. Easily and without self-consciousness, he moved among the dregs of his society, prostitutes, and tax extortionists. Healing, helping people out of chasms of despair, counseling them in their crises, he went about doing good. He went about doing it with such single-mindedness and effectiveness, in fact, that the people who were with him from day to day found their estimate of him modulating to a new category. They found themselves thinking: if God is pure goodness, if he were to take human form this is the way he would act.

"Never Spake Man Thus"

It was not only what Jesus did, however, that made his contemporaries think of him in new dimensions. It was also what he said.

There has been a great deal of controversy over the originality of Jesus' teachings. Possibly the most balanced view is that of the great Jewish scholar Klausner. If you take the teachings of Jesus separately, he wrote, you can find every one of them paralleled in either the Old Testament or its commentary, the Talmud. If, on the other hand, you take them as a whole, they have an urgency, an ardent, vivid quality, an abandon, and above all a complete absence of second-rate material that makes them refreshingly new.

The language of Jesus, in fact, is a fascinating study in itself, quite apart from its content. If simplicity, concentration, and the sense of what is vital are marks of great religious literature, these qualities alone would make Jesus' words immortal. But this is just the beginning. They carry an extravagance of which wise men, mindful of capacity for balanced judgment, are incapable. Indeed, their passionate quality has led one poet to coin a special word for Jesus' language, calling it "gigantesque." If your hand offends you, cut it off. If your eye stands between you and the best, gouge it out. Jesus is always talking about camels going through needles' eyes, of men who fastidiously strain the gnats from their drink while oblivious of the camels humping down their gullets. His characters go around with timbers protruding from their eyes looking for tiny specks in the eyes of their neighbors. He talks of people whose outer lives are stately as mausoleums while their inner lives stink as of bodies in putrefaction. This is not rhetorical technique skillfully added for effect. The language is part of the man himself, stemming from the urgency and passion of his driving conviction.

And what did he use this language to say? Not a great deal, quantitatively, as far as our records have it. All the words of Jesus as reported in the New Testament can be spoken in two hours. Yet they are the most repeated words in the world. "Love your neighbor as yourself." "Whatsoever ye would that men should do unto you, do ye also unto them." "Come unto me, all ye that labor and are heavy laden, and I will give you rest." "Ye shall know the truth, and the truth shall make you free." Most of the time, however, he told stories—parables we call them: of buried treasure, of sowers who went out to sow, of pearl merchants, of a good Samaritan, of a young man who blew his entire inheritance on one huge binge and then found himself cadging scraps from the pigs, of a man who had two sons—the world knows them well. People who heard these stories for the first time were moved to exclaim, "Never spake man thus!"

They were astonished. And small wonder—if we are not it is only because we have heard his words so often that their edges have been worn smooth by familiarity. If we could recover their original impact, we too would be startled. Their beauty would not cover the fact that they are "hard sayings," a scheme of values so radically at odds with those by which we live that they would rock us like an earthquake.

We are told that we are not to resist evils; we are to turn the other cheek. The world assumes that evil must be battled by every means available. We are told to love our enemies and bless them that curse us. The world assumes that friends are to be loved and enemies hated. We are told that the sun rises on the just and the unjust alike. The world resents this, feeling that the sun ought to rise only on the just. It is offended when the wicked go unpunished, and would prefer to see them living under perpetual clouds. We are told that the publican and the harlot go into heaven before many who are outwardly righteous, whereas the world assumes that the good people, the respectable people, the people who fulfill the norm and have nothing to be ashamed of, will, lead the heavenly procession. We are told that the path and gate that lead to salvation are narrow. The world, wrapped in convention and conformity, assumes that it is safest to follow the crowd. We are told to be as carefree as birds of the air and the lilies of the field. The world assumes that we should take infinite care to build our security. We are told that it is as difficult for the rich to enter the Kingdom as for camels to go through the eye of a needle. The world esteems wealth above all. We are told that the happy people are those who are meek, who weep, and are merciful and pure in heart. The world assumes that it is the rich, the powerful, the wellborn who are happy. There blows through these teachings, Berdyaev has said, a wind of freedom and liberty that frightens the world and makes it want to deflect them by postponement; not yet, not yet! H. G. Wells was evidently right; either there was something mad about this man or our hearts are still too small for what he was trying to say.

And what, precisely, was he trying to say? Taken together, his parables and beatitudes, indeed everything he said, form the surface of a burning glass which focuses man's awareness on the two most important facts about life: God's overwhelming love for man, and the need for man to receive this love, then let it flow outward again toward his neighbors.

Jesus was an authentic child of Judaism, heir to the best in her magnificent religious heritage as we have tried to sketch this in the preceding chapter. As such he inherited the Jewish vision of a God of infinite loving kindness whose entire being is bent on man's salvation. If Jesus differed from his compatriots, it was only in taking this vision of God more seriously and sensing it more directly, not in believing something different. God had "smote Egypt" and delivered Israel from her bondage before the Israelites were even a nation to receive his law. This amazing grace had continued to bless the Jews right down through their history. Despite the recurrent apostasy of his people, God had been unswerving in his loving kindness and stubborn love. Time after time, as in his story of the Shepherd who risked ninety-nine sheep to go after one that had gone astray, Jesus tries to convey God's absolute love for every single one of his children. To perceive this love, nay to feel it to the very marrow, was to respond in the only way possible, in profound and total gratitude for the wonders of God's grace.

The only way to make sense of Jesus' extraordinary admonitions as to how we should behave toward our fellow men is to see them as cut to fit this understanding of the God who loves man absolutely without pausing to calculate his worth or due. We are to give others our cloak as well as our coat if they need it—why? Because God has given us what we need. We are to go with others the second mile—again why? Because we know, deeply, overwhelmingly, that God has borne with us not only for a second, but a third, and a fourth, and a fifth. Why should we love not only our friends but our enemies, and pray for those who persecute us? Jesus' answer is explicit: "So that you may be sons of your Father who is in heaven, for he makes his sun to rise on the evil and on the good, and sends rain on the just and on the unjust. . . . You, therefore, must be perfect, as your heavenly Father is perfect." (Matt. 5:44-45, 48.) Paul Ramsey has spelled out this final injunction as follows: "Be ye therefore entirely indifferent to the qualities of character in particular men which usually elicit preference or lack of preference for them"; or, what is the same thing, "Be therefore completely self-giving and redemptive in any single case of your good will, even as your heavenly Father disinterestedly cares for all."[2] Plainly the crater from which Jesus' strenuous perfectionism issues is God's astonishing love for man. Correlatively the reason we find his ethic incredible is that we do not share the premise on which it was based. The reason the love Jesus proposed is so demanding is that it is to be absolutely free, geared entirely to our neighbor's needs, not his due. And the reason this seemed to Jesus the natural way to look at the matter is that this is the way God's love has come to us.

For anyone who proposes to live by Jesus' teachings there are many problems to be faced, of which we can allude to only two. The first is a problem of theory. While Catholics believe that Jesus was omniscient from the moment of conception, most Protestant scholars hold that the New Testament evidence shows that he accepted the apocalyptic view of his day, which held that God was on the verge of intervening in history to establish his Kingdom by divine and dramatic fiat.[3] If so, he was obviously wrong—many Protestants will say this right out loud, adding that he would not have been fully human as the Creeds assert if in certain respects his understanding had not been limited. But would not such an error cancel his ethic? Surely if we believed the world were coming to an end tomorrow, we too could bring ourselves to act nobly and urge others to do the same. Insofar as the doctrine of an imminent Second Coming has been exploded, has not Jesus' ethic lost its validity as well?[4]

Validity has nothing, essentially, to do with genesis. How a thought comes into being is irrelevant to its truth. Let us suppose for the sake of argument that Jesus could not have spoken with the force and clarity he did about the extent to which man should love his neighbors except by believing that God would support this love by his early intervention; even so, would this preclude his teaching from being the supreme truth on the subject, the means by which God established a bridgehead for the view in history? Christians could still see the fact as simply one more evidence of the way God uses lowly things, partial error along with mangers and criminal crucifixions, by which to make his home among men.

The second main problem connected with the ethic of Jesus is not theoretical but practical. We have not one neighbor to love, but many. Suppose I give my neighbor both my coat and my cloak, only to find that another who is less vocal deserves one of them. Suppose I do not resist evil when the target of this evil is not myself but my neighbor? The point is clear enough. Jesus' teachings contain no simple rule of thumb as to what overt acts are required of us. To be a follower of Christ is not to be relieved of the responsibility to think. All that we know in advance of the complex demands of any actual situation is that we must respond to our neighbors, all of them insofar as we can envision the outworkings of our acts, not in proportion to what we judge to be their due but in proportion to their need with the question of the cost to us an irrelevance. In this much the words of Jesus are plain.

"We Beheld His Glory"

We have spoken of what Jesus did and what he said. But these alone would not have been enough to force his associates to the conclusion that he was divine had it not been for a third factor: what he was.

"There is in the world," writes Dostoyevsky, "only one figure of absolute beauty: Christ. That infinitely lovely figure is . . . an infinite marvel." Certainly the most impressive thing about the teachings of Jesus is not that he taught them but that he lived them. His entire life was one of complete humility, self-giving, and love which sought not its own. The supreme evidence of his humility, as E. C. Colwell has pointed out,[5] is that it is impossible to discover precisely what Jesus thought of himself. He was not concerned that men should know what he was. His concern was for people to know God and his will for their lives. By indirection this tells us something about what Jesus thought of himself too, but it is the obvious; he thought infinitely less of himself than he did of God. It is impossible to read what Jesus said about selflessness without sensing at once how free he himself was of pride. The same is true of his observations on sincerity—they could not have been uttered by anyone tinctured by deceit. Truth was to him as the air, falsity as suffocating as a tomb.

Through the pages of the Gospels Jesus emerges as a man of surpassing charm and winsomeness who bore about him, as someone has said, no strangeness at all save the strangeness of perfection. He liked people, and they liked him in turn. They loved him; they loved him intensely and they loved him in numbers. Drawn to him irresistibly, they surround him, flock about him, follow him. He stands by the Sea of Galilee and they press so hard about him that he has to speak to them from a boat. He sets out for the day and a crowd of several thousands accumulates, missing their lunch, staying right through until suddenly they discover they are famished. To say that Jesus responded to these multitudes with an equal love puts the matter the wrong way around—it was the people who were responding to the love which he first had for them. He felt the appeal of people, whether they were rich or poor, young or old, saints or sinners. Mary Magdalene had known many men to love her body, but here was one who loved, instead, *her*—the difference was overwhelming. Jesus had not let even her reputation as a prostitute stand between them. Indeed, whenever conventions raised barriers between person and person, he ignored them. He loved children. He hated injustice because of what it did to what he called, tenderly, "the least of these." Above all, he hated hypocrisy because it hid a man even from himself and precluded that wealth of fellowship he sought to build among men. In the end, especially when he laid down his life for his friends, it seemed to those who knew him best that here was a man in whom the human ego had disappeared completely, leaving his life so completely under the will of God that it became perfectly transparent to that will. It came to the point where they felt that as they looked at Jesus they were looking at the way God would be if he were to assume human form. This is what lies behind their final lyric cry: "We beheld his glory, the glory as of the only begotten son of the Father, full of grace and truth."

Shakespeare was no great Christian, but he too was moved to tribute:

> Some say that ever 'gainst that season comes
> Wherein our Savior's birth is celebrated,
> The bird of dawning singeth all night long;
> And then, they say, no spirit can walk abroad;
> The nights are wholesome; then no planets strike,
> No fairy takes, nor witch hath power to charm,
> So hallow'd and gracious is the time.

THE END AND THE BEGINNING

The way Jesus' active ministry ended is known to everyone. After mingling with the people and teaching them for a number of months he was crucified.

That might well have been the end of the story. History abounds with visionaries who proposed schemes, died, and that is the last that was heard of them. In this case, however, it was just the beginning. Within a few weeks his followers were ardently preaching the gospel of Christ the Risen Lord.

The New Testament supplies few details concerning the Resurrection. Three days after Christ's crucifixion, Mary, going to his tomb, found its stone rolled away and the tomb empty. Thereafter Jesus appeared to her and sporadically to a few other followers. That is all; the accounts are meager. Yet there is no question but that faith in the Resurrection gave the impetus to the rise of the Apostolic Church and the Christology that supported it. The word that flashed across the Mediterranean world was not Jesus' admonition to "Love your neighbor." It was the news that Christ had risen, and with it the implication that those who believed in him could, like him and with him, triumph over sin and death to new life. The message was irresistible.

That the first Christians believed that Jesus' body had literally been restored to life is beyond question. To say this is only to begin to understand what this fact meant to them. Others before them had believed that someone they had known or heard of had returned from the dead, but this had not produced a fraction of the dynamic it touched off in the disciples. Standing by itself the resurrection could easily have been dismissed as a freak of nature or an act of wizardry.

To see the disciples' resurrection faith in its fullness we must see it as the resurrection of *Christ*. In his life, as we have noted, the disciples had found pure goodness incarnate. To this goodness, now, was added the supreme exemplification of power. What the resurrection disclosed, therefore, was the juncture of goodness with power—the disciples would not have put it in such abstract terms, but this was its central meaning. If Golgotha's cross had been the end, the goodness Christ embodied would have been tragically beautiful, but how significant? A fragile blossom afloat on a torrent, soon to be dashed—how relevant is goodness if it has no purchase on reality, no power at its disposal? The resurrection completely reversed the cosmic status in which goodness had been left by the crucifixion. Instead of being pitiful it was victorious, triumphant over everything, even the end of all ends, death itself.

Thus the resurrection faith did not deal merely with the fate of a good man. Its full referent was the character of God and the nature of ultimate reality. For if Christ's life and death had convinced the disciples of God's love, his resurrection convinced them of his power, demonstrating conclusively that neither the worst men can do (crucify the one who loves them most) nor even the seemingly inexorable laws of nature (death) can block God's work. Power as well as goodness are completely his. If the disciples' encounters with Christ's perfect life had ended with his death, their whole conception of God would have been left where it rests in most men's thought whether they admit it or not; either God doesn't care or he doesn't count—indifferent power has the last word. As it was, they had proof that the God who so loved the world that he sent his only begotten son was likewise the Lord of lords. To the first Christians the resurrection meant this in a very personal way, for they had individually experienced Christ's love for each of them. If, as the resurrection proved, this love was backed by a power that was absolute, what harm could possibly befall them? They stood supported by Christ's sovereign power forever.

Most Christians today continue to believe in the bodily resurrection of Christ, but even of those who do not, most claim to share in the resurrection faith. For if the ultimate referent of this faith is not what happened to a particular human frame but rather the status of God—his absolute lordship over both nature and history—"modernist" Christians claim to be in full accord with the original Christians on the central point in question. The faith of these moderns entails the belief that God could have resurrected Christ's body if it had been essential to his purpose, and the further belief that something equally contrary to our usual estimates of how little God and his goodness avail did happen in that Holy Week gestalt that climaxed in Easter and led on from there to Pentecost. They grant, further, that if these beliefs cannot take hold of us without our believing that Jesus' body actually rose from the tomb, we come closer to the truth about God if we believe that it did than that it did not. But to insist that despite the scantiness of our evidence there is only one legitimate view as to what happened in nature and history that first Easter is to focus the resurrection faith on physical externals instead of on the central point.

THE GOOD NEWS

But back to the original Christians. Whether or not Jesus' body actually rose from the grave, no one can doubt that his spirit jumped dramatically to life, transforming a dozen or so disconsolate followers of a slain and discredited leader into one of the most creative groups in human history. We read that tongues of fire descended upon them. It was a fire destined to set the whole Mediterranean world aflame. Men who were not speakers became passionately eloquent. They exploded across the Græco-Roman world, preaching what has come to be called the Gospel, but which, if translated literally, would be called the Good News. Starting in an upper room in Jerusalem, they spread their message with such ardor that in the very generation in which Jesus lived, it took root in all the leading cities of the region.

And what was this Good News that snapped Western history like a dry twig into B.C. and A.D. and left its impact through the Christian Church? Was it Jesus' ethical teachings—the Golden Rule, the Sermon on the Mount? Not at all. There is no teaching of Jesus that could not already be found in other literature of his day. Paul, whose letters epitomize the concerns of the early church, knew a great deal about what Jesus had taught, but he almost never quotes him. Obviously the news he found so exciting was neither Jesus' ethical precepts nor even the phenomenal way in which his life had exemplified them. It was something quite different.

What this other something was may be approached through a symbol. If we had been living around the eastern Mediterranean in the early centuries of the Christian era we might have noticed scratched here and there on the sides of walls and houses or simply on the ground the crude outlines of a fish. Even if we had seen it in several places we would probably have dismissed it as a doodle—these were mainly seaport towns where fishing entered naturally into the lives of the people. If we had been Christians, however, we would have seen these fish as symbols of the Good News; their heads would have pointed us toward the place where the local Christian group held its underground meetings. For in those years of catacombs and arenas, when to be known as a Christian meant that one might be thrown to the lions or made into a human torch, Christians were forced to more cryptic symbols than the cross. The fish was one of their favorites, for the Greek letters for the word fish are also the first letters of the words "Jesus Christ, Son of God, Savior." This was the Good News, epitomized in the crude outline of an ordinary fish.

But what does the phrase itself mean: Jesus Christ, Son of God, Savior? Those who have grown up with it every Sunday may know the answer well. Our task, however, is to go behind the immense history of this phrase and try to work our way into what it meant to the men and women who first uttered it, for the entire subsequent history of Christianity grew out of their understanding of its significance.

In doing so one is tempted to plunge at once into ideas, definitions, and theology, but it will be wise to begin otherwise. Ideas are important in life, but they seldom, of themselves, provide starting points. They grow out of facts and experiences, and torn from this soil lose their life as quickly as uprooted trees. We shall find ourselves quite incapable of understanding Christian theology unless we manage to see clearly the experience it tried to account for.

The man in the street who first heard Jesus' disciples proclaiming the Good News was as impressed by what he saw as by what he heard. He saw lives that had been transformed—men and women ordinary in every way except for the fact that they seemed to have found the secret of living. They evidenced a tranquillity, simplicity, and cheerfulness that their hearers had nowhere else encountered. Here were people who seemed to be making a success of the greatest enterprise of all, the enterprise of life itself.

Specifically there seemed to be two qualities in which their lives abounded. The first of these was mutual affection. One of the earliest observations about Christians we have by an outsider was, "See how these Christians love one another." Here were men and women who not only said that all men were equal in the sight of God but who lived as though they believed it. The conventional barriers of race and status meant nothing to them. For in Christ there was neither Jew nor Gentile, Greek nor barbarian, bond nor free. As a consequence, in spite of differences in function or social position, their fellowship was marked by a sense of real equality.

Just before his crucifixion Jesus told his disciples, "My joy I leave with you." This joy was the second quality that pervaded the lives of the early Christians. Outsiders found this baffling. These scattered Christians were not numerous. They were not wealthy or powerful. If anything, they faced more adversity than the average man or woman. Yet in the midst of their trials they had laid hold of an inner peace that found expression in a joy that was almost boisterous. Perhaps radiant would be the more exact word, though Paul himself describes the Holy Spirit as intoxicating. Radiance is hardly the word we would use to characterize the average religious life, but none other fits so well the life of these early Christians. Paul is an example. Here was a man who had been ridiculed, driven from town to town, shipwrecked, imprisoned, flogged until his back was covered with stripes. Yet here was a life whose constant refrain was joy: "Joy unspeakable and full of glory." "Thanks be to God who giveth us the victory." "In all things we are more than conquerors." "God who commanded the light to shine out of darkness has shined in our hearts."

"Thanks be to God for his unspeakable gift." The joy of these early Christians *was* unspeakable. As the Fifth Chapter of Ephesians suggests, they sang not out of convention but from the irrepressible overflow of their direct experience. Life for them had ceased to be a problem to be solved and had become a glory discerned.

What produced this love and joy in these early Christians? The qualities themselves are universally coveted—the secret is how they are to be had. The explanation, insofar as we are able to gather it from the New Testament record, is that three intolerable burdens had suddenly and dramatically been lifted from their shoulders. The first of these was fear, even the fear of death. We have the word of Carl Jung that he has yet to meet a patient over forty whose problems did not root back to fear of his approaching death. The reason the Christians could not be intimidated by the lions and even sang as they entered the arena was that this fear had lost its hold. "Grave, where is thy victory? Death, where is thy sting?"

The second burden from which they had been released was guilt. Some persons contend that it is difficult for contemporary man to understand the ancients on this score because they assume guilt to be a vanishing phenomenon. Psychologists do not agree. They see modern man as weighted down by enormous guilt feelings. Indeed, it seems impossible for man to by-pass guilt feeling. No one can live without drawing distinctions of some sort between what he judges to be better and worse. Out of these distinctions there arises in every life a concept of what that life might be. Paralleling this, inevitably, runs the sense of failure. The times that we violate our norms are not confined to ones in which we treat other people less well than we should; they include opportunities for ourselves that we let slip irretrievably. Guilt may keep its distance while the sun is up, but there are times when alone in the night it comes upon us all, "when you wake up cold and all you did seems awful, whatever it was, and shame to make you shake."

> I wake and feel the fell of night, not day . . .
> Self-yeast of the spirit a dull dough sours. (G. M. Hopkins)

We think of Keats as the silver-tongued poet, but how did he think of himself? The epitaph he proposed was, "Here lies a life that was written in water." Unrelieved guilt always reduces creativity. In its acute form it can rise to a fury of self-condemnation that stifles creativeness completely and brings life to a standstill. Paul had felt its force before he gained his personal release: "Wretched man that I am, who will deliver me from this body of death?" (Rom. 7:24.)

The third release the Christians experienced was from the cramping confines of the ego. There is no reason to suppose that prior to their new life these men and women had been any more self-centered than the next person, but this was enough for them to know that their love was radically infected with failure. They knew, in the words of a contemporary poet, that "the human curse is to love and sometimes to love well, but never well enough."[6] Now this curse had been dramatically lifted. In Paul's "I live, yet not I, but Christ liveth in me," the circle of self was broken, leaving love to flow freely from its former, self-demanding constraints.

It is not difficult to see how release from guilt, fear, and self could give men a new birth into life. If someone were actually to save us from these devastating drags against our love and joy, we too would call him savior. But this only pushes our question back a step. How did the Christians *get* free of these burdens? And what did a man named Jesus, now gone, have to do with the process that they should credit it as his achievement?

The only power that can effect transformations of the order we have described is love. It remained for our generation to discover that locked within the atom is the energy of the sun itself. For this energy to be released, however, the atom must be bombarded from without. So too there is, locked within every human life, a wealth of love and joy that partakes of God himself, but it too can be released only through external bombardment, in this case the bombardment of love. We see this clearly in child psychology. No amount of threat or preachment will take the place of the parents' love in nurturing a loving and creative child. We are beginning to see the point likewise in psychotherapy where love is coming to be a key term in theories of treatment. The best evidence, however, is that of personal experience. As reality rather than fiction is what is needed here, let me relate an actual experience of a student in the hope of triggering a comparable memory from the reader's own recollection.

He was a diffident freshman in a small mid-western college when one morning the instructor he most respected opened the class by saying, "Last night I read some of the most significant words I have ever come across, and I want to share them with you." As he proceeded to read, the boy's heart leapt into this throat as he recognized his own words from a paper he had submitted the previous week. As he relates the incident:

"I don't remember another thing that happened during that hour.

But I shall never forget my feelings when I was brought to my senses by the closing bell. It was noon, and October was never so beautiful. I was exultant. If anyone had asked me for anything, I would have given it gladly, for I wanted nothing—I ached only to give to a world that had given so much to me."

The point is: If a boy found himself changed to this extent by the interest a mere man had shown in him, is it difficult to imagine the change that would have come over the early Christians if they really knew themselves to be loved by God? Take his experience and multiply it by the distance between interest and love plus the distance between man and God and we have the measure of the experience that should have been theirs. Imagination may fail us at this point, but logic need not. If we too really felt loved, not abstractly or in principle but vividly and personally, by one who united in himself all power and perfection, the experience could melt our fear, guilt, and self-concern forever. As Kierkegaard says, if at every moment both present and future it were eternally certain that nothing has happened or can ever happen, not even the most fearful horror invented by the most morbid imagination and translated into fact, which can separate us from God's love, here would be the reason for joy.

This love of God is precisely what the first Christians did feel. They became convinced that Jesus was God and they felt directly the force of his love. Once it reached them it could not be stopped. Melting the barriers of fear, guilt, and self, it poured through them as if they were sluice gates, expanding the love they had hitherto felt for others until the difference in degree became a difference in kind and a new quality which the world has come to call Christian love was born. Conventional love is evoked by lovable qualities in the beloved—beauty, gaiety, friendliness, cheerfulness, personal charm, or some other. The love men encountered in Christ needed no such virtues to release it. It embraced sinners and outcasts, Samaritans and enemies; it gave not prudentially in order to receive, but because giving was its nature. Paul's famous description of Christian love in the Thirteenth Chapter of *First Corinthians* ought never, as Paul Ramsey has acutely pointed out, to be read as if he were making a few supplementary observations about a "love" with which we are already familiar. It defines by indication, pointing not to something generally experienced by all men everywhere, like greenness or warmth, but to Jesus Christ. In phrases of classic beauty it describes the divine love which the Christian, insofar as he feels himself encompassed by the love of God, will reflect toward others. The reader should approach this chapter as if he were encountering the definition of some new conception, a quality which, as it had appeared "in the flesh" only in Christ, Paul was describing for the first time.

Love is patient and kind; love is not jealous or boastful; it is not arrogant or rude. Love does not insist on its way; it is not irritable or resentful; it does not rejoice at wrong, but rejoices in the right. Love bears all things, believes all things, hopes all things, endures all things. Love never ends. . . . (I Cor. 4-8.)

So astonishing did the first Christians find this love and the fact that it had actually entered their lives that they had to appeal for help in describing it. Paul, in closing one of the earliest recorded sermons on the Good News, turned back to the words of one of the prophets who in turn was speaking for God: "Look at this you scornful souls and lose yourselves in wonder, for in your days I do such a deed that, if men were to tell you this story, you would not believe it."

THE MYSTICAL BODY OF CHRIST

The first Christians who preached the Good News throughout the Mediterranean world did not feel themselves to be alone. They were not even alone together, for they believed that their Leader was in their midst as a concrete, energizing power. They remembered his having said, "Wherever two or three are gathered together in my name, there am I in the midst of them." So, while their contemporaries were nicknaming them Christ-ians (literally the Messiah-folk), they began to call themselves a church. This is an interesting word in itself. Coming from the Greek word *ekklesia*, it means literally "called out," "those who are called apart." The choice of this name points up how unlike a self-help society the early Christian community thought it was. This was no human association in which men of goodwill banded together to encourage one another in their good works and lift themselves by their collective bootstraps. Though it was composed of human members, it was guided and energized by the power of God himself.

Totally convinced of this, the disciples went out to possess a world which they were convinced God had already possessed for them. Images came to mind to characterize the intense corporate experience they felt. One of these came from Christ himself: "I am the vine, you are the branches." This is obviously a metaphor, but we shall miss the Church's understanding of itself if we do not see the exact sense in which it took it. Just as through a vine there flows a physical substance, sap, which entering into the branches enlivens them and causes them to bear fruit, so a spiritual substance, the Holy Spirit, was flowing from the resurrected Christ into his followers, empowering them with the love which bore good works as its fruit. In this understanding the early Christians read Jesus' full statement on the theme: "I am the true vine. . . . Abide in me and I in you. As the branch cannot bear fruit of itself unless it abide in the vine so neither can you unless you abide in me. I am the vine, you are the branches: he that abideth in me, and I in him, the same beareth much fruit, for without me you can do nothing. If anyone abide not in me he shall . . . wither." (John 15:1 ff.)

Saint Paul adapted this image by using the human body instead of a vine as the life form with which to compare the Church. This preserved the vine's image of a central life-substance animating the parts, but had the added advantage of making a greater place for diversity than a vine's branches suggest. Though the offices and talents of individual Christians might differ as much as eyes and feet, said Paul, they still draw their spiritual life from a single source. "For as the body is one and hath many members and all the members of the body, whereas they are many, yet are one body, so also is Christ."

This seemed to the early Christians to be the completely apposite image of their corporate life. The Church was the Mystical Body of Christ. Mystical in this usage meant supernatural and mysterious, but in no sense did it mean unreal. The human form of Christ had left the earth, but as his work on earth was incomplete he was continuing it, his physical body being now replaced by his mystical body of which he was the head. This Mystical Body was brought into life in the Upper Room in Jerusalem at Pentecost by the power of the Holy Spirit which was its animating force. For "what the soul is to the body of man," writes Saint Augustine, "that the Holy Ghost is to the Body of Christ, which is the Church."

If Christ was the head of this body and the Holy Spirit its soul, individual Christians were its cells, few at first but increasing as the body came of age. The cells of a physical body do not live unrelated; a single life vivifies the whole with each cell sharing in it. Similarly, the Holy Spirit was flowing through and vivifying each Christian, all of whom together constituted the Church's natural form. As man lives through each of his individual cells, so Christ was living in each member of his Mystical Body. The entire aim of Christian worship was to say those words and to do those things that, in helping Christians to realize their inclusion in the Body of Christ, would enable his life to course through their own more potently.

In describing themselves as Christ's body, then, these Christians were not using metaphor loosely, as we do when we speak of a crowd as a "body" of people. They believed themselves to be genuinely "incorporated" into Christ's person. In any given Christian the divine life might be flowing fully, partially, or not at all, according to whether he was active, perfunctory, or apostate in his faith, the latter condition being comparable to paralysis. Some cells might even turn like cancer to devour their host—these are the Christians Paul speaks of as bringing disrepute upon the Church by falling into scandals. But to the degree that a member was in Christian health, the pulse of God coursed through him and the Holy Spirit was his animating power. Not only was each Christian bound to others as part of a common life, but each stood in the closest conceivable relation to Christ himself.

Building upon this early conception of the Church, Christians have generally defined it as having a double aspect. Insofar as it consists of Christ and the Holy Spirit dwelling in men and suffusing them with grace and love, it is perfect;[7] insofar as it consists of human members affected by sin, it is always short of perfection. The worldly face of the church is always open to criticism—joking criticism over its lotteries and interminable chicken dinners, serious criticism over its crusades, inquisitions, and the morals of some of its leaders. But insofar as there have been mistakes, Christians hold that these have been due to the human material through which it has had to work; the divine persuasion itself never wavers.

In what sense there is salvation apart from the Body of Christ is a question on which Christians differ. Some Protestant liberals reject Christianity's historic claim that "there is no salvation outside the Church" completely as indicative of religious imperialism. At the other extreme are the "mushroom sects" that insist that no one but those who are knowingly and formally Christians will be saved. Most Christians, however, answer the question by drawing a distinction between the Church Visible and the Church Invisible. The Church Visible is composed of those who are formally members of the Church as an earthly institution. Pope Pius IX spoke the views of the overwhelming majority of Christians when he rejected membership in the Church Visible as indispensable to salvation. "Those who are hampered by invincible ignorance[8] about our Holy Religion," he said, "and, keeping the natural law, with its commands that are written by God in every human heart, and being ready to obey him, live honourably and uprightly, can, with the power of Divine light and grace helping them, attain eternal life. For God, who clearly sees, searches out, and knows the minds, hearts, thoughts, and dispositions of all, in his great goodness and mercy does not by any means suffer a man to be punished with eternal torments, who is not guilty of voluntary faults." This statement clearly allows for those who are not members of the Visible Church to be saved. Beyond the Church Visible, however, stands the Church Invisible, composed of all who, whatever their formal persuasion, follow as best they are able the lights they have. Most Christians continue to affirm that in this second meaning of the Church there is no salvation apart from it. Most of them would add to this their belief that the divine life pulses more strongly through the Visible Church than through any alternative institution. For they concur with the thought John Donne put poetically in his sonnet on the Resurrection where he says of Christ,

> He was all gold when He lay down, but rose
> All tincture. . . .

Donne was referring to the alchemists whose ultimate hope was to discover not a way of making gold but a tincture that would transmute into gold all the baser metals it touched. A Christian is a man who has found no tincture equal to Christ.

THE MIND OF THE CHURCH

The mind was not the first part of man to respond to Christ. As we have seen, experience came first—the experience of living in the actual presence of a life which drew from the disciples the conviction that if God were to take human form this is what he would be like. But though Christianity did not spring primarily from an act of the intellect, the mind soon found itself involved. This was inevitable. Religion always involves more than man's mind; nevertheless, being a response of his total self, the mind is never omitted. Once Christian experience had occurred, it was only a matter of time until the mind would seek to interpret this experience and Christian theology would be born. From then on the Church would be mind as well as heart.

Forced in this brief survey to choose, we shall confine ourselves to Christianity's three most distinctive tenets: the Incarnation, the Atonement, and the Trinity. From the very names of these doctrines it is apparent that our discussion must be theological, and before going further a word should be said about this discipline. Although our generation is witnessing a theological revival, the discipline is still a long way from her mediæval position as Queen of the Sciences. Modern man is more interested in ethics than in theology. Within Christianity this means that he appreciates the ethical teachings of Jesus more than the theological arguments of Paul. However little he may care to live by the Sermon on the Mount, he at least respects it. Doctrines like those we are about to discuss, on the other hand, he not only disbelieves but also finds tedious or annoying. Even New Testament study in the first third of this century fell in step with this mood to the extent of trying to draw a sharp line between the "religion *of* Jesus" and "the religion *about* Jesus," between the forthright ethics of Jesus and the involved theology of Paul, between the human Jesus and the cosmic Christ, with strong insinuations that in each case the former was the nobler.

Notwithstanding the fact that even seminaries can succumb to this view that the essence of religions is ethics, it is a fatal mistake; so much so, in fact, that it is scarcely too much to say that it can only arise as the result of a kind of religious blindness. For there are persons who are religiously blind just as there are those who can see nothing in painting. Such persons are not found only among skeptics and the unchurched; they number among the conventionally orthodox as well.

High religion always includes, of course, a summons to above-average morality, but it is a fatal blunder to assume that its eyes are fixed primarily on this summons. Its attention is on a vision which, almost incidentally and as a by-product, sets morality in motion. A child growing up in a home has two questions. One of them is, How should I behave? The other, so much the more important that it may never be consciously asked, is, What will happen to me if I fall below my parents' expectations? What are the limits beyond which I will be rejected?

Theology is concerned with this second type of question. Its primary interest is not in how men should behave but in the character of the human situation. This being the more difficult question of the two, theology is often complicated and obscure. But the question with which it deals is basic. Moreover—and here is the paradox of the ethicist's neglect of it—the quality of man's morality depends on the answer he reaches regarding it.

When we apply these considerations to Christianity, we can understand why the New Testament did not close with the Four Gospels. These Gospels present Christ's teachings as to the way men should live. They show the perfection with which he himself exemplified this way.

They are very, very great books. But they fail to tell us how we can act as Christ admonished. How can I become the kind of person who *can* take no thought for the morrow, turn the other cheek, and love without reserve?

This question was left for the other books of the New Testament to answer. We have already sketched the momentous sequence of experiences out of which they grew. Beginning with the disciples' conviction that Jesus was God and the direct experience of his love for them, they were brought to a radical realization that God loved them completely. The idea of God's love was not new, but in Christ's presence it ceased to be an idea and became a living reality. And the experience of its force was revolutionary. By loosing the strictures of guilt, fear, and self-centeredness, it enabled the disciples to love their neighbors to a degree of which they had never before been capable.

This brings us to the creeds, for these are attempts of the early Christian mind to understand conceptually the happening which had produced this change in their lives. The impact of Christ on their lives led simultaneously in two directions. Overtly it led to acts of loving kindness toward their fellow men; intellectually it led to the creeds.

We may begin with the doctrine of the Incarnation. Holding as it does that in Christ God assumed a human body, it affirms that Christ was God-Man, simultaneously both fully God and fully man. To say that such a contention is paradoxical seems a charitable way to put the matter —it looks more like a straight contradiction. If the doctrine held that Christ were half human and half divine or that he was divine in certain respects while being human in others, our minds would not balk. But such concessions are precisely what the creeds refuse to grant. In the words of the Creed of Chalcedon, Jesus Christ was "at once complete in Godhead and complete in manhood, truly God and truly man . . . of one essence with the Father as regards his Godhead, and at the same time of one essence with us as regards his manhood, in all respects like us, apart from sin."

The Church has always admitted that such assertions are anomalous to man's present understanding. The question is whether this is the last word on the matter. Actually we can ask the same question of science. There are so many findings in contemporary physics that refuse to be correlated in a single logical framework that Robert Oppenheimer has proposed a Law of Complementarity as the basic working concept in the field, meaning by this (in part) that opposing facts must be held in tension even where logically they are at odds if they can help account for phenomena observed. In more than one field, it seems, reality can be more subtle than man's logic at any given moment. Whenever we are forced to sacrifice either logic or evidence it would seem wise to stick with evidence, for this can lead to a wider logic whereas a rigid adherence to consistency can easily close the doors to ampler truth.

In suggesting that the early Christians were pressured by evidence into the logic-taxing assertion that Christ was both human and divine, we are of course speaking of religious evidence—intuitions of the soul concerning ultimate issues of existence. Such evidence cannot·be presented with an obviousness that will compel assent, but if we try we can arrive at some intimation of the experiential leads the Christians were following. When in the year 325 the Emperor Constantine summoned the Council of Nicea to settle whether Christ was of the same substance as God or only of like substance, three hundred bishops and attendants came rushing in a frenzy of excitement from all over the empire, many of them with the eyeless sockets, disfigured faces, and twisted and paralyzed limbs they had gotten from Diocletian's persecution. Obviously more than mere words were at stake in such deliberations.

The Nicean decision that Christ was "of one substance with the Father" claimed both something about Jesus and something about God. Note first a claim it implied about Jesus. Among the many possible meanings the word "God" carries, none is more important than "that to which a man gives himself without reservation." In saying that Jesus was God, one thing the Church was saying is that his life provides the perfect model by which men may order their lives. Slavish imitation of details is, of course, never creative, but in proportion as Christ's love, his freedom, and the daily beauty of his life can find their authentic parallels in our own, these too approach the divine.

This much is obvious. But as we enter more deeply into the Incarnation we must be prepared for surprise. To begin with, we usually assume that its most startling claim concerns Jesus. That the son of a Jewish carpenter is to be identified with God—what could be more fantastic than this? Actually, however, the Greeks and Romans who heard the doctrine were more astounded by its other side; it was what the Incarnation asserted about God that they found disturbing. The thought that God might walk the earth in human form was not foreign to their thinking, but that he would voluntarily suffer for man's sake—this was the incredible part of the Christian claim. A God willing to proceed unmajestically, strength willing to become weakness, goodness good enough to be unmindful of its own repute, love plenteous enough to give and ask not for return—the revolutionary feature of the Christ-claim was not what it claimed for Jesus but what it claimed about God. This is why the early Christians seldom spoke of God without specifying that they were talking about "the God and Father of our Lord Jesus Christ." His relation to Christ had brought them a new understanding of his character. Christ was God's mirror; to know what God is like, the creeds were saying, look at him.

We would suppose that the difficult task confronting the Apostles would be to convince their listeners that Christ was God. Actually it proved to be harder to keep his humanity in view. So fast and completely did people accept his divinity that the first creed of the Church had to be directed almost entirely against the Marcion-sponsored, gnostic view that he was this only and not human as well.

I believe in God the Father Almighty, Maker of heaven and earth; and in Jesus Christ our Lord, who was *conceived* by the Holy Ghost, *born* of the Virgin Mary, *suffered* under Pontius Pilate, was *crucified, dead,* and *buried.* . . .

How casually this Apostle's Creed touches on Christ's divinity! Even in the second century A.D. the point had no longer to be argued; it was assumed. The Creed's burden, carried by the words we have italicized, was to hammer home forever the fact that Christ was man as well. He *really* was born, it says; he really suffered, he really died and was buried. These incidents were not just make-believe, a sequence through which God merely gave the illusion of brushing with man's estate. Christ endured these experiences as fully as do we. He was "truly man."

It is not difficult to see why even at the cost of infinite logical awkwardness the Church insisted on Christ's humanity as well as his divinity. A bridge must touch both banks, and Christ was the bridge between God and man. To have said that Christ was man but not God would have been to deny that his life was fully *normative* and concede that other ways might be as good. To have said that he was God but not man would have been to deny that his example was fully *relevant;* it might be a realistic standard for God but not for men. To say that Christ was God is to say that the absolute love he embodied is the ultimate fact in the universe. To say that he was man as well is to insist that God's love is really love, being willing to assume the full conditions of humanity and to suffer. At each point the Christians could have relaxed their claims to relieve the strain on logic, but driven by what they had experienced, they refused to do so.

Turning to the doctrine of the Atonement, we find that its root meaning, of course, is reconciliation, the recovery of at-one-ment. Christians were convinced that Christ's life and death had effected an unparalleled *rapprochement* between God and man. In the words of Saint Paul, "God was in Christ reconciling the world unto himself." The Roman Catholic interpretation of this doctrine is couched in legal language. By voluntarily disobeying God's order not to eat of the forbidden fruit in Eden, Adam sinned. As his sin was directed squarely against God, it was of infinite proportion. Sins must be compensated for, otherwise God's justice is outraged. An infinite sin demands infinite recompense, and this could only be effected by God's vicarious assumption of our guilt and payment of the ultimate penalty it required, namely death.

Leading Protestant interpretations draw more on psychological than on legal concepts. All reconciliation presupposes an estrangement that has been overcome. In the Atonement this antecedent estrangement is between man and God, and its name is sin. It is with sin, therefore, that explication of the Atonement must begin.

Asked on his deathbed whether he had made his peace with God, Thoreau replied, "I didn't know we had quarreled." If there has been no quarrel, no reconciliation is needed; if there is no sin, no atonement is required. Christianity, however, maintains that sin is universal. In asserting this Protestant theology does not mean that everyone transgresses one or more of a bill of particulars, whether blue laws or the Ten Commandments. Kin to the word "sunder," sin in its Protestant interpretation means basically estrangement. By saying that all men are involved in it, this interpretation asserts that quite apart from any individual act of wrongdoing men are strangers to one another more than they should be. We are alienated from each other. We sense this alienation in the stab of jealousy rather than pleasure we feel in another's good fortune. We are tense in the presence of others, anxious as to the impression we shall make upon them. Our eyes are slits, narrowly squinting on ourselves instead of open to the scene of creation as a whole. We are lonely, and, as we look out upon the great unknown, immense, opaque, we are afraid, for we are alienated not only from other men but from the ground of our being which is God. All this is sin. Who can say when the human animal first fell from God's lap into this vast imbalance? The point is simply that it is here, around us, in us, through us, to the very core of our being.

The Christian view that all men are sinners is widely considered a morbid belief. Certainly it asserts a discrepancy between the actual and the ideal in man. But whether this admission is morbid depends on where the ideal is pegged. The New Testament writers who spoke of man's sin were not incompetent observers. The juices of life flowed as strongly in them as in anyone, and man's behavior struck them as embodying roughly the same proportions of good and bad others saw in it. But this, writes Paul Ramsey, "has been their misfortune, their burden and their ultimate hope: no longer to compare men with one another, or one day's deeds with another, but in all things to compare themselves first and secondly mankind in general with the glory of God and the image of perfect manhood seen in Jesus Christ."[9] In Christ the disciples had caught a new vision of what man might be, of the extent to which a love deeper than any they had known might pervade his whole life. John Wesley brings out the difference in the quality of this Christian love when, in saying that we should love our neighbor as he loves himself, he catches himself immediately and adds, "Nay, our Lord hath expressed it still more strongly, teaching us to love one another even as He hath loved us. 'As I have loved you, so love ye one another.' Now herein perceive we the love of God, in that he laid down his life for us."

Who will question that by this standard of love all men are found wanting, which is to say, are in sin, sundered from the life of love? In their encounter with Christ, however, the original Christians found this alienation removed. As we have seen, they felt close to God, loved by him, and loving him in return. As a consequence they found their fear, guilt, and selfishness—all of which are aspects of sin—overcome. And all this had been accomplished by Christ! Back of their theories as to why or how men were saved through Christ was the fact that they had experienced what it was like to *be* saved by him. The Church's theories of the Atonement likewise vary, but they too have sprung from the actual experience of life renewed by exposure to Christ.

The third crucial Christian concept is that of the Trinity. It holds that while God is fully one he is also three. The basis of this doctrine, like the two preceding ones, is contained in the New Testament. Jesus spoke of God. He also said, "The Father and I are one."[10] In addition he speaks of a third party in the Godhead: "I will ask the Father and he shall give you another Paraclete that he may abide with you for ever: the Spirit of Truth, . . . the Holy Ghost whom the Father will send in my name, he will teach you all things." In his final commission to the Apostles he collects these three persons of the Godhead into a single statement: "Go ye therefore into all the world, baptizing in the name of the Father, and of the Son, and of the Holy Ghost."

No concept of Christendom has enjoyed a greater reputation for obscurity than this. The Church itself has confessed it to be a mystery, true but beyond the reach of mind to fathom completely. Nevertheless, as nothing important in religion is entirely removed from human experience, here again it is possible to suggest by analogy something of what the doctrine involves. Some of the analogies that have been proposed are crudely physical (that water can retain its chemical identity while in the distinct states of ice, liquid, and steam); others are subtly psychological. Three that are closer to the latter variety may be mentioned.

Every instance of seeing is a real unity. Nevertheless three distinguishable aspects are involved: the object seen, the act of vision, and the mental interpretation. Similar triune patterns can be discovered in numerous other domains of human experience. Apparently the idea of three-in-one, whatever difficulties it may throw up for the understanding, is not foreign to our experience.

In the religious sphere man confronts God in three places, in the splendor and order of nature, in the historical person of Christ, and in the depth of his own heart. These are equally God; nevertheless they are distinct. They are, respectively, God the Father, God the Son, and God the Holy Spirit.

Dorothy Sayres' play, *The Zeal of Thy House*, proposes the analogy of the artist's creative act. First there is the Creative Idea, effortless and serene, beholding the entire work in an instance, a complete and timeless whole; this is the image of the Father. Next, not in time but in enumeration, there is the Creative Energy, working out the Idea in space and time with sweat and passion; this is the image of God incarnate, the Son, the Divine Word. Finally there is the Creative Power, the response the work elicits from the lively soul that perceives it; this is the image of the in-dwelling Spirit. "And these three are one, each equally in itself the whole work, whereof none can exist without other: and this is the image of the Trinity."

From the standpoint of Christian orthodoxy, it is important not to water down the Trinity by interpreting it as referring to three roles of a single person, as a man may simultaneously be a son, a husband, and a father. As the Athanasian Creed put the matter, "We worship one God in Trinity, and Trinity in Unity, neither confounding the persons nor dividing the Substance." Oneness is needed to insure simplicity and wholeness in man's devotion—there can be no compromise with monotheism. Distinctness is needed, from man's perspective, to do justice to the distinct ways in which this oneness comes to him. But before this, distinctness is required by the Godhead itself. For God is love, and love is meaningless except between persons. "The Godhead," writes a contemporary Roman Catholic theologian, "is a society of three divine persons, knowing and loving each other so entirely that not merely can none exist without the others, but in some mysterious way each *is* what the other is. In the deepest communion of man and woman, each desires to surrender so completely to the other as to be absorbed in that other. But in man, even the closest intimacy remains partial and incomplete. In the Godhead, the separate persons possess one nature. Each person remains himself, yet there is nothing of the divine essence that is not fully shared by each."[11]

Roman Catholicism

We have been speaking of Christianity as a whole. This does not mean that every Christian will agree with all that has been said. Christianity is such a complex phenomenon that it is difficult to say anything significant about it that will carry the assent of all Christians. So it must be stressed that what has gone before is an interpretation. Nevertheless it has sought to be an interpretation of the points which, substantially at least, Christians hold in common.

When we turn from the early Christianity we have been considering thus far to Christendom today, we find the Church divided into three great branches. Roman Catholicism focuses in the Vatican in Rome and spreads from there, being dominant, on the whole, through central and southern Europe, Ireland, and South America. Protestantism dominates Northern Europe, England, Scotland, and North America. The third great division, Eastern Orthodoxy, has its major influence in Greece, the Slavic countries, and the U.S.S.R.

Up to 313 A.D. the Church fought an uphill battle in the face of official Roman persecution. In that year it became legally recognized and enjoyed equal rights with other religions of the empire. Before the century was out, in 380, it became the official religion of the Roman Empire. With a few minor splinterings, like the Nestorians, it continued as a united organization up to 1054. That is slightly more than half the time span from Jesus to ourselves—for roughly half its history the Church remained substantially one institution. In 1054, however, its first great division appeared, between the Eastern Orthodox Church in the East and the Roman Catholic Church in the West. The reasons for the break were complex—geographical, cultural, linguistic, and political as well as religious—but it is not our concern to detail them here. Instead we move to the next great division which occurred in the Western Church with the Protestant Reformation in the sixteenth century. Protestantism follows four main courses—Baptist, Lutheran, Calvinistic, and Anglican—which themselves subdivide until the current census lists over two hundred and fifty denominations in the United States alone. Currently the ecumenical movement is bringing some of these denominations back together again.

With these minimum facts at our disposal we can proceed to our real concern, which is to try to understand the central perspectives of Christendom's three great branches. Beginning with the Roman Catholic Church, we shall confine ourselves to what are perhaps the two most important concepts for the understanding of this institution: the Church as Teaching Authority, and the Church as Sacramental Agent.

First, the Church as Teaching Authority. This concept begins with the premise that God came to earth in the person of Jesus Christ to teach people the way to salvation—how they should live in this world so as to attain eternal life in the next. If this is true, if his teachings really are the door to salvation and if the opening of this door was one of the prime reasons why he came to earth, it seems unlikely that he would have held this door ajar for his generation only. Would he not want his saving teachings to continue to be available to mankind?

The reader might agree but add, "Don't we *have* his teachings—in the Bible?" This, however, raises the question of interpretation. The Constitution of the United States is a reasonably unambiguous document, but our social life would be chaos without some authority—the Supreme Court—to interpret it. Just so with the Bible. Leave it to private interpretation and whirlwind is sure to be the harvest. Unguided by the Church as Teaching Authority, Biblical study is certain to lead different students to different conclusions even on subjects of the highest moment. And since the net effect of proposing alternative answers to the same question is to make it impossible to believe in any as certain, the result of this approach must necessarily be to reduce the Christian faith to hesitation and stammer.

Let us take a specific issue for illustration. Is divorce moral? Surely on a question as important as this any religion that proposes to guide the conscience of man may be expected to have a definite view. But suppose we try to draw the Christian answer from the Bible directly. Mark 10:11 tells us that "Whosoever shall put away his wife and marry another, committeth adultery against her." Luke 16:18 concurs. But Matthew 5:30

enters a reservation: ". . . except it be for the cause of fornication." Saint Paul accepts the stricter view. What is the Christian to think? What are the probabilities that the Matthew text has been tampered with? May an innocent party remarry or not?

The question is only a sample of the many that must remain forever in doubt if our only guides are the Bible and private conscience. Was Christ born of a virgin? Did his body really rise after death? Is the Fourth Gospel authentic? Are impenitent sinners punished forever in hell? Without a sure court of appeal, moral and theological disintegration seem inevitable. It was precisely to avert such disintegration that Christ established the Church to be his continuing representative on earth, that there might be one completely competent authority to adjudicate between truth and error on life-and-death matters. Only so could the "dead letter" of scripture be continually revivified by the living instinct of God himself. This is the meaning of Jesus' words to Peter, "I tell you, you are Peter, and on this rock I will build my church. . . . I will give you the keys of the Kingdom of heaven, and whatever you bind on earth shall be bound in heaven, and whatever you loose on earth shall be loosed in heaven." (Matt. 16:18-19.)

Ultimately this idea of the church as Teaching Authority shapes the idea of papal infallibility. Every nation has its ruler, be he emperor, king, or president. The earthly head of the Church is the Pope, successor of St. Peter in the bishopric of Rome. The doctrine of papal infallibility asserts that when the Pope speaks officially on matters of faith or morals, God stays him against the possibility of error.

This doctrine is so often misunderstood that we must emphasize that infallibility is a strictly limited gift. It does not assert that the Pope is endowed with extraordinary intelligence of any kind. It does not mean that God helps him to know the answer to every conceivable question. Emphatically it does not mean that Catholics have to accept the Pope's views on politics. The Pope can make mistakes. He can fall into sin. The scientific or historical opinions he holds may be quite wrong. He may write books that are full of errors. Only in two limited spheres is he infallible, and in these only when he speaks officially as the supreme teacher and lawgiver of the Church, defining a doctrine that must be held by all its members. When, after studying a problem of faith or morals as carefully as possible and with all available help from expert consultants, he emerges with the Church's answer—on these occasions it is not strictly speaking *an* answer, it is *the* answer. For on such occasions the Holy

Spirit protects him from the possibility of mistake. These answers constitute the infallible teaching of the Church and as such are binding on all Roman Catholics.

The second idea central to Roman Catholicism is the idea of the Church as Sacramental Agent. This supplements the idea of the Church as Teaching Authority. It is one thing to know what we should do, another to be able to do it, which is why there is a need for the Sacraments. The Church helps with both problems. It points the way we should live, and it also supplies us with the power to live in this way.

The second gift is as important as the first. Christ called his followers to live lives far above the average in charity and service. No one would claim that this is easy. The Catholic, however, insists that we have not faced our situation squarely until we realize that without help such a life is impossible. For the life to which Christ called men is supernatural in the exact sense of being contrary to the pull of man's natural instincts. By his own efforts man can no more live above his nature than an elephant can live a life of reason. Help, therefore, is obviously necessary. The Church, as God's representative on earth, is the agency to provide it, and the Sacraments its means for doing so.

Since the twelfth century the number of Sacraments in the Roman Catholic Church has been fixed at seven. In a striking way these parallel the great moments and needs of man's natural life. Man is born, he comes of age, he marries or dedicates himself completely to some purpose, he dies. Meanwhile he must be reintegrated into society when he deviates, and he must eat. The Sacraments provide the spiritual counterparts to these natural events. As birth brings a child into the natural world, *baptism* (by planting God's first special grace in his soul) draws him into the supernatural order of existence. When he reaches the age of reason and needs to be strengthened for mature and responsible action, he is *confirmed*. Usually there comes a solemn moment when he is joined to a human companion in *holy matrimony*, or dedicates his life entirely to God and his work in *holy orders*. At the end of his life, *extreme unction* closes his eyes to earth and prepares his soul for its last passage.

Meanwhile two sacraments need to be repeated frequently. One of these is *confession* or *absolution*. Being what he is, man cannot live without falling into error and straying from the right. These aberrations make necessary definite steps by which he may be restored to the human community and divine fellowship. The Church teaches that if a man confesses his sin to God in the presence of one of his earthly delegates, a priest, truly repents of the sin committed, and honestly resolves (whether or not this resolve proves effective) to avoid it in the future, he will be forgiven. God's forgiveness depends on the sinner's penitence and resolve being genuine, but the priest has no infallible means for determining whether or not they are. If the penitent deceives himself or the priest, the absolution pronounced is inoperative.

The central Sacrament of the Catholic Church is the *Mass*, known also as the Holy Eucharist, Holy Communion, or Lord's Supper. The word Mass derives from the Latin *missa*, which is a form of the verb "to send." The ancient liturgy contained two dismissals, one for persons interested in Christianity but not yet baptized which preceded the sacrament of the Lord's Supper, and a second for fully initiated Christians after it had been celebrated. Coming as it did between these two dismissals, the rite came first to be called the *missa* and then, by transliteration, the Mass.

The central feature of the Mass is the re-enactment of Christ's Last Supper in which, as he gave his disciples bread and wine, he said, "This is my body that was broken for you. . . . This is my blood that was shed for you." (Mark 14:22 ff.) It is totally false to the Catholic concept of this Sacrament to think of it as a commemoration through which priest and communicants elevate their spirits by symbolic remembrance of Christ's life and death. The Mass provides a literal transfusion of spiritual energy from God to man. In a general way this holds for all the Sacraments, but for the Mass it holds uniquely. For the Catholic Church teaches that in the Host and the Chalice, the consecrated bread and wine, Christ's human Body and Blood are actually present. They consider his words, "This is my body. . . . This is my blood," explicit on this point. When a priest utters these words of consecration, therefore, the change they effect in the elements is not one of significance only. The elements may appear no different; analysis would register no chemical change. In technical language this means that their "accidents" remain as they were. But their "substance" is transubstantiated. As Ronald Knox puts it, the other sacraments convey God's grace not as a boat conveys its passengers but as a letter conveys meaning. For the letter to have meaning intelligence is required in addition to the paper and ink marks, as in the sacraments God's power is necessary in addition to the instruments of the sacrament. But in the Mass spiritual nourishment is literally to be had from the elements themselves. It is exactly as important for the Christian's spiritual life to feast upon them as it is for his bodily life to partake of food. Opening your mouth for the Bread of Life, writes Saint Francis de Sales,

. . . full of faith, hope, and charity, receive Him, in whom, by whom, and for whom, you believe, hope and love. . . . Represent to yourself that as the bee, after gathering from the flowers the dew of heaven and the choicest juice of the earth, reduces them into honey and carries it into her hive, so the priest, having taken from the altar the Savior of the world, the true Son of God, who, as the dew, is descended from heaven, and the true Son of the Virgin, who, as a flower is sprung from the earth of our humanity, puts Him as delicious food into your mouth and into your body.[12]

This physical presence of God in the elements of the Mass distinguishes it significantly from the other sacraments, but it does not vitiate the common bond that unites them all. Each is a means by which God, through his agent on earth, the mystical body of Christ, literally infuses into man the supernatural power that enables him so to live in this world that in the world to come he may have life everlasting.

EASTERN ORTHODOXY

The Eastern Orthodox Church, which today has somewhere in the neighborhood of 200,000,000 communicants, broke officially and permanently with the Roman Catholic Church in 1054 A.D., each charging the other with responsibility for the break. Eastern Orthodoxy includes the Churches of Albania, Bulgaria, Georgia, Greece, Poland, Romania, Russia, Serbia, and Sinai. While each of these churches is self-governing, they are in full communion with one another, and their members think of themselves as belonging primarily to the Eastern Church and only secondarily to their particular division within it.

In most ways the Eastern Orthodox Church stands close to the Roman Catholic, for during more than half their histories they were formally a unit. It honors the same seven Sacraments and interprets them in fundamental respects exactly as does the Roman Church. The only noticeable difference here is a surface one; whereas in Holy Communion the Roman Church reserves the Cup, the Eastern Church offers it to its communicants along with the Bread.

On the Church as Teaching Authority there is more difference, but even here the premises are the same. Left to private interpretation the Christian faith would disintegrate into a babble of conflicting claims and uncertainties. It is the Church's responsibility to insure against this, and

God enables it to do so; the Holy Spirit preserves its official statements against the possibility of error. This much is identical with Rome. The differences are two. One of these has to do with extent. The Eastern Church considers the issues on which unanimity is needed to be far fewer in number than does the Roman Church. In principle, only issues mentioned in scripture can qualify (that is, the Church can interpret doctrines but it cannot initiate them); in practice, the Church has exercised her prerogative as interpreter only seven times, in the Seven Ecumenical Councils, all of which were held before 787 A.D. This means that the Eastern Church assumes that though the articles a Christian must believe are of decisive importance, their number is relatively few. Strictly speaking, all the decisions of the Ecumenical Councils are embodied in the Creeds; beyond these there is no need for "innovations" like purgatory, indulgences, the immaculate conception, or the bodily assumption of Mary, all of which were defined by the Roman Church as dogmas after the Great Schism. For nearly twelve hundred years the Church has not needed to exercise her right as teaching authority. The other side of this fact is that the Eastern Church leaves many more points open to individual judgment than does the Roman.

The other way in which the Eastern Church's understanding of its role as teaching authority differs from the Western pertains to the means by which her dogmas are reached. The Roman Church, as we have seen, holds that in the final analysis they come from the Pope; it is his decisions that the Holy Spirit preserves from error. The Eastern Church has no pope—if we want *the* distinguishing difference between the two churches, this is it. Instead, it holds that God's truth is disclosed through "the conscience of the church." By this phrase it means the concensus of Christians in general. This consensus needs, of course, to be focused, which is what ecclesiastical councils are for. When the bishops of the entire Church are assembled in Ecumenical Council, their collective judgment establishes God's Truth in unchangeable monuments.[13] It would be correct to say that the Holy Spirit preserves their decisions from error, but it would be truer to the spirit of the Eastern Church to say that the Holy Spirit preserves Christian minds as a whole from lapsing into error, for the bishops' decisions are assumed to do no more than focus the thought of the latter.

This brings us to one of the special emphases of the Eastern Church. Standing (as in many ways it does) midway between Roman Catholicism and Protestantism, it is more difficult to put one's finger on features within it that are sharply distinctive. But if, as in our sketch of Roman Catholicism, we were to select two, one of these would be its strong corporate feeling about the Church.

Common to all Christians is the view of the Church as the mystical body of Christ. Just as the parts of a body are joined in a common well-being or malaise, so too are the lives of Christians interrelated. All Christians accept this doctrine that all are "members one of another," but while matters of degree are notoriously difficult to determine, it seems safe to say that the Eastern Church has taken it more seriously than either Roman Catholicism or Protestantism. Each Christian is working out his salvation with the rest of the Church, not individually to save his own soul. A saying has been preserved in the Russian branch of Eastern Orthodoxy: "A man can be damned alone, but he can only be saved with others." The Eastern Church goes even farther; it takes seriously St. Paul's theme of the entire universe as "groaning and in travail" as it awaits redemption. Not only is the destiny of the individual bound up with the entire Church; he is responsible for helping to sanctify the entire world of nature and history. The welfare of everything in creation is affected to some degree by what each individual contributes or detracts from it.

Though the most important consequence of this strong corporate feeling is the spiritual one just stated—the down-playing of that "holy selfishness" that puts its own personal salvation before everything else—the concept comes out in two other very practical ways. One of these we have already noted. In identifying the Church's teaching authority with the Christian conscience as a whole—"the conscience of the people is the conscience of the Church"—Eastern Orthodoxy maintains that the Holy Spirit's truth enters the world diffused through the minds of Christians as a whole. Individual Christians, the laity as well as the clergy, are cells of the "mind of Christ" which functions through them all collectively.

The other side of this point concerns administration. Whereas the administration of the Roman Church is avowedly hierarchical, the Eastern Church rests more of her decisions in the laity. For example, the laymen of each congregation elect their own clergymen; without such election the Bishop is powerless to appoint them. The Roman Church may argue that this confuses the offices of laity with clergy, but the strong corporate feeling in the Eastern Church has led her to feel, again, that divine guidance, even when it reaches down to touch practical issues of church administration, is more generally diffused among Christians than Rome will allow. The clergy has its uninfringeable domain, the administration of the sacraments; but beyond these the line that separates them from the laity is thin. Priests need not remain celibate and laymen may read the Bible in formal worship and even preach. Even the titular head of the Eastern Church, the Patriarch of Constantinople, is no more than "first among equals," and the laity is known as the "royal priesthood."

In the discussions of the religions of the East it was suggested that spiritual union has meant more for the East as whole, and individuality less, than have these for the West—Hinduism and Buddhism, where complete merger with the undifferentiated One is the preponderant goal, are only the clearest examples of a pervasive orientation. If we are right in regarding this accent on unity as an authentic trait of Eastern mentality, it helps to explain why it is the Easternmost branch of Christianity that has most stressed the corporate nature of the church, both in the equality (as against Catholicism) and solidarity (as against Protestantism) of Christians. Certainly it accounts for her second trait, namely, her mystical emphasis.[14]

Like all the other religions we have considered, Christianity believes reality to be composed of two realms, the natural and the supernatural. Following death, man's life is translated fully into the supernatural domain. But even in this world it is not insulated from it. For one thing, the Sacraments, as we have seen, are channels whereby supernatural grace is made available to man even in his current condition.

This much virtually all Christianity teaches. The differences come when we ask to what extent it should be a part of the Christian program to try to partake of supernatural life while still within the body. Roman Catholicism holds that the Trinity actually dwells in every Christian soul, but its presence is not normally felt. By a life of prayer and penance it is possible to dispose oneself for a special gift whereby the Trinity discloses its presence and the seeker is lifted to a state of mystical ecstasy. But as man has no *right* to such states, they being wholly in the nature of free gifts of grace, the Roman Church neither urges nor discourages their cultivation. The Eastern Church has encouraged the mystical life more actively. From very early times when the deserts near Antioch and Alexandria were filled with hermits seeking illumination, the entire mystical enterprise has occupied a more prominent place in her life. As the supernatural world intersects and impregnates the world of sense throughout, it should be a part of Christian life in general to develop the capacity to experience directly the glories of God's presence.

> Does the fish soar to find the ocean,
>   The eagle plunge to find the air,
> That we ask of the stars in motion
>   If they have rumour of thee there?
>
> Not where the wheeling systems darken,
>   And our benumbed conceiving soars,
> The drift of pinions, would we hearken,
>   Beats at our own clay-shuttered doors.
>
> The angels keep their ancient places;
>   Turn but a stone, and start a wing:
> 'Tis ye, 'tis your estranged faces
>   That miss the many-splendoured thing.[15]

Mysticism is a practical program even for laymen. The aim of every life should be union with God, actual deification to the point of sharing the Divine Life. As our destiny is to enter creatively into the life of the Trinity, the love that circulates incessantly among the Father, Son, and Holy Spirit, movement toward this goal should be a part of every Christian life. For only as we advance toward increasing participation in the Trinity are we able to love God with our whole heart and soul and mind, and our neighbor as ourselves. The mystical graces are open to everyone and it is incumbent for each to make of his life a pilgrimage toward glory.

PROTESTANTISM

The causes that led to the break between Roman Catholicism and what came to be known as Protestant Christianity are complex and still in dispute. Political economy, nationalism, Renaissance individualism, and a rising concern over ecclesiastical abuses all played their part. But they do not camouflage the fact that the basic cause was religious, a difference in Christian perspective between Roman Catholicism and Protestantism. With time and space the various factors that contributed to the Reformation could be weighed with reasonable care, but we shall not attempt to do so here. Ideas rather than history being our immediate concern, we shall be content to treat the sixteenth century—Luther, Calvin, the Ninety-five Theses, the Diet of Worms, King Henry VIII, the Peace of Augsburg—as a vast tunnel. The Western Church went into it whole; it emerged in two sections. More accurately, it emerged in several sections, for Protestantism is not so much a church as a movement of churches. But in this brief sketch we shall not go into the differences that distinguish the various denominations that make up the movement as a whole.

Protestantism shares much with Roman Catholicism and Eastern Orthodoxy. Appearing as it does within the general outlines of history, faith, and worship of Christendom as a whole, it is primarily Christian rather than Protestant. Here, however, we must simply take this common Christian substance for granted and attend to her two most distinctive features, namely, Justification by Faith, and the Protestant Principle.

Faith in the Protestant conception is not simply a matter of belief, an acceptance of knowledge held with certainty yet not on evidence. It is a response of the entire man, in Emil Brunner's phrase "a totality-act of the whole personality." As such, it includes a movement of the mind in assent: specifically a conviction of God's limitless, omnipresent creative power. But this is not its all. To be truly faith it must include as well a movement of the affections in love and trust, and a movement of the will in desire to be an instrument of God's redeeming love. When Protestantism says that man is justified—that is, restored to right relationship with the Ground of his being and his fellowmen—by faith, it is saying that such restoration requires a movement of the total self, in mind, will, and affections all three.

Thus defined, faith is a personal phenomenon. "Right beliefs" or "sound doctrine" can be accepted second-hand and largely by rote, but service and love cannot. Faith is the response by which God, heretofore a postulate of philosophers or theologians, becomes God to me, my God. This is the meaning of Luther's statement that "Everyone must do his own believing as he will have to do his own dying."

To feel the force of the Protestant emphasis on faith as response of the whole man we need to see it as a passionate protest against religious perfunctoriness. Luther's protest against indulgences which when bought were thought to help the buyer toward salvation is only a symbol of this wider protest which extended in a number of directions. No number of religious observances, no record of good deeds, no roster of doctrines believed could guarantee that an individual would reach his desired state. These things were not irrelevant to the Christian life, but unless they helped to transform the believer's heart (his attitudes and response to life) they were inadequate. This is the meaning of the Protestant rally cry, "justification by faith alone." It does not mean that the Creeds or the Sacraments are unimportant. It means that unless these are accompanied by the experience of God's love and a return in love for him they are inadequate. Similarly with good works. The Protestant position does not imply that good works are to be taken lightly. It means that in the full sense they are correlatives of faith rather than its preludes. If one really does have faith, good works will flow from it naturally,[16] whereas the reverse cannot be assumed; good works do not necessarily lead to faith. To a large extent both Paul and Luther had been driven to their emphasis on faith precisely because a respectable string of good works ground out fearfully had not succeeded in quieting their hearts.

Once more, and for a last time, we need to draw here on the analogy of the child in his home, an analogy which speaks so directly to one aspect of man's religious situation that we have had occasion to refer to it several times already. After the child's physical needs have been met, or rather while they are being met, the child needs more than anything else to feel the enveloping love and acceptance of his parents. Paul, Luther, and Protestants in general say something comparable for man as a whole. Since he is always a child compared with the power that confronts him, his greatest need to his dying day is to know that his basic environment, the Ground of Being from which he has sprung and to which he will return, is for him rather than against him. If he can come to know this to the extent of really feeling it he is released from the basic anxiety which causes him to try to elbow his way to security. This is why, just as the loved child is the cooperative child, the man or woman in whom God's love has awakened the answering response of faith is the one who can truly love his fellowmen. The key is inward. Given faith in God's goodness, everything else of importance follows. In its absence, nothing can take its place.

The other controlling perspective in Protestantism has come to be called the Protestant Principle. Stated philosophically, it warns against absolutizing the relative; stated theologically it warns against idolatry.

The point is this. Man's allegiance belongs to God—this all religions (with allowance for terminology) will affirm. God, however, is beyond nature and history. He is not removed from these, but he cannot be equated with either or any of their parts, for while the world is emphatically finite, God is infinite. With these truths all the great religions in principle agree. They are, however, very hard truths to keep in mind; so hard that men continually let them slip and proceed to equate God with something they can see or touch or at least conceptualize more precisely than the infinite. Of old they equated him with statues, and men called Prophets—the first "protestants" or protesters on this decisive point—rose up to denounce their transpositions, dubbing their pitiful substitutes idols, or "little pieces of form." Later men stopped deifying wood and stone, but this did not mean that idolatry had ended. While the secular world proceeded to absolutize the state or the self or man's intellect, Christians fell to absolutizing dogmas, sacraments, the church, the Bible, or personal religious experience. To think that Protestantism devalues these or doubts that God is involved in them is to seriously misjudge its stance. But it does determinedly insist that none of them *is* God. All of them, being involved in history, are mixtures of the divine with the human; and since the human is never perfect, these instruments partake of relativity and imperfection too. As long as each points beyond itself to God, it is invaluable. But let any claim man's absolute or unreserved allegiance—which is to say claim to usurp God's place—and it becomes diabolical. For this, according to tradition, is what the devil is,—the highest angel who, not content to be second, determined to be God himself.

In the name of the sovereign God who transcends all the limitations and distortions of finite existence, therefore, every human claim to absolute truth or finality must be rejected. Some examples will indicate what this Principle means in practice. Protestants cannot accept the dogma of papal infallibility because this would involve removing from criticism forever opinions which, being channeled through a human mind, can never (in the Protestant view) wholly escape the risk of limitation and partial error. Creeds and pronouncements can be believed; they can be believed fully and wholeheartedly. But to place them beyond the cleansing cross fire of challenge and criticism is to absolutize something finite—to elevate "a little piece of form" to the position that should be reserved for God alone.

Instances of what Protestants consider idolatry are not confined to other sects or religions. Protestants admit that as the tendency to absolutize the relative is universal, it occurs among them as much as anywhere, bringing the need for continual self-criticism and reformation within Protestantism itself. The chief Protestant idolatry has been Bibliolatry. Protestants do believe that God speaks to man through the Bible as in no other way. But to elevate it as a book to a point above criticism, to insist that every word and letter was dictated directly by God and so can contain no historical, scientific, or other inaccuracies, is again to forget that in entering the world God's word must speak through human minds. Another common instance of idolatry within Protestantism has been the deification of private religious experience. Protestant insistence that faith must be a living experience has often led her constituents to assume that any vital experience must be the working of the Holy Spirit. Perhaps so, but again it is never pure Spirit. The Spirit must work through man so that what is received is never uncompounded.

By rejecting all such absolutes Protestantism tries to keep faith with the First Commandment, "Thou shalt have no other gods before me." The injunction contains a negative, and for many the word Protestant too carries a predominantly negative ring. Is not a Protestant a person who protests against something? This, as we have seen, is certainly true; he protests without ceasing the usurpation of God's place by anything less than God. But the Protestant Principle can just as well be put positively, which is how it should be put to get its full point. It protests against idolatry because it testifies for (pro-testant = one who testifies for) God's sovereign place in human life.

But how is God to find his way into man's life? To insist that he cannot be equated with anything in this tangible, visible world only leaves man at sea in God's ocean. God doubtless surrounds him always, but to gain access to man's awareness, his presence must be concretized and focused.

This, for Protestants, is where the Bible comes in. In its account of God working through Israel, through Christ, and through the early Church, we find the clearest picture of God's great goodness and how man may find new life in fellowship with him. In this sense the Bible is for Protestants ultimate. But note with care the sense in which this is so. It is ultimate in the sense that when man reads this record of God's grace with true openness and longing for God, he stands at the supreme intersection between the divine and the human. There more than anywhere else in this world of time and space he has the prospect of catching, not with his mind only but with his whole being, the truth about God and the relation in which he stands to his life. No derivative interpretation by church councils, popes, or theologians can replace or equal this. The Word of God must speak to each individual soul directly. It is this that accounts for the Protestant emphasis on the Bible as the *living* Word of God.

Is not this concept of Christianity freighted with danger? The Protestant readily admits that it is. First, there is the danger of misconceiving God's word. If, as the Protestant Principle insists, all things human are imperfect, does it not follow that each individual's vision of God must at least be limited and possibly quite erroneous? It does. Protestantism not only admits this; it insists on it. But as the fact happens to be true, how much better to recognize it and open the door to the corrections of the

Holy Spirit working through other minds than to saddle Christendom with what is in fact limited truth masquerading as finality. As Jesus himself says: "I have yet many things to say to you, but you cannot bear them now. When the Spirit of truth comes, he will guide you into all the truth." (John 16:12-13.) One very important reason for restricting final loyalty to the transcendent God is to keep the future open.

The other danger is that Christians will see God and his will through the Bible differently. The 255 denominations of Protestantism in the United States are witness not only to the fact of Protestant diversity but to its danger, the danger that the church will evaporate into complete individualism. Protestantism admits this, but adds three points.

First, Protestant diversity is not as great as its hundreds of denominations suggest. Most of these are of negligible size; actually 85% of all Protestants belong to twelve denominations. Considering the freedom of belief Protestantism affirms in principle, the wonder lies not in its diversity but in the extent to which Protestants have held together.

Second, Protestant divisions reflect differing national origins in Europe or differing social groupings in the United States more often than differing theologies.

The third point, however, is the most important. Who is to say that diversity is always bad? Man is a varied creature and differences in historical circumstances cause his needs to vary even more. "New occasions teach new duties." Protestants have taken their understanding of the gospel so seriously that they have been willing to create new forms of the church and forms differing from their neighbors'. For life and history are too fluid to allow God's redeeming word to be enclosed in either single or unchangeable form. Protestants are concerned about the brokenness of Christ's "body" and are taking stronger steps than ever before in their history toward Church union. But though differences that have become meaningless have no point in continuing, Protestants are determined not to cuddle up to one another just to keep warm. They insist that longing for the comforts of union must not lead to structures that will restrict the dynamic character of God's continuing revelation. If united, the Church must still provide a framework flexible enough to enable the gospel to speak with different accents to different individuals and especially to different historical situations. "The Spirit bloweth where it listeth."

Protestants agree, then, that their perspective is loaded with dangers; the danger of uncertainty as the individual wrestles with his soul to ask if he has heard God's word distinctly; the danger of schism as fellow

Christians see God differently. But they accept these dangers because, risk for risk, they prefer the precarious freedom entailed by their direct encounter with God to the comfortable authority proffered by persons or institutions which, even when they look toward God, remain finite. In the last resort they can carry the burden of this freedom because of their faith. Luther voiced the spirit of this faith when, asked where he would stand if the church were to excommunicate him, he is said to have replied, "Under the sky."

SUGGESTIONS FOR FURTHER READING

In view of the sea of literature surrounding the reader on the subject of Christianity, I shall confine myself here to listing some of the items I have found most immediately helpful in writing the present account. This gives me an opportunity to acknowledge my sizeable indebtedness to these authors while recommending them to the reader.

For the life of Jesus: John W. Bowman, *The Intention of Jesus* (Philadelphia: Westminster Press, 1943), and C. J. Cadoux, *The Historic Mission of Jesus* (New York: Harper & Brothers, 1943).

For the teachings of Jesus: T. W. Manson, *The Teachings of Jesus* (Cambridge: University Press, 1931), and Paul Ramsey, *Basic Christian Ethics* (New York: Charles Scribner's Sons, 1952).

For the impact of Jesus on his contemporaries, three little books by John Knox: *The Man Christ Jesus* (Chicago: Willett and Clark, 1941), *Christ the Lord* (Chicago: Willett and Clark, 1945), and *On the Meaning of Christ* (New York: Charles Scribner's Sons, 1947).

On Christian doctrine: Ronald Knox, *The Creed in Slow Motion* (London: Sheed and Ward, 1949), D. M. Baillie, *God was in Christ* (New York: Charles Scribner's Sons, 1948), and Alan Richardson, *Christian Apologetics* (New York: Harper's, 1947).

For Roman Catholicism: R. A. Knox, *The Belief of the Catholics* (London: Sheed and Ward, 1939), Thomas Corbishley, *Roman Catholicism* (New York: Longmans and Green, 1950), and parts of a number of works by M. C. D'Arcy.

For Eastern Orthodoxy: George Mastrantonis, *What is the Eastern Orthodox Church?* (Chicago: OLOGOS, 1956).

For Protestantism: John Dillenberger and Claude Welch, *Protestant Christianity Interpreted through Its Development* (New York: Charles Scribner's Sons, 1954).

9

A Final Examination

THE most obvious question that suggests itself at the close of this kind of inquiry is: What have we gotten out of it? Has it done us any good?

It would be surprising if we had not picked up some facts about man's religious heritage: what the *yogas* mean for the Hindus, Buddha's analysis of the cause of life's dislocation, Confucius' ideal of the Gentleman, who Lao Tzu was, Islam's Five Pillars, what the Exodus meant to the Jews, the substance of the Good News for the early Christians, and so on. These are not to be belittled. But are they all?

We may have caught some sense of what an important part in the human venture religion has played. It may have left us with dismay at how far short of its finest embodiments religion often falls. We may see how important the quality of religion is to the way civilization goes.

Perhaps, too, we have emerged with a new appreciation of faiths not our own. Not that we now agree with them all. There is nothing in the study of man's religions that requires that they cross the line of the reader's acceptance in a photo finish. But perhaps we are able to see them more as faiths of real people, people who are asking the same basic questions that we are, seekers like us of the illumined life.

These, however, are matters of personal attitude. We may leave them, therefore, for our second question. How do these religions fit together? In what relation do they stand to one another?

This is the most difficult question in the field of comparative religion today, and as such has no one answer that would be universally accepted as correct. Consequently at this stage of our understanding the worth of an answer depends more on the adequacy with which it is defended than on whether it is right or wrong in any objectively demonstrable sense.

There are today three main answers that can be defended enough to find advocates among knowledgeable scholars in the field. The first is that in the midst of all the religions of man there stands one so incomparably superior that no significant religious truth is to be found in any of the others which is not present in equal or clearer form within this religion itself. That this view is both held and challenged by so many truly learned men is clear evidence that it is impossible to prove, flatly, that it is either right or wrong. Evaluation turns, instead, on the adequacy with which it is maintained. Has the answerer, let us suppose him to be a Christian, faced up to the extent to which identical claims are made by equally knowing proponents of other faiths, Muslims and Jews for example? What does he do with this paradox? Is it clear that his answer has not been prompted by an unconscious fear that should he acknowledge the possibility of some unique and significant truth in other religions he may be mounting the slippery incline that slopes toward conversion? Fear is never an adequate base for faith; the man who is afraid of being converted to another religion does not really believe that his contains the truth about God. Above all, in comparing his faith with others does he really know what he is talking about. Has he genuinely tried to unite himself with others in spirit before making the judgment?

Laying aside condescension and contempt, and even that sort of "objectivity" which, while it may depict, never truly understands, has he learned to see and feel the world and God as others have seen and felt these? Grant that success in such an undertaking can only be proximate, has he really tried to find in other religions something besides what his preconceptions have unconsciously deposited there in advance? In the language of religion, has he sought to draw some of the water, tasting which man thirsts not again, from some well other than his own? If his answer acquits itself well before these cross-questions, it stands.

A second possible answer to the question of the relation between religions is that in all important respects they are the same. Does not each contain some version of the Golden Rule? Do they not all regard man's self-centeredness to be the source of his troubles and seek to help him in its conquest? Does not each acknowledge a universal Divine Ground from which man has sprung and in relation to which his true good is to be sought? If all truth essential to salvation can be found in one religion, it can also be found in each of the other great ones. Edward Steichen, the great photographer of *The Family of Man*, summarized his creed by saying, "I believe that in all the things that are important, in all of these we are alike." The words are tailor-made for this second hypothesis. Religion is important; in religion all the peoples of the world are fundamentally alike. The differences are but dialects of a single spiritual language that employs different words but expresses the same ideas. If it be true as Michael Scott has recently suggested that "humanity has never before stood so desperately in need of a universal religion, a living, cohesive force that will emancipate mankind, that will overcome the dangers of arrogant nationalism and the doctrines of self-interest, hatred and violence," we need only open our eyes to see this universal religion embedded in the heart of each of the world's great existing religions, the *philosophia perennis* of St. Augustine's "wisdom uncreated, the same now that it ever was, and the same to be forevermore."

It is an appealing doctrine, and, like the previous one, may be true. Everything depends on what is essential to salvation and what is husk and cultural accident. But before its advocate goes hiking off too quickly to Baha'i, the current syncretistic faith that is making the most serious attempt to institutionalize this conviction, several questions again must be raised. The main one, interestingly enough, is the same as that which challenged the previous hypothesis; namely, how seriously and fully have the various faiths of mankind been entered into before the judgment was reached? How fully has the proponent tried and succeeded in understanding Christianity's claim that Christ was the *only* begotten Son of God, or the Muslim's claim that Muhammed is the *Seal* of the Prophets, or the Jews' sense of their being the Chosen People? How does he propose to reconcile Hinduism's conviction that this will always remain a "middle world" with Judaism's promethean faith that it can be decidedly improved? How does Buddha's "*anatta* doctrine" of no-soul square with Christianity's belief in man's individual destiny in eternity? How does Theravada Buddhism's rejection of every form of personal God find echo in Christ's sense of relationship to his Heavenly Father? How does the Indian view of Nirguna Brahman, the God who stands completely aloof from time and history, fit with the Biblical view that the very essence of God is contained in his historical acts? Are these beliefs really only accretions, tangential to the main concern of spirit? The religions of man may fit together, but they do not do so easily.

A great historian of religion devoted forty years of his life to determining what the world's religions have in common and came up with two things: "Belief in God—if there be a God," and "Life is worth living—sometimes." There is also the story of an English M.P. who, after the 1928 debate in the Commons on the Revised Prayer-Book, emerged from the House muttering that he didn't see what all the fuss was about. "Surely," he said, "we all believe in some sort of something." Quips do not defeat a position, and to raise the questions we have does not mean that they cannot be answered. They have been introduced only to indicate that the advocates of the essential unity of man's religions must meet the charge of superficiality. Their answer stands or falls with their ability to convince us that the charge is ill-founded.

A third possible answer to the question of the relation between religions is best defined in contrast to both preceding ones. It does not find all religions saying the same things, though the unity is in certain respects both striking and impressive. But neither, in the presence of differences, does it assume that all important truths can be found in any single tradition. If God is a God of love, it seems most unlikely that he would not have revealed himself to his other children as well. And it seems probable that his revelation would have taken different facets and different forms according to the differences in nature of individual souls and the differences in character of local traditions and civilizations. This is one possible contemporary meaning of Paul's statement about "one spirit, many gifts." One who holds this view will find many things in other religions that puzzle and disturb, but will see their light as deriving basically from the same source as his own. As they too come from God, God may in certain respects speak to him through them.

"Isn't it ironical," remarked G. K. Chesterton upon hearing of the first round-the-world wireless communication, "that we have learned to talk around the world at precisely that moment when no one has anything to say." For the advocate of this third hypothesis this is far from true of religion. Here the people of the world have a great deal to say to one another, and they have drawn close at precisely the time when man's spiritual life, facing severe threats from nationalism, materialism, and conformity, stands in desperate need of the stimulus that searching conversation can encourage.

Where this conversation will lead cannot be fully predicted, but it looks as though it will be less toward an amalgamated world religion than toward certain emendations and restored emphases while each religion continues to maintain its historic identity. Vision, genius, and the will and capacity to follow the light where it leads will be needed. And there will be risks, for some pioneers may, like Jawaharlal Nehru, "become a queer mixture of East and West, out of place everywhere, at home nowhere." The chief question anyone who presumes to pioneer in this direction must answer is whether his personal, autonomous reason is qualified to stand judgment on matters as important as these, picking and choosing what in other traditions is authentic and what is spurious? To the extent that he can satisfactorily meet this question, his answer too, in the present state of man's religious knowledge, may stand.

Our last question is: What should be our approach to the religions of man from this point on? Whereas the preceding question did not permit a single answer, this one seems to require it. The only defensible reply must be continued listening, for we have had little more than a brief glimpse of these faiths we have passed through so hurriedly. We must listen first to our own faith, for every heritage is inexhaustible and the ways of spirit, even as channeled through a single tradition, are beyond the wit of anyone to master completely. Though a man sink himself into his faith as deeply as he can, there will remain the persistent challenge of more to be experienced than has been known or told.

But we must also listen to the faiths of others. This holds however we may have answered the question of their relation to our own—even if we assume that they have no truth that cannot be found in our own.

We must listen to them, first, because as said at the outset of this book, our times require it. The community today can be no single tradition; it is the planet. Daily the world grows smaller, leaving understanding the only bridge on which peace can find its home. But the annihilation of distance has caught us unprepared. Who today stands ready to accept the solemn equality of nations? Who does not have to fight an unconscious tendency to equate foreign with inferior? We live in a great century, but if it is to rise to its full opportunity, the scientific achievements of its first half must be matched by comparable achievements in human relations in its second. Those who listen in the present world work for peace, a peace built not upon ecclesiastical or political empire, but upon understanding and the mutual involvement in the lives of others that this brings. For understanding, at least in realms as inherently noble as the great faiths of mankind, brings respect, and respect prepares the way for a higher power, love—the only power that can quench the flames of fear, suspicion, and prejudice, and provide the means by which the peoples of this great earth can become one to one another.

Understanding then can lead to love. But the reverse is equally true. Love brings understanding; the two are reciprocal. So we must listen in order to further the understanding the world so desperately needs, but we must also listen in order to practice the love which our own religion (whichever it be) enjoins, for it is impossible to love another without listening to him. If then, we are to be true to our own faith we must attend to others when they speak, as deeply and as alertly as we hope they will attend to us. We must have the graciousness to receive as well as to give. For there is no greater way to depersonalize another than to speak to him without also listening.

Said Jesus, blest be his name, "Do unto others as you would that they should do unto you." Said Buddha, blest be his name as well, "He who would, may reach the utmost height—but he must be anxious to learn." If we do not quote the other religions on these points it is because their words would be redundant.

Notes

Chapter One: POINT OF DEPARTURE

1. Perhaps the best of these for the general reader is John B. Noss' *Man's Religions* (New York: Macmillan Co., 1956). Detailing as it does the facts from which my concern has been to distill meaning, it would make an excellent companion to the present essay.

2. *Katha Upanishad*, I. iii, 14.

3. *Civilization on Trial* (New York: Oxford University Press, 1948), p. 156.

4. Erwin Schrodinger, *Science and Humanism* (Cambridge: The University Press, 1952), p. 9.

Chapter Two: HINDUISM

1. The Sanskrit word here is *artha* which literally means "thing, object, substance" and so is usually translated "wealth" or "material possessions." I have translated it "worldly success" because the Hindu texts when discussing this second pursuit deal in fact with this larger theme, not just wealth, which is natural considering the usual connection of prestige and power with material possessions.

2. *Waiting for God* (New York: G. P. Putnam's Sons, 1951), p. 210.

3. D. G. Mukerji, *The Face of Silence* as paraphrased in Romain Rolland *The Life of Ramakrishna* (Mayavati, Almora, Himalayas: Advaita Ashrama, 1954), p. 80.

4. See Alain, Daniélou, *Yoga: Method of Reintegration* (New York: University Books, 1949) for a brief, uncritical summary of the methods and claims of this school.

5. Let me cite just one example taken from *The Reporter*, one of the most responsible journals in America. In its issue of Sept. 14, 1954, Jean Lyon tells of seeing a buried *yogi* whose air supply Western medical doctors said should not suffice for more than one or two days live for eight.

The most thorough scientific investigation of this subject to date was made in 1957 by Professors M. A. Wenger of the University of California at Los Angeles and B. K. Bagchi of the University of Michigan. As these pages go to press it has not been determined in which professional journal their report, tentatively titled "A Psychophysiological Investigation of Yoga," will appear.

6. Heinrich Zimmer, *The Philosophies of India* (New York: Pantheon Books, 1951), pp. 80-81.

7. A refrain which, with minor variations, runs throughout the *Upanishads*.

8. Song by Tukaram. Translated by John S. Hoyland in *An Indian Peasant Mystic* (London: Allenson and Co., 1932).

9. *The Art of Mental Prayer* (London: S.P.C.K., 1950), pp. 29-30.

10. Translated by R. M. French (New York: Harper & Brothers, 1955).

11. *Bhagavad-Gita*, Prabhavananda & Isherwood translation (New York: Harper & Brothers, 1944-51), p. 60.

12. Hubert Benoit, *The Supreme Doctrine* (New York: Pantheon Books, 1955), p. 22.

13. There is here something paralleling Luther's determination to obliterate the distinction between clergy and laity by sanctifying the common life. One recalls him crying to magistrate, farmer, soldier, artisan, and servant girl that if they approach their station in the right spirit none on earth can be higher; indeed, any of these can be "a status higher than that of a bishop."

14. *Bhagavad-Gita*, V: 10.

15. *Bhagavad-Gita*, IX, 27-28.

16. *Bhagavad-Gita*, III:19, 30.

17. Swami Swarupananda, *Srimad-Bhagavad-Gita* (Mayavati, Himalayas: Advaita Asharama, 1933), p. 125.

18. *Bhagavad-Gita*, Chap. VI, translation by Prabhavananda & Isherwood.

19. For parallel advice in the Christian tradition, see Bede Frost, *op. cit.*, p. 146.

20. *Bhagavad-Gita*, Chap. XII. See also Chap. XIV.

21. Heinrich Zimmer, *op. cit.*, 303-04.

22. St. Thomas however defined mysticism as experimental knowledge of God.

23. Quoted in Heinrich Zimmer, *op. cit.*

24. Interestingly, Kagawa, the famous Japanese Christian, retains the Eastern perspective on this point, being said to advocate not closing the eyes in prayer.

25. *Bhagavad-Gita*, Prabhavananda & Isherwood translation, Ch. VI.

26. Prabhavananda & Isherwood translation, Ch. V.

27. *Katha Upanishad*, II, iii, 10.

28. Paul Deussen, *The Philosophy of the Upanishads* (New York: Charles Scribner's Sons, 1908).

29. A description which, with minor variations, recurs throughout *The Upanishads*.

30. For description of a man who spent six months in this condition, see Romain Rolland, *The Life of Ramakrishna* (Hollywood: Vedanta Press, 1952), pp. 77-78.

31. Heinrich Zimmer, *op. cit.*, p. 44.

32. *Ibid.*, pp. 157-58. This entire description of the four stages has drawn heavily on Zimmer's account.

33. So little has this fact been recognized in recent discussions of caste that it will be well to document it through three quotations. An ancient and authoritative lawgiver writes: "Learn supreme knowledge with service even from the man of low birth; and even from the *chandala* [outcaste]; learn by serving him the way to salvation." Quoted in *The Complete Works of Swami Vivekananda* (Mayabati, India: Advaita Ashrama, 1932), Vol. III, p. 381. Swami Tyagisananda's translation of the seventy-second aphorism of Narada's *Bhakti-Sutras* (Madras: Sri Ramakrishna Math, 1943) reads, "In [the lovers of God] there is no distinction based on caste or culture." Most forceful of all is Sri Krishna's statement in the thirteenth chapter of the *Mahabharata*: "The devotees of the Lord are not Sudras [the lowest caste]; Sudras are they who have no faith in the Lord whichever be their caste. A wise man should not slight even an outcaste if he is devoted to the Lord; he who looks down upon him will fall into hell."

34. For one of the most thoughtful of such defenses, see "What has India Contributed to Human Welfare?," the first chapter of Ananda Coomaraswamy's, *The Dance of Shiva* (Bombay: Asia Publishing House, 1948).

35. The Sanskrit word *kshatrya* originally connoted warrior as well as ruler, be-

cause the latter were expected to protect the weak and subdue the wicked.

36. I am indebted to Gerald Heard for this analogy.

37. Ananda Coomaraswamy, *op. cit.*, p. 168.

38. Compare Thomas à Kempis: "There is a distance incomparable between the things men imagine by natural reason and those which illuminated men behold by contemplation."

39. Western parallels of this *via negativa*, the way to God through radical negation, are to be found in the writings of most of her great mystics and theologians. There is St. Bernard's *"nescio, nescio,"* and Angela of Foligno's "Not this! Not this! I blaspheme" as she struggles to put her overwhelming experience of God into words. "Then only is there truth in what we know concerning God," says St. Gregory, "when we are made sensible that we cannot know anything concerning Him." And Meister Eckhart insists that God must be loved "as not-God, not-Spirit, no-person, not-image, just be loved as He is, a sheer pure absolute One, sundered from all twoness, and in whom we must eternally sink from nothingness to nothingness."

40. A Western parallel to the Hindu view on this point occurs in Simone Weil's *Waiting for God*, p. 32: "A case of contradictories, both of them true. There is a God. There is no God. Where is the problem? I am quite sure that there is a God in the sense that I am sure my love is no illusion. I am quite sure there is no God, in the sense that I am sure there is nothing which resembles what I can conceive when I say the word." See also Paul Tillich, "Religious Symbols and the Knowledge of God," *The Christian Scholar*, Vol. XXXVIII, No. 3 (September 1955), pp. 193-194.

41. Abbreviated from Shankara's Commentary on *The Brahma Sutram*, II, iii, 46.

42. See *Katha Upanishad*, II, ii, 15; *Mundaka Upanishad*, II, ii, 10; *Svetasvatara*, V, vi, 14.

43. *Brihadaranyaka Upanishad*.

44. "The Wishing Tree," *Vedanta for the Western World* (Hollywood: Marcel Rodd Co., 1946), pp. 448-51.

45. *Mundaka Upanishad*, I, i, 7.

46. Prema Chaitanya, "What Vedanta Means to Me," *Vedanta and the West* (Los Angeles: Vedanta of Southern California, 1955), p. 33.

47. The remainder of this section consists of teachings of Sri Ramakrishna as compiled by Swami Abhedananda in *The Sayings of Sri Ramakrishna* (New York: The Vedanta Society, 1903), with minor editorial changes.

Chapter Three: BUDDHISM

1. The wording in the case of Jesus was different, but the direction of the question was the same.

2. The precise date has never been agreed upon. 1956 was widely celebrated throughout Buddhist lands as the 2500th anniversary of Buddha's death, which would put his birth at 624 B.C. I have given here the date usually cited by Western scholars.

3. Cf. Clarence H. Hamilton, *Buddhism: A Religion of Infinite Compassion* (New York: The Liberal Arts Press, 1952), pp. 14-17.

4. Cf. *ibid.*, pp. 3-4.

5. Quoted from *Digha Nikaya* in J. B. Pratt, *The Pilgrimage of Buddhism and a Buddhist Pilgrimage* (New York: The Macmillan Co., 1928), p. 10.

6. Related in J. B. Pratt, *op. cit.*, p. 12.

7. Quoted in *ibid.*, p. 8.

8. Quoted in *ibid.*, p. 9.

9. Quoted in *ibid.*, p. 10.

10. *Majjhima*, LXXII. Quoted in *ibid.*, p. 13.

11. Thomism holds that the existence of God and the soul can be demonstrated

by exact science, but even it acknowledges that the nature of these exceeds demonstration. The word "speculation" is being used here in a loose sense to cover all issues in religion that exceed rational empirical demonstration without regard to whether they are covered by revelation.

12. Quoted in B. L. Suzuki, *Mahayana Buddhism* (London: David Marlowe Ltd., 1948), p. 2.

13. E. A. Burtt, ed., *The Teachings of the Compassionate Buddha* (New York: Mentor Books, 1955), pp. 49-50.

14. *Ibid.*, p. 18.

15. See, e.g., *ibid.*, p. 32.

16. I have paraphrased slightly the discourse as it appears in Majjhima Nikaya, Sutta 63, as translated by E. J. Thomas in *Early Buddhist Scriptures* (London: K. Paul, Trench, Trubner & Co., 1935), pp. 64-67.

17. Quoted in F. L. Woodward, *Some Sayings of the Buddha* (London: Oxford University Press, 1939), p. 283.

18. Quoted in E. A. Burtt, *op. cit.*, p. 50.

19. Quoted in Christmas Humphreys, *Buddhism* (Harmondsworth, England: Pelican Books, 1951), p. 120.

20. Quoted in F. L. Woodward, *op. cit.*, p. 283.

21. Quoted in A. Coomaraswamy, *Hinduism and Buddhism* (New York: The Philosophical Library, no date), p. 62.

22. F. L. Woodward, *op. cit.*, p. 294.

23. E. A. Burtt, *op. cit.*, p. 49.

24. Sir Edwin Arnold, *The Light of Asia* (Boston: Roberts Brothers, 1892).

25. *Brother to Dragons* (New York: Random House, 1953).

26. Sigmund Freud, *General Introduction to Psychoanalysis* (New York: Liverwright, 1935), p. 344.

27. Christmas Humphreys, *op. cit.*, p. 91.

28. Quoted in J. B. Pratt, *op. cit.*, p. 40.

29. *Altars of the East* (Garden City: Doubleday & Co., 1956), pp. 90-91.

30. Precisely this indescribable character of Nirvana caused later Buddhists to speak of it as *Sunyata* or Emptiness. It is not void or a negation of existence, but is empty in a way analogous to the way suprasonic is empty of sounds our ears can detect.

31. Quoted in E. A. Burtt, *op. cit.* p. 115.

32. *Iti-vuttaka*, 43; *Udana*, VIII, 3. Cf. J. B. Pratt, *op. cit.*, pp. 88-89, and E. A. Burtt, *op. cit.*, p. 113.

33. *Buddhism: Its Essence and Development* (New York: Philosophical Library, 1951), p. 40.

34. Compare, for example, its relation to Paul Tillich's "God above God" in *The Courage to Be* (New Haven: The Yale University Press, 1952).

35. All three examples quoted in René Grousset, *The Rise and Splendour of the Chinese Empire* (Berkeley and Los Angeles: University of California Press, 1952), p. 153.

36. Vairacchedika, 32; *Sacred Books of the East* (Clinton, Mass.: The Colonial Press, 1900), p. 144.

37. This, in passing, was one of the ways in which Buddha's understanding of reincarnation differed from most of the Hindus' of his day. The standard Hindu doctrine attributed rebirth to *karma*, the consequences of actions set in motion during previous lives. As these actions were innumerable, innumerable lives were assumed to be needed to work off these consequences and gain ultimate release. Buddha characteristically took a more psychological view. Rebirth, he maintained, was due not to *karma* but to *tanha*. As long as the wish to be a separate self existed,

the wish would be granted. It follows that since desire is the key it is possible to step permanently out of the cycle of rebirth at any point that one develops the wholehearted wish to do so.

38. Quoted in J. B. Pratt, *op. cit.*, p. 86.

39. Quoted in *ibid.*, p. 91.

40. From the *Bodhicharyavatara* of Shantideva.

41. This section, begun under the influence of Dr. D. T. Suzuki's writings and lectures and helped in progress by the criticisms of Drs. Henry Platov and George Fowler, received its final shape from six weeks of Zen study in Kyoto during the summer of 1957, including daily *sanzen* (consultation concerning meditation) with the eminent Zen master Goto Roshi, celebration of a Gematsu O-Sesshin (week of intensive looking into mind and heart) with the monks in the monastery of Myoshinji (Temple of the Marvellous Mind), access to the manuscripts and meditation hall of the Kyoto branch of the First Zen Institute of America, Inc., and a number of invaluable conversations with Mrs. R. F. Sasaki, its director.

42. A western professor, wishing to show that he had grasped Zen's determination to pass beyond forms, expressed surprise when the abbot of the temple he was visiting bowed reverently to images of the Buddha they were passing. "I thought you were beyond such things," he said. "I am," he continued. "Why, I would just as soon spit on these images." "Very well," replied the abbot. "You spit, I bow."

43. Heinrich Dumoulin and Ruth F. Sasaki, *The Development of Chinese Zen after the Sixth Patriarch* (New York: The First Zen Institute of America, Inc., 1953), p. 5.

44. Though *koans* are Zen's most distinctive feature, they are not its distinguishing one, for they are not universally employed. Of the two Zen schools that retain their vigor as living sects in Japan today, Rinzai uses the koan whereas Soto does not.

45. Dylan Thomas, "Light Breaks Where No Sun Shines."

Koans are actually of quite different types, geared to different stages in Zen development. As the mind works differently according to the kind of *koan* being studied, it is difficult to give any phenomenological description of *koan* study as a whole. What I have said here applies to the early *koans*. The first attempt at an English exposition of *koan* training as a whole is scheduled to appear this year: Miura Roshi's *Zen Dust* (New York: First Zen Institute of America, Inc., 1958).

46. Quoted in *Cat's Yawn* (New York: The First Zen Institute of America, Inc., 1947), p. 32.

47. Quoted in *Zen Notes* (New York: The First Zen Institute of America, Inc., Vol. I, No. 5), p. 1.

48. The great Zen master Daie Osho reported, "I have experienced Great *Satori* eighteen times, and lost count of the number of small *satoris* I have had." The contemporary Miura Roshi puts the point generally: "The more *satoris* you have experienced the more you must repeat; the clearer your understanding becomes, the more you must study." (From the manuscript of Miura Roshi's *Zen Dust*, to be published by The First Zen Institute of New York in 1958.)

49. *Zen Dust.* The point is so important for the understanding of Zen that a second quotation is in order. In its discussion of "the four maladies," the *Sutra of Perfect Awakening*, after naming activity and dependence, continues as follows: "The third is the malady of cessation. Someone may say: 'I have now brought my mind to cessation and have attained the universal nature. Now I am in perfect quietude and uniformity. Now I seek perfect awakening.' But the nature of perfect awakening is not to be found in cessation. The mind fuses with the state of awakening without an intentional cessation. Therefore this cessation is called a malady.

"The fourth is the malady of annihilation. Someone may say: 'I have now annihilated forever all [defilements]. After all, my body and mind are non-existent and empty, to say nothing of the objects of sense. All existences, therefore, can be reduced to the state of eternal extinction. By this comprehension I now seek perfect awakening.' But the nature of perfect awakening is not to be found in the state of extinction. Therefore this annihilation is called a malady." (Quoted in Sokei-an Roshi's *Rinzai Roku Commentary* to be published within the next two years by The First Zen Institute of America.)

50. From *The Sayings of the Lay Disciple Ho*. Not published in English.

51. Reprinted in E. A. Burtt, *op. cit.*, pp. 227-230.

52. From "Zen—A Religion," an unpublished essay by Mrs. R. F. Sasaki.

53. *Majjhima-Nikaya*, 3.2.22.135. Quoted in H. Zimmer, *op. cit.*, pp. 477-78.

54. Cf. Edward Conze, *Buddhism: Its Essence and Development* (New York: Philosophical Library, no date), p. 136.

55. Ramprasad. Quoted in H. Zimmer, *op. cit.*, p. 602.

Chapter Four: CONFUCIANISM

1. *The Analects*, VII, 1, 20.

2. *Ibid.*, VII, 33.

3. *Ibid.*, *passim*.

4. Arthur Waley, *The Way and Its Power* (London: George Allen & Unwin, 1934), p. 32.

5. The position of the Realists I shall present comes to us primarily through the eyes of orthodox Confucian historians. How far their characterization may involve caricature is a question scholars are still debating but one that does not promise to alter the main tenor of the succeeding paragraphs.

6. Quoted in Arthur Waley, *Three Ways of Thought in Ancient China* (Garden City: Doubleday, 1956), p. 199.

7. Han Fei Tzu. Quoted in Waley, *The Way and Its Power*, p. 74.

8. Han Fei Tzu. Quoted in Waley, *Three Ways of Thought in Ancient China*, p. 162.

9. Han Fei Tzu. Quoted in Waley, *The Way and Its Power*, p. 73.

10. Cf. John B. Noss, *op. cit.*, p. 372.

11. *Ibid.*, pp. 371-72.

12. *Ibid.*, p. 372.

13. *Ibid.*, pp. 373-74.

14. *Ibid.*, p. 372.

15. Mo Tzu himself lived in the generation following Confucius. We are speaking here of the Mohist idea rather than Mo Tzu the man. It remained for Confucius' greatest disciple Mencius to champion the Confucian alternative against Mo Tzu in person.

16. This is a major thesis of Ralph Linton's last book before his death, *The Tree of Culture* (New York: Alfred A. Knopf, 1955).

17. Walter Lippmann, *The Public Philosophy* (Boston: Little, Brown & Co., 1955).

18. Arthur Waley, *The Way and Its Power* (London: George Allen & Unwin, 1949), p. 161.

19. Chiang Monlin, *Tides from the West* (New Haven: Yale University Press, 1947), pp. 9, 19.

20. Walter Lippmann, *op. cit.*

21. Confucius. Quoted in Arthur Waley, *The Analects of Confucius* (London: George Allen & Unwin), p. 28.

22. *The Great Learning*.

23. Lucien Price, ed., *Dialogues of Alfred North Whitehead*, p. 339. Quoted in Frederic Spiegelberg, *Living Religions of the World* (Englewood Cliffs: Prentice-Hall, 1956), p. 325.

24. Related in Lady Hosie's Introduction to W. E. Soothill, *The Analects* (London: Oxford University Press, 1937), pp. xxxii-xxxiii.

25. *The Analects*, XVII, 9.

26. *Ibid.*, II, 17.

27. *Ibid.*, XI, 11.

28. *Ibid.*, IX, 5.

29. *Ibid.*, III, 13.

30. Chiang Monlin, *Tides from the West* (New Haven: Yale University Press, 1947), p. 77.

31. Charles Galton Darwin, *The Next Million Years* (Garden City: Doubleday, 1953).

32. By this time Confucianism had changed into Neo-Confucianism, but the influence of the Master was, with diminished force, still coming through.

33. F. S. C. Northrop, *The Taming of the Nations* (New York: The Macmillan Company, 1953), p. 117.

34. Quoted in René Grousset, *The Rise and Splendour of the Chinese Empire* (Berkeley: University of California Press, 1953), p. 207.

35. Charles Galton Darwin, *op. cit.*, p. 199.

36. *An Historian Looks at Religion* (London: Oxford University Press, 1956), p. 70.

Chapter Five: TAOISM

1. A number of contemporary scholars think that the *Tao Te Ching* emerged in the fourth and third centuries B.C. as a product of joint authorship and repeated editing.

2. Quoted by Arthur Waley, *The Way and Its Power*, pp. 48-49.

3. *Tao Te Ching* (Waley Tr.), Chs. 2, 7.

4. Witter Bynner's *The Way of Life According to Laotzu* (New York: John Day, 1944) is the best translation in this third mode of reading the *Tao Te Ching*. It is relatively pointless to argue which reading is most accurate as the text is so laconic that it lends itself to all three interpretations and has been so read in Chinese history. Better simply to acknowledge that there have been in China three Taoisms, each of which claims the *Tao Te Ching* as its spiritual base.

5. Unless otherwise specified, chapter references in this section and the next are to the *Tao Te Ching*, Bynner translation.

6. Related by Arthur Waley in *Three Ways of Thought in Ancient China*, pp. 7-8.

7. *Tao Te Ching*, Chapter 80. Fung Yu-lan's translation, as quoted in *A Short History of Chinese Philosophy* (New Jersey: Princeton University Press, 1953), p. 20.

8. Related by Arthur Waley, *Three Ways of Thought in Ancient China*, p. 11.

9. *Ibid.*, p. 33.

10. *Ibid.*, p. 6.

11. Quoted in K. L. Reichelt, *Meditation and Piety in the Far East* (New York: Harper and Brothers, 1954), p. 102.

12. Quoted by Arthur Waley, *Three Ways of Thought in Ancient China*, p. 7.

13. Witter Bynner, *op. cit.*, pp. 12-13.

14. Adapted from K. L. Reichelt's translation of the Twenty-fifth Chapter of the *Tao Te Ching*, *op. cit.*, p. 41.

Chapter Six: ISLAM

1. *History of the Arabs* (London: Macmillan, 1940), pp. 3-4.

2. Carlyle's description in "The Hero as Prophet," *Heroes and Hero-Worship* (Chicago: W. B. Conkey, 1900).

3. The Koran, Surah xcvi, 1-4.

4. Quoted in Ameer Ali, *The Spirit of Islam* (London: Christophers, 1923), p. 18.

5. *Ibid.*, p. 32.

6. *Ibid.*

7. Sir William Muir, quoted in Ameer Ali. *op. cit.*

8. Quoted without source in *ibid.*, p. 52.

9. *Ibid.*

10. Philip Hitti, *The Arabs: A Short History* (Princeton: Princeton University Press, 1949), p. 32.

11. *Ibid.*, p. 21.

12. Today the language of Islam is among Muslims a matter of sharp controversy. Many, notably the Ulemas, insist that it must remain Arabic. Others argue that divine words retain their divine character in any tongue.

13. "She [Mary] said: My Lord! How can I have a child when no mortal hath touched me? He [the angel] said: So. Allah createth what He will. If He decreeth a thing, He saith unto it only: Be! and it is" (iii:47, Mohammed Pickthall's translation). Subsequent quotations from the Koran in this chapter are as translated by Ameer Ali.

14. Ameer Ali, *op. cit.*, p. 150.

15. Sir Muhammad Iqbal, *The Secrets of the Self* (Lahore: Muhammad Ashraf, 1920-1944), p. xxx.

16. Quoted in Ameer Ali, *op. cit.*, p. 199.

17. Ameer Ali, *op. cit.*, p. 170.

18. Cf. J. Christy Wilson, *Introducing Islam* (New York: Friendship Press, 1954), p. 12.

19. Hunter, *Our Indian Musalmans*, p. 179. Quoted in Ameer Ali, *op. cit.*, p. 165.

20. *Ibid.*, p. 114.

21. *Ibid.*, p. 173.

22. Quoted in *ibid.*, p. 249.

23. "Turn away evil with that which is better" (xlii:37).

24. Quoted by Ameer Ali, *op. cit.*, p. 212.

Chapter Seven: JUDAISM

1. *The New Yorker*, December 4, 1954, pp. 204-05.

2. Henri Frankfort, *The Intellectual Adventure of Ancient Man* (Chicago: University of Chicago Press, 1946), p. 363.

3. *Rediscovering the Bible* (New York: Haddam House, 1954) pp. 27-28.

4. William Shakespeare, *Julius Caesar*, Act. IV, Sc. 3, Line 217.

5. W. F. Albright in *Approaches to World Peace* (New York: Council on Science, Philosophy and Religion, 1943), p. 9.

6. See I Kings 18:46 and II Kings 2:16.

7. Quoted by Abba Hillel Silver, *Where Judaism Differed* (New York: The Macmillan Company, 1956), p. 109.

8. Abraham Heschel.

9. G. Ernest Wright, *The Old Testament Against its Environment* (Chicago: Alec R. Allenson, 1950), p. 60.

Chapter Eight: CHRISTIANITY

1. There is a shroud in Italy bearing a photographic imprint caused by bodily chemicals which is claimed to be that in which Jesus was wrapped when he lay in the tomb. Though it has passed what appear to be some extraordinary tests, it has not been generally accepted by Christendom.

2. *Basic Christian Ethics* (New York: Charles Scribner's Sons, 1952), p. 16.

3. Cf. Matthew 10:23, "When they persecute you in one town, flee to the next; for truly, I say to you, you will not have gone through all the towns of Israel, before the Son of man comes."; Mark 9:1, "Truly, I say to you, there are some standing here who will not taste death before they see the kingdom of God come with power"; and Luke 22:18, "For I tell you that from now on I shall not drink of the fruit of the vine until the kingdom of God comes."

4. The fact that few Christians today look forward to Christ's imminent and literal return does not mean that the doctrine of the Second Coming has lost all meaning for Christendom. It retains important symbolic meaning, to wit, that what Christ began, that he will also complete. In addition to being the author of the Christian faith, he is its finisher.

5. *An Approach to the Teachings of Jesus* (Nashville: Abingdon-Cokesbury Press, 1947), pp. 72-75.

6. Robert Penn Warren, *Brother to Dragons* (New York: Random House, 1953).

7. Strictly speaking, Roman Catholic and Eastern Orthodox Christianity limit the word "Church" to this divine aspect of the institution.

8. Invincible ignorance is defined as "that which has not been capable of being overcome or removed by reasonable care; whether because no thought or doubt concerning such matters ever entered the mind; or because, even if such a thought had come into the mind, this ignorance could not have been overcome or removed by the use of reasonable and common care, nor could a knowledge of the truth have been obtained."

9. *Basic Christian Ethics*, p. 291.

10. This does not contradict our earlier statement that we cannot derive from the Gospels a clear idea of who Jesus thought himself to be, for it remained for the Church to crystallize what these words mean. The vehement controversies in early Christendom concerning Christ's nature is clear proof that the meaning of his words is not unambiguous, to say nothing of whether he himself actually said all the things that are ascribed to him in the Gospels. A significant number of Christians believe that, as forty years intervened between his death and the first Gospel, some of his sayings represent convictions of the early church which were so fully believed that it became assumed that Jesus must have said them.

11. Thomas Corbishley, *Roman Catholicism* (London: Hutchinson House, 1950), pp. 40-41.

12. *Introduction to the Devout Life* (Garden City: Doubleday Anchor Book, 1955), pp. 113-114.

13. The Roman Church agrees on this point with, of course, the Pope as Bishop of Rome included in such councils. It also holds that the Bishops are infallible when, in the absence of formal definition, they nevertheless teach unanimously that a given doctrine is divinely revealed and to be believed by all their faithful. The differences lie in the sharp line the Roman Church draws between clergy and laity in the reaching of its doctrines and (as stated) in the absence in the Eastern Church of the authoritative voice of a single individual, the Pope.

14. It is interesting to reflect on how much both these emphases of Eastern Orthodoxy, its mysticism, and its sensitivity to the interrelatedness of lives, are embodied by the Russian novelists, especially Dostoyevsky and Tolstoy.

15. Francis Thompson, "The Kingdom of God."

16. Paul is explicit on this point: "Faith without works is dead."

Index

325

About the Author

Huston Smith was for ten years Professor of Philosophy at Washington University in St. Louis. He is now Professor of Philosophy at the Massachusetts Institute of Technology. He is the author of *The Purposes of Higher Education*.

COLOPHON BOOKS ON PHILOSOPHY AND RELIGION

*In Preparation